DATE DUE

THE ARAB AWAKENING
THE STORY OF THE ARAB NATIONAL MOVEMENT

by

GEORGE ANTONIUS

Arise, ye Arabs, and awake!
Ode by Ibrahim Yazeji.

WITH FIVE MAPS

CAPRICORN BOOKS
NEW YORK

To

CHARLES R. CRANE,

*aptly nicknamed Harun al-Rashid,
affectionately.*

CONTENTS

CHAPTER V

CHAPTER VI

CHAPTER VII

CHAPTER VIII

CHAPTER IX

CHAPTER X

CHAPTER XI

CHAPTER XII

CHAPTER XIII

＊

PAGE

LIST OF MAPS

The maps have been drawn by Mr. Tom Wrigley.

FOREWORD

THE object of this book is primarily to tell a story and mark its significance. It aims at giving, not the final or even a detailed history of the Arab Movement, but an account in outline of its origins, its development and the main problems it has had to face, in the form of a continuous narrative interspersed with such analysis as seemed necessary to elucidate the problems.

The story has never been told in full before. Accounts have appeared of this or that phase of the Movement; but there appears to be no work, in any of the languages with which I am acquainted, in which the story is told from the beginning, that is to say from the earliest stirrings of the Arab awakening one hundred years ago, down to the present day. Nor is there in existence, to the best of my knowledge, an account that derives its authority from an equal reference to the Arab and the foreign sources. Just as the Arabic histories rely almost exclusively on Arab sources, so the works published in the European languages will be found to have been mainly based on Western sources. It has seemed to me that there was room for a work to be drawn from both founts of knowledge, in which the texture of the story and of the problems of the Movement might be more solidly woven by crossing the woof of Arab sources and interpretation with the warp of European documentation.

The task of examining all the relevant sources has taken me several years of research in European and American libraries, and a great deal of travelling and personal inquiry in the Arab world. I have made a particular point of obtaining the testimony of persons who have had a hand in the actual shaping of the Movement or in one or other of its significant activities – a task which has not been easy but which was greatly facilitated by the willingness and the helpful kindness of a large number of people, both Arab and non-Arab, whose name is legion and to whom I am deeply indebted.

I have tried to discharge my task in a spirit of fairness and objectivity, and, while approaching the subject from an Arab angle, to arrive at my conclusions without bias or partisanship. If I have failed, it is not for want of trying or for any uncertainty as to the seriousness of my responsibilities towards my readers.

It would have been impossible for me to have carried out that research had it not been for my connexion with the Institute of Current World Affairs of New York. The Institute has not participated in any form or degree in the drawing up of my conclusions, or in any sense influenced them. For these, I am wholly and solely responsible. My gratitude goes to the Trustees and the Director (Mr. Walter S. Rogers) of the Institute, not only for the exceptional and generous facilities without which this work could not have been written, but also for the complete absence of any restriction as to time or method or freedom of expression.

I ask all those who have helped me with information and guidance, or who have otherwise facilitated my research, to accept this acknowledgement of my gratitude. It was only after I had actually begun the task of composition that I realised its difficulties. On re-reading the book in proof, it seemed to me that its primary asset was that it contained certain information which was not generally known and which might be of use in the elucidation of the problems confronting the Arab world in its relations with the Powers of the West. For that, the credit goes mainly to those who have helped me to trace it and understand its meaning.

October 1938   G. A.

THE ARAB AWAKENING

CHAPTER I

THE BACKGROUND

1.

THE story of the Arab national movement opens in Syria in 1847, with the foundation in Bairut of a modest literary society under American patronage.

The frequent risings and upheavals which, in the preceding three centuries, had stirred the Arab world from its torpid passivity under Ottoman dominance do not properly belong to the story. Even such movements as the rise of Fakhruddin in Syria, the establishment of the Wahhabi power in Arabia, and the campaigns of Mehemed-'Ali against his Turkish suzerain, must be relegated to the background as being isolated movements due to particular causes rather than steps in the march of an advancing Arab nationalism. For all their importance at the time, and their ultimate bearing on the destinies of Arab populations, they represent the achievements of individual genius goaded by great ambition or great faith, not the exertions of suffering idealists moved by the pride of race.

All the same, a sketch of the background to which those upheavals belong is necessary to the understanding of the story.

2.

The geographical setting calls for definition at the start, and with it, the exact connotation of the expression the *Arab world*

During the centuries which followed the rise and expansion of Islam, the term *Arab* gradually acquired a wider meaning. Originally, as far back as the oldest inscriptions go, pagan Arabia was inhabited by two races, of which the one, mainly nomadic, had as its roaming-ground the country comprised between the Euphrates and the centre of the Peninsula, down to the southern confines of the Hejaz and Najd; while the other, largely sedentary, had established itself in the uplands of the south, roughly corresponding to the Yaman and the Hadramaut. In its narrower ethnographical sense, the term *Arab* denoted only the first of those races; but that meaning is now obsolete, and is only of service in the science of racial origins. The present use of the word *Arab* and of the expression *the Arab world* has a much wider application which will become clear presently.

With the preaching of the Moslem faith, a process of expansion began which was destined to lead to one of the most spectacular human conquests the world has ever seen. The forces of Islam, emerging from the heart of the Peninsula shortly after the death of the Prophet Muhammad, pressed forward in every direction open to a land advance. Northwards, they overran Syria and advanced into Anatolia to threaten Constantinople. To the east, they conquered Iraq, Persia, the greater part of Afghanistan, and crossed the Oxus into what is now known as Turkestan. To the west, they captured Egypt, the whole of the North African coast and, reaching the shores of the Atlantic, turned northwards at Gibraltar, overran Spain and crossed the Pyrenees into France, where they occupied Avignon, Carcassonne, Narbonne and Bordeaux. In barely one hundred years from the death of Muhammad, an Arab empire had been founded which extended without a break from the Iberian Peninsula in the west, along the southern shores of the Mediterranean, to the banks of the Indus and the Aral Sea in the east. In the centuries which followed, this empire gained and lost ground at both its extremities. But it maintained itself long enough within those broad frontiers for the Arabs to have left their permanent impress upon it. Under their rule a brilliant chapter in the history of mankind was to unfold itself, and their real claim to greatness was not that they conquered such a vast portion of the known world, but that they gave it a new civilisation.

3.

The cultural evolution which the Arabs set in motion was the resultant of two processes, the one purely religious and the other essentially social, which, although they ran in parallel courses, were nevertheless distinct and differed greatly from each other in point of appeal and of reach.

The first was the process of *islamisation* whereby the new faith preached by the Prophet Muhammad, commending itself for a variety of reasons to millions of new adherents, transformed their spiritual life. The other was the process of *arabisation* which had two aspects: linguistic arabisation, that is to say the process by which the populations of the conquered countries gradually acquired Arabic as their mother tongue; and racial arabisation, caused by the entry into those countries of masses of immigrants of pure Arab stock, whose absorption by fusion and inter-marriage gave the conquered races a certain, in some cases a predominant, admixture of Arab blood.

The process of arabisation was the older of the two. For centuries before the rise of Islam, Arab tribes had poured or penetrated, according as the urgence of their economic wants was more or less pressing, into Syria[1] and Iraq[2]; and, in the two centuries before the Christian era, had founded dynasties in Homs, Edessa and in the regions bordering the Mediterranean coast. The third century A.D. had even seen the establishment of flourishing Arab kingdoms at Palmyra and Hira. Considerable bodies of Arabs migrated into

[1] Except where otherwise specified, the term Syria will be used to denote the whole of the country of that name, which is now split up into the mandated territories of (French) Syria and the Lebanon, and (British) Palestine and Transjordan.

[2] The Arabic name for Mesopotamia, now universally adopted.

15

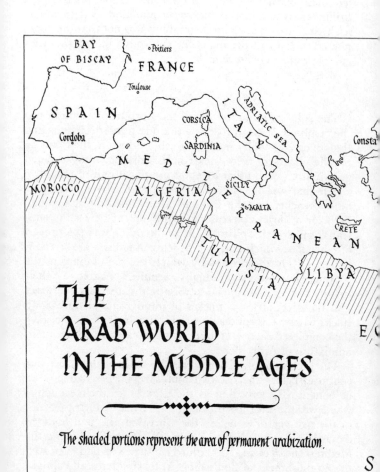

THE ARAB WORLD IN THE MIDDLE AGES

The shaded portions represent the area of permanent arabization.

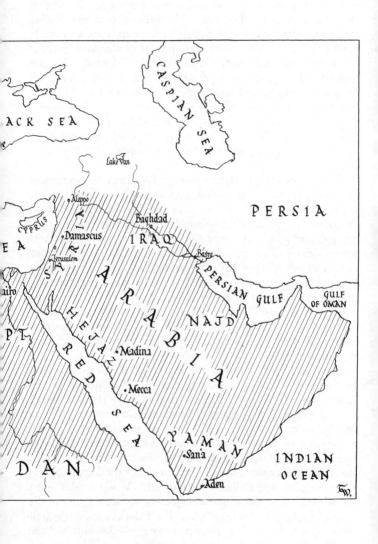

Syria and Iraq in the wake of those invasions, who settled there and became absorbed. The influence of the Arabic language, although it did not go very deep, had also made itself felt. But the essential structure of civilisation in those countries had not been fundamentally altered. In the seventh century, however, under the impetus of Islam, the invaders came armed with a moral force such as they had not possessed in any previous emergence. It proved irresistible, and the old order of hybrid and debilitated cultures – Greco-Aramaic in Syria, Sassanian in Iraq, Greco-Coptic in Egypt – gave way before the onset of the new faith.

The two processes, islamisation and arabisation, were now at work together, but, although intimately interconnected, were by no means identical. Nor did they halt at the same frontiers. Islamisation, essentially a spiritual force, progressed much further afield and was able to sweep barriers which arabisation, involving material displacement, could not always overstep. Broadly speaking, every country which became permanently arabised became also permanently islamised. But the converse is not true. There are countries, such as Persia and Afghanistan, where, notwithstanding a thorough and lasting islamisation, the progress of arabisation remained so restricted as to be, for our purposes, negligible.

Similarly, though not to the same extent, the two aspects of the process of arabisation, namely, the spread of the Arabic language and the infiltration of Arab stock, differed both in range and in reach. There are physical and economic limits to the capacity of a country to admit and absorb migrations from the outside, even when, as happened with those waves of Arab colonisation, the process is carried through by superior force. The spread of the language was not circumscribed by those limitations. While Arabic went on advancing until it had completely enthroned itself, the tide of racial penetration found itself dammed within narrower confines. Of the countries lying on the fringe of the Arabian Peninsula, the portions now known as Palestine and

Transjordan received and absorbed the largest proportion[1] of Arab stock, and Egypt the smallest, while Syria and Iraq occupy a midway position.

4.

In less than three generations, the life of those countries was completely transformed. While the new religion preached by the invaders was far from being universally accepted, the whole population, with a few scattered exceptions, adopted their language and, with their language, their manners and ways of thought. The new civilisation which arose in place of the old was in no material sense imported by the newcomers. It was a compound product resulting from a process of reciprocal assimilation; from the impulse which the Moslem conquerors gave to the resources of intelligence and talent which they found, disused and moribund, and quickened into life. In its external manifestations the new civilisation varied in each country, in keeping with the variations in the cultural aptitude of the local populations. But two features were common to all: its faith and its language, with all that these implied of new standards and new outlook. And while the religion of Islam allowed large communities in the conquered countries to retain their old faith, and had itself to suffer a schism as between its Sunni and Shi'i adherents, the Arabic language had unity and became uniformly dominant everywhere. Before the end of the seventh century, it had become the language of the State, as well as of the majority of the population, at any rate in Syria and Iraq.

Thanks to their extraordinary powers of diffusion, the Moslem faith and the Arabic language continued, throughout the centuries which followed, to advance in rapid strides. Thus two worlds, one considerably more extensive than the other, were created: the Moslem world and the Arab world,

[1] In a brilliant essay published in the *Revue du Monde Musulman*, Vol. LVII (1924), Professor Louis Massignon estimates that nearly two-thirds of the settled Moslem population of Palestine is of original Arab stock. In Transjordan, the percentage is still higher.

of which the first contained the second. In course of time, the world of Islam reached out to India, China and the westernmost recesses of Africa; whereas the Arab world remained confined to those countries in which the process of arabisation had progressed so far and so deep as to have achieved three lasting results: the enthronement of Arabic as the national language, the introduction of Arab manners and ways of thought, and the implantation of an appreciable Arab stock in the racial soil.

The Arab world of to-day is made up of those countries in which a great majority of the population has remained impressed with those cultural and social influences. It does not include Spain or the Mediterranean islands in which, after the disappearance of Arab domination, other forces arose to efface or submerge the results of arabisation. It does not include Persia or Turkey or Afghanistan, or any of the countries beyond the Indus and the Oxus, where Arabic never became the national language. What it does include is that continuous chain of countries stretching from the Atlantic seaboard in the west, along the southern shores of the Mediterranean, to the Persian border in the east: the North African coast from Morocco to Egypt, Syria and Iraq, and the Peninsula of Arabia.

The connotation of the word *Arab* changed accordingly. It is no longer used solely to denote a member of the nomad tribes who peopled the Arabian Peninsula. It gradually came to mean a citizen of that extensive Arab world – not any inhabitant of it, but that great majority whose racial descent, even when it was not of pure Arab lineage, had become submerged in the tide of arabisation; whose manners and traditions had been shaped in an Arab mould; and, most decisive of all, whose mother tongue is Arabic. The term applies to Christians as well as to Moslems, and to the off-shoots of each of those creeds, the criterion being not islamisation but the degree of arabisation.

Such are, in broad outline omitting scattered fractions, the confines of the Arab world to-day. And such, save for slight differences, were its confines at the beginning of the sixteenth century, when a Turkish conqueror, pressing forward from the fastnesses of Anatolia, marched into Cairo and laid the foundations of the modern Ottoman Empire.

5.

The conquest of Egypt by Selim I in 1517 marks a definite stage in the extension of the Ottoman sway over the Arab world. Selim's crushing victories over the Shah of Persia in 1515 and the Sultan of Egypt in the following year had made him master of Iraq and Syria and enabled him to enter Cairo and, in the space of a few months, to establish his rule over Egypt. During his brief stay there, a deputation from the Sharif of Mecca came to pay him homage and offer him the keys of the Holy City and the title of Protector of the Holy Places,[1] a dignity calculated to enhance his prestige in the Moslem world. Some doubt exists as to his having secured the title of caliph as well.[2] Whether he did so or not, he returned to Constantinople in triumph as virtual master of the Arab world and the ruler whose name was reverently uttered in the prayers of all Moslem worshippers in his empire.

Under Selim's successor, Soliman the Magnificent, the subjection of Arab countries to Ottoman rule was extended westward along the North African coast and southward as far as the Yaman and Aden. When Soliman's reign – the most glorious in the annals of Turkey – came to an end with his death in 1566, the Ottoman dominion over the Arab world extended without a break from Algeria to the Persian Gulf,

---

[1] *Khadem al-haramain al-sharifain*, literally 'servant of the two Holy Sanctuaries' (i.e., Mecca and Madina), a title which thereafter became one of the designations of the Caliph of Islam.

[2] There is a widely-accepted report that Selim had obtained the formal cession of the title from al-Mutawakkel, the last of the Abbasid caliphs. The report appears to have first arisen in the eighteenth century and has gained currency among both Eastern and Western historians; but, as the late Sir Thomas Arnold has shown in *The Caliphate* (Oxford University Press, 1924), it rests on insufficient, and certainly on no known contemporary, evidence. The unquestioned fact is, however, that from the beginning of the eighteenth century onwards, the sultans of Turkey have styled themselves Caliph of the Prophet and have generally been so recognised.

and from Aleppo to the Indian Ocean. It included the heart as well as the head of Islam. In addition to the sacred cities of Mecca, Madina and Jerusalem, it embraced Damascus, the first capital of the Arab empire, and Baghdad, whose science had once illumined the world.

With varying fortunes, frequently accompanied by wars, revolts and massacres, the Ottoman dominion maintained itself in those frontiers until the close of the eighteenth century. Its authority was generally loose and insecure and was sometimes openly flouted, whenever a rebellious vassal would successfully defy the ruling Sultan. Sensational figures stalk across the stage of those three centuries, now martial and heroic like Fakhruddin and Daher al-'Umar, now merely brutal and sanguinary like Ahmad al-Jazzar and the Mamelukes of Cairo; but always solitary and self-seeking. They appear and disappear in tedious succession, with the clatter of operatic tyrants, blowing the trumpets of their local triumphs but never overthrowing or seriously threatening the hold which Soliman the Magnificent had fastened upon the Arab world. In any case, their exploits had no perceptible bearing on the rise of the Arab national movement. The only exceptions were Muhammad ibn 'Abdul-Wahhab, an earnest reformer, whose preaching led to an important religious revival; and Mehemed-'Ali who, had it not been for the Powers of Europe, might have wrested the throne and the caliphate from the hands of his suzerain in Constantinople and founded an Arab empire.

CHAPTER II

A FALSE START

I.

MEHEMED-'ALI came to Egypt, from his birth-place in Cavalla, as an officer in the Albanian force detailed in 1799 by the Sultan of Turkey to put an end to Bonaparte's invasion. He was then a young man of thirty, whose remarkable gifts had not yet had scope to reveal themselves. The Albanians were easily defeated by Napoleon, but it was this defeat that gave Mehemed-'Ali his chance. He succeeded to the command of the force so that when, two years later, the French had evacuated Egypt, he found himself at the head of a small army and in a position of authority. This he used to his best advantage, in resourceful and astute ways, in which he displayed political as well as soldierly talents. By 1805, he had become the military master of Egypt and been recognised as its titular governor.

His next opportunity was to occur in Arabia, and he spent the intervening six years on the task of consolidating his position in Egypt by breaking the power of the Mamelukes and putting some order into the prevailing anarchy. By 1811, he had so far entrenched himself as to be able to turn his attention to Arabia where the religious revival started by another great figure had led to a movement of military expansion on such a scale as to become a menace to the Caliph's authority in the Holy Land of Islam.

This revivalist movement of the eighteenth century, which came to be known as the Wahhabi movement, originated in the teachings of Muhammad ibn 'Abdul-Wahhab, a native of Najd, who had travelled widely in the Moslem world, studying

21

theology, and become imbued with a passionate zeal for reform. In his view, Islam had sunk into impiety. With the passage of the centuries, new practices had crept into use, for which there was no warrant in the doctrine preached or the precedents established by the Prophet. Innovations had obtained currency and superstitious uses had spread, that seemed to Muhammad ibn 'Abdul-Wahhab indistinguishable from idolatry. He began a campaign of purification. He was a reformer not in the sense that he desired a change in the doctrines of Islam or even a new interpretation of its tenets, but in the sense that he felt it his mission to denounce innovations and accretions, and preach a return to Islam's former purity.

He found an ally in a scion of the House of Sa'ud, who accepted his teaching and became his secular champion. The formation of their partnership in 1747 marks the birth of the Wahhabi movement. It grew rapidly enough in Central Arabia where it had sprung, but it was not until some forty years later that it made itself felt outside. Muhammad ibn 'Abdul-Wahhab died in 1792, and his ally who had died thirty-three years before him had been succeeded by his son 'Abdul-'Aziz ibn Sa'ud, ancestor and namesake of the present Wahhabi king; and it was during the reigns of that ruler and of his son Sa'ud that the forces set into activity by the new teaching emerged out of Najd to denounce and dispute the Caliph's authority. Their first excursions were directed against Iraq and brought them to the gates of Baghdad where, in 1799, they compelled the Turkish governor to conclude a treaty with them. Two years later, they renewed their attack and sacked Karbala, a holy city of the Shi'a. They then turned westwards and northwards, occupied Madina and Mecca, and invaded Syria to threaten Damascus and even Aleppo. There they still were in 1811 when Mehemed-'Ali, yielding at last to the Sultan's pressing demands, despatched an army under the command of one of his sons to recover the Holy Cities.

The Egyptian campaign in Arabia lasted seven years and ended in a victory for Mehemed-'Ali. The Holy Cities were delivered; and an expeditionary force under the command of another son, Ibrahim, advanced eastwards and succeeded, in 1818, in capturing Dar'iya[1] and forcing the surrender of the Wahhabi ruler. Ibrahim's advance into the heart of Najd, which involved a long march across inhospitable country, was a military achievement of outstanding merit, and stamped him as a greater general even than his father. He had crushed, although he had not killed, the Wahhabi movement. His victories had rid the Sultan of a formidable menace and restored his authority over the Holy Places of Islam. They had added lustre to the fame of Mehemed-'Ali and prestige to his name throughout the Arab world. And, what is more significant still, they had brought him and his son into touch with the pulse of the Arab world and given them both, who were in no sense Arabs, the vision of an Arab empire and the ambition to be its architects.

2.

Mehemed-'Ali's project of carving out for himself an Arab empire from the Sultan's dominions was never realised: it crashed on the rock of Palmerston's opposition. But he came within sight of it with his conquest of Syria.

His triumph in Arabia had been followed by other successes. With an energy and a determination which compel wonder, he organised his somewhat nondescript forces into a regular army and acquired a fleet. In 1820, an expeditionary force under the command of yet another son advanced into the Sudan and conquered it, and the indefatigable Mehemed-'Ali did not flinch at the task of setting up an administration in that vast and chaotic territory. He sent expeditions into the Red Sea to put an end to piracy and bring its ports, on both the Arabian and African seaboards, under his control. In response to the Sultan's entreaties, he

---

[1] The ancestral home of the Sa'ud dynasty in Najd, whither Muhammad ibn 'Abdul-Wahhab had taken refuge in 1747 to seek help from the head of the clan of Sa'ud.

lent his assistance to the Turkish forces sent to quell the insurrection which had broken out in Greece. In 1822, he despatched a naval force to occupy Crete; and, two years later, a much greater military and naval force led by the redoubtable Ibrahim who landed in the Morea, conquered the peninsula and captured Athens. The Egyptian army, incomparably more efficient than the Turkish forces, repressed the revolt and were occupying the greater part of Greece when a combined British and Russian squadron destroyed the Turco-Egyptian fleet at Navarino (1827). This defeat was a serious blow to Mehemed-'Ali; but, far from damping his ambition, it incited him to press his claim to the overlordship of Syria as a reward for his intervention in Greece. When the Sultan had definitely refused to recognise his title to the province, he proceeded to take it. And once more, his victorious instrument was Ibrahim.

The conquest of Syria was speedily effected, once the fortress of Acre had surrendered in May 1832. From there, Ibrahim moved on in swift strides to occupy Damascus, rout the Turkish forces near Homs, and inflict another defeat on them in the neighbourhood of Aleppo. By the end of July he was master of the whole of Syria. The Sultan, taking alarm, despatched emissaries to Mehemed-'Ali to open negotiations. Ibrahim, curbed by his father, waited; and when, five months later, the negotiations had broken down and a strong Turkish army marched against him, he resumed the offensive and won a crushing victory. The road to Constantinople lay undefended before him, and he pressed forward. But again he was stopped by orders from his father. The Powers had intervened and brought pressure on Mehemed-'Ali. At last, in the spring of 1833, an agreement was arrived at by which the Sultan formally recognised Mehemed-'Ali as Governor of Syria. For the next seven years, Ibrahim administered the country on behalf of his father, until the end of 1840 when he was compelled, owing to European pressure combined with local discontent, to surrender the governorship and evacuate Syria.

3.

It was during the Egyptian occupation of Syria that Mehemed-'Ali's plans for setting up an Arab empire became a matter of public concern. He had cherished the dream for many years, but had not yet taken steps to enlist popular support for his designs. The conquest of Syria, however, and his recognition as governor of it gave him his opportunity. He was now in actual, if not titular, possession of an important portion of the Arab world, that contained Mecca and Madina, Cairo, Jerusalem and Damascus; and, by an act of prevision which was not foreign to his ambitious nature, saw himself extending his sway over the remaining portions of it and then wresting a title to the whole.[1]

It is on record that he intended to make a bid for the caliphate as well, and that he made no secret of his intention. He knew that France would look with favour on the establishment of an independent and stable kingdom in the Arab countries lying, as Syria, Egypt and Arabia lay, on the highway to the East, that is to say on England's route to India. He had had encouragement from Austrian sources, in the form of concrete suggestions placed before him by Count Prokesch-Osten, who arrived in Cairo on a special mission. In a note dated May 17, 1833, the Austrian diplomat outlined his suggestions in some detail. It provided for Mehemed-'Ali's assumption of the caliphate, and the building up by him of an Arab empire to include Egypt and the Sudan, the Arabian Peninsula, Syria and Iraq. The suggestion appears to have carried with it, at any rate in Mehemed-'Ali's mind, an implication that it was backed by the Austrian Government. But whatever may have been the measure of foreign support in prospect, the opportunity before him was

---

[1] The British Consul-General at Alexandria, writing in January 1832, reported that: 'His immediate object is to establish his authority firmly in the Pashaliks of Acre and Damascus; after which to extend his dominion to Aleppo and Baghdad, throughout the provinces, where Arabic is the language of the people, which he calls the Arabian part of the Empire.' Public Record Office, *F.O. 78/213.*

in itself alluring enough. He controlled the Holy Places of Islam; the Sharif of Mecca looked up to him rather than to the Sultan; the Sultan himself was unpopular with his Moslem as well as his Christian subjects: and as for the Turkish forces, they were, in comparison with the reorganised Egyptian army, contemptible. The ground was propitious, so far as conditions in the Arab world went. But, elsewhere, there was one formidable obstacle: Lord Palmerston, who was adamant in his opposition to the idea of an Arab empire. Mehemed-'Ali realised that he would have to proceed warily, and he sought to improve the prospects of his scheme by gaining the Syrians over to an open espousal of it.

In this, he was ably, perhaps too zealously, seconded by his son. An inkling of his father's plans had penetrated into Syria some time before Ibrahim began his advance and had predisposed the population in his favour. The Moslems, already stirred by the boldness of the Wahhabis' defiance of the Sultan, were prepared to welcome this fresh challenge to the detested rule of the Turk. The Christians, envious of the fair treatment which Christians in Egypt enjoyed under Mehemed-'Ali, were no less expectant. The powerful Amir Bashir of the Lebanon, who was in touch and in sympathy with Mehemed-'Ali, played upon the feelings of the Moslems by skilfully dangling before them the alluring prospect of an Arab empire to be set up after the expulsion of the Turk from Syria. Based though it was on flimsy grounds, a belief arose and became widespread that an Egyptian conquest would bring freedom to the Arabs; and, long before he had begun his advance, Ibrahim might detect signs of the welcome which awaited him, for his championship of Arab liberation: revolts had broken out in Damascus; secret emissaries appeared in Cairo with earnests of Syrian support. When Ibrahim had at last overcome the obdurate resistance of the Pasha of Acre, he found that his progress across the rest of Syria, far from being opposed, was acclaimed and abetted by the whole population.

Here a parallel suggests itself between Ibrahim's advance

in 1832 and Allenby's victory in 1918. Both campaigns
started in Egypt and had as their end the expulsion of the
Turks from Syria. On each occasion, the invading army
crossed Sinai into southern Syria and there, breaking the
enemy's back with a well-timed blow, marched almost unopposed into Damascus, Homs, Hama and Aleppo, with the
active assistance of the Arab inhabitants. In both cases, the
military advance had been heralded by promises of political
emancipation, and the progress of the conquerors abetted by
a people whom the prospect of liberty had turned into eager
allies. And in both cases, too, the frustration of those hopes
had its roots in the complexities of the European political
system.

The assumption by Ibrahim of the governorship of Syria
in 1833 placed him for a time in a position of unquestioned
authority, and he applied himself from the start to the
furtherance of his ideas in regard to an Arab revival. In the
way of tangible results, his efforts came to nothing. But
they were the product of vision as well as of ambition, and
had the added grace of sincerity. In the fallow conditions of
the age, they were doomed to remain sterile, yet the causes
of his failure deserve closer study.

4.

In their attempt to create an Arab movement, Mehemed-
'Ali and his son laboured under weighty handicaps. They
were not Arabs and had not mastered Arabic, although
Ibrahim had learnt to speak it with a certain fluency; and
their advocacy of an Arab national revival, wanting in the
incentive of race and the eloquence of a rich language, lacked
the force of spontaneity. Their driving motive was personal
ambition, and their desire to revive the Arab Empire sprang
primarily from their desire to acquire an empire. Whatever
may have been the other causes of their failure, one lay in
that inherent principle of weakness.

Father and son were not altogether at one in their conceptions of the future empire. They were united in their

desire to transform their Arab conquests into a single king-dom, with themselves and their descendants for its dynasty, and to assume the title of Caliph. But they differed in their estimates of Arab capacity and of the reliance which could be placed on Arab co-operation. Mehemed-'Ali's aims were entirely acquisitive. He had set his heart on becoming caliph and the ruler of an independent kingdom, and knew that, in the attainment of those ends, he would need the goodwill and perhaps the active support of the Arabs. But he had no real sympathy with them, did not speak their language, and had no high opinion of their talents. In his empire-to-be, his Turks and Albanians were to support the edifice of sovereignty, and the Arabs to figure as dutiful subjects. Ibrahim went further than his father in that he desired to see an Arab revival as well as to found an empire. He had come to Egypt as a boy and had grown up in Arab surroundings. His acquaintance with Arab history and culture had come to him with the first rudiments of know-ledge. His sojourn in Arabia had brought him into contact with the virtues and defects of the race in their unalloyed state. His imagination had been touched and his sym-pathies awakened. He acquired the conviction that the empire dreamed of by his father would rest on more lasting foundations if its groundwork were to be the regeneration of the Arab race. The divergence between father and son answered to a difference in their vision as well as in their temperaments. As a contemporary observer said, Mehemed-'Ali's genius was of a kind to create empires, while Ibrahim had the wisdom that retains them.

Ibrahim arrived in Syria wearing, as it were, his sympathies on his sleeve, and impressed foreign observers with the sin-cerity of his professions. He spoke of himself as an Arab and liked to be regarded as one. 'I came to Egypt as a child,' he once remarked, 'and my blood has since been coloured completely Arab by the Egyptian sun.'[1] He spoke openly of his aims and exerted himself to spread his ideas among the

[1] G. Douin, *La mission du baron de Boislecomte*, Cairo, 1927, to which I am indebted for some of the other facts about Ibrahim.

humble as well as the influential in Syria. A French envoy, the Baron de Boislecomte, who paid him a visit at that time was struck with the breadth of his views and the freedom with which he professed them. He relates that Ibrahim made no secret of his intention to revive Arab national consciousness and restore Arab nationhood, to instil into the Arabs a real sense of patriotism, and to associate them in the fullest measure in the government of the future empire; that he regarded his father's ideas as narrow and merely imperialistic, and more suited to the state of enslavement into which the Arab world had sunk than to the politically independent status to which he proposed, on Mehemed-'Ali's death, to lead the Arab race. The enlightened Frenchman was favourably impressed and, in a despatch to his Government, paid homage to the general's vision. Ibrahim Pasha's idea of making the empire entirely Arab, he wrote in substance, is undoubtedly more satisfying to the mind and holds greater guarantees of stability and permanence than does his father's narrower conception; the only question is whether the Arabs are capable of governing themselves: Mehemed-'Ali thinks they are not, Ibrahim holds the opposite view.

Both during his advance and in the course of his first two years in Syria, Ibrahim was active in spreading his ideas of national regeneration and trying to convince the population that a new age had dawned for them with the advent of Mehemed-'Ali's rule. In his army proclamations, he had frequently referred in stirring terms to the glorious periods of Arab history and had infected his troops with his own enthusiasm. He had surrounded himself with a staff who shared his ideas and worked for their dissemination. And when he assumed the governorship, one of his first cares was to set up a new machinery of administration which was a marked improvement on the old in most of the fundamental branches of state organisation, such as taxation, justice, education, law and security. In the space of barely a year, he succeeded in establishing a new order, based on religious and civil equality and on the protection of lives and property, such as Syria had not known since the days of Arab rule in

Damascus. A new era had dawned indeed, and Ibrahim, pointing to his achievements, tried to show by concrete proof that, with the passing of Turkish rule, the Arabs could confidently look to a better future under the rule of Mehemed-'Ali and his dynasty.

In spite of this auspicious start, the new order did not live very long but achieved its own destruction in an effort to attain permanence. The underlying cause was Europe's hostility. Ibrahim's march into Asia Minor had aroused the concern of the Powers as well as alarmed the Sultan. It had opened the eyes of the world to the ease with which Egypt might overpower Turkey. The European Concert, by nature discordant, had one tune on which it always harped in unison: the maintenance of the Ottoman Empire. By the pressure it exerted on Mehemed-'Ali, it compelled him to come to terms with the Sultan and accept the governor-ship of Syria on a life-tenure instead of on the basis of hereditary rule. This arrangement was highly distasteful to Mehemed-'Ali, but he was not strong enough to resist; and he accepted it with the settled intention of challenging it in due time. He needed to replenish his treasury and strengthen his fighting services, and it was in the pursuit of those two objectives that he committed the blunders which contributed to his downfall in Syria.

In execution of his father's orders, Ibrahim took measures which aroused widespread discontent. He imposed new taxes and introduced conscription. Two more unpalatable measures could scarcely have been devised. To make mat-ters worse, he decided, as a prelude to general recruitment, to disarm the population; and that, to a community in which a man's gun was his main security, came as the crowning provocation. Revolts broke out all over the country, first at Nablus and Hebron, then in the Lebanon and the regions east of Jordan. For several months, Ibrahim was mainly engaged on putting down the insurrection. Although he succeeded in restoring order for a time, he had lost his popularity and, with it, the place he had won for himself and his plans in the public affection; and when, in 1840, European pressure forced him to evacuate Syria, he had scarcely a friend left in a population which, eight years before, had welcomed him as a liberator.

5.

In the complex of causes which led to Mehemed-'Ali's failure in Syria, two factors stand out as bearing directly on his plans for an Arab empire. Palmerston's opposition was one; the other – a negative factor – was that Arab national consciousness was non-existent.

A clash between Mehemed-'Ali and England was perhaps inevitable. The growth of his power in Egypt and its extension into Arabia and the Red Sea had placed him in a commanding position astride one of the most important of the world's trade-routes and one which was of special value to English commerce. His advance into Syria whence he threatened Constantinople had given Russia a pretext for intervention which none of the other Powers, least of all England, could brook. And now, with his scheme for an Arab empire, he was proposing to weld his conquests together into a solid whole in which transit facilities for European commerce would depend on his pleasure instead of on the facile consent of an enfeebled Turkey. Palmerston had shown himself vigilant and inflexible whenever the fluctuations of Mehemed-'Ali's duel with the Sultan had threatened to place Russian influence at Constantinople in the ascendant. He was equally alert over the Arab kingdom. In a letter dated the 21st of March 1833, to the British Minister at Naples, he wrote: 'His [Mehemed-'Ali's] real design is to establish an Arabian kingdom including all the countries in which Arabic is the language. There might be no harm in such a thing in itself; but as it would imply the dismemberment of Turkey, we could not agree to it Besides Turkey is as good an occupier of the road to India as an active Arabian sovereign would be.'[1] Thus it was not merely fear of Russian hegemony that had moved Palmerston

[1] Sir Henry L. Bulwer, *Life of Palmerston*, Vol. II.

to oppose the growth of Mehemed-'Ali's power and caused him, in the crisis of 1840, to despatch a fleet to expedite the expulsion of Ibrahim's forces from Syria.

This was the first occasion in modern times on which the idea of an Arab empire had presented itself as a problem in world politics, and on that occasion, at any rate, England's hand was against it.

6.

The other factor was the lack of anything approaching national solidarity in the Arab world. Centuries of decadence and misrule had debilitated the collective spirit of its population and loosened its former cohesion. The unifying force generated by the genius of the Prophet Muhammad had remained a force so long as Arab power had remained supreme. As that power waned, its cohesive influence weakened; and the diverse peoples it had welded together into a cultural whole fell gradually asunder to form separate entities, regional and sectarian, according to the district, clan or creed to which they belonged. Side by side with that disintegration, a process of religious evolution was going on, which had led not only to the birth of new confessions, among both Moslems and Christians, but also to an increased emphasis on sectarian differences and to the growth of confessional loyalty as a substitute for cultural solidarity.

In Syria, a country notable for the diversity of its sects, the process of disintegration had gone very far. At the time of the Egyptian conquest, its social edifice rested mainly on sectarian distinctions. The Moslems, who numbered considerably more than one-half of the total population, were in the ascendant. They alone had the status of full citizens, and they had a monopoly of privileges which were denied the followers of the other creeds. The Christians, who formed approximately one-third, were in a position of distinct inferiority and had become subjected to invidious laws of exception which operated to their detriment in matters of taxation, justice and other rights of citizenship. The heterodox Moslem sects – Druze, Nusairi and Mutawali – formed separate entities which, although small, were none the less resolute in their jealous attachment to their own social and confessional traditions. Patriotism in the national sense was unknown. All creeds and sects, had, it is true, much in common: language, customs, racial kinship; and, above all, hatred of Turkish rule of which they all desired to be rid. But in their aspiration towards freedom they were moved by different impulses; and their motives in welcoming Ibrahim's advance were selfish and divergent. The Moslems desired it mainly because they believed that the establishment of an Arab empire and the restoration of the caliphate to Arab hands would strengthen their predominance. The Christians welcomed it from exactly opposite motives. They had seen that Mehemed-'Ali's rule in Egypt was founded on toleration and equality, and they hoped that his conquest of Syria would bring the same blessings to them. In this they were not disappointed. Ibrahim did abolish the laws of exception and all other discrimination in force against the Christians. But in doing so, he alienated the Moslems and provided them with fresh incentive to revolt. Displayed as it was in a fanatical age, his tolerance does him all the greater credit; but because the age was fanatical and knew nothing of patriotism, the strongest sentiment it evoked was that of jealousy.

7.

Thus the ambitious plan of an Arab empire, conceived by Mehemed-'Ali and nurtured by Ibrahim, failed to find in Syria the sustenance it needed and was the more easily stifled by England's hostility. Its great weakness was that it was formed out of time, in advance of the birth of Arab national consciousness. It was sponsored by two men who were not of the race and whose efforts, notwithstanding the energy of the one and the enthusiasm of the other, had found no fire to kindle into flame. It vanished with their retreat, not to be heard of again as a problem in world politics until the War of 1914, when it emerged once more as the dream of one man and his son, of Arab race this time, whose purpose was to be strengthened by the very forces that had been denied Mehemed-'Ali: the fire of Arab nationalism and the strong arm of England's backing.

The tale of the events which led the Sharif Husain and his son 'Abdullah to plot a revolt with British connivance is the story of the Arab national movement. It opens in Syria shortly after Ibrahim's withdrawal, and its first episode was, as I have said, the foundation of a literary society in Bairut.

CHAPTER III

THE START: 1847–68

I.

THE rule of tolerance established by Ibrahim had one unpremeditated result: it opened the door to Western missionary enterprise; and, by so doing, it gave free play to two forces, one French and the other American, which were destined between them to become the foster-parents of the Arab resurrection.

Foreign missionaries had settled in Syria as far back as the beginning of the seventeenth century, but their activities had had little scope, and had remained confined to the establishment of a few scattered schools and seminaries, and the dissemination of devotional books. They were all Catholics and mostly French, and belonged to one or other of the Jesuit, Capuchin or Carmelite orders. Owing to the strong prejudices of the age, they found it difficult to work outside their own fold, and they had therefore to confine themselves mainly to the care of those Christian communities which were in communion with the Church of Rome.

The most active were the Jesuits whose connexion with Syria dates from 1625. Labouring under great difficulties caused by persecution and at times by their own penury, they managed by tenacity and perseverance to maintain themselves and prosecute their work with some success, until the suppression of their order in 1773, when they dispersed, shutting down most of their establishments and leaving it to missionaries of the Lazarist order to succeed them in the others. Not until 1831 did they return, and one of the reasons which dictated their second coming was that American missionaries had arrived in Syria and had begun to convert members of the Catholic communities to Protestantism.

The first Americans had come in 1820. They were Presbyterians working under the auspices of the American Board of Control for Foreign Missions who, having previously founded a station in Malta, had now felt called to carry their evangelical activities further east. They landed in Bairut, which was their first station and has remained their most important centre. In addition to encountering all the obstacles which had beset the path of their Catholic predecessors, they were confronted by a difficulty which was peculiar to their mission: there was no Protestant community in Syria, so that their only means of gaining adherents was to convert members of the other sects. This meant that their activities could not fail (as, in fact, they did not fail) to arouse the hostility of the local ecclesiastics. But, undeterred by that handicap, they entered on their evangelising campaign with zeal. The pioneers of 1820 were followed by others, amongst whom was Eli Smith, a young man of twenty-six, whose activities in Syria were to lead to distant results.[1]

But such were the disabilities under which foreign missions had to work before the Egyptian conquest of Syria, that all their efforts were doomed to remain, if not paralysed, at any rate cramped. The Americans had, since their arrival, been confined to Bairut which was then a walled city of barely 9,000 souls. The Jesuits and the Lazarists, with a start of two hundred years, had established schools in Damascus, Aleppo and the Lebanon, and had certainly made an appreciable contribution to the spread of education. But their main effort had borne on proselytising and on theological culture and had done nothing to revive the Arabic language from the torpor of its decrepitude; and, despite two centuries of teaching, they can scarcely be said to have weakened sec-

---

[1] Eli Smith was born at Northford (Conn.) in 1801, and educated at Yale and Andover. After taking holy orders, he joined the Presbyterian Mission and volunteered for foreign service. He was first sent to Malta to take charge of the missionary printing-press. He came to Bairut in 1827, left a year later in the general exodus of missionaries caused by the threat of war, but returned in 1834 and devoted the rest of his life to his work in Syria. A man of high ideals and of indefatigable energy, he died in Bairut in 1857.

tarian hatred or to have made any contribution towards a movement of ideas.

The changes brought about by Ibrahim's policy gave the foreign missions their chance. They flocked to Bairut and thence radiated to the rest of Syria. The year 1834 appears to date a turning-point. The Jesuits had returned, the small American contingent was swelled by fresh arrivals, and a competition began between Catholic and Presbyterian, which attaining at times to the asperity of a duel, caused them to vie with each other for influence and supremacy; and, in so striving, to set in train a revival of the Arabic language and, with it, a movement of ideas which, in a short lifetime, was to leap from literature to politics.

2.

Four events occurred in that year, which deserve special notice. One was the re-opening of the men's college at 'Aintura by the Lazarist Fathers. The second was the removal of the American mission's printing-press from Malta to Bairut. The third was the establishment by Eli Smith and his wife of a school for girls in that town, in a building of its own. The fourth was the initiation by Ibrahim Pasha of a wide programme of primary education for boys, modelled on the system inaugurated by his father in Egypt.

A glance at the state of cultural activity in Syria in those days will throw into relief the novelty and the significance of those events.

The general intellectual level was very low. Such schools as existed were of an elementary type and, whether Moslem or Christian, were mainly dedicated to the narrower branches of religious studies; and, even in those studies, their standard was poor and their horizon close. Efforts had been made by the Maronite Church to provide higher education, notably at 'Aintura, a village in the Lebanon, where a seminary for the training of ecclesiastics had been founded in 1728, and its management entrusted to the Jesuits. It closed down when the order was suppressed in 1773. The only other institutions of higher education were the colleges at Zegharta (1735) and of 'Ain-Waraqa (1789), both founded at those localities in the Lebanon by Maronite ecclesiastical enterprise. Of the two, the college of 'Ain-Waraqa which had the advantage of being a monastic foundation, was easily the more important. It made a point of encouraging the study of Arabic literature. Most of the men who in the first half of the nineteenth century rose to distinction in the world of letters and scholarship had had their schooling in it.

The scarcity of books was another factor in the retardment of cultural development. The Arabic printing-press was practically non-existent. A few hand-presses had made their appearance in monasteries during the eighteenth century, but their output had remained meagre and almost entirely limited to devotional books. At the beginning of the nineteenth century the position had been improved by the establishment of Arabic printing-presses in Constantinople (1816) and in Cairo (1822), both of which gave out books of literary or scientific value in Arabic.[1] A number of those books found their way into Syria, but only in limited quantities, and Dr. John Bowring, who was sent by Palmerston to study conditions in Syria in 1838, reported that the demand for books was so small that he could not find a bookseller in Damascus or Aleppo.[2] As for Arabic newspapers and periodicals, they were totally unknown.

The language itself had degenerated. Even in the early stages of the spread of arabisation, a divergence had appeared between the Arabic spoken in rural or tribal districts and the more grammatical idiom used by the literate classes

[1] Of these, the printing-press in Cairo, known to this day as the Bulaq Press, was the more important from the point of view of Arabic culture. Between 1822 and 1830 its publications amounted to over fifty books in Arabic, Turkish and Persian. By 1850, it had issued some 300 books in those three languages, of which an appreciable proportion were in Arabic and related to medicine, surgery, mathematics and literature.

[2] 'An estimate of the general want of instruction may be formed from the fact that the demand for books is so small in Syria that I could not find a bookseller in Damascus or Aleppo. . . . Some of the books printed by the Egyptian Government, at the Bulaq Press, are sent to Syria, and are sold there, but the demand is small; they, however, have made their way into some of the schools, and into a few private families.' *Report on the Commercial Statistics of Syria*, by John Bowring (Parliamentary Papers, 1840).

in the towns. With the passage of the centuries, the cleavage had become more marked and had led to the growth of a set of spoken idioms showing considerable deviations from the standard forms. This process was a natural one, and harmless enough so long as Arabic culture remained active and flourishing and the traditions of the classical age alive. But with the decay of Arab power and civilisation, which received their death-blow with the Ottoman conquest, those traditions were lost and the live spoken idioms threatened to swamp the standard language and taint it with their own debasement. At the beginning of the eighteenth century, the damage wrought to literary Arabic had taken such proportions, at any rate in Syria, as to cause a serious degeneracy, especially in the Arabic used by Christians,[1] as is amply revealed in the known works of 'educated' writers of the period. To make matters worse, the literature of the classical ages had vanished from memory and lay buried in oblivion. The patterns of literary expression were lost and the spiritual influence of a great culture removed; and, however missionaries might exert themselves to teach, minds remained starved and ideas stagnant.

Those being the conditions at the time of Ibrahim's arrival in Syria, the activities which were set in train in 1834 deserve to be regarded as the starting-point of the progress which was afterwards achieved. The revived college of 'Aintura, which is still in existence, began to play an important part in the formation of writers and thinkers. The scholastic system introduced by Ibrahim, although short-lived, gave a powerful stimulus to national education, particularly among the Moslem community; and the start he gave it was all the more far-reaching as his system aimed deliberately at awakening Arab national consciousness among the pupils. The school established by Mrs. Eli Smith was the first in Syria that had ever had a building constructed to serve as a school for girls; and, in a country where female education was almost universally neglected, the departure was startling and impressive,

---

[1] The standard of literary scholarship and purity of expression has, in general, been higher among Moslem than among Christian Arabs, largely because of the influence of the Qoran and of the profoundly humanistic value of the Islamic sciences.

and was widely copied. Lastly, the installation of a printing-press equipped to emit books in the Arabic language opened out new horizons to educators; and, by providing teachers and pupils with text-books on the essential branches of learning, it revolutionised in the first few years the educational methods of the age.

Without school or book, the making of a nation is in modern times inconceivable. In Syria, the work initiated in 1834, involving as it did new standards for schools and text-books, was at any rate an experiment in essentials. In retrospect, its consequences appear to have been decisive. It paved the way, by laying the foundations of a new cultural system, for the rehabilitation of the Arabic language as a vehicle of thought.

3.

From that year onward, the spread of education progressed by leaps and bounds. There were three main agencies at work. The Egyptian administration with its programme of State schools; the foreign missions, French and American; and the local ecclesiastics whose instincts of self-preservation as well as of charity had been aroused by the activities of the missionaries. The achievements of each were in various ways remarkable, and may briefly be summarised as follows.

First, the Egyptian system. It provided for the establishment of primary schools throughout the country and of secondary colleges in certain of the principal towns. Ibrahim's intention was not only to propagate education for its own sake, but also to use the school as an instrument to serve his political aims and military needs. He was keen on sowing, even more than his father had in the schools of Egypt, the seed of Arab national consciousness, and he invited a distinguished French educationist[1] who was in Mehemed-'Ali's

[1] Dr. A. Clot, usually known as Clot bey, a French surgeon who rendered eminent services in the fields of public hygiene and of medical education in Egypt during Mehemed-'Ali's reign. He was genuinely devoted to his master and to the cause of national regeneration in Egypt; and one of his concerns in the higher schools which he directed was to inculcate a true sense of Arab national sentiment. cf. Douin, *loc. cit.*, p. 138.

service to advise on the methods to be pursued. He also wanted by special education to fit the youth of the country for military service. In addition to the primary schools which he established all over Syria, he founded large colleges in Damascus, Aleppo and Antioch, in which the pupils, who were all Moslems, were boarded, clothed and taught at government expense, and received a stipend into the bargain. The Damascus college had some 600 pupils, its counterpart in Aleppo over 400. The pupils wore uniform and received instruction in the military profession.[1] Although much was accomplished in the time, the new system lived barely six years, for it collapsed with the evacuation of Syria by the Egyptian army in 1840. But it had one lasting result. Moslem parents had looked with apprehension on Ibrahim's recruitment of their sons for military training, and their fears roused them into activity. They opened schools to compete with those of Ibrahim and provide their children with an escape from the military career which they dreaded for them. And, with this incentive at work, an active interest in secular education was created, which remained alive after Ibrahim's departure, and gathered strength as the years went by.

4.

In the second place came the American missionaries whose contribution was all the more productive as it was governed by ideas as well as by enthusiasm. They realised that what the country needed above all was a system of education consonant with its traditions, and they had the imagination to perceive that a nation's lost inheritance may not be recovered except through its literature. The first requisite was a supply of Arabic text-books and school manuals: Eli Smith and his colleagues decided to create one. While they were transferring their printing-press from Malta to Bairut, they applied themselves to the task of learning Arabic.

Within a few years they had printed enough books to supply the schools they had founded, and other schools besides

[1] Bowring, *Report etc.*, pp. 107-8.

their own. Finding that they were handicapped by the inadequacy of their Arabic fount, Eli Smith travelled to Egypt
and Constantinople in quest of a design for new characters,
and eventually to Leipzig where a new type, henceforth
known as *American Arabic*, was cast under his direction.[1]
With this addition to its equipment, the American Press was
able to undertake a more ambitious programme of Arabic
printing and, in particular, to carry into execution the
laborious task of issuing a new translation of the Bible. They
secured the services of two scholars, Nasif Yazeji and Butrus
Bustani, whom they commissioned to compose manuals on a
variety of subjects for the use of schools. As soon as the
books were written and approved, they had them printed in
their own establishment and disseminated all over the country. The avidity with which these books were seized upon
showed not only that they filled a want, but that minds were
awakening to knowledge.

Meanwhile, the missionaries were rapidly opening schools
in various parts of Syria. Their first foundations were in
Bairut, Jerusalem and the Lebanon. The excellence of
their education was recognised by Dr. Bowring who, in his
report to Palmerston, spoke of the comparatively high standard attained.[2] Having remedied the shortage of books,
they turned their attention to the problem of training qualified teachers, which they did by converting the high school
they had founded at 'Abay in the Lebanon into a training-
college for teachers. By 1860 they had established thirty-
three schools attended by approximately one thousand pupils,
of whom nearly one-fifth were girls.

[1] cf. H. H. Jessup, *Fifty-three Years in Syria* (New York, 1910), to which
I am indebted for other information used in this chapter.

[2] 'In Bairut the Americans have also schools of some reputation. One
large one attached to the premises of the mission is stated to be more de-
serving of the name of college than any other institution in Syria. . . . I
had an opportunity of seeing many of the Syrian youths who are educated in
the American missionary school, and found them more advanced than any
other boys of their age in Syria. They are all taught English. The expense of the establishment is from 6,000 to 7,000 dollars per annum, and it is
wholly paid by public subscriptions in the United States. . . . They have
also had several female schools at different times. The result is that a
greater proportion of the Christian population of Bairut can read and write
than in any other town in Syria.' Bowring, *loc. cit.*, p. 106.

Their crowning work in the educational field came in 1866, when they founded the Syrian Protestant College in Bairut. The problem of higher education had engaged their attention for some years, and in 1862 a resolution was passed at one of the Mission meetings, by which the proposal of establishing an appropriate centre for it was finally voted. Daniel Bliss[1] was charged with the task of proceeding to England and then to the United States in order to solicit financial support for the scheme. He was so far successful that the Mission found it possible to proceed with the scheme, and the Syrian Protestant College, as it came to be known, opened its doors to sixteen students in October 1866. At first the studies were confined to courses of higher secondary education and of medicine; and the language of instruction was Arabic throughout. But as time went the range and the standard of instruction were extended. The college has grown steadily since its foundation, and has now attained university status. Thus came into being an institution which was destined to play a leading part in the country's future. When account is taken of its contribution to the diffusion of knowledge, of the impetus it gave to literature and science, and of the achievements of its graduates, it may justly be said that its influence on the Arab revival, at any rate in its earlier stage, was greater than that of any other institution.

The educational activities of the American missionaries in that early period had, among many virtues, one outstanding merit; they gave the pride of place to Arabic, and, once they had committed themselves to teaching in it, put their shoulders with vigour to the task of providing an adequate literature. In that, they were the pioneers; and because of that, the intellectual effervescence which marked the first stirrings of the Arab revival owes most to their labours.

[1] Rev. Daniel Bliss, D.D., born in 1823 in the United States, came to Bairut in 1856. When the Syrian Protestant College was founded in 1866 he became its first president until 1902, when he retired and was succeeded by his son, Howard Bliss.

5.

The Catholic missions were not less active and, in course of time, their influence became as widespread as that of their Presbyterian competitors. But they were slower in starting and their efforts took longer to mature.

The most enterprising in the field of male education were the Jesuits. As we have seen, they had returned to Syria in 1831. Two years later they had re-opened two of their former establishments in the Lebanon, to each of which a school was afterwards attached. They founded schools in Bairut (1839), Ghazir (1843), and Zahleh (1844), and then extended their range as fast as their resources permitted to neighbouring localities, and eventually to more distant centres like Damascus (1872) and Aleppo (1873), where they had previously worked. Of the schools they founded during that period, the school at Ghazir in the Lebanon is histori-cally interesting as having become, on its transfer to Bairut in 1875, the University of St. Joseph – an institution which like its American sister, has exerted a decisive influence on the rising generations.

In the field of printing, too, the Jesuits started later than the others. They established their first press in 1847; it operated on the lithographic process and its output was very limited. It was not until 1853 that they began to print with movable type. In later years, their press expanded steadily and, by the time they transferred their centre of higher edu-cation to Bairut, they had an admirably-equipped plant in being. Its output of classical texts and other books of learn-ing, together with the excellence of its type and the care brought to the editing of its publications, entitles it to the first place in that field.

Other foreign Catholic missions became active in that period in Syria. Besides the Lazarists who had re-opened the college at 'Aintura and had started a school in Damascus, the Sisters of Charity and other orders established schools for girls and young boys in Bairut, Baalbek, Damascus and in various localities in the Lebanon.

In general, save for the Jesuits and the Lazarists, the activities of the Catholic missions in those early days, creditable though they were in the circumstances, remained localised and restricted in their influence. Several of their establishments were, if not actually ravaged, at any rate menaced and compelled to shut down in the disturbances which intermittently shook the country, notably in 1860. After that year, their activities, being less exposed to molestation, were considerably extended. Their contribution to the general progress of education was indeed valuable; but whatever influence they may have had on the Arab revival in its literary aspect was only slight and incidental.[1]

6.

It is time now to take cognisance of two great figures who dominate the intellectual life of the period.

Nasif Yazeji was the older of the two. He was born in 1800 in a hamlet of the Lebanon, of a Christian family who had known better days. The instruction he received in his childhood was of the formal, uninspiring kind in vogue at the time, but it did not succeed in stifling his genius. His natural curiosity, whetted without being satisfied by the lessons of the village priest, drove him to seek knowledge elsewhere. Books were not available in print, so that his only recourse was to the manuscripts stored in monastic libraries. Thanks to the name he had earned for himself by his diligence and his importunity, he was allowed to have access to manuscripts and even to borrow them. He made the fullest use of this facility. He had a great capacity for work and a prodigious memory; and whenever he encountered a text that seemed to him worthy of close study he would learn it by heart or copy it out patiently in his

[1] Several other foreign missions, of which the earliest were the British Syrian Mission led by Mrs. Bowen Thompson and the Prussian Mission of the Deaconesses of Kaiserswerth, came to work in Syria after the massacres of 1860, and have since carried on extensive and valuable activities in the fields of education and medical relief. But their influence, great as it became in the succeeding generations, had not made itself felt to an appreciable extent in the period with which we are here concerned.

festooned handwriting.[1] His exploration of libraries took him into the heart of the lost world of classical Arabic literature, and revealed to him the desolation wrought by the centuries. From that moment the problem of how to revive the past became his dominant interest. The beauty of the buried literature had awakened the Arab in him and bound him as by a spell. He became the apostle of its resurrection.

The salient facts of his career may be briefly noticed. At the age of sixteen, he was singled out for the post of secretary to a high ecclesiastic, but his tenure of it lasted only two or three years, and he went on from that to pursue his studies independently. In his late twenties, he accepted employment in the chancery of the Amir Bashir, the autocrat of the Lebanon, in whose service he remained until 1840 when the Amir had, in consequence of Ibrahim Pasha's withdrawal from Syria, to leave the country and go into exile. By that time he had achieved fame as a master of the Arabic language. He had already written a good deal, chiefly in verse of which several volumes were afterwards published and wrongly described as poetry, for the poetic quality was lacking. The outstanding excellence of his works lay in their purity of style and the example they set in new standards of literary expression. It was only natural that the Americans should have turned to him for help in the production of books dealing with the science of the Arabic language. He was better qualified for the task than any of his contemporaries. The books he wrote on grammar, logic, rhetoric and prosody were intended for the use of schools and, in the first place, for the schools of the American Mission. But they were adopted by a far larger circle of teachers and students and continued, long after his death in 1871, to govern the teaching of the science of Arabic.

Nasif Yazeji's influence, however, was not confined to the diffusion of his printed works. When he left the service of the ruler of the Lebanon and came to live in Bairut, his house became the haunt of an ever-growing crowd of admirers

---

[1] Several of the copies made by him at the time are extant in the archives ᷇ Yazeji family.

who, in accordance with the ancient custom of Arabs every-where, would flock to hear him discourse on the beauties of their mother-tongue. He was by nature reserved and spar-ing of words and he had all the inflexibility of the purist; but on the subject of Arabic, the only love of his intellectual life, his tongue was loosened and he spoke abundantly. It was the only language he knew: he died without learning another; and this limitation, constraining the movement of his mind into a single channel, gave it the force of a torrent. He was untiring in his advocacy of a revival of the old literature, and he succeeded in convincing a large circle of disciples that that way alone lay salvation. The novelty of his preaching was all the more striking as it addressed itself to Arabs of all creeds, to Christians as much as to Moslems, and urged them, at a time when religious fanaticism was still violent, to remember the inheritance they had in common and build up a fraternal future on its foundations. He brought up his twelve children, boys and girls, on those ideas, infecting them with his own enthusiasm; and one of them, as we shall see, was afterwards moved by the lessons of his father to utter the first call to Arab national emancipation.

7.

The other great figure was Butrus Bustani, born in 1819. He, too, was a Christian Arab and came from the Lebanon; but unlike Yazeji, he had received the best education which was then available and learnt other languages besides Arabic. At the age of ten, he entered the monastic college at 'Ain-Waraqa where he was taught Syriac and Latin, as well as the canonical sciences and the science of his mother tongue. At school, he stood out among his contemporaries, both for his character and for the brilliance of his attainments; and the monks selected him for a scholarship at the Maronite College in Rome. He was willing to go, but his widowed mother wept at the thought of her son being sent so far and entreated him to stay. He remained and took to a life of teaching, during which he found time to learn English; and, having gone to Bairut in 1840, he made the acquaintance of Eli Smith and of another American, newly arrived in Syria as a medical missionary, Dr. Cornelius van Dyck[1].

The acquaintance ripened not only into friendship but also into spiritual communion, and Bustani adopted the Presbyterian faith. From that moment, his activities became intimately linked to those of the Mission and his energy found unrestrained scope. He accepted employment as teacher of Arabic in the training-college at 'Abay, and wrote books for the use of schools. On being asked to help Eli Smith in the work of translating the Bible, he applied himself to learning Hebrew, Aramaic and Greek, in addition to perfecting himself in Syriac and Latin, thus mastering all the languages of the earliest scriptural texts. Italian he had learnt at school, and he appears at some period of his life to have learnt French as well. He was able to take up his task in the translation of the Bible with all the implements of the craft.

He had a remarkable power for assimilating knowledge, and yet his output was as abundant as his appetite was insatiable. In the early years of his association with the Americans, he had taught in their colleges, learnt new languages, devoured books in English on the physical sciences, and written manuals for the use of schools. He had lectured, preached and composed papers for the literary society which they had founded at his instigation. Then began his collaboration with Eli Smith in the translation of the Bible, which formed his principal occupation for some ten years, and he had barely brought it to an end than he started on the first

[1] Born at Kinderhook in the State of New York, in 1818. Studied medicine at Jefferson College in Philadelphia. Came to Bairut in 1840 as a lay doctor in the Presbyterian Mission, where one of his first acts was to begin the study of Arabic, in which he acquired an astonishing proficiency. He learned to speak and write it with the ease of a cultured Arab. He wrote text-books in it on various scientific subjects, some of which remained in use for two or three generations. He died in 1895, having spent 55 years of unremitting effort in Syria. Of all the foreigners who came to work in Syria in the nineteenth century, he entered more intimately into the life of the people than any other. So far as the power of example went, his was probably the most valuable and effective single influence ever exerted by a foreigner in the cultural development of the country.

of his two *magna opera*: the compilation of a dictionary of the Arabic language which appeared in 1870 in two volumes, under the name of the *Circumference of the Ocean*.[1] While he was busy, almost single-handed, with its compilation, he realised that its size would place it beyond the reach of the large majority of young students; so he prepared an abridgement as he went along, which appeared soon after as the *Diameter of the Ocean*.[2] His second great work was an Arabic encyclopaedia. He began this task a few years after the publication of his dictionaries, and made full use of the available European sources. But it was much more than a mere compilation and translation, for it contains a great deal of information drawn from Arabic literary and historical sources and shows evidence of original and industrious research. Six volumes had appeared at the time of his death in 1883. The work involved was so great, the quality of its production so good in spite of many serious imperfections, that it seems scarcely credible that one man alone could have directed such an undertaking, revised every entry and written a great part of it himself.[3]

Meanwhile his energy had been spending itself in other activities of which love of his country provided the main incentive. The upheaval of 1860, accompanied as it was by a savage massacre of Christians in Damascus and the Lebanon, had roused the passions of religious hatred to a murderous pitch. Bustani sought to work for its appeasement by means of a newspaper which he founded in Bairut in that year. It was a small weekly publication called the *Clarion of Syria*,[4] the first political journal ever published in the country, and was mainly devoted to the preaching of concord between the different creeds and of union in the pursuit of knowledge. For knowledge, he argued week after week in the earnest columns of his paper, leads to enlightenment; and

[1] *Muhit al-Muhit.*
[2] *Qutr al-Muhit.*
[3] This encyclopaedia, known as *Dairat al-Ma'aref*, was continued after his death by his sons and other members of his family. In all, eleven volumes have appeared.
[4] *Nafir Suriya.*

enlightenment, to the death of fanaticism and the birth of ideals held in common. A platitude, perhaps, but one that Syria had not heard before, and which contained the germ of the national idea. Three years later, in pursuance of the same doctrine, he founded a school which he called the National School,[1] to provide boys of all creeds with an education based on religious tolerance and patriotic ideals. He was fortunate enough to secure Nasif Yazeji as principal teacher of Arabic. The school achieved fame rapidly, and attracted pupils from all parts of Syria, including some who were afterwards to achieve distinction in the service of their country. In 1870, having published his great dictionary, he founded *al-Jenan*, a fortnightly political and literary review, of which the purpose was, again, to fight fanaticism and preach understanding and unity for the sake of the national welfare. He gave it for motto: *Patriotism is an article of faith*, a sentiment hitherto unknown in the Arab world, which appeared as an epigraph on the title-page of each issue. The review was published with fair regularity during the rest of his lifetime. It drew contributions from a number of writers from the neighbouring Arab countries as well as from Syria itself; but its value lay mainly in its exposition of the precepts of its founder and the impulse it gave to the movement of ideas towards breadth of view and tolerance.

As with Yazeji, Bustani's influence derived as much from the example of his life as from the diffusion of his published works. He practised what he preached with effortless consistence and with the serenity of disinterested conviction. Even during the massacres of 1860, when a paroxysm of religious hatred was convulsing the country, he had kept his head, not from indifference – his own parish was amongst the sufferers – but because he saw, what his contemporaries did not, that the fundamental cause of the trouble was the intolerance that is born of ignorance, and that the only way to peace among the sects lay across the untilled field of knowledge. From 1860 to the day of his death, he laboured to show the way with a diligence and a perseverance which

[1] *al-Madrasa al-wataniya.*

compel admiration. He worked indefatigably, and as he grew older became still more assiduous. He was fifty-six when he began to compose his encyclopaedia in the midst of multifarious other occupations. The world around him was showing signs of responding to his voice and a clamour for more light was filling the air. But the task he had set himself was more than his strength would stand. He died suddenly of heart-failure one night, as he was working at his encyclopaedia, and was found prostrate on the floor of his room, with his pen in his hand and a litter of books around him.

8.

In the early days of their association with the American Mission, Yazeji and Bustani had come forward with a proposal for the foundation of a learned society. I have not been able to find any trace of their ideas as to how that society should be formed or of the specific ends which they had in view. In all probability, they had felt that, side by side with the spread of education in the schools and the birth of a new interest in the sciences, some effort ought to be made to promote knowledge among adults by bringing them into touch with Western culture. In any case, it is on record that they placed their suggestion with some insistence before their new friends and induced them in 1842 to appoint a committee to give it effect.[1] The project matured in January 1847, when a society came into being in Bairut, under the name of the *Society of Arts and Sciences*. Yazeji and Bustani were both members, as were Eli Smith, Cornelius van Dyck and several other Americans. An Englishman, resident in Syria, the celebrated Colonel Churchill, also belonged. Within two years of its foundation, the Society had

---

[1] This committee, as recorded in an unpublished minute, dated April 21, 1842, in the archives of the American Mission in Bairut, was composed of Dr. Cornelius van Dyck and two other missionaries, and its terms of reference were 'to take the preparatory steps for the formation of a society for scientific purposes'. I am indebted to the Mission authorities in Bairut for allowing me to consult their unpublished records as well as their library.

fifty members, of whom the majority were Christian Syrians domiciled in Bairut. There was no Moslem or Druze membership. It had a modest but useful library,[1] of which Yazeji was librarian. The secretary was Bustani. Meetings of the Society at which papers would be read by one or other of the members were held once a fortnight at first, and less frequently as time went on. It lived five years and, in its last year, issued a volume of transactions, edited by the indefatigable Bustani, which contained an account of its activities and summaries of the papers read at its meetings.

This was the first society of its kind ever established in Syria or in any other part of the Arab world. The idea of promoting knowledge by an organised collective effort was foreign to the individualistic nature of the Arab whose method of approaching higher learning was akin to that of Plato's Greece, where a Master would hold his academic court and disciples flock, sometimes from great distances, to sit at his feet. But it turned out to be a fruitful innovation. Other societies were formed after its pattern, which were to play an important part in the growth of the Arab national movement. It was, in fact, in one of those early societies, the direct descendant of that which had been founded at the instigation of Yazeji and Bustani, that the first cry of the infant movement was uttered.

The Jesuits were the first to imitate the example set by the Americans. In 1850 they founded the *Oriental Society* on similar lines, of which the moving spirit was the active Father de Prunières.[2] The records which have remained of its activities are unfortunately incomplete; it is known, however, that it held periodical meetings at which papers were read, and that, as with its American-formed predecessor, its membership was partly Syrian, partly foreign and exclusively

[1] The statutes of the Society and a report on the state of its library were communicated to the Deutsche Morgenländer Gesellschaft by Dr. Eli Smith, and published in *Z.D.M.G.*, II, pp. 378–88.

[2] Henri de Prunières, a French Jesuit born in 1821, arrived in Bairut in 1849 and at once began the study of Arabic. His great erudition and remarkable activity gave him a wide influence in Syria. He distinguished himself by the part he took in the relief of distress during the massacres of 1860. He was obliged, owing to ill-health, to return to France where he died in 1872.

Christian.[1] It appears to have died out at the same time as the *Society of Arts and Sciences*, or at any rate shortly after.

The last society with which we shall deal in this chapter was founded in 1857, after the dissolution of the other two. It was the largest of the three and differed from its predecessors in two ways: its members were all Arabs, and its membership included Moslems and Druzes as well as Christians.

These two points of difference are more indicative of change than may appear at first sight. When the first two societies were formed, religious prejudice was still dominant, and the Moslems and Druzes had stood out. The fact that those societies were founded under the auspices of missionaries had made them still more unpalatable to the non-Christian elements. But as time went on, ideas moved and the unwholesome mists of prejudice had begun slowly to dissolve in the healing light of knowledge. The fervour with which Yazeji had been appealing to Arabs of all creeds to unite in the service of their language, and the sincerity of Bustani's campaign for the overthrow of barriers, had not been without effect. The Moslems came forward with a proposal: provided missionary influence was eliminated, they would join in the formation of a new society to unite all creeds in the service of learning.

Thus the *Syrian Scientific Society* (*al-Jam'iya al-'Ilmiya al-Suriya*) came into being in 1857. Its membership rose to 150 and included the leading Arab personalities of all creeds. On its board were the erudite Druze Amir Muhammad Arslan who was for several years its president; Husain Baihum, head of an influential Moslem family; and Christians of all sects amongst whom was one of Bustani's sons. Its aims, its methods and even its statutes were closely modelled on the society of 1847. The massacres of 1860 naturally caused a set-back to its activities; but it was re-constituted shortly after on a still wider basis, obtained official recognition in 1868 and extended its membership to include a large

[1] An account of the activities of the *Oriental Society* is to be found in *al-Mashreq* (Bairut), XII (1909), pp. 32-8.

number of personalities living outside the country, notably in Constantinople and in Cairo. For the first time, probably, in the history of Syria, certainly for the first time in the 350 years of the Ottoman domination, a common ideal had brought the warring creeds together and united them in an active partnership for a common end. An interest in the progress of the country as a national unit was now their incentive, a pride in the Arab inheritance their bond. The foundation of the Society was the first outward manifestation of a collective national consciousness, and its importance in history is that it was the cradle of a new political movement.

9.

It was at a secret gathering of certain members of the *Syrian Scientific Society* that the Arab national movement may be said to have uttered its first cry.

One of the members, Ibrahim Yazeji, a son of the great Nasif, and himself destined to achieve fame in the world of letters, had composed a poem in the form of an ode to patriotism. In substance, the poem was an incitement to Arab insurgence. It sang of the achievements of the Arab race, of the glories of Arabic literature, and of the future that the Arabs might fashion for themselves by going to their own past for inspiration. It denounced the evils of sectarian dissensions, heaped abuse on the misgovernment to which the country was a prey, and called upon the Syrians to band together and shake off the Turkish yoke. It was all the more seditious as it was couched in stirring terms, and it was recited in a hushed voice to eight members of the Society who had assembled in a private house one night and were known to one another to be of the same way of thinking.

The poem had a wide circulation. It was too treasonable to be safely committed to anything but memory. But such is the talent of Arabs for memorising poetry and for secret conspiracy that it was spread by word of mouth throughout the town and, later, throughout the country, without a hint to betray its origin. It made a particular appeal to the students and stamped their minds in their receptive years with the impress of racial pride.

The poem did much to foster the national movement in its infancy. It owed its vogue to its easy cadence and the neatness of its rhymes, and above all to the fact that, echoing sentiments unconsciously felt, it could awaken true emotion in the people for whom it was intended. With its utterance the movement for political emancipation sang its first song. It was the direct outcome of that earliest muster of all the creeds uniting to revive their ancient culture, which was once the burden of Nasif Yazeji's appeals and now the reward of Bustani's lifelong exertion.

10.

It would be well, before closing this chapter, to cast a retrospective glance at the political fortunes of Syria in the years which followed the termination of the Egyptian occupation in 1840.

The period was one of general restlessness and muddle, punctuated by outbreaks of disturbance. Before the Egyptian conquest, the population was, as we have seen, divided against itself into creeds and sects which, although they were occasionally brought together in the pursuit of material interests, were fundamentally divergent in their outlook and their loyalties. They had, nevertheless, attained a working stability in their relations, and outbreaks of sectarian violence were rare. One of the consequences of the Egyptian occupation, however, had been that it upset that balance as between the three principal elements, the Christians, the Druzes and the Moslems.[1] This was due partly to Ibrahim Pasha's emancipation of the Christians, which had disturbed the Moslems, and partly to the activities of foreign emissaries, chiefly from England, who had stirred up rivalry between

[1] It is impossible to furnish statistics with any certainty. The available sources give tentative and contradictory estimates. But it is probably reasonably near the truth to say that the total population of Syria amounted to $1\frac{1}{2}$ million and that the percentages of Moslems, Christians and Druzes were, respectively, 65%, 31% and 4%.

Druzes and Christians. When the Egyptian forces had evacuated Syria, and the country had reverted to Turkish rule, the three elements found themselves face to face, with their feelings ruffled into a new animosity against each other, but without Ibrahim's heavy hand to restrain them. In less than a year after the Egyptian withdrawal, serious trouble had broken out in the Lebanon between the Christians and the Druzes.

In the meantime, the Sultan of Turkey had promulgated a decree, known as the *Hatti Sherif* of Gulhaneh (1839), which provided amongst other things for a reform of the administration. In consequence of this and of the disorders of 1841, a new administrative régime was established in the Lebanon. The time-honoured practice of naming a feudal chieftain as governor of it was abandoned; a Turkish official was appointed; and the Lebanon was parcelled out into two separate districts, one of which was predominantly Christian and the other predominantly Druze. This cantonisation, however, was somewhat artificial and did nothing to reduce the friction. To make matters worse, the rivalry between England and France, which furnished these two Powers with increasing pretexts for interference in the affairs of the Lebanon, had crystallised into partisanship, of the Maronites (who formed the majority of the Christians in the Lebanon) by France, and of the Druzes by England. Disorders broke out again in 1845, accompanied by acts of massacre and pillage in which Catholic convents suffered considerably. The Sultan despatched his Minister of Foreign Affairs, Shekib Efendi, with instructions which gave him a wide latitude. He introduced changes into the administrative system, which, while they went a step further in diminishing the power of the feudal chiefs, left the Lebanon cantonised into two districts and administered on a system with which no one was satisfied.

Still, the settlement put into force by Shekib Efendi was followed by years of comparative tranquillity, at any rate so far as outward violence went; and the attention of the Porte and of the European Powers shifted to Jerusalem, where disputes among the Christian sects over privileges relating to the custody of the Holy Places had broken out and set a train of diplomatic passions on fire which led eventually to the Crimean War. The conclusion of peace was followed by the promulgation, in 1856, of another decree by the Sultan, known as the *Hatti Humayun*, which is important as containing an explicit recognition of the complete equality of all creeds in the Ottoman Empire in matters of taxation, justice and the privileges and obligations of citizenship. In that respect it adopted and consecrated the principles introduced into Syria by Ibrahim Pasha, and gave the Christians a legal and absolute right of equality with the Moslems. The *Syrian Scientific Society* which, as we have seen, was the first to include members of both creeds, was founded in the year following the promulgation of the decree. It could scarcely have been founded before.

But this tranquillity was only a phase, as forces were at work which threatened to bring about civil war. The two main influences were the discontent of the peasantry striving to liberate themselves from the remaining vestiges of the feudal system, and the growing power of the ecclesiastics, more particularly the Maronite clergy, who, not content with the powers granted them under the settlement made by Shekib Efendi, were trying to extend their influence in the direction of effective political ascendancy. These two forces allied themselves against the landed gentry who, although divided against themselves, were capable of a show of unity when their privileges were threatened. A revolt broke out in the northern Lebanon in 1857, in which the Maronite peasantry, incited by their clergy, rose against their feudal overlords of the same sect. The movement extended to the southern Lebanon and there, owing to the existence of a large Christian peasantry in the service of Druze overlords, it took the aspect of a sectarian conflict. To make matters worse, the Porte happened to be represented by a governor, Khurshed Pasha, who saw in the growing volume of internecine hatred a promise of violence which, if it were to result in an outbreak, might be used as a pretext for the consolidation of the Turkish hold on the country. While in the background, the competition for influence between England and France, conducted in a spirit of narrow partisanship, added to the general effervescence.

At last in the spring of 1860, trouble broke out in the form of Druze attacks on parties of Christians in the southern Lebanon. In a few weeks it had attained the dimensions of a conflagration. The Druze peasantry, acting in concert with their own feudal lords, organised a general onslaught on Christians – peasantry, gentry and clergy alike: and although the aggressors were far inferior in numbers, they were better armed and more warlike. In many places the Christians offered an heroic resistance, in others they retaliated as murderously as they were attacked. But what with the violence of the Druze offensive and the treachery of the Turkish soldiery who, when they did not actually side with the aggressors, left the victims to their fate, thousands of Christians were overwhelmed or driven to seek refuge in the towns. The wave of hatred spread to other parts of the country. Early in July, the Moslems of Damascus rose in a body and, rushing to the quarter inhabited by the Christians, committed one of the most savage massacres in history. The toll of lives in the Lebanon and Damascus reached the appalling total of 11,000, and there was a correspondingly large destruction of property. Among the worst sufferers were the Catholic missions, and more particularly the Jesuits, who were subjected to atrocious acts of murder and pillage.

The indignation aroused by these outrages caused the Porte and the Powers to act. Foreign warships were promptly despatched to Syrian waters. At the end of August, a French expeditionary force landed at Bairut. By that time, the disorders had practically come to an end, but the presence of the French troops contributed to the final pacification. The Sultan had despatched one of his ablest ministers, Fuad Pasha, with wide powers and with instructions to respect no guilty person in the meting out of punishment. Having discharged this duty with a great show of zeal, Fuad Pasha was ordered to concert measures with the representatives of the Powers who had assembled in Bairut, for the better government of the Lebanon; and their deliberations resulted in the drawing up of a protocol which was later expanded into an instrument known as the *Règlement Organique* of 1864. In that year, a law recasting the administrative system of the Ottoman Empire was promulgated. Syria was divided into two provinces, each administered on highly centralised lines by a governor-general who was no longer a feudal chieftain or semi-independent pasha, but an official appointed by the Sultan and directly responsible to the central government in Constantinople; while the Lebanon, separated from the rest of the country, was placed under a privileged régime based on a large measure of autonomy which allowed it to have its own system of local government, administered by a Christian Governor with the help of a representative council.

The consequences of the upheaval of 1860 and of the settlement which followed it were very far-reaching. It had served to discredit the clergy in their exercise of political power and to drive another nail into the coffin of the feudal system. In the international sphere, it had provided the European Powers with a pretext to justify their meddling openly in the internal affairs of Syria – a precedent which they were to invoke constantly in the next fifty years. Its outstanding political result was to give the Lebanon, what it had never enjoyed before, a form of government designed to suit the peculiar structure and needs of its society and rendered more stable by the international guarantee on which it rested.

But apart from its political and international consequences the upheaval of 1860 deserves to be regarded, in the history of the movement of ideas in Syria, as the decisive event of the nineteenth century. It awakened men's minds to the horrors of their moral stagnation and rekindled the zeal of those who saw that at the root of the country's tribulations was the sectarian hatred that thrives on ignorance. It led to a renewal of activity in the establishment of schools and to an intensification of effort in favour of breaking down the

barriers of obscurantism. And, not least among its consequences, it drove a band of young thinkers to begin an agitation for the liberation of their country from Turkish rule.
They were the pupils of Yazeji and Bustani, the first generation to have been nurtured on the recovered cultural inheritance; and, in the contemplation of its beauty, their
minds had drawn closer to the Arab spirit and felt the warmth
of its passion for freedom. The seed of patriotism was sown,
and a movement came into being whose inspiration was
Arab and whose ideals were national instead of sectarian.
The Arab national movement was born, and the story of its
infancy is in the record of the next forty years in which it
remained weak and impotent, but alive and growing, and
borne slowly towards its destiny on the wings of a renascent
literature.

CHAPTER IV

THE HAMIDIAN DESPOTISM: 1876–1908

I.

THE story of the next forty years unfolds itself, for the most part, in the shadow of 'Abdul-Hamid II's tyranny and covers the two grants of constitutional government to his subjects, which marked the beginning and the end of his reign.

At the opening of the period, the ruling Sultan was 'Abdul-'Aziz, an erratic and extravagant monarch who had ascended the throne in 1861. His reign, which ended with his deposition fifteen years later, was not less turbulent than his predecessor's: apart from his own excesses, the dishonesty and the incompetence of his principal ministers and officials sufficed to make his rule intolerable. There were serious insurrections in several of the European (though not in the Arab) provinces of the empire, of which the last, in Bulgaria, was repressed with such brutal ferocity that it evoked a storm of protest in Europe and formed the starting-point of Gladstone's fulminations against Ottoman misrule. In the Arab provinces, no concerted outbreaks of violence occurred. Unrest and disaffection were increasing, and there was a growing impatience with the corrupt vagaries of the administration. But the movement of ideas towards national emancipation, of which we have seen the birth in the preceding chapter, was still in its infancy and had scarcely had time to do more than awaken a few minds here and there. While in Arabia itself, the occupation of al-Hasa in 1871 and of the Yaman in the following year had extended without consolidating the hold of the Turks in the Peninsula over an increasingly reluctant people.

61

The deposition of 'Abdul-'Aziz was accomplished on May 30, 1876, when he was compelled to abdicate in favour of a nephew who succeeded him as Murad V. The latter, an incurable epileptic, was deposed three months later, on account of his infirmities, and was succeeded by a younger brother, 'Abdul-Hamid II, who was proclaimed sultan on August 31 of that year.

'Abdul-Hamid's reign lasted thirty-three years, until 1909 when he was deposed in his turn. During that period, the movement of ideas of which we have seen the birth in the preceding chapter made decisive strides, and the seed of Arab national consciousness which had taken root in Syria, threw out shoots into the neighbouring Arabic-speaking countries, and finally blossomed forth, after his deposition, into a deliberate and widespread agitation.

2.

'Abdul-Hamid came to the throne at a moment when the outlook for the Ottoman Empire seemed unusually gloomy. A spirit of insurrection was abroad, Russia threatened war, Europe was hostile and dictatorial, especially after the atrocities in Bulgaria; as for financial resources, the public chest was empty and the treasury had already defaulted. The reputation he enjoyed at his accession was that of a devout, liberal-minded and progressive prince, and both the Powers and his subjects had occasion to put it to the test in the first year of his reign.

The Powers were loud in their insistence on reforms in the provincial administration. An influential group of his subjects, led by Midhat Pasha,[1] were pressing for the introduc-

---

[1] One of the greatest Turkish statesmen of modern times. Born in Constantinople in 1822, he served in various posts in the administration until he became, at the age of forty, governor of the province of Bulgaria and later of the Danubian province. In 1868 he was appointed to govern the province of Baghdad. In those posts, he revealed himself a gifted administrator and a patriotic and enlightened statesman. He became Grand Vizir in 1873; but, finding it impossible to serve 'Abdul-'Aziz and retain his self-respect, he retired into private life and joined the group of statesmen who brought about that ruler's deposition.

tion of constitutional government. 'Abdul-Hamid began by appearing to live up to his reputation, revealing at the same time a foxy talent for subterfuge. He made Midhat Grand Vizir, granted a constitution, and chose to have it announced, with a fine show of ceremonial, on the very day (December 23, 1876) on which the representatives of the Powers were assembling in conference to draw up proposals for the better government of his empire. An astute move, so far as its immediate consequences went; for it not only gave his subjects a deceptive earnest of good intentions, but also stole the thunder of the European conference.

The constitution was originally the work of Midhat himself and was stamped with his liberal ideas. One of his deepest beliefs was that a check on the autocratic power of the Sultan was indispensable to the welfare of the empire, and indeed to its existence. Another was that equality of treatment, as between the different subject races, was a necessary prelude to the enlistment of popular support for constitutional government. The first of those two objectives was unexceptionable. The second seems now to have been based on an imperfect estimate of the forces at work. For the disaffection prevailing among the subject races was as much a sign of incipient national consciousness as the product of tyranny and misgovernment. Midhat saw the one motive but failed to discern the other; or, if he perceived it, seems to have misjudged its implications. In any case, the remedy he sought to apply, in providing for the fusion of the different races into a single and coherent democracy, does greater credit to his sense of justice than to his powers of discernment. In the form in which it was issued, after modification by the Sultan, the constitution did not ensure real equality; but it paid due homage to it as a principle of government. Its main virtue, however, was that it provided for some check, though not to the extent of Midhat's desire, on the unfettered caprice of the Sultan.

The victory, however, was short-lived. 'Abdul-Hamid's democratic leanings, such as they were, seemed less pronounced after his accession, and it soon became evident that he was granting a constitution not because he desired or believed in that form of government, but because circumstances had made some such gesture necessary, both as a sop to his subjects and as a torpedo to fire at the European conference. Both those aims had now been achieved: the Sultan had become the idol of his people, and the conference, badly winded, had broken up. He set out to destroy the constitution. The only serious obstacle that remained was Midhat. Early in February, 'Abdul-Hamid abruptly dismissed him and sent him to Europe in exile. Then, having early in March inaugurated the new Parliament with a grandiloquent speech from the throne, he seized the pretext of Russia's declaration of war to decree the suspension of the constitution. It remained 'suspended' for thirty-one years.

The Russo-Turkish War of 1877 ended with the arrival of the Russian armies at the outskirts of Constantinople and the imposition upon the Sultan of the onerous Treaty of San Stefano. But as a result of Great Britain's intervention, Russia had to consent to a revision of its terms and its replacement by the Treaty of Berlin, concluded in July 1878. The settlement thus arrived at affected the European provinces of the Ottoman Empire considerably; but it left the Arab provinces untouched so far as territorial re-adjustment went. The main effect of the war upon their populations was to add to the general discontent and intensify the grievance caused by the levying of Arab recruits to fight, on alien battleships and in conditions of incredible hardship, a remote enemy who was little more than a name to them.

Henceforth, with the constitution suspended and the Treaty of Berlin concluded, 'Abdul-Hamid was free to rule as he liked, and an era began which, for its tyranny and corrupt abuse of power, has scarcely been surpassed in history. There is no need to attempt a chronicle of the main events of his reign: all we need do is to make a brief survey of those features of it which affected the fortunes of the Arab world.

3.

This is a convenient place for taking stock of the Sultan's Arab possessions and the system on which they were administered.

The administrative reorganisation which had begun in the late thirties of the nineteenth century had been carried several steps forward in a succession of enactments passed during the reigns of 'Abdul-Mejid and 'Abdul-'Aziz, one of the results of which had been to give the sultan's ministers a greater degree of control. The new system aimed at uniformity. The Empire was divided into provinces (*vilayet*) each of which was administered by a governor-general (*vali*) directly responsible to the central government in Constantinople. The vilayet was sub-divided into a number of counties (*sanjaq*), each of which had at its head a lieutenant-governor (*mutasarref*) who was a subordinate of the vali's; while the sanjaq was itself made up of numerous smaller units each of which was administered by an official (*qaimmaqam*) whose immediate chief was the mutasarref. In a few exceptional cases, a county which for some reason did not fit into the normal provincial scheme was erected into a separate administrative entity known as an 'independent sanjaq', which meant that its mutasarref enjoyed the prerogatives of a vali so far as executive powers and direct reference to Constantinople went. The Lebanon, as defined in the *Règlement Organique*, was an example in point.

When 'Abdul-Hamid came to the throne, his Arab possessions in Asia were Syria, Iraq and the Arabian Peninsula. In its application to Syria, the administrative system provided for the division of the whole of the geographical expression which went by that name into two vilayets and one sanjaq. But the arrangement proved to be unwieldy and was replaced in 1887 by another one which gave Syria three vilayets and two sanjaqs. These were the Vilayet of Aleppo in the north; the Vilayet of Bairut in the west; the Vilayet of Syria in the east; the Sanjaq of the Lebanon, detached from the Vilayet of Bairut to form a special administrative unit; and the Sanjaq of Jerusalem in the south, which was likewise administratively distinct. In Iraq, after a similar period of trial, the system finally led to the formation of three vilayets, the Vilayet of Mosul in the north, the Vilayet of Baghdad in the centre, and the Vilayet of Basra in the south.

In the Arabian Peninsula, however, conditions were far from favourable to the establishment of a uniform and highly-centralised system. A vali had been appointed to the Hejaz as far back as 1841, in an endeavour to bring the holy land of Islam under direct administration based on a form of dyarchy in which the vali's powers were qualified by the prerogatives of the Grand Sharifs, the traditional lords of Mecca and Madina. In the Yaman, two military expeditions had tried to establish effective Turkish rule, the first in 1849, and the second – carried out on a larger scale thanks to the facilities provided by the opening of the Suez Canal – in 1872. On the Persian Gulf side of the Peninsula, the Turkish penetration had remained limited to the coastal province of al-Hasa which had come under military occupation in 1871. But further inland, in the principalities of Najd and Shammar the Houses of Ibn Sa'ud and of Ibn Rashid, vying with one another as to which could increase its power and its possessions at the expense of its neighbour, cared little for Turkish claims to sovereignty and conducted their affairs and their wars with the freedom of independent dynasties. The difficulties confronting Turkey in the task of asserting her authority in the interior of the Peninsula were insuperable: distance, lack of communications, and the fierceness of the peninsular Arab in the defence of his freedom.

Turkey's task was less difficult in the coastal regions, but there she was finding herself faced with a competitor. The needs of her Indian empire were causing Great Britain to look for allies and coaling-stations on the Arabian seaboard. Napoleon's bid for the conquest of Egypt had caused her to occupy the island of Perim at the mouth of the Red Sea. Almost simultaneously, for reasons connected with Bombay's trade, she had concluded an agreement with the principality of Masqat at the entrance of the Persian Gulf. Strategy and commerce required that the highway be securely guarded, and the freedom of the seas that encircle Arabia became an axiom of British policy. Aden was occupied in 1839 and subsequently acquired as a possession of the British Crown. Then Perim was re-occupied in 1857, permanently this time. And step by step, throughout the nineteenth century, the shadow of British influence crawled northwards towards the head of the Persian Gulf to the discomfiture of the Turk who, moving southwards from Basra, endeavoured in vain to assert his authority on the fringes of Arabia, since the interior was beyond his grasp.

In Africa, the Ottoman Empire as 'Abdul-Hamid found it comprised only Tunisia, Libya, Egypt and the Sudan, since Algeria had been seized by France in 1830; and, so far as retaining his Arab possessions in that continent goes, the Sultan began his reign badly. In 1881, he lost Tunisia to France. In the following year, England occupied Egypt and subsequently the Sudan. His nominal suzerainty was acknowledged by Great Britain in Egypt and the Sudan, but not by France in Tunisia; in both cases he ceased to exercise any control on the administration. This meant that the whole of the North African coast had passed out of Turkish hands, with the single exception of Libya of which a substantial part was to fall to Italy in 1912. For the moment, it remained the Sultan's only possession in Africa; and, so far as its administration went, it was divided into two provinces, the Vilayet of Tripoli and the Vilayet of Benghazi.

4.

The foundations of 'Abdul-Hamid's rule were laid on a basis of espionage and repression. A system grew up in which the spies employed by the Sultan for his political ends became a powerful oligarchy of corrupt ruffians against whom no one, however eminent or innocent, was safe, except perhaps by the timely use of bribery. A censorship was imposed and grew more rigorous and stifling, until it succeeded in taking the life out of all journalistic or any kind of literary enterprise. The courts of justice became the subservient instruments of the Palace clique and could generally be counted upon to find the required judicial grounds for the imposition of a pre-ordained penalty. Such punishments as internment, deportation or exile were currently inflicted on mere suspicion or delation.

Having laid the groundwork of his power internally, 'Abdul-Hamid proceeded to raise upon it the edifice of an imperial and foreign policy. He was not blind to the weakness of Turkey's position among the nations, and was shrewd enough to realise that her only security lay in the rivalry and jealousies of the Powers amongst themselves. The Russian advance to the gates of Constantinople had left him with no illusion as to his military strength; and the Treaty of Berlin, despite the mitigating effect of England's curbing of Russia, was itself a humiliating reminder that his empire existed only on sufferance. As for the financial position, it had reached the stage of bankruptcy. The remedies which 'Abdul-Hamid devised were characteristic of his realistic and unenlightened mind. First, he obtained money by mortgaging to foreign capitalists the principal resources of the empire. Next, he devoted a large share of the money thus obtained to the reorganisation of his army, spending vast sums on military academies and training, while real education remained half starved. And thirdly, in an attempt to strengthen his position internationally, he invoked the power of religion to his aid in the political field. Of the three, the last was in many ways the most important.

5.

When 'Abdul-Hamid ascended the throne, the attention of Islam had for some years been captured by a voice calling it to a new life. It was the voice of Sayyed Jamaluddin al-Afghani, one of the most ardent and most eloquent preachers the Moslem world has ever heard. His ultimate aim was to raise the Moslem peoples to the status of free and progressive nations by a wide process of education and by the adaptation of the religion of Islam to the conditions of the age; but he believed that, as a means to that end, revolutionary action was unavoidable. He wanted to see the Moslem countries freed from foreign domination, as a prelude to their moral regeneration, and then united under one universally acknowledged caliph, as in the golden age of Islam. In the eight years (1871-9) of his sojourn in Egypt, he had formed a small but active following of disciples and acquired such a say in the fortunes of that country that he was invited to leave it. He was already a force in the world of Islam and one with which the Powers of the West had to reckon. The remaining years of his life, which he spent in Europe, in Persia and in Turkey, until his death in 1896, were devoted to an intense and indefatigable propagation of his ideas. The movement known as the pan-Islamic revival, which stirred the Moslem world in the last quarter of the nineteenth century, was largely his creation; and it was while Jamaluddin was at the height of his powers and his activity that 'Abdul-Hamid began to lay the foundations of his own Islamic policy.

'Abdul-Hamid's policy was in no sense an espousal of Jamaluddin's ideas. In essence, it was an attempt on the part of the sultan-caliph to strengthen his authority as sultan of the Ottoman Empire by a greater display of his prerogatives as caliph of Islam. His predecessors had held the dual title continuously for at least two centuries and had been generally recognised in Europe as the lawful bearers of it. But they had not succeeded in staying the process by which the *caliph* attribute had gradually lost its original significance and come to be regarded as a merely spiritual dignity, an appanage of the *sultan* attribute, fit only to be invoked in matters of religious import. This view of the caliphate, partly derived from a false analogy with the papacy, was altogether erroneous since it overlooked that, in Islam, church and state were closely interwoven, and the term 'caliph' synonymous in practice with that of 'ruler'. 'Abdul-Hamid's plan was to restore the caliphate to its proper place, to identify it with the sultanate in the popular

69

mind and use it, when thus rehabilitated, now as a prop and then as a lever for the attainment of political ends. His policy had thus points of apparent contact with the revival preached by Jamaluddin. The contact was outward and not real, but 'Abdul-Hamid skilfully exploited it to his uses.

'Abdul-Hamid had two distinct policies in view, the one domestic and the other foreign. Within the empire, he sought to strengthen the hold of the sultanate on the minds of his Moslem subjects by emphasising its identity with the caliphate and harping on the sacred attributes of his office: shadow of God on earth, commander of the Faithful, servitor of the Holy Places; to stimulate loyalty to his throne by playing on the feelings of the devout millions; to build up a reserve of energy, in the form of religious fervour, for possible use in war. In its foreign aspect, his plan aimed at buttressing Turkey's position among the nations. His assumption of the role of pious caliph would earn him not only the more willing allegiance of millions of his own subjects, but the reverence as well, and perhaps a good deal more than the mere reverence of many more millions of Moslems outside his empire – subjects of Great Britain, France and Russia. He aspired to become the head of Islam, in influence as well as in name. Whatever success this policy might achieve would mean so much more strength to his position in the international game.

In the execution of this plan, 'Abdul-Hamid displayed a resourceful versatility and a nice sense of showmanship. On the principle that true sanctity begins at home, he started by giving his private life an appearance of devout austerity. He took to practising the religious observances strictly and with discreet ostentation. The habits of drunkenness and debauchery which former sultans had carelessly indulged were rigorously suppressed in the Palace, or at any rate screened from knowledge. He surrounded himself with theologians and holy men, amongst whom were some of wide renown and influence, and used them as almoners, mentors or propagandists. A college was founded for the training

of missionaries who were presently despatched in batches
to the furthest corners of Islam to preach the good tidings
and extol the piety of the caliph. He won the Sharif of
Mecca over to active support in the form of propaganda and
exhortation among the pilgrims who, on returning to their
countries, carried the message and, in some cases, founded
cells for its further diffusion. Subsidies to theological schools
and colleges, both within and without the empire, were
liberally provided. The newspapers were made to play
their part, and periodicals founded to further the publicity.

An important feature of 'Abdul-Hamid's plan was that it
was specially designed to influence the non-Turkish elements and more particularly the Arabs. The Turkish
masses, composed mainly of Anatolian peasants, were by
nature submissive and loyal to the Padishah. The Arabs,
with their ingrained love of independence, were less amenable and (what was more serious) had been showing disquieting symptoms of a budding national consciousness.
'Abdul-Hamid made special efforts to win them over. He
showered bounties on Arab institutions of learning, and
honours and office on Arab chiefs and dignitaries. He spent
lavish sums on the repair and decoration of the mosques at
Mecca, Madina and Jerusalem, the three principal shrines
of Islam, and all three in Arab custody. One of the battalions which formed his personal bodyguard was entirely composed of picked Arab recruits. He took Arabs into his own
personal service at the Palace and used them to organise and
direct those of his agents who were working to combat Arab
nationalist tendencies. A few of those acquired such influence with the Sultan that courtiers, concession-hunters,
ministers of state and even the grand vizir found it expedient
to humour them and to observe the golden rule of canvassing
their goodwill beforehand for all important transactions. It
was said, not without truth, that while the Sublime Porte
and the Ministries were still a hunting-ground for Turks, the
Palace had fallen entirely into the hands of Arabs.

Wherever his policy of favours and blandishments failed
of its effect, 'Abdul-Hamid had recourse to criminal means.

71

He had a number of picked emissaries scouring the Arab world in the guise of preachers whose real mission was to sow or fan discord between feudal chiefs and the heads of the larger nomadic confederations. Family quarrels, tribal disputes and blood-feuds were exploited and promoted. He subsidised agents to provoke disturbances of the peace in order to provide visible pretexts for the punishment of some recalcitrant chieftain or leader marked down for vengeance. He tolerated, and in certain instances ordered, a resort to assassination. If the victim happened to be too eminent for summary vengeance, 'Abdul-Hamid would compel him to reside in Constantinople, and there would not only abstain from having him murdered, but arrange for his living in ease and dignity under the watch of his spies.

One of such 'guests' was Husain ibn 'Ali, a scion of the House of Bani Hashem, the noblest of all Arab families, for they traced their descent in the male line back to the Prophet's daughter, and generations of holders of the dignity of Grand Sharif of Mecca had been recruited from their ranks. Reports had reached 'Abdul-Hamid, depicting young Husain as a wilful and recalcitrant person whose views, on the rare occasions when he consented to express them, revealed a 'dangerous' capacity for original and independent thinking. The family's standing in the Moslem world was so high that the sultans of Turkey, in their dealings with its members, moved with circumspection and maintained an outward show of regard. Husain was courteously invited to bring his household and come to reside in Constantinople. He arrived there in 1893, a comparatively young man in his late thirties, with his wife and three sons just old enough to be put to school: 'Ali (afterwards King of the Hejaz), 'Abdullah (afterwards Amir of Transjordan), and Faisal (afterwards King of Iraq). The family's captivity was to last over fifteen years, and during that time, Husain who was a deeply religious man, led a quiet, meditative and outwardly inert life which to the Sultan's spies seemed unexceptionable, but which made 'Abdul-Hamid, with his keen sense of unseen forces, increasingly uneasy.

6.

Among the adventurers who had intrigued their way into 'Abdul-Hamid's favour was 'Izzat Pasha al-'Abed, a Syrian Arab, who served thirteen years (until his downfall in 1908) as the Sultan's second secretary, and who rose to become the most powerful official in the empire, second only to his master in wealth, rascality and influence. He was, even for the Constantinople of Hamidian days, an extraordinarily astute man, cunning and agile, but not exempt from that obtuseness which is so often the background of a nimble mind. His outstanding quality was his unerring insight into the less reputable traits of the human character: in that lay the secret of his amazing success, for it enabled him to understand the cowardice and the vanity of his master with true discrimination and a nice sense of the mood of the moment. Inwardly, he held 'Abdul-Hamid in utter contempt, which partly explains the ease with which he could play upon his feelings. His career is of interest for the general reason that he became the pivot of the Sultan's Arab policy, and also for a particular reason – the construction of the Hejaz Railway.

There are indications to show – although it is not certain – that the idea of laying a railway line to the Hejaz originated in 'Izzat Pasha's mind; in any case it was he who became mainly instrumental in carrying it into fruition. The project was to build a railway from Damascus to Madina and on to Mecca, ostensibly with the sole object of facilitating the pilgrimage, but in reality for reasons which were primarily political and strategic. A board presided over by 'Izzat was set up, and an appeal to the Moslem world issued stressing the pious motive which had inspired the caliph to build the railway, and asking for contributions towards the cost. The appeal met with a handsome response. At the same time, a special tax in the form of a stamp duty was levied throughout the empire, while officials in the Hejaz were 'invited' to contribute a percentage of their salaries.

The work of construction which was entrusted to German engineers began in the spring of 1901, and by the autumn of 1908 the line had been laid to Madina – a distance of close upon 900 miles. Of the total cost, amounting to some £3,000,000 over one-third was made up of voluntary donations from all parts of the Moslem world.

The project was a master-stroke of policy in more than one way. It evoked a great deal of enthusiasm throughout Islam, and did more, probably, than any of 'Abdul-Hamid's other schemes to add to the prestige of the caliphate. Strategically, it had provided him, at relatively small cost to his treasury, with a much-needed means of overland transport for his troops to and from Arabia. Hitherto, he had had to depend on the slower and costlier sea-transport through the Suez Canal; now he had a railway running entirely in his territory, and he could look forward to the day when the line would be carried southwards to Mecca and possibly beyond, to strengthen his hold on turbulent Yaman.

But the most important result, and one which 'Abdul-Hamid had perhaps not envisaged was the speeding up of communications for travel and therefore for ideas, in the western Arab provinces. Before the operation of the line, it would take a quick caravan not less than forty days to travel from Damascus to Madina; while the sea-journey from Syria to the Hejaz took from ten to fifteen days, according to the sailings which were infrequent and capricious. With the railway, the two cities were brought to within five days of each other; and this abbreviation was destined, as we shall see, to make an incalculable difference to the fortunes of the Arab movement when at last it found an opportunity for breaking into open revolt.

In his annual report for 1907, the British Ambassador at the Sublime Porte wrote:

'There are only two factors in the general political situation that show forth with any clearness during, at all events, the last ten years. The one is the astute policy which induced the Sultan to pose before 300,000,000 of Mohammedans as the Caliph and spiritual head of his religion, and in bringing home to his subjects the fervour and energy of his religious feelings by the construction of the Hejaz Railway, which, in the near future, will afford facilities to every Moslem to perform the pilgrimage to the holy places of Mecca and Madina, and throw open to them in the next life the joys and delights of paradise. The effect has been that he has commanded, to an unprecedented degree, the blind obedience of his subjects, and reconciled them to a despotism more absolute than has perhaps ever been known in the whole course of history. The will of the "Padishah" has become the law of the land, and the unfortunate Moslem who feels the cruel oppression and tyranny of the Government lays his grievances at the door of the officials, and attributes no evil action to the Caliph.'[1]

The other factor which the ambassador had in mind was 'Abdul-Hamid's relations with the Kaiser.

7.

'Abdul-Hamid's accession coincided roughly with the birth of a new orientation in Germany's foreign policy, the *Drang nach Osten.* For some time, economists and political writers in Germany had been devoting a good deal of attention to the possibilities of Asia Minor as a field for colonisation, and the idea that it might become a predominantly German field had begun to make headway. In course of time, it was adopted as the basis of a new policy which was to establish German ascendancy in Constantinople and lead Kaiser Wilhelm II to make, in favour of 'Abdul-Hamid's Islamic policy, one of his strangest demonstrations.

A chapter was opened in 1883 when a German military mission arrived in Constantinople to undertake the modernisation of the Sultan's army. It was headed by Colonel von der Goltz, a capable and conscientious officer, who for the next thirteen years worked indefatigably at his task. His passion for efficiency, however, was not altogether to the Sultan's liking; for, although he wanted his army improved, 'Abdul-Hamid did not want too strong an army – he lived

[1] Gooch and Temperley: *British Documents on the Origins of the War,* Vol. V, p. 43.

in dread of a military revolution – and he and his camarilla worked in secret against von der Goltz.   While the latter was putting his unflagging energy to overhauling every branch of the gimcrack military machine, agents of the Palace were seeing to it that his efforts, in so far as they aimed at making the army into a strong, self-contained instrument, remained within the bounds of 'safety'.   Nevertheless, von der Goltz was able to achieve a great deal; and in one branch – that of military education – his work had important political results.   It was thanks to him that a system of military colleges came into being, whose standard was so far above the general educational level that it drew – from among Arabs as well as Turks – many of the best brains of the coming generation. Of the men who were afterwards to play a part in the revolution which overthrew 'Abdul-Hamid's tyranny, and in the Arab Revolt a few years later, the graduates of those military colleges were the most prominent.

The military mission was, naturally enough, instrumental in placing orders for arms and munitions with German firms but its activities were not confined to its professed task. Some of its members, acting on orders issued by Bismarck himself, busied themselves with a variety of other interests and sent home periodical reports on conditions and prospects in Turkey.   Then agents of financial houses appeared, to be followed by powerful banks intervening to secure, first, one concession, then another, for railways in Anatolia; so that, between 1888 and 1896, the existing line from Haidar Pasha (on the Asiatic shore of the Bosphorus) was extended down to Konia.   Meanwhile, the idea of exploiting Asia Minor had crystallised into a principle of *Realpolitik* sponsored by the German Government, which included plans for the economic invasion of the Ottoman Empire.   It was part of those plans that a concession be sought for the construction of a railway to the Persian Gulf; and the Kaiser came in person to obtain it.

In the autumn of 1898, after four or five years of diplomatic preparation, Wilhelm II arrived in Constantinople on a state visit to the Sultan, and succeeded in obtaining the desired concession. The Baghdad Railway was to be a continuation of the German-built line from Haidar Pasha to Konia and was planned to skirt the southern fringe of Anatolia eastwards to Mosul, thus following almost exactly the racial boundary between Turks and Arabs, and then, turning southwards to Baghdad, to run down to Basra and reach its terminus somewhere on the Persian Gulf. Branch lines were contemplated at various points, including one to Alexandretta, so as to provide direct communication between the Mediterranean and the Persian Gulf. It was a bold and ambitious scheme, and a menace to British interests in the East. It raised problems of a strategic, as well as political and economic, nature. To Germany, it would mean the acquisition of a great sphere of influence, rich in markets and raw materials, secure against the menace of sea-power, pregnant with the promise of empire; to Great Britain, the installation of a formidable competitor for her trade and a challenge to her supremacy in the Persian Gulf.

From Constantinople the Kaiser went to Jerusalem and on to Damascus, to lay the foundations of the new edifice of German influence in Syria. During his tour, he took pains to stress – and, as was usual with him, to overstress – his benevolence to the Sultan and his sympathy for Islam and its caliph. In a speech he delivered in Damascus, he said: 'His Majesty the Sultan and the three hundred million Moslems who revere him as the Caliph may rest assured that they will always have a friend in the German Emperor.' Then, with great ceremonial, he repaired to the tomb of Saladin, laid a wreath, and ordered that a silver lamp be made for the mausoleum, as a personal gift from one of the Moslem hero's fervent admirers. These gestures were widely advertised, and the Kaiser returned to Berlin amidst the plaudits of the inspired Press in the Moslem world.

'Abdul-Hamid was far too shrewd to be dazzled by the heroics of his new protector. But he saw the value of an ally of that calibre in the councils of Europe, and he had confidence in his own ability to ward off the dangers implied in the German bid for influence. He welcomed the Kaiser's

77

flourish of friendship to Islam, not for its own sake, but rather for the uses to which it might be put as an advertisement and a diplomatic prop. As for Germany's ambitions in Turkey, so long as they did not imply political control, he felt disposed to bargain, and even to be generous, with assets which had never brought him any revenue. Over the Baghdad Railway, he was particularly eager to adopt the German scheme because to him, haunted as he was by his exaggerated fears of a rising of the Arabs, it seemed above all – like the Hejaz Railway – a means of tightening his hold on restive Arab populations. Trusted advisers, like 'Izzat Pasha had played on those fears; and von der Goltz, in whose sincerity he believed, had for years urged him on to a forward and progressive policy in the Arab provinces.[1]

So, while the rival Powers looked frowningly on, 'Abdul-Hamid held out his hand and lent his cheek to the Kaiser's kisses, without anyone but himself knowing to what lengths he would ultimately go in the sordid bestowal of his favours. His reign of personal rule came to an end on the 23rd of July 1908, when a revolution of army officers – the graduates of military colleges, it need scarcely be added – compelled him to restore Midhat Pasha's Constitution which had remained suspended for thirty-one years.

[1] Von der Goltz's views on this subject are to be found in his article: *Stärke und Schwäche des Türkischen Reichs,* in *Deutsche Rundschau,* October 1897.

CHAPTER V

THE INFANT MOVEMENT: 1868–1908

I.

THE first organised effort in the Arab national movement can be traced back to the year 1875 – two years before 'Abdul-Hamid's accession – when five young men who had been educated at the Syrian Protestant College in Bairut formed a secret society.   They were all Christians, but they saw the importance of getting Moslems and Druzes to join, and managed after some time to enlist the membership of some twenty-two persons belonging to the different creeds and representing the enlightened *élite* of the country.   Freemasonry on the European pattern had just found its way into Syria, and the promoters of the secret society were able, through one of their number, to interest the recently-founded Lodge in its activities.

The centre of their organisation was Bairut, and they established branches in Damascus, Tripoli, and Sidon. Their aims being frankly revolutionary, they could scarcely indulge in any of the pleasures of publicity, and their procedure was at first entirely confined to secret meetings at which they would exchange views and discuss plans, and to the dissemination of their political ideas through personal channels. At last, after three or four years of whispered conspiracy, they realised that to continue preaching to themselves would serve only to increase their own ardour, and they decided to broaden their appeal.   The method they chose – the only one open to them under a vigilant Turkish bureaucracy – was that of posting anonymous placards in the streets.

Once this decision was taken, they set to work with the

agility of youthful conspirators. Having drafted the text of
an appeal they would spend long nightly vigils making out
innumerable copies of it in disguised handwritings. Then
at an agreed hour at dead of night, the younger members
would go out, with pots of glue in their pockets, and stick
as many placards as they found time for on the walls of
the city. In the morning, a crowd would collect around
each poster while som'eone read it out aloud, until the
police would come, tear it down, and make arrests among
the innocent bystanders. Before the excitement had died
down in Bairut, reports would come of the appearance
of similar placards in Damascus. Tripoli or Sidon. Their
contents furnished a topic of hushed conversation at
private gatherings; and the members of the society,
carefully guarding their secret, would circulate among their
friends and acquaintances, take part in the discussions, and
inwardly note the comments. They would then compose
their next appeal in the light of the effect caused by the last.
By a refinement of the art of disguise, they varied the style and
literary standard of their compositions, and committed
deliberate errors of grammar, thus rendering conjecture as
to authorship still more uncertain.

The placards contained violent denunciations of the evils
of Turkish rule, and exhorted the Arab population to rise in
rebellion and overthrow it. The authorities, in Constantinople as well as in Syria, were puzzled and perturbed, and
the Sultan despatched secret emissaries of his own to Bairut
to investigate. Houses were searched and a number of
people imprisoned on suspicion. Rumour had it that the
Governor-General of Syria, who was none other than
Midhat Pasha, the former Grand Vizir and author of the
Constitution of 1876, was privy to the existence of the society
and, if he had not actually created it, was at any rate shield-
ing it. The intention was even assigned to him of wishing
to foment trouble in Syria in the hope of wresting it from the
Sultan's rule and, like Mehemed-'Ali in Egypt, founding a
dynasty of his own. The available evidence can scarcely
support this accusation. Yet such was the effervescence

caused by the proclamations of the Bairut society that the
Sultan recalled Midhat. It is pretty certain that he was
innocent of any connexion with it. The society remained in
existence for three or four years after his recall, until the
weight of 'Abdul-Hamid's tyranny became so heavy that it
was thought prudent to suspend its activities. Its scanty
records were destroyed, and several of its most active members emigrated to Egypt. The secret was well kept to the
end, and the identity of the conspirators was never known to
the Government or to the public.

2.

No account exists of the activities of the Bairut secret
society in any of the published sources I have consulted; and
I am greatly indebted, for the narrative I have just given, to
one of its original founders, Dr. Faris Nimr Pasha[1] who, at
the ripe age of eighty and in the fullest enjoyment of his
faculties, remembered the main facts and the names of the
twenty-two members. I spent several sittings with him,
drawing on his prodigious memory and accumulating fact
after fact about those occurrences in which he had first become involved close upon sixty years previously, until I had
the narrative complete, save in one important respect: the
texts of the placards. Dr. Nimr was able to give me an idea
of their general trend and purport, of the increasing violence
of their tone, of the trouble the writers took to disguise their
handwritings and vary the style. But the wording of the
appeals, so material to a proper appreciation, he could not
at such an interval recollect. No copies had been kept at the
time, nor was any divulgation possible during 'Abdul-
Hamid's reign, even on the part of the exiles, for it might
have led to reprisals. The only other member of the society
who is still alive was able to furnish me with a good deal of

---

[1] One of the most outstanding figures in the Arab world. Born in the
Lebanon, he emigrated to Egypt in 1883 and has lived there ever since. He
was one of the founders of al-Muqtataf, a scientific monthly, and of al-
Muqattam, a daily newspaper, both published in Cairo, and both still
widely read in the Arabic-speaking countries.

corroborative evidence; but he, too, did not remember the texts. It seemed as though I would have to resign myself to writing the story without them.

For over a year, in the course of my travels in search of material for this book, I followed the faint trail of the secret society of 1875, and I questioned people in all parts of Syria, and in Cairo and Baghdad. There were many who remembered the appearance of the placards, and some who could from personal knowledge testify to the deep effect which the fervent appeals they contained had on the minds of the rising generation. But of the texts there was still not a trace.

A year later, as I was pursuing my research in the Public Record Office in London, I came upon a telegram from the British Consul-General in Bairut, dated June 28, 1880.[1] It read as follows:

> 'Revolutionary placards have appeared in Bairut. Midhat suspected as the author. Tranquillity, however, prevails. Details by next post.'

There followed several despatches, some from Bairut and others from Damascus, which told the story as it became known to the British consular agents at the time, with their conjectures as to the origin of the placards. But what was more valuable still was that the consul-general in Bairut had thought it worth while to transmit as enclosures to his despatches the texts of three different placards, in the Arabic in which they were written. Of these, one was an original which had been taken away before the arrival of the police, while the other two were copies. With these texts before us, we can form a clearer idea of the aims and tendencies of the society. Taking them in the order in which they appeared, they reveal an interesting progression in their range and literary quality.

The first, which accompanies a despatch dated July 3, 1880[1] is the shortest and the least interesting. Although it is

[1] Public Record Office, *F.O. 195/1306.*

the first to have been noticed by the British consulate, it was obviously not the first placard issued by the society, for it refers to a previous appeal and seeks to assert the sincerity and the patriotism of its authors in connexion with some former pronouncement. It rebukes the people of Syria for their lethargy under the tyranny of the Turks and for their habits of dissension which make them a prey to European ambitions. It stresses the importance of unity and incites the people to sink their differences and unite against their tyrants under the inspiration of their 'Arab pride'. It is surmounted with a device representing a drawn sword below which is this line of verse: '*By the sword may distant aims be attained; seek with it if you mean to succeed.*'

The second, which is enclosed in the same despatch, is more specific in its condemnation of the Turks. It indicts them for their failure to carry out the reforms which for twenty years – that is to say since 1860, the year of the massacres in Syria – they had promised to introduce, and brands them as incorrigible and hopeless. It goes further than the preceding text in that it explicitly advocates a régime of autonomy, or possibly independence, for Syria; and it ends with a rhetorical assertion of resolve on the part of its authors to serve their country at whatever cost.

The third, which is described in a covering despatch[1] as having been posted up on the night of December 31, 1880, is the most significant of the three, since it contains the first recorded statement of an Arab political programme. It opens with another indictment of the Turks as rulers, to whose other misdeeds is now added that of attempting to stifle the Arabic tongue. It strikes a religious note in describing the Sultan's tenure of the caliphate as a usurpation of Arab rights and accusing the Turks of habitually transgressing the laws of Islam. It states that, after consultation 'with our colleagues all over the country', a programme had been drawn up which it was intended to carry out, at the point of the sword if necessary. The main points of that programme were:

[1] Public Record Office, *F.O. 195/1369.*

(1) the grant of independence to Syria in union with the Lebanon;
(2) the recognition of Arabic as an official language in the country;
(3) the removal of the censorship and other restrictions on the freedom of expression and the diffusion of knowledge;
(4) the employment of locally-recruited units on local military service only.

Taken together, the three texts show a definite progression from the general towards the particular, from a rhetorical denunciation of Turkish misrule to the formulation of a specific programme of national aspirations, and a programme in which the fruits of Yazeji's efforts for the enthronement of the Arabic language and of Bustani's campaign against ignorance are clearly discernible. Ibrahim Yazeji, the son of Nasif, was himself a member of the society; and it adds to the interest of the three texts that each of them should have ended with a quotation from the poem which, twelve years previously, he had recited at a clandestine meeting of the Syrian Scientific Society.

3.

It is not easy at an interval of some sixty years to gauge with any certainty the impulse given by the Bairut secret society to the movement of ideas. The evidence in the despatches of British consular agents tends to minimise its importance, and to represent its revolutionary placards as damp squibs which did no more than excite an apathetic population to a faint show of curiosity. The testimony of Arab contemporary observers, on the other hand, asserts that the appeals had a widespread effect. The consular despatches have the double merit of having been written at the time and by comparatively neutral observers; but the fact that they deal with matters of treasonable conspiracy, in which both actors and spectators were afraid to speak their minds, takes away from the value they might otherwise have had.[1] Even when

[1] Certain palpable errors in those despatches show that the truth about the activities of the society remained largely hidden from the British consular representatives.

proper allowance is made for the passage of time, the factor of exaggeration, and the inconstancy of human memory, the testimony of the eye-witnesses I have in recent years consulted seems convincing and acceptable.

However that may be, the society's appeals were the first trumpet-call emitted by the infant Arab movement. It was the earliest organisation to be founded with a primarily political object. Viewed in the light of subsequent events, as well as of the conditions of the period, its activities appear to have been premature, in the sense that they presupposed a more widespread development of the national consciousness than the country at large could boast of; and thus its call to political agitation – to be reinforced by armed revolt, if need were – had come too soon to rally a nation. In that aspect the attempt was doomed to failure; but it bore fruit in other ways. And not the least of its achievements was that the society's repeated appeals did serve to hammer into shape desires that were still too vaguely felt and hopes as yet unformulated; and, by so doing, to give the drifting tide of ideas not only added impetus but a sense of direction as well. The programme announced in the third of its placards stands out as a model for those which came later. It is the first statement of political aims of which there is any record in the history of the movement, and it merits attention as the only document of the period that provides us with an authentic picture of the nature and the tendencies of Arab nationalism in its earliest days.

Hitherto, the movement had kept within the narrow limits of its environment. It had come into being, as we have seen, thanks to a cultural and social awakening of which the mainsprings were the literary revival and the revulsion of feeling caused by the massacres of 1860. The forces that had set it in motion were not only of a moral order, unaffected by economic needs or political theories; but they were also forces of spontaneous origin, generated by emotions from within. The movement had derived its ideas from the familiar sources of its environment, long before it took to borrowing the Western notions of political

85

evolution. The innovations of Mehemed-'Ali in Egypt and
of Sultan Mahmud II in Turkey had had as their primary
aim to re-model the fighting services and modernise certain
branches of the administration, and had served to introduce
the forms and patterns rather than the abstract ideology of
European institutions. Practical devices are assimilated
more rapidly than ideas, and the concept of a nation, that is
to say of a homogeneous population forming a coherent
whole and governed by a common national outlook and purpose, had not penetrated to any depth in the Arab provinces
of the Ottoman Empire. Even as late as 1876, the enthusiasm evoked by Midhat's Constitution, with its ideal of a
piebald state formed of the fusion of different racial elements
pursuing totally divergent aims, showed how far minds still
were from grasping the ideas underlying the Western concept
of the nation-state. It was only during the last quarter of the
nineteenth century that that concept invaded the world of
ideas in Syria, to graft itself on the indigenous tree of Arab
nationalism. Until then, the movement which had sprung
in a soil of its own had derived its main sustenance from the
earth in which it had its roots. And the programme pla-
carded by the Bairut society in 1880 has this added historical
value, that it enables us, while recognising the cultural tendencies implicit in the very birth of the movement, to discern
the first symptom of a new conception, namely, that of a
politically independent state resting on a truly national basis.

4.

The first plank in that programme aims at the achievement
of independence based upon the unity of Syria and the
Lebanon. The special régime of local autonomy established
in the Lebanon by the *Règlement Organique* of 1864 had endowed that province with an administration of its own which
had virtually detached it, in point of political structure, from
the rest of Syria. Whatever its beneficial effects in other
directions may have been, this disseverance was altogether
hostile to the spirit of the Arab revival, to its hatred of barriers

and divisions, and to its fervent belief in the virtues of unison and concord which it regarded as the principle of salvation. The fact that the Arab character, with its strongly individualistic strain, was conspicuously deficient in those virtues and had proved an easy prey to the dangers of clannishness and faction gave added stimulus to the zeal of the leaders in extolling their merits.   In the Bairut programme, the emphasis put upon the community of interests and the political identity of the Lebanon with the rest of Syria was only the natural reflection of that revulsion against the mere idea of partition and separatism.   Here, too is the root of the idea of Arab unity which, spreading outward from Syria, has embraced the whole of the Arab nationalist world and taken a place in the forefront of Arab aspirations.   It was in the pursuit of that idea as it bore on the problem of Syria that the authors of the programme of 1880 adopted, for the first time on record, the plank of an independent state embodying the national (as against the sectarian) concept of a political entity.

In the same way, the second point in the programme is the direct reflection of the earliest phases of the revival, namely the rehabilitation of Arabic as a medium of literary expression and the campaign against ignorance and fanaticism.   From 1864 onwards, as the policy of greater centralisation in the Ottoman Empire developed, the use of Turkish as the language of government became more widely imposed in Syria.   The higher officials were all Turks and the majority of them totally unacquainted with Arabic. The business of administration, in the law-courts and the principal public services, was conducted in Turkish; and a knowledge of that language which had remained a foreign tongue despite centuries of Ottoman sovereignty was now becoming an indispensable medium for official transactions.   This change was taking place at a time when, as we have seen, the educational efforts of the foreign missions and the activities of scholars who were resuscitating the forgotten culture of the past had led to the regeneration of Arabic as a vehicle of thought and to a vigorous movement of literary and scientific production in the national language.

87

The spreading imposition of Turkish ran counter to this movement and wounded the pride of its enthusiastic adherents. Nor was this all: there was also the censorship, introduced by 'Abdul-Hamid soon after the suspension of the constitution, which was gradually growing in severity and stupidity, extending its withering hand to ban foreign books as well as stifle local expression. To none could such shackles appear more galling than to the members of the Bairut secret society, with its varied membership of scientists and men of letters, most of them the pupils, all of them the disciples, of Yazeji and Bustani. Like their appeal for unity, their plea for language and intellectual freedom was but the echo of the impassioned doctrines of their masters and was destined, likewise, to be the battle-cry of the coming generations.

Unlike the first two, the third point in the programme deals with a matter of incidental rather than fundamental origin. It was a protest against the newly-introduced practice of detailing the Arab troops recruited in Syria to fight the Arabs of the Yaman. The reconquest of that province by the Ottoman forces in 1872 had opened a long and costly chapter of enmity between Turk and Arab, and the imperial troops in occupation of it could scarcely, from the very start, hold their own against the hostile population. It was thought that regiments formed of Arab troops might meet with less determined resistance, and orders were issued to draft the conscripts enlisted in Syria for service in the Peninsula. The first batch, amounting to several thousands, had been forcibly embarked in 1874 amid general consternation. Three years later, battalions recruited in Syria had been despatched to the theatres of the Russo-Turkish War, to fight for a cause with which they had not the remotest connexion.

5.

The publication of the programme was the outward climax of the society's activities. It continued to exist over the next three or four years and, according to oral report, it issued further appeals. But of these, no trace has yet come to light; and in any case, on the testimony of one of the society's founders, they did not add materially to the earlier ones. The agitation had served its main purpose: to translate racial sentiment into a political creed, and in doing so had not merely unfurled a flag, but, what was more needed still, had set an arrow to point the way.

It is in the nature of the Arab temperament to conceive action in spasms rather than on a plan of sustained effort, and the history of the national movement is in a sense a chronicle of vivid outbursts with periods of recovery and preparation between them. It unfolds itself in a pattern of flames shooting upwards from a dull fire of smouldering feeling. The revolutionary effort of the Bairut secret society was the first of a series of waves which were to follow each other at irregular intervals; and the programme of 1880, quite apart from its intrinsic importance, is historically notable as marking the furthest advance of that earliest wave. In the way of tangible results, it accomplished nothing visible: its achievement remained hidden in the secret recesses of the national consciousness whose signpost it became. The minds who had shaped it out of the blurred longings of an inarticulate people were thinking ahead of their time. But they had seen the problem clearly and seen it whole, and one of the tributes afterwards paid to their insight is that their programme, in its essentials, was never superseded.

6.

Both the movement of ideas in Syria and the political ferment which it fostered are vividly described in the following quotations from the writings of contemporary observers.

A French writer who visited Syria in 1882 has left a record of his impressions of the new spirit:

' . . . . A spirit of independence is abroad. During my stay in Bairut, young Moslems were busy organising societies to promote the establishment of schools and hospitals and to

work for the regeneration of the country. An interesting
feature of this activity is its freedom from all taint of sectarian-
ism. The societies which are being formed are designed to
admit Christians and enlist their co-operation in the national
task. The Turks were left out of account. . . .'[1]

Another Frenchman who, after extensive travels in the
Arab countries of North Africa and along the shores of the
Red Sea and the Persian Gulf, sailed up the Tigris as far as
Baghdad in 1883, found symptoms of unrest in all parts of
the Arab world:

'. . . . Everywhere I came upon the same abiding and universal sentiment: hatred of the Turks. . . . The notion of
concerted action to throw off the detested yoke is gradually
shaping itself. . . . An Arab movement, newly-risen, is looming
in the distance; and a race hitherto down-trodden will presently claim its due place in the destinies of Islam. . . .'[2]

In the Arabian Peninsula itself, the germ of political combination was already discernible. Writing on the 10th of
May 1882, the British Political Agent at Jedda reports that

'It is within my knowledge, however, that the idea of freedom does at present agitate some minds even in Mecca. . . .
I have had a hint of a supposed scheme for combining Najd,
the Arabs of Mesopotamia under Mansour Pasha, and 'Asir
and Yaman under 'Ali ibn 'Ayed, and I shall know before
long whether there is more in this than castle-building. . . .'[3]

These reports by foreign observers, so far as they go,
corroborate the evidence of contemporary Arab witnesses.
The unrest was no longer confined to Syria: it had spread to
other parts of the eastern Arab world. Although its immediate causes were not everywhere identical, its outward
manifestations tended to one end – liberation from Turkish
rule – and gave it the deceptive appearance of a concerted
insurgence. In actual fact, there was as yet no conscious co-
operation between the varied and scattered regions of the
Arab world. Speedy means of communication had scarcely

[1] Gabriel Charmes, *Voyage en Syrie*, pp. 171-2.
[2] Denis de Rivoyre, *Les vrais Arabes et leur pays*, pp. 294-5.
[3] Public Record Office, *F.O. 78/3415.*

begun to develop, railways in the Arab world were practically non-existent, and the obstacles set up by distance were still formidable. The Press was muzzled. While news and ideas could travel with their customary indifference to barriers, the movements of individuals were restricted and the business of concerting a revolt over so wide an area lay outside the bounds of possibility.

Thus the signs of unrest which appeared in the early eighties may not be read as the premature eruption of an organised Arab plot. They were rather the first manifestations of new ideas which, born in Syria, had drifted in haphazard flight over the vast surface of the Arab world and fanned the discontent with Turkish rule into episodes of separate flares, like incidental bonfires in a vast landscape of hills. The organised plot, with its ensuing conflagration, was not to come till thirty years later, not until 'Abdul-Hamid's tyranny was overthrown and succeeded by another form of Turkish rule, constitutional in name, but in fact more despotic and provocative.

7.

In the interval, the Arab national movement stood still, so far as its visible manifestations went. Not only were the censorship, the spies and the unseen terrors of the Hamidian régime driving most of its ardent spirits into voluntary exile; it was also debilitated by a variety of influences – and more particularly by three – of which 'Abdul-Hamid's Arab policy was the most insidious. The other two were offshoots of the progress of Western education and the growing power of the clergy.

The sultan's Arab policy has been described in a preceding chapter. Based as it was on a skilful exploitation of the instincts of greed and of fear, it was bound to achieve at least partial and temporary success; and although it did not kill the movement or arrest its subterranean growth, it did reduce it to impotence: by offers of office and other favours on the one hand, and terrorisation on the other.

Nowhere was this policy adhered to more assiduously than in Syria. Whether on account of its being the cradle of the Arab movement, or because it was culturally more advanced than his other Arab possessions and geographically the key to them, Syria did get the lion's share of 'Abdul-Hamid's favouritism; and, getting it, denied the prophets of her freedom.

It may seem paradoxical to say, but it is only too true, that the progress of Western education had also a stultifying effect. Its development in Syria during the Hamidian reign was on a much larger scale than in the preceding generation, and led to the establishment of a network of schools and colleges spread over the whole country. These were no longer solely dependent on French, American and British enterprise, for Russian, Italian and German missions had come to add their activities to those of their forerunners. In a country which was already a prey to internal divisions, this very diversity was an added mischief, as some of the missions had become the tools of political ambitions and brought in their trains the evils of international rivalry as well as the benefits of education. The French Government, anxious to strengthen their influence, subsidised the French ecclesiastical missions; and these, entering into an alliance with the Maronite and Melchite clergy, strove to give the rising generation an education which, although well enough in itself, aimed also at shaping their minds in a French mould and turning their outlook and their mental allegiance towards France. The Russians, through the agency of an ecclesiastical mission and a richly-endowed pedagogic society, cultivated the Orthodox Arab population and the Orthodox Patriarchates of Antioch and Jerusalem, with similar ulterior aims. There is no evidence that British or American schools were inspired by political motives. But as a counterweight to French and Russian influence with the Christians, Great Britain supported the Druzes and encouraged them, through her consular offices, to regard her as their political godmother; while the influence of the Americans, who took no part whatever in the political game but confined their activities to education and evangelisation, had led to the creation of a new religious denomination – the Syrian Presbyterian Church –which, although it included some of the most enlightened elements in the country, added yet another source of discord to the existing diversity. German and Italian schools also contributed to the general variegation, but their efforts were comparatively restricted.

Thus the progress of Western education was not an unmixed blessing. Although it raised the cultural standard to a relatively high level and made Syria into the most advanced portion of the Arab world, in other ways it did harm. It emphasised sectarian divisions and added to them, in a country where their existence was, as we have seen, one of the main obstacles to national progress. It became an instrument of political penetration as well as a vehicle of culture; and, more reprehensibly still, it facilitated and sometimes deliberately encouraged the acquisition of political power by the clergy. In those two directions, it was nullifying the work of the Arab reformers of Bustani's generation, who had made the first stand against sectarian dissension and its evil counsellor – the political ambition of the ecclesiastics. It was striking at the root of the Arab national movement.

8.

One of the lasting contributions which the development of Western education in Syria made to the Arab national movement was that it helped to transfer the leadership from Christian to Moslem hands. It did this mainly by its indirect attack on the position of the Arabic language as the instrument of national culture.

The activities of foreign schools and colleges led naturally to the acquisition by their pupils of the foreign language predominating at each. But the significant thing is that, as time went on, proficiency in the foreign tongue was increasingly gained at the expense of Arabic. This was due to two distinct causes. One was that certain institutions –

those in which a political objective was being deliberately pursued – purposely gave the first place to their own national tongue. The other was that, as education spread, and spread very fast, it was found that the rapid introduction of the modern sciences with their unfamiliar terminology was taxing the resources of the Arabic language and rendering the translation of text-books increasingly difficult. Rich and resilient though Arabic is, it could not, without an organised and sustained effort on the part of scholars and lexicographers, respond adequately to the calls suddenly made upon it to supply equivalents for the new words and phrases. The needed effort was not made, or even seriously attempted; and foreign educationists decided to dispense with Arabic and teach in a European language. Even the Americans who had hitherto led the field in reviving the resources of Arabic took the line of least resistance and, about 1880, made English the medium of instruction in the Syrian Protestant College. And in course of time a generation grew up who felt more at home in French, English or Russian than in their mother Arabic.

This phenomenon had an important – in some ways a decisive – bearing on the future of the national movement. The *clientèle* of the foreign schools was overwhelmingly Christian, since the Moslems, fearing proselytisation, preferred to send their children to the less efficient but religiously orthodox schools managed by the State or by their own community. The education which pupils received at foreign schools was, from the academic standpoint, incomparably better; but, being cast in a Western mould, it weakened the spiritual hold of Arabic culture on their minds and weaned them away from the sources which had nourished the Arab movement in its infancy. The Moslems, keeping aloof from foreign schools, grew up in closer contact with the traditional way of life; and even when they had to resort to Turkish colleges for their higher studies, their minds remained strongly imbued with the spirit of the Arab revival. The education they received was in many ways narrower, but its language was Arabic and its values familiar, and it had, from the point of view of the national movement, the virtue of consistency.[1]

So it came to pass that the ideas which had originally been sown by Christians were now – roughly at the turn of the century – finding an increasingly receptive soil among the Moslems. The evolution was scarcely noticeable at the time, since the movement had fallen into a phase of outward inactivity. The change was none the less real and decisive; and its effects came rapidly to light when 'Abdul-Hamid's tyranny, was overthrown and the leadership in the Arab movement revealed itself as predominantly Moslem.

9.

An attractive figure appears on the scene towards the end of the century, in the person of al-Kawakebi, whose contribution to the progress of the movement was as valuable as it was original and witty. It took the form of two brilliant books and a great deal of lively, entertaining talk.

'Abdul-Rahman Kawakebi was a Moslem Arab born (1849) in Aleppo of a well-known Syrian family, and educated in the unscientific but profoundly humanistic tradition which prevailed at the time, at the leading Moslem college in his native town. His career began in journalism and the law, then he entered the public service where he earned for himself, first the frowns of his chiefs, and later a term in prison, by his outspoken denunciations of tyranny. On his release (1898), he left Syria and went to live in the freer atmosphere of Egypt. Two years later, he started on a journey to study the life of some of the remoter Arab populations and visited Somaliland, Zanzibar and the hinterland of the Yaman. After a long sojourn in Mecca, he returned to Cairo where he died suddenly, at the age of fifty-four (1903).

Little has been written about Kawakebi but there are, fortunately, a few people alive who knew him well, whose

[1] It is not to be inferred that all the Christians and none of the Moslems went to the foreign missionary schools; or that there were no Christian Arab schools. But allowing for exceptions, and bearing in mind that there were important exceptions, the broad result was as described above.

impressions of him seem to fit the personality reflected in his writings. From the accounts of those who knew him best – no one seems to have known him intimately – he emerges as a man of deep feeling whose main impulses came from a truly compassionate heart, and whose thoughts were calm and clear in spite of the fire within him. It is certain that he had a profound belief in the destinies of Islam and of the Arab race, and a profound hatred of intolerance and injustice – injustice to the poor especially. He is described as a brilliant talker who charmed his audiences, at daily sittings in the *Splendid Bar* café in Cairo, with the novelty and the daring of his opinions, and the humour with which he could express them. His circle of friends was large and varied: it included Christians and Jews as well as Moslems, for he practised what he often proclaimed, namely, that patriotism was above distinctions of creed. But his real friends were the poor, and perhaps no episode of his life affords a truer insight into his nature than that of the office he had established at his own expense in Aleppo, to give free legal advice and help to the poor of all communities. His nickname in Aleppo was Father of the Weak *(Abul-Du'afa),* and he had earned it in years of unremitting effort at that noblest of all pursuits – the fight against injustice.

His first book, entitled *Umm al-Qura,*[1] is a symposium on the destiny of Islam. Twenty-two fictitious characters, representing scholars and divines from as many parts of the Moslem world, are imagined to have assembled in Mecca for the pilgrimage and, after an exchange of views lasting over a dozen formal meetings, to have agreed on founding a society for the regeneration of Islam. The greater part of the book is taken up by what purports to be a *verbatim* record of the imaginary proceedings; it then gives the statutes of the new society and concludes with a digression on the caliphate. It is a distinguished, witty and delightful composition, and its form lends itself admirably to the presentation of Kawakebi's daring views. His other book[2] is

---

[1] A name occuring in the Qoran as one of the designations of Mecca.
[2] *Taba'i' al-Istibdad* (The Attributes of Tyranny).

a reprint (with additions) of articles he had published in the Egyptian Press, on the subject of Tyranny. It is a thoughtful and profound work in which the author's hatred of despotism enlivens without disturbing the even flow of his philosophy.

Both books were published anonymously in Cairo in the author's lifetime and were widely read and discussed. Copies were smuggled into Syria and distributed in secret. Taken together, they form a profound and brilliant analysis of the decrepitude of the Moslem world in general and of the Arab portions of it in particular, of its causes and of possible remedies, with an impassioned plea for the adoption of the right remedy. Two requisites seemed to him of fundamental importance: one was that a serious and organised effort be made to combat the obscurantism of the theologians and the ignorance of the masses; the other, that the function of the Arabs in the destinies of Islam be restored to its proper place. He believed that some such society as he had imagined in *Umm al-Qura*, with branches in all parts of the Moslem world, would be adequate for the one; and for the other, his digression on the caliphate and his book on Tyranny furnished an eloquent appeal. As contributions to the Arab movement, his books stand in a class apart, for their originality, their range and their audacity.

The campaign initiated by Kawakebi was chiefly original in this, that it differentiated between the Arab movement and the general pan-Islamic revival preached by Jamaluddin al-Afghani and adapted to his own ends by 'Abdul-Hamid. He was undoubtedly influenced by his predecessor, and there are points of similarity, both of form and of substance, which show a close connexion between the two minds. But whereas Jamaluddin regarded the whole world of Islam as one field to be united under the sceptre of no matter what caliph – be he Turk, Afghan or Egyptian – provided he were powerful enough to be master in his own house, Kawakebi drew a sharp distinction between the Arab and the non-Arab Moslem peoples. This distinction he derived from the lessons of history, that is to say from the part

played by Arabs in the rise and spread of Islam, from the
intimate connexion between the Arab genius and the spirit
of Islam, and from the special place to which the Arabs were
entitled in the fortunes of Islam by their language and their
descent. So that, while fully upholding the doctrine of the
unity of Islam, he advocated the abolition of the sultan's
title to the caliphate and the setting up of a Quraish-born[1]
Arab as caliph in Mecca.

The doctrines preached by Kawakebi contributed, as was
inevitable, to the gradual transference of the leadership in
the Arab movement to Moslem hands. Far from being inspired by prejudice, his campaign was on the contrary a
plea against sectarian dissension; and his writings contain
passages in which he pleads for equality between the creeds
for the sake of national solidarity, with fervour and unmistakable sincerity. At the same time, it was a campaign for
the regeneration of all Islam as well as that of the Arab race;
and, as such, it was bound to move the Moslems more profoundly and spur them on with a double incentive.

10.

The only other instance of political incitement under
'Abdul-Hamid was the campaign begun by Najib 'Azuri, a
Christian Arab, who became active in the closing years of
the reign. It was launched in Paris in 1904 when he founded
a society known as *Ligue de la Patrie Arabe*, of which the declared object was to free Syria and Iraq from Turkish domination, and which issued several fiery appeals calling upon the
Arabs to rise in revolt. In the following year, he published
(in French) a book under the title of *le Réveil de la Nation
Arabe*. Two years later, having secured the collaboration of
certain French writers of note, he began the publication (in
French) of a monthly review entitled *l'Indépendance Arabe* of
which the first number appeared in April 1907. The object

[1] It is one of the traditional requirements for a candidate to the caliphate,
though one that has been honoured as often in the breach as in the observance,
that he should be able to trace his descent back to the Arab tribe of Quraish
– the clan to which the Prophet belonged.

of the review was to spread knowledge about the Arab countries and arouse an interest in the problem of their emancipation. Its publication was discontinued when the Ottoman constitution was proclaimed in July 1908.[1]

'Azuri's campaign attracted some attention in Europe at the time, but so far as the Arab movement itself was concerned its effect was negligible. Independently of its merits, the fact that his campaign was conducted from a foreign capital and in a foreign language was in itself a crippling restriction. It never reached the heart of the movement. And its main value in this history is that it provides an example of the extent to which, as a result of foreign education, certain advocates of the Arab Revolt had strayed from the sources of its inspiration.

II.

In the main, the period of 'Abdul-Hamid's reign was for the Arab national consciousness one of slow and almost imperceptible growth. Only on two occasions had the infant movement reared its head: once, at the beginning of the reign, with the campaign of the Bairut secret society; and once, in its closing years, when al-Kawakebi had stirred up eddies of agitation. Except for those two manifestations, the movement had lain prone as though in sleep, held down by 'Abdul-Hamid's tyranny and drugged with the opiates of his Arab policy.

It was during that period that Egypt detached herself from the Arab movement and evolved a nationalist policy of her own. The change had begun in the seventies of the nineteenth century, during the reign of the Khedive Isma'il, when that ruler's extravagance and his entanglements with European finance had brought about a wave of popular discontent. Hitherto, the movement of ideas in Egypt, so far as the Arabic cultural revival and the birth of the Arab national consciousness went, had marched hand in hand

---

[1] A set of fifteen issues (April 1907 to June 1908) of *l'Indépendance Arabe* is preserved at the Bibliothèque Nationale in Paris.

with the same process in Syria; and the lead given by the one country evoked a ready response in the other. Cairo and Bairut had been centres of parallel activities, and the influence exerted by each sprang from a common cultural source and radiated concurrently to the rest of the Arabic-speaking world. When Great Britain occupied Egypt in 1882, at a time when the national awakening had already begun to translate itself into a politically-minded movement, a new current of ideas emerged whose inspiration was specifically Egyptian and whose aim was, first and foremost, to agitate for the withdrawal of the British army of occupation.

Thus was Egyptian nationalism born and thus did its leaders adopt a course which, as the years went by, made it increasingly distinct from the general Arab movement. Cultural ties continued to link Egypt to the rest of the Arab world, all the more so as the Nile Valley, growing prosperous and secure under England's protective tutelage, became a refuge for all manner of students, writers and political thinkers from those Arab countries that had remained subject to the Sultan's rule; and there was still, as there is to-day, a great deal of common ground as between Egyptian and Arab aspirations. But in the field of specific nationalist activity the disseverance was complete. The same applied to Tunisia in its subjection to a French Protectorate. To a greater degree than ever before, the Arab national movement was finding itself confined to Syria, Iraq and the Arabian Peninsula.

The fact that Egypt was out of 'Abdul-Hamid's reach caused Cairo to become one of the centres of conspiracy against the tyrant's rule. Paris was another. In those two capitals, groups of political refugees – Young Turks they called themselves – were plotting and secretly corresponding with confederates in Salonica to put an end to the Sultan's despotism; and, on the 24th of July 1908, the conspiracy bore fruit.

CHAPTER VI

YOUNG ARABS AND YOUNG TURKS:
1908–14

I.

ON the 24th of July 1908, in a panic caused by the sudden outbreak of a military revolution, 'Abdul-Hamid granted his subjects a constitution. On the following day, he abolished the censorship, released all political prisoners and disbanded his army of 30,000 spies. Like a carnival queen, Liberty – or at any rate a paper incarnation of her – made her entry from round the corner and bowed, scattering her favours by the armful.

The revolution was the work of the Committee of Union and Progress,[1] a secret association which the Young Turks had formed in Salonica with the object of overthrowing the Sultan's despotism. It is not necessary for our purposes to trace the rise of the Young Turk party back to its origins, for there was no inter-connexion between its aspirations and those of the Arab movement save in so far as hatred of the Hamidian despotism was common to both. Although a few Arabs, most of them army officers, had joined the party and worked hand-and-glove with its leaders, they had done so as Ottoman citizens rather than as Arab nationalists. The C.U.P. were a medley of races and creeds, in which Turks predominated and Jews came second, with Ottoman nationals of other races in tow, and political refugees and exiles abroad in the background; and while it is true that the motives which prompted the party were as mixed as its composition, its first object was to put an end to 'Abdul-Hamid's autocratic rule and secure good government for

---

[1] Henceforth referred to as the C.U.P.

the empire on the basis of racial fusion as envisaged in the 1876 Constitution. The military members were influential in the councils of the party, as became a generation in which military education was held in high honour, and it was perhaps inevitable that it should have resorted, for its sudden *coup d'état*, to a revolution proclaimed by the army – the very thing that 'Abdul-Hamid had dreaded most.

The constitution of 1908 was none other than Midhat's project of 1876, resuscitated by a stroke of the pen, with its old imperfections rendered more incongruous by the passage of time and the growth of national sentiment. But its revival was greeted with enthusiasm, and nowhere perhaps was the jubilation greater than among the Arab nationalists who, in the first flush of deliverance, had mistaken it for real liberty. There was rejoicing all over the empire, in which Turks fraternised deliriously with Arabs, and Moslems with Christians, in the genuine belief that the constitution would meet everybody's wants. Its incompatibility with cultural aspirations seems to have passed unperceived. The fact that it provided for the fusion of the different races into a single, Ottoman democracy with Turkish for its distinctive language was in itself the very negation of the doctrine of cultural identity. But such was the intoxicating effect of the mere appearance of freedom that few were left with the power to think clearly; and months were to elapse before those few could get a hearing for their misgivings.

It was during this Turco-Arab honeymoon that the first Arab society was founded under the name of *al-Ikha' al-'Arabi al-'Uthmani*.[1] At a large meeting of the Arab colony in Constantinople, held on the 2nd of September, and attended by members of the C.U.P., the society was formally and enthusiastically inaugurated. Its main objects were to protect the Constitution, unite all races in loyalty to the Sultan, promote the welfare of the Arab provinces on a footing of real equality with the other races of the empire, spread education in the Arabic tongue and foster the observance of Arab customs. Its membership was open to Arabs of all creeds,

[1] The Ottoman Arab Fraternity.

and branches of it were to be founded throughout the Arab provinces, and a newspaper was actually started to promote the diffusion of its ideas which, as we have seen, rested on a confusion of thought.

Two measures were taken at the time, which deserve our notice. One was the formal inauguration in September of that year of the Hejaz Railway line which had been completed to Madina. The other was the appointment of the Sharif Husain ibn 'Ali to be Grand Sharif of Mecca.[1]

Husain was still living in Constantinople, in that enforced quietude to which the Sultan's guests were bound. He had been a captive for nearly sixteen years, and his captivity had restrained but not deadened his spirit. He was by nature keen and talkative; but the caution he had had to exercise, sharply driven home by an episode of confidences betrayed, had taught him a wary reserve. In public life – the Sultan had appointed him to be a member of the Council of State – he was a conspicuous and venerated figure, as a descendant of the Prophet could scarcely escape being in the capital of Islam. In addition to his descent, his piety, his exquisite manners and the irreproachable pattern of his life had earned him the reverence of a large circle of admirers. Because of that, and still more because they knew him to be unbeloved of the Sultan, the C.U.P. in power chose him to be Sharif of Mecca, in place of the ruling Sharif. 'Abdul-Hamid opposed the appointment, urging with canny foresight that Husain in an office of that importance would be no mere tool, but a force and possibly a danger. But his warnings went unheeded, and Husain sailed for the Hejaz. He was a man of 53 at the time.

Then elections were held for the first parliament under the new constitution, and it was over this question that the unnatural alliance of Turks and Arabs received its first jolt.

---

[1] The title of *Sharif* was borne by all descendants of the Prophet and carried no function with it. The post to which Husain was now appointed, of which the full designation was *Sharif and Amir of Mecca*, carried with it a definite and important function of which the main attribute lay in the custody of the Holy Places of Islam in the Hejaz, and the supervision of the pilgrimage and other observances.

The electoral machinery was controlled by the C.U.P., and had been so geared as to ensure the return of a great majority of their nominees. But more than that, the electoral con-constituencies had been demarcated in such a way as to favour the Turkish element at the expense of the other races. The Turks were by no means the largest element in the empire, and were actually outnumbered by the Arabs, roughly in a ratio of three to two.[1] Yet in the Chamber of Deputies which assembled in December, out of a total of 245 elected representatives, 150 were Turks and 60 were Arabs, a ratio of five to two to the advantage of the Turks. In the Senate which numbered forty members appointed by the Sultan, there were only three Arabs. This was the first of a series of measures which were to reveal an ever-widening gap between what the Turks professed and what they practised in the matter of racial equality. It gave the sceptics among the Arabs their chance, and this time, their misgivings met with a ready hearing.

In April of the following year, another revolution broke out with the same suddenness as in the preceding July. This time it was 'Abdul-Hamid trying to overthrow the C.U.P. On the 13th of April, incited by agents of the Sultan, the troops forming the garrison of Constantinople broke into mutiny, rushed the Parliament buildings and killed, besides several of their own officers, the Minister of Justice and an Arab deputy.[2] When the news of the outbreak reached Salonica, Mahmud Shaukat Pasha decided to march on the capital. He was an Arab who had risen to high rank in the Turkish army and was then in command of the army corps stationed in Salonica. He entered Constantinople, after some stiff fighting, on the 24th and restored the authority of the C.U.P. Three days later, the Senate and the Chamber sitting together pronounced the deposition of 'Abdul-Hamid and proclaimed his brother Prince Reshad sultan in his stead.

---

[1] No accurate statistics exist. A fair approximation would give the total population of the Ottoman Empire in 1908 (excluding Egypt) as amounting to 22 million, of whom 7½ were Turks by race, 10½ Arabs, and the remaining 4 Greeks, Albanians, Armenians, Kurds and smaller elements.
[2] The Druze Amir Muhammad Arslan, one of the deputies for Syria.

The new sovereign who took the name of Mehemed V, was sixty-four years of age, and a gentler, more self-effacing and ineffectual old man was never girded with the sword of Othman. He had none of the ambition or the vices of his predecessors and was willing to let others rule him as well as rule in his name. With his accession, the C.U.P. found themselves in absolute mastery, and in the five years which elapsed before the outbreak of the World War, they held office with but few breaks and established a tyranny which, albeit different in kind from that of 'Abdul-Hamid, was not less despotic and, so far as the Arabs were concerned, a good deal more detested. One of their first acts after they had overcome the outbreak in April was to ban the societies founded by the non-Turkish racial groups, amongst them *al-Ikha' al 'Arabi* which, barely eight months before, had been inaugurated with vows of everlasting fidelity, at an impassioned meeting of Arabs and Turks in the gaudy radiance of their honeymoon.

2.

It must be said in fairness to the Young Turks that the legacy they inherited from the Hamidian régime was not only damnable in itself: they had come into it at a particularly inauspicious moment. The separatist forces at work in the Balkan provinces were in the ascendant, the covetousness of two European Powers lurked menacingly behind a thin diplomatic veil, and a series of disasters occurred before the Young Turks had had time to prove their worth: the annexation by Austria-Hungary of Bosnia and Herzegovina in October 1908, the simultaneous secession of Bulgaria, Italy's aggression on Libya in the autumn of 1911 and the Balkan War of 1912. In those few years, the Ottoman Empire lost all its provinces in Europe (except for eastern Thrace); that part of Libya which comprised the provinces of Tripoli and Benghazi; Crete and the islands of the Dodecanese. In addition to the territorial losses, a burden of military expenditure had to be incurred which made serious inroads on Turkey's budgetary resources.

But in other ways, the Young Turks had only themselves to blame for their insuccess. In accomplishing their revolution, they had undoubtedly been moved by patriotic and liberal ideals, and been sincere in their professions of equality for all under the Constitution. But they were far from equal to the task they had set themselves. The first mistake they made – and, as we have seen, they were not alone in making it – was that they failed to perceive the serious flaw in Midhat's Constitution in its relation to the racial problem. Later on, as its implications dawned gradually upon them, they made another and, this time, fatal mistake. They threw the principle of equality overboard and used their power, often in foolish and vexatious ways, to promote the Turkish interest to the detriment of their fellow-Ottomans, and to rule the empire on the basis of racial supremacy for the Turkish element.

In itself, the desire to exalt the Turkish above the other races was only natural in an empire which, after all, had been created by Turks. It sprang, however, from other motives than mere egotism. A movement of purely Turkish nationalism was beginning to assert itself. It had its roots in a new assertion of the Turanian origins of the Turkish people, which had given birth to the creed that the path to the regeneration of the Turkish race lay towards reunion with the kindred populations of Turanian descent, of whom the majority were under Russian rule. The C.U.P., without adopting the doctrine of *Pan Turan* in all its irredentist implications, were powerfully influenced by its teaching. But here again, they were guilty of confused thinking. Turanianism, with its ideal of exalting the Turkish nationality and stressing the affinity of the Turks in the Ottoman Empire with their racial brothers in central Asia, was the negation of the doctrine of Ottomanism which aimed at uniting the different races of the empire into one nation on a basis of equality for all. The C.U.P. failed to see the incompatibility of the two policies; or, if they perceived it, adopted the hopeless course of trying to reconcile them. In that attempt, they only succeeded in alarming the other races, and more particularly the Arabs, into a belief that the Ottomanism which they were asked loyally to accept was a sham and that, if it meant anything, it could only mean that they would have to abandon their Arab cultural aspirations and allow themselves to be Turkified for the sake of unity.

A worse mistake still was the C.U.P.'s adoption of a policy of centralisation. It was borrowed, as were many of their guiding ideas, from the tenets of the French Revolution, but borrowed without regard to a fundamental difference between the France of 1789 and the Ottoman Empire of 1908. The centralisation in Paris of the republican administration was the continuation of an historical process and was in harmony with the forces which, for centuries, had made Paris a cultural and economic centre and driven France towards political and administrative unity in that centre. In the Ottoman Empire, the position was the very opposite. The forces generated by the national awakening were at work in directions pointing away from the centre; differences of language, customs and culture were still the mainsprings of those forces; and Constantinople, melting-pot though it was, was in no sense a centre of cultural unity. The diversity of races within the empire called for a decentralised form of government, which should have given the Arab and other non-Turkish provinces a large measure of home rule and the freedom to pursue their political and cultural development as autonomous members of the empire. The policy followed by the C.U.P. was the very opposite. They adopted the centralised form of government which they found in existence when they came into power, and proceeded to tighten instead of relaxing the hold of the central bureaucracy. In that alone, their attempts at strengthening the unity of the empire were doomed to fail; and the clumsy and vexatious steps which they took in pursuance of that policy made its failure more conspicuous and intensified the bitterness it engendered.

3.

By their suppression of *al-Ikha' al-'Arabi*, the C.U.P.

drove the Arab leaders to underground methods, and a series of societies came into being, among which were some whose existence never became known to the Turks. The propagation of Arab national ideas was henceforth conducted on two planes; that of the open platform, functioning through the agency of recognised clubs and associations; and that of the subterranean channel, fed by secret, conspiratorial organisations. A number of those societies were formed and became active between 1909 and 1914; and four of them, of which two were public and two secret, deserve special mention.[1] The activities of each group were to a great extent complementary to each other, and it would perhaps make their inter-connexion clearer if, taking liberties with their chronological sequence, we were to review the two recognised societies first, and then pass on to the activities of the two secret groups.

The earliest, *al-Muntada al-Adabi* (i.e., the Literary Club), was an association founded in Constantinople in the summer of 1909 by a group of officials, deputies, men of letters and students,[2] to serve as a meeting-place for Arab visitors and residents in the capital. Its club-house was equipped with a library and a hostel, and it did become the busy and useful centre it was intended to be. The C.U.P. tolerated it, and for a time gave it their patronage, since its objects were not avowedly political. In actual fact, it exerted a good deal of political influence, and there came a time when its committee became the recognised intermediary in negotiations for the settlement of differences between the Arabs and the C.U.P. But its function was essentially that of a clearing-house rather

---

[1] I have collected from numerous written and oral sources – in most cases from the founders themselves – enough material for a fairly complete record of those societies. But since a full inventory would take too long and make for redundancy, I am confining myself here to an account of those societies whose contribution to the history of the movement formed an essential link in the chain of its development.

[2] Among whom were: *'Abdul-Karim al-Khalil (Moslem from the Lebanon); *Saleh Haidar (Moslem from Baalbek); *Rafiq Sallum (Christian from Homs); Jamil Husaini (Moslem from Jerusalem); Yusuf Mukhaiber (Moslem from Baalbek); *Saifuddin al-Khatib (Moslem from Damascus).

* An asterisk denotes that he was hanged by the Turks during the War on a charge of treasonable nationalistic activities.

than a factory of ideas, and its contribution to the Arab movement did more to strengthen its appeal and extend its reach than to give it a new impulse. It had an enormous membership running into thousands of whom the majority were students, and it established branches in various towns of Syria and Iraq; and not the least of its uses was that it provided centres in which Arabs from all parts of the Empire felt at home and talked freely in an atmosphere in which minds relaxed and the traffic of ideas could move.

The other important public society was founded in Cairo towards the end of 1912, with the name of 'The Ottoman Decentralisation Party'.[1] Its objects were twofold: to impress upon the rulers of Turkey the need for decentralising the administration of the empire; to mobilise Arab opinion in support of Decentralisation. Its founders were, for the most part, men of experience and good standing, who had made their mark in public life.[2] The statutes of the society provided for an elaborate party machine. The control was vested in a powerful committee of twenty members domiciled in Egypt and a smaller executive body of six of their own number. Branches were established in every town of Syria and smaller agencies in a number of other localities; and the closest contact was maintained between its branches and other Arab political associations in Syria and Iraq, and of course with *al-Muntada al-Adabi* in Constantinople. In about a year, the committee of the Decentralisation Party had become the best-organised and most authoritative spokesman of Arab aspirations.

The importance of this society in the history of the Arab movement was that it provided its first essay in the science of organised effort. The battle between the C.U.P. with their policy of unification at the centre and the Arabs clamouring

---

[1] *Hizb al-Lamarkaziya al-Idariya al-'Uthmani.*

[2] Among them were: Rafiq al-'Azm (Moslem from Damascus); Rashid Rida (Moslem from Tripoli in Syria); Iskandar 'Ammun (Christian from the Lebanon); Fuad al-Khatib (Moslem from the Lebanon); *Salim 'Abdul-Hadi (Moslem from Jenin); *Hafez al-Sa'id (Moslem from Jaffa); *Naif Tellu (Moslem from Damascus);*' Ali Nashashibi (Moslem from Jerusalem)

* An asterisk denotes that he was hanged by the Turks during the War on a charge of treasonable nationalistic activities.

for home rule had gone on for three years in that intermittent dispersed way which is characteristic of Arab warfare; and the foundation of the society was an attempt at co-ordinating the efforts into one, concerted and continuous pressure.

Meanwhile, the two secret societies had come into being. One was *al-Qahtaniya*[1] which was established towards the end of 1909, not long after *al-Muntada al-Adabi*. Its founders were men of a bolder stamp, and its objects were to promote a new and daring project – that of turning the Ottoman Empire into a dual monarchy. This was yet another attempt to grapple with the problem created by the C.U.P.'s centralising policy. The Arab provinces were to form a single kingdom with its own parliament and local government, and with Arabic as the language of its institutions; the kingdom was to be part of a Turco-Arab empire, similar in architecture to the Austro-Hungarian edifice; and the Ottoman sultan in Constantinople would wear, in addition to his own Turkish crown, the crown of the Arab kingdom, as the Hapsburg emperor in Vienna wore the crown of Hungary. Thus unity could be reached through separation, and the destinies of Turks and Arabs linked together on a more lasting, because more realistic, basis.

Here was a concrete plan with a definite idea behind it, and the authors of it were a band of practical and determined men who saw the impossibility of carrying it through by public advocacy. They were led by 'Aziz 'Ali al-Masri, an officer in the Turkish army, of whom we shall hear more hereafter. The members of *al-Qahtaniya* were chosen with care, only those being admitted whose patriotism was above question and who could be trusted to guard a secret.[2] Its membership included several Arab officers of high rank in

[1] Named after Qahtan, one of the legendary ancestors of the Arab race.
[2] Among them were: *Salim Jaza'iri (army officer, Moslem from Damascus); the Amirs Amin and 'Adel Arslan (Druzes from the Lebanon); Khalil Himadeh (Moslem from Bairut); Amin Kazma (Christian from Homs); Safwat al-'Awwa (army officer, Moslem from Damascus); *'Ali Nashashibi (army officer, Moslem from Jerusalem); *Shukri al-'Asali (Moslem from Damascus).

* An asterisk denotes that he was hanged by the Turks during the War on a charge of treasonable nationalistic activities.

the Turkish army, and two of the founders of *al-Muntada al-Adabi*. The society had a password and a signal for identification, and branches were established in five centres besides Constantinople. It derived its strength from the personalities of some of its members, and its importance in the history of the movement was that it made the first known attempt to win the Arab officers serving in the Turkish army over to active co-operation in the national movement.

The society was very active in the first year of its existence, until the founders were given cause to fear a betrayal. Despite the care with which candidates were chosen, one member – his name is not in the preceding footnote – was found to have betrayed confidences, and the rest of the company became uneasy. The society was not actually dissolved, but its leaders found it impossible to continue with a presumed traitor in their midst, and it died of wilful neglect.

The other secret society was *al-Fatat*,[1] which was founded in Paris in 1911. No other society has played as determining a part in the history of the national movement. Its founders were seven young Arabs, all of them Moslems, who were pursuing their higher studies in the French capital,[2] and who, by reason of their youth, their keenness and the unanimity of their views, gave it unity and vigour. In that respect, its foundation recalls that of the Bairut secret society of 1875, with this difference that the initiative had passed into the hands of Moslems. The objects of the society were to work for the independence of the Arab countries and their liberation from Turkish or any other alien domination – a significant advance on those programmes which aimed at autonomy within the empire, and an unconscious return to the ideals of the Bairut secret society.

The influence of *al-Fatat* on the march of events will appear presently. Here, we are concerned with its development,

---

[1] Its full name was *Jam'iyat al-'Arabiya al-Fatat*, i.e., the Young Arab Society.

[2] They were: 'Auni 'Abdul-Hadi (Jenin); Jamil Mardam (Damascus); *Muhammad al-Mihmisani (Bairut); Rustum Haidar (Baalbek); *Taufiq al-Natur (Bairut); Rafiq Tamimi (Nablus;); *'Abdul-Ghani al-'Urayisi (Bairut)

* An asterisk denotes that he was hanged by the Turks during the War on a charge of treasonable nationalistic activities.

which was cautious yet rapid, and which made it into the most effective of the Arab societies of the time, remarkable alike for its objects and methods as for the admirable discipline of its members. Membership was made subject to a long period of probation. Each recruit was introduced by one of the sworn members but was kept in ignorance of the identity of all the other members until he had been tried and proved, when he would be invited to take an oath to serve the ends of the society, to the point of forfeiting his life, if need be, in its service. For the first two years, its centre was Paris; and its membership remained small: then, as its founders graduated and returned to their homes, it was shifted to Bairut in 1913 and in the following year to Damascus. Its membership rose to over 200, most of whom were Moslems, with but a few Christians. The secret of its existence was guarded to the end, and the Arab countries had gained their liberation from Turkish rule before it was disclosed. During the War, when the Turks were prosecuting Arab nationalists for treason, one member of *al-Fatat* was driven by physical torture to attempt suicide, and another went to the gallows rather than betray the society's secret. The oath its members had had to take may seem a trifle melodramatic, but there is little harm in melodrama when it can inspire fidelity.

4.

These four societies, and a few others of lesser importance, were in existence when a fresh wave of the Arab movement broke against the Turkish resistance. It began in Bairut in the last days of 1912, but the same tide carried it to Paris where an Arab Congress was held six months later.

In Bairut, the initiative was taken by an influential body who formed themselves into a Committee of Reform composed of eighty-six members of all creeds and drew up a scheme for the grant of home rule to the Arab provinces of the Ottoman empire. The motives prompting them were those which had led to the foundation in Cairo of the Party of Decentralisation with whom they acted in close contact, and their scheme was no more than the practical expression of the principles advocated by the seekers after autonomy on the basis of decentralisation.

The scheme fitted into the framework of existing administrative divisions and fully recognised Turkish domination. But it drew a distinction between questions of an imperial character, such as foreign affairs, defence, trunk communications and national finances, and questions of a regional character, such as provincial administration and revenues and local services; and it provided for the devolution of all regional services in the province of Bairut to bodies representative of the province. Among other reforms, the scheme provided for the recognition of Arabic as the official language and for its adoption in Parliament on a footing of equality with Turkish; while, on the subject of military service, it required that the practice of conscripting soldiers for peace-time service outside their province be abandoned. In these last provisions, we find an echo of the appeals of the Bairut society of 1875.

About the middle of February 1913, the Committee of Reform gave publicity to their scheme. It was greeted with demonstrations of popular favour not only in the Syrian provinces, but also in Iraq. Public meetings were held in Damascus, Aleppo, Acre, Nablus, Baghdad and Basra, and telegrams acclaiming the scheme as being the expression of the universal desire in the Arab provinces poured into Constantinople. The C.U.P. in power, hostile to the thought of decentralisation, took measures to repress the agitation. One day when the Committee of Reform were in session, on the 8th of April, the police came to inform them that the Government had decreed their dissolution and the closure of their headquarters. There was general dismay and anger: all the shops and business premises in Bairut were closed, and the newspapers appeared framed in borders of black, with the order of dissolution as their sole announcement. Adopting the 'strong line' so dear to unpopular governments, the authorities arrested the principal leaders and suspended newspapers. The agitation increased and evoked demonstrations of solidarity in other parts of Syria. The Government compromised: it released the arrested leaders and announced that reforms in the sense desired would be introduced; and actually on the 5th of May the governor-general promulgated a new Law of the Vilayets giving increased powers to representative bodies in the provinces, but falling so far short of the Committee's scheme that it came to be looked upon, and not without reason, as a veiled step towards further centralisation, tightening the grip of Constantinople on the Arabs and its stranglehold on liberty.

5.

Then the centre of agitation shifted to Paris. For some time, the young founders of *al-Fatat* had entertained the thought of bringing the Arab question to a head by a public ventilation of it in some neutral and free atmosphere. The method they chose was that of holding an Arab congress, and, after some hesitation as to whether it should be held in Switzerland or France, their choice fell on Paris. They accordingly wrote, on the 4th of April 1913, to the committee of the Party of Decentralisation in Cairo, to invite them and their affiliated societies to attend the congress. It is important to note that, foremost among the reasons given, was the plea that the denial of Arab claims was carrying the Arab provinces towards chaos and exposing them to foreign (i.e., European) intervention. The idea was approved and the invitation readily accepted. In Bairut, the Committee of Reform, smarting under the repression of their movement by the C.U.P., warmly sent their adhesion. So great was the general alacrity that preparations were rushed, only scant notice being given to the outlying Arab provinces, and the congress held its inaugural sitting on the 18th of June in a hall in the Boulevard St. Germain.

The list of delegates bore the names of twenty-five accredited persons of whom twenty-four attended. The membership was almost exactly divided between Moslems and Christians, and the delegates were preponderantly Syrian. Iraq was represented by two members, and three others came on behalf of Arab communities in the United States. With the exception of Syria, the Arab provinces were scantily represented. The congress lasted over six days during which four formal sittings were held and a list of resolutions passed unanimously. The sittings were attended by some 200 Arab listeners, and on the last day the doors of the congress were thrown open to all visitors without restriction and the deliberations were held in French.

The proceedings were marked by frankness and a conciliatory tone, and the resolutions showed a desire for moderation. They amounted to a re-statement of the principles uttered by the Party of Decentralisation, and of the concrete proposals put forward by the Bairut Committee of Reform with emphasis on the Arab claim to full political rights and to an effective share in the administration of the affairs of the empire. Throughout the proceedings, references were made – prudently veiled, since they related to French ambitions – to the possibility of foreign intervention as a danger to be resolutely warded off. There was no talk of separatism or secession. Indeed, speakers had been at pains to stress the general desire to maintain the integrity of the empire provided the rights of the Arabs as partners were recognised and their cultural aspirations given free scope in a decentralised form of government. Some of the speeches showed political sense and insight. One speaker, reviewing the causes of dissension, touched the core of the problem when he exposed the fallacy in the C.U.P.'s doctrine of centralisation, as borrowed from the French Revolution, and, in a lucid analysis, demonstrated why it would be suicidal for the Arabs to accept it.

The C.U.P. were in power at the time and their attitude was naturally hostile. They set a movement on foot, fed by their newspapers and by provoked demonstrations, to discredit the congress and sow dissension among its promoters. They tried to move the French Government to prohibit its convocation on French soil. Having failed in this, they deputed their party secretary to Paris with instructions to enter into negotiations with the heads of the congress, which he did with success. An agreement on principles was arrived at, which the Arab leaders felt they could accept as a basis for further negotiation; and three of them travelled to Constantinople to press their gains home.

The agreement reached in Paris, so far as it went, was outwardly a victory for the Arabs. It granted them their points about regional military service, the use of Arabic as the official language of the Arab provinces, and its use as the medium of instruction in primary and secondary schools. It provided for the appointment of European inspectors to take a hand in the reform of the administration. But on the issue of decentralisation, the concessions embodied in it were more apparent than real. It extended the powers of the provincial bodies in a few secondary services and reserved certain posts in the higher offices of the state to Arab holders. There were henceforth to be not less than five Arab governors-general in constant employment and a minimum of three Arab ministers in any Ottoman cabinet.

It is not known whether, in concluding such an agreement the emissary of the C.U.P. had acted on instructions or had sought to conciliate the Arabs by a piece of self-contrived trickery. He may have been doing both. For, subsequently, when the terms of the agreement were whittled down to a negligible level, it was realised that the C.U.P. leaders had never intended to ratify it. But they kept up the comedy for two months. They gave the three Arab leaders who came from Paris a warm welcome, receptions and banquets sprouted up, eminent Turks were entertained at the Arab Literary Club, and the facile fraternisations of 1908 verbosely repeated.

On the 18th of August, an imperial decree was issued, purporting to enact the provisions of the Paris agreement. The concessions had been scaled down considerably, and most of what was left was hedged with reservations and ambiguity. On the subject of language, the decree did rule that Arabic was henceforth to be the medium in primary and secondary schools; but it added that secondary schools in provincial capitals – and all secondary schools were in those capitals – would continue to teach in Turkish. The concession with regard to military service was similarly qualified. No mention was made of the adoption of Arabic as the official language, or of its admission as one of the official languages, in the Arab provinces; or of offices in the cabinet and governorships being reserved to Arabs.

The appearance of the imperial decree caused dismay which presently turned to despair. For it gradually dawned upon the watchful Arabs that it, too, was only a blind, and that the C.U.P.'s game was to sidetrack the issue. Perfunctory instructions were sent to the valis in certain Arab provinces to 'pave the way for the eventual enforcement of the august Imperial Decree'; and, meanwhile, emissaries of the C.U.P. approached certain Arab personalities with offers of office, to buy their acquiescence. Five of them accepted nomination as senators, and of those, four were strangers to the national movement, while the fifth, 'Abdul-Hamid al-Zahrawi, was of its heart, for it was he who had presided over the congress in Paris. His professed motive in accepting the nomination was one of tactics: he felt that the congress, coming as it had just after the Bairut campaign, had brought Turco-Arab relations dangerously near breaking point, and that, as a senator, he might usefully exert his influence there to improve them and to persuade the C.U.P. into a more liberal policy. In this he was probably sincere, judging by correspondence published after his death; and some (though by no means the majority) of his closest associates supported him in this view. But among the rank and file of the movement his acceptance of the nomination was regarded as a betrayal. The appointment was gazetted on the 4th of January 1914, and the revulsion it caused marks a turning-point. The Bairut agitation and the Paris congress had both failed of their main objectives, and the wave of feeling that had borne them along receded in a backwash of bitterness and despair. No further attempt was made to come to an agreement with the C.U.P.; and, to make matters worse, the latter, having won the hand by a piece of chicanery, went on to press their advantage by a singularly ill-devised piece of severity.

6.

On the 9th of February of that year, as he was leaving the Tokatlian Hotel after lunch, Major 'Aziz 'Ali al-Masri[1] of the general staff was accosted by three detectives and invited to the central police-station in Constantinople. There, without any charge being preferred against him, he was taken into custody, and rumours began to float about that he was to be tried for treason. The news of his arrest caused consternation among the Arab community, and then anger which found its expression in mass demonstrations in the streets.

'Aziz 'Ali was already, at the age of thirty-five, a well-known figure. Born in Cairo where his father was domiciled, he had entered the military academy in Constantinople and then the staff college whence, passing out with distinction in 1904, he was posted to the staff of the Third Army in Macedonia. There he joined the C.U.P. and was one of the officers who had led the military revolution in 1908 and taken part in the march on Constantinople in April of the following year. But his adherence to the C.U.P. had been prompted as much by his Arab national ideals as by his devotion to the welfare of the Ottoman Empire; and when he realised, in the months which followed the counter-revolution of 1909, that the C.U.P.'s policy was to oppose the one and mismanage the other, he began to look around for more worthy allies.

His influence was far greater than his rank implied, for he had had at one time to lecture at the staff college and, during those months, had won the hearts of the coming generation of army officers. In the service, he had shown character, dash and judgment; and, being single-minded and resolute in his patriotism, was readily accepted as a leader by men older than himself. It was he who, with the help of another

[1] Now 'Aziz 'Ali al-Masri Pacha, Inspector-General of the Egyptian Army.

remarkable patriot – his brother officer Salim al-Jaza'iri – had founded *al-Qahtaniya* with its programme of a dual monarchy, in which Arab aspirations were to be reconciled with loyalty to the Ottoman Empire. In 1910, he was sent to the Yaman on active service, scored a triumph by inducing the Imam to compose his differences with the Porte, volunteered to Libya where he covered himself with glory, leading the Arab resistance to Italian aggression, and returned to Constantinople in the summer of 1913, only to witness the slow extinction of Arab hopes in the months that followed the Paris congress. At the Ministry of War, he found disorder and corruption enthroned, an envious belittlement of his successes in Africa, and a disposition on the part of the C.U.P. to order the wholesale transfer of Arab officers stationed in the capital – including himself – to outlying provincial garrisons. He resigned his commission in disgust.

Early in 1914, 'Aziz 'Ali carried into execution a plan which had been maturing since the days of *al-Qahtaniya*, when the discovery that the society harboured an eaves-dropper had killed his interest in it. His plan was to turn it into an association for army officers only. Eventually, he founded a separate organisation, independent of the earlier one, but with a somewhat similar programme. The new society was called *al-'Ahd* (i.e., the Covenant), and its objects were those of *al-Qahtaniya* expressed in soldierly parlance. Only two civilians, chosen for the incorruptibility of their patriotism, were admitted; and one of them, the Amir 'Adel Arslan, had been one of the first members of the parent society. The Iraqi element, being the most numerous in the Ottoman army, was particularly strong in the councils of *al-'Ahd*, and founded branches in Baghdad and Mosul. It became to the soldiers what *al-Fatat* was to the civilians; and, although neither society was aware of the existence of the other at first, their activities, each in its field, became complementary to each other; until 1915, when they established contact in Damascus and pooled their resources together to provoke the Arab Revolt.

The C.U.P. may have had wind of the formation of *al-*

'*Ahd* when they ordered the arrest of 'Aziz 'Ali, but they had no certain knowledge, and the charges preferred against him made no mention of his connexion with secret societies. His trial began *in camera* on the 25th of March before a military court of discipline, and it became known that the charge-sheet accused him of having committed the wildly improbable crimes of embezzling army funds, of surrendering Cyrenaica to the Italians in return for a bribe, of having tried to set up an Arab kingdom in North Africa. By that time, the commotion aroused by his arrest had spread far afield. In Egypt, the land of his birth, the indignation vented itself in a general chorus of protest. Mass meetings were held, a vehement Press campaign broke out, a committee headed by the Rector of al-Azhar was formed, and deputations visited Lord Kitchener, the British Agent in Cairo, to ask for British diplomatic intervention.

Early in April, it became known that 'Aziz 'Ali had been secretly condemned to death. The agitation became more vociferous, and wherever Arab officers gathered oaths were taken to avenge his death in blood. Fortunately for 'Aziz the voice of Europe and in particular of England, spoke in his defence. Kitchener moved the Foreign Office to act, Sir Louis Mallet made representations in Constantinople, and *The Times*, in a series of four leaders spread over six weeks, pleaded outspokenly in his favour.

In its issue of April 9, *The Times* wrote:

'. . . should the injustice which has already been done to the gallant Arab officer be followed by what would be neither more nor less than a judicial murder, the relations between the Ottoman Government and Egypt would be seriously affected, and probably not only the relations between Turkey and Egypt.'

On the 15th it was announced that 'Aziz 'Ali had been condemned to death but that the Sultan had commuted the sentence to one of fifteen years with hard labour. There was general relief, but the agitation against the injustice of the trial continued. At last on the 21st, 'Aziz 'Ali was pardoned and set free; and, on the following day, he sailed for Egypt and received an enthusiastic welcome on his arrival. His trial had shaken the Arab world more profoundly, perhaps, than any single act of Turkish tyranny, and greatly hardened the Arab will to freedom, for it had moved the masses as well as the thinkers.

7.

Meanwhile, important changes had taken place in the out-lying parts of the sultan's Arab Empire, and this was the position in the Arab world as it appeared in the summer of 1914.

In Africa, that part of Libya which contained the Vilayets of Tripoli and Benghazi had been lost to Italy in the war of 1911, and Turkey had had formally to renounce her sover-eignty over them in the Treaty of Ouchy. There remained, however, the sparsely-inhabited plateau of Cyrenaica which had not been conquered by the Italian forces. This region had a political importance of its own, for it was the home of the Sanusi fraternity and of their energetic chief, Sayyed Ahmad al-Sharif, whose influence in Northern Africa went far beyond the confines of his immediate domain.

The Sanusi order had been founded in Cyrenaica in the middle of the nineteenth century by a devout Algerian who had spent the greater part of his life in Mecca and devoted it to preaching a reform of the Moslem faith. The tenets of the order had much similarity with those of the Wahhabi movement, in that they both preached a return to the ways and usages of early Islam. It had missionary aims, and its organisation into *zawias* (i.e., centres of worship and theo-logical instruction) scattered about the country gave it the means of exerting political influence as well, and of recruiting volunteers for military purposes. One feature of the move-ment was that it encouraged settlement and cultivation of the land. In the half-century of its existence, the fraternity had acquired strength and cohesion, and had founded colo-nies of adherents over an extensive area in central Africa.

Sayyed Ahmad, himself a descendant of the founder, was now at the head of the movement. He was on no very good terms with the C.U.P., but when the Italians made their first attempts to penetrate into the interior, he joined hands with 'Aziz 'Ali in organising a spirited Arab resistance, and he was still directing it when the War broke out.

In Asia, the Arab possessions of the Sultan were in 1914 substantially what they were when we last reviewed them in the early years of 'Abdul-Hamid's reign. The spread of British influence had continued and led to the conclusion of a number of treaties between the Government of India and certain Arab Chiefs along the southern and eastern seaboards of the Peninsula. In the hinterland of Aden, a zone of nine petty states (known as the Aden Protectorate) had come under British influence and protection; the treaties with Masqat and Bahrain had been renewed, and other treaties (notably that with Kuwait in 1899) concluded, on terms which gave the Government of India a virtual protectorate and practically ignored the sultan's sovereignty. Officers of the Indian political service were accredited to the Arab Chiefs, a Resident to direct their activities was stationed at Bushire on the Persian coast, and the Gulf became, to all intents and purposes, a British preserve in which freedom of transit was now all the more vital as the exploitation of the rich oil-fields in south-western Persia had been conceded to a British company.

On the mainland, the Turkish hold had on the whole increased. Taking the Persian Gulf side, the last thirty years had seen the ups and downs of the duel between the dynasties of Rashid and Sa'ud, the expulsion of the latter from Najd, and its recapture, in the first years of the present century, by a doughty scion of the latter House, 'Abdul-'Aziz Ibn Sa'ud. At one stage in the contest, the Rashid ruler of the day had thrown himself on the Turkish mercy and asked for help, and the Turks had sent an expeditionary force and shown their flag in Central Arabia for the first time since Ibrahim Pasha's advance. Then 'Abdul-'Aziz Ibn Sa'ud's power grew, and by an audacious *coup* in 1913 he put an end to the Turkish occupation of the maritime province of al-Hasa – a blow to the Sultan's prestige, but one which was partly compensated for the Turks by the establishment of closer ties between them and the House of Rashid in the Shammar region.

On the Red Sea side, things had gone very ill with 'Abdul-Hamid in the Yaman, but the Young Turks had more than retrieved the position. The expeditionary force of 1872 had occupied San'a but had not subdued the interior which had remained unsettled and rebellious. In 1891, a serious insurrection had broken out, which had necessitated the despatch of large forces; then again, in 1903, another revolt, inspired and led by the Imam Yahya, opened a fresh chapter of military reverses and disasters in the history of the Turks in Arabia. The rebels had occupied San'a and held it for over a year. This they did a second time in 1911, until the Turks, weary of the endless drain, were ripe for a compromise. An agreement negotiated in the first instance by 'Aziz 'Ali commended itself to the Turkish commander-in-chief; and it led to peace and to the grant of substantial powers to the Imam, with a liberal subsidy to enhance their validity.

Immediately to the north of the Yaman lay the province of 'Asir in which a new star was in the ascendant – Sayyed Muhammad Ibn 'Ali, commonly known as the Idrisi. He came from a family which had but recently become established in the Peninsula, and his rise to power had begun in the early years of the century. His ancestors were Moroccan Arabs who, in the last years of the eighteenth century, had come to Mecca on a pilgrimage and afterwards settled in the uplands of 'Asir. The original migrant was Ahmad al-Idrisi, a man of piety and learning, who had earned a reputation for holiness and died bequeathing his heirs the privileges and profits which, in the Moslem society, often devolve on the members of a family accounted saintly. The Idrisis made 'Asir their home and multiplied, and lived contentedly in that state of affluence which is all too seldom the reward of saintliness. Until one of them, abler and more ambitious, had set out to consolidate the family's assets into those of a ruling dynasty, free from Turkish dominance. This was the present Idrisi, Sayyed Muhammad. His horizon was not limited to Arabia, for he had lived in Cairo as a student at al-Azhar University and stayed with the Sanusi Chief in Cyrenaica; and, on his return home, had built up an administration of his own devising in the uplands of 'Asir. Then, in 1909, a young man of thirty-five, he had risen against the Turks, gone to the aid of the Imam Yahya in his own revolt, suffered defeat, risen again with Italian help, only to end in a stalemate which left him, as he had begun, master of the hill-country but of scarcely more. In 1914, he was still nominally a vassal of the Sultan, but in fact an unappeased rebel, mustering his forces for another trial of strength with the Turks.

In the Hejaz, the Sultan's authority was – thanks largely to the completion of the Hejaz Railway line to Madina – more secure than elsewhere in Arabia, and might have been absolute had it not been for the new Grand Sharif. Husain had turned out to be a good deal more wilful than the gentle and pacific aristocrat whom the C.U.P. had chosen for the dignity. He had found on his arrival in 1908 that his predecessors had suffered several of the old prerogatives of the office to lapse, and he had set out to revive them. In particular, he had succeeded in restoring the hegemony of the Sharifate over the tribes of the Hejaz; and, going eastwards to outside the confines of the Hejaz, had tried to impose his authority on tribes whose allegiance Ibn Sa'ud claimed as his due. When the C.U.P. announced that the administration of the Hejaz was henceforth to be adapted to that of the rest of the empire, on the centralised pattern, and that conscription would be introduced, Husain objected with good reason that the project was unfeasible. On that, the C.U.P. decided to depose him, but he was too firmly entrenched for them to have risked a summary dismissal; and they sent out, to pave the way for the Sharif's punishment, a governor-general known for his bluntness and the shortness of his temper. But against him, Husain pitted his own tenacity and resourcefulness, and won. Matters came to a head in the spring of 1914 when, after a long tussle which threatened to bring about an insurrection, the *vali* was bidden make his peace with the Sharif, which he had to perform at a public ceremony, kissing the hem of Husain's garment in token of obeisance to the sanctity of his office.

CHAPTER VII

THE WAR AND THE HOLY WAR: 1914

I.

FOREMOST among the Arab deputies in the Ottoman Parliament was the Amir 'Abdullah, the second son of the Sharif of Mecca. This young man, then scarcely aged thirty, was already a figure in political circles. Early in life he had stood out among his kin as an independent spirit, proud of his descent and eager to champion the merits of his race. His long sojourn in Constantinople during the Sharif's detention had enabled him to acquire the Turkish tongue and enough of the manners of well-bred Turks to soften without emasculating his native Arab bluntness. His natural aptitude for tribal politics and his ardour to promote the family fortunes had caused his father to prefer him to a function of trust, as emissary and mediator, for which he seemed better fitted than either his elder brother, the gentle and diffident 'Ali, or the younger Faisal who had hitherto sought and won his laurels in exploits of military valour. 'Abdullah was easily the most famous and the most popular of the three. Not the least of his assets was his charm; and he had one passion, amongst many, that endeared him to his fellow-workers in the Arab cause: his love of Arabic poetry. He read and remembered a lot, and with such a quick feeling for niceties in literature that his conversation was thereby enriched and his thought, even at that early age, attired in an apparel of wisdom.

Outside the Hejaz, 'Abdullah made the fullest use of his opportunities as the Sharif's son and right-hand man. As deputy for Mecca, he had tried to use his status and influence with the Porte to consolidate his father's position in the Hejaz,

which was none too secure in the spring of 1914; and the
C.U.P., suspecting him of being the instigator as well as the
apologist of the Sharif's obduracy, had tried to deflect him
with offers, first of a seat in the Cabinet, then of the post
of Governor-General of the Yaman. Scenting the bait,
'Abdullah had asked to be excused and had retained his
independence. Like his father, he was bent upon a trial
of strength with the Turks. They were both ambitious,
and they both dreamed of an autonomous Hejaz which
should in course of time lead the rest of the Arab provinces
to a like autonomy. The main difference between father
and son was one of tactics or, more exactly, of temperament.
Husain was interminably cautious until the moment should
come when he would risk everything with a fine recklessness.
'Abdullah was impatient, self-confident and hasty, with little
of his father's depth or foresight; and he boldly went to Lord
Kitchener to sound him on England's attitude.

This was in the first week of February 1914. Kitchener
was then British Agent in Egypt and 'Abdullah who was
staying in Cairo on his way from Mecca to Constantinople
called on him, ostensibly to return a visit of courtesy. In
the presence of Mr. (now Sir) Ronald Storrs, then Oriental
Secretary at the British Agency, 'Abdullah gave Kitchener
an account of the strained relations between the Turkish
authorities and the Sharif. He knew that the C.U.P. had
secretly decided to depose his father, and he gave Kitchener
to understand that if they carried out their intention there
would probably be a revolt in the Hejaz. In guarded language, he tried to sound Kitchener as to the British Government's attitude in the event of a conflict breaking out openly
between Turks and Arabs. Kitchener's answer, although
non-committal, was discouraging. He gave it as his opinion
that, since England's traditional policy was one of friendship
with Turkey, it was not likely that she would intervene. At
the same time, guessing that his visitor had more to say than
he cared in a formal interview to divulge, he instructed
Storrs to pay a return call two days later and give 'Abdullah
an opportunity of speaking his mind more fully.

With Storrs, 'Abdullah was more explicit. Storrs had some knowledge of Arabic and a talent for making a little go a long way; and he had at least one hobby in common with 'Abdullah – a passion for chess. The two men made friends at once, and on that foundation of intimacy – so rare between Englishmen and Arabs – 'Abdullah felt at home and became expansive. He told his visitor a great deal more than he had said to Kitchener about the gravity of the issue in the Hejaz, and about the preparations which his father was making against the final rupture that seemed to him inevitable. He spoke at length of the aims of the Arab movement, of the hopes of its leaders and of their growing despair. Then, with characteristic directness, he asked whether Kitchener would help the Sharif to obtain machine-guns.

Storrs's answer, naturally enough, was as discouraging as his chief's, and the conversation came to a close. Towards the end of April, 'Abdullah passed through Cairo again, did not see Kitchener, but had another meeting with Storrs, at which the latter made it plainer than ever that no encouragement was to be expected from the British Government; and 'Abdullah returned to the Hejaz. Although nothing was achieved, these conversations were nevertheless to have a determining effect on the course of events. They opened Kitchener's eyes to the strength and the depth of Turco-Arab animosity and to the reality of the Arab desire for independence, and caused him, a few months later, to take the first of a series of steps which ultimately brought the Arabs into the War as England's allies against the Turks.

2.

The importance of those conversations lay in this, that the Amir 'Abdullah's approaches happened to synchronise with certain speculations which were agitating Kitchener's own mind. As British Agent in Cairo, his primary responsibility was for Egypt and the Sudan. But his vision ranged beyond the confines of his immediate beat. His campaigns in the Sudan, his term of service as commander-in-chief in

India, and the close acquaintance he had there acquired with the problems of the north-western frontier and Afghanistan, had brought him into direct touch with militant Moslem forces and developed in him a keen sense of the political importance of the religious bond in Islam. During his three years in Cairo, he had kept an anxious eye on Constantinople, the seat of the caliphate. He had watched the growth of German influence, the ominous advance of the Baghdad Railway line, and become keenly aware of, not to say obsessed by, the implied threat to Great Britain's position in the Persian Gulf and India. He made no secret, among his few intimates, of his belief that British diplomacy had committed an unpardonable error in suffering Germany to establish her political and military ascendancy in the capital of the Ottoman Empire, and the problem of how that menace was to be parried had become one of his constant pre-occupations.

Different solutions presented themselves to his mind. One was that a portion of southern Syria, roughly from the Haifa-Acre Bay in the Mediterranean Sea to the Gulf of 'Aqaba on the Red Sea, might in course of time be detached from the Ottoman Empire and made to come under British protection, so that the belt of British influence might stretch uninterruptedly from Egypt to the Persian Gulf. Another was that the Arab provinces of the Ottoman Empire might be encouraged to form themselves into an autonomous state or chain of states friendly to Great Britain and extending all the way from the Mediterranean seaboard in the west to the Persian frontier in the east – an Anglo-Arab dam to stem the Turco-German tide. In other words, he had come, by an independent process of reasoning, to a point where he was envisaging the very possibilities that were being contemplated by Arab nationalist leaders; and it was at a time when his mind was busy with those speculations that the Amir 'Abdullah, himself a member of one of the secret societies and an enthusiastic believer in the fruitfulness of an Anglo-Arab understanding, called upon him and supplied him with fresh food for thought.

3.

When war broke out in August, Kitchener was in England on leave and started back at once to return to his post. But he had not proceeded beyond Dover before he was recalled by the Prime Minister and appointed Secretary of State for War. He found himself faced, literally overnight, with the task of improvising a British army on an unprecedented scale, and while he gave himself over wholly to the pursuit of that task, one compartment of his mind remained obsessed by the dangers lurking in the German diplomatic hold on Turkey and engrossed in the problem of how to meet them. Outwardly, Turkey seemed bent on a policy of neutrality; at least, so the C.U.P., who were the party in power at the time, kept proclaiming. But, his anxieties being what they were, Kitchener could scarcely bank on such dubious professions. He felt that the risk was too great, and when a suggestion came to him from Storrs about the middle of September, he persuaded the Cabinet to let him act.

Storrs, who had returned to Egypt without his chief, had not been idle. The frankness with which 'Abdullah had spoken to him a few months previously had helped his quick mind to fasten upon the wider implications of the Arab discontent. He saw, perhaps more clearly than anyone at the time, the possibility of turning it to useful account; and the consultations which, as Oriental Secretary, he had occasion to hold with the numerous Arab leaders residing in Egypt, had strengthened him in his view. He wrote privately to Kitchener, to something like this effect: 'Would you authorise me to ascertain from 'Abdullah which way the Arabs are going to jump if and when Turkey comes into the War: apart from broader considerations, it would clearly improve our flank position if we could get them in on our side.' These may not have been his actual words, but that was the sense of what he wrote.

Kitchener adopted the suggestion at once and telegraphed to Storrs the instructions which he had solicited. More specifically, he directed Storrs to inquire from 'Abdullah whether, in the event of Germany prevailing upon Turkey to enter the War on her side, the Sharif of Mecca would follow Turkey's suit or join Great Britain against her. These instructions were issued in the last week of September, that is to say, about six weeks before the declaration of war on Turkey. It took Storrs a few days to find a reliable messenger who could be counted upon to travel secretly to the Hejaz and insinuate himself into 'Abdullah's presence without attracting notice. The messenger – an Egyptian known as 'Ali Efendi – arrived in Mecca about the middle of October, delivered his message and returned to Cairo before the end of the month, bringing with him a written reply from 'Abdullah.

The receipt of Kitchener's message had placed the Sharif of Mecca in an extremely delicate posture. He had been seeking an opportunity to assert his authority in the Hejaz, even at the cost of a breach with the Turks. This was several months before the outbreak of the War, at a time when the prospect of a general conflagration in which Turkey might be drawn was practically non-existent and when his differences with the Turks related solely to affairs in the Hejaz. Now that war had broken out and that Turkey's participation seemed imminent, the problem had become much broader and involved the future of all the Arab provinces of the Ottoman Empire. If Turkey were actually to be drawn into the War, might not her absorption in it give the Arabs their long-awaited opportunity? Two courses seemed open to them: to stand by Turkey in her hour of trial and earn her grateful recognition, or to rise against her and seek their freedom at the point of the sword. Which of those alternatives to take?

The two sons he consulted were of opposite minds. Faisal favoured the first alternative: he was convinced that France had designs on Syria and England on the southern regions of Iraq, and Kitchener's offer contained no guarantee against those dangers; moreover, he did not think that the Arabs were sufficiently prepared and feared that a revolt would misfire.[1] 'Abdullah thought otherwise. His admission to one of the secret Arab societies had given him an insight into the strength of the revolutionary feeling, and, being of an optimistic turn, he was confident that Damascus and Baghdad would respond handsomely to a call to revolt. He felt that the proper course would be not to reject Kitchener's offer as insufficient, but to find out by negotiation whether it was intended as an absolute guarantee of Arab independence.

The two brothers stuck tenaciously to their opinions, in the whispered conferences to which their father kept summoning them, and neither of them would budge. Husain was inclined on the whole to share Faisal's views on the unpreparedness of the Arabs in the other provinces; yet there was that in 'Abdullah's insistence that made him pause. Eventually he came to an interim decision. On the one hand, he would send emissaries to Syria and the principal Arab rulers, to discover the true state of national feeling and preparedness and sound the leaders; and on the other, he would give Kitchener just enough (but no more) encouragement to keep him in play. He composed a letter to Storrs for 'Abdullah to sign, in which he defined himself as being willing to come to an understanding with Great Britain, but unable yet to depart from the neutrality which his position in Islam bound him to observe. He confined his remarks to the Hejaz, carefully avoiding to commit the rest of the Arab world, and hinted that he might find it possible to lead his immediate followers to revolt, in the event of the Turks bringing matters to a head, provided England were to promise effective support.[2]

This letter reached Storrs before the end of October and was telegraphed to London at once. Its text must have

[1] T. E. Lawrence, in *Seven Pillars of Wisdom*, and other writers have stated that Faisal was already a member of a secret Arab society and won to the idea of a revolt. I have it on Faisal's own authority that he had not joined any such society before the War and that it was only when he went to Damascus in 1915 that he became converted to the idea of an Arab revolt.

[2] So far as I am aware, the text of this letter has never been made public. After numerous conversations with the late King Husain and his sons I am satisfied that the summary given above is a fair condensation of it. This observation holds good for all the correspondence which passed between Kitchener and 'Abdullah at that stage.

reached Kitchener about the same time as a letter from his old friend Sir John Maxwell who was then commanding the British Forces in Egypt and who, writing from Cairo on the 16th October, advised; '. . . . I do not know what the policy of the Foreign Office is, but I think the Arabs about Mecca and the Yaman ought to be approached and set against the Turks.' Maxwell had served long in the East, and his advice was weighty with Kitchener. On the 31st, Kitchener telegraphed to the British Agency in Cairo the text of a message to be despatched to 'Abdullah in reply. The message opened with an announcement of the news of Turkey's entry into the War. It contained a definite promise to Husain, that if he and his followers were to side with England against Turkey, the British Government would guarantee his retention of the dignity of Grand Sharif with all the rights and privileges pertaining to it and would defend it against all external aggression. It held out a promise of support to the Arabs in general in their endeavours to secure freedom, on condition that they would ally themselves to England. It concluded with a hint that, in the event of the Sharif being proclaimed caliph, he could count on England's recognition.

This message reached 'Abdullah on November 16, at a critical juncture as will appear hereafter, and caused him the liveliest satisfaction. On the subject of the Hejaz, it gave Husain the very assurance he had solicited; while, on the question of the other Arab provinces, it opened out an alluring prospect of national liberation. The terms of the message were studiously general, it is true; but in the form in which it reached 'Abdullah[1] it spoke of 'the Arab nation' and of the 'emancipation of the Arabs'. Whatever these phrases may have meant to the pre-occupied Kitchener when he used them, to the Sharif they conveyed an unmistakable invitation to foment a revolt of all the Arabs. In that sense did he read the letter addressed to his son in the name of Kitchener, whose fame in the East was then greater than that of any living Englishman and whose word was accepted without

[1] i.e., in an Arabic translation made at the British Agency in Cairo.

question; and to that end, henceforth, did he direct his activities.

He caused an answer to be sent to Cairo, in which 'Abdullah definitely committed his father to a policy of un-avowed alliance with England. 'Abdullah stressed again the inability of the Sharif, before the requisite preparation, to commit any act of overt hostility against the Turks, and he asked for time in which to find his bearings, muster his forces and then seize a favourable opportunity for a rupture. He promised Storrs that he would send a further communication in due course. This reply reached Cairo in the early days of December, and with it the first chapter in the Anglo-Arab conspiracy came to a close. The second chapter was to open eight months later, in the following July, as soon as Husain had completed his inquiries among Arab leaders and his negotiations with them. It opened with a note from the Sharif to Sir Henry McMahon, the first of an important series of diplomatic notes which make up what is known as the McMahon Correspondence.

4.

The mere fact that the Ottoman Empire had sided with the Central Powers meant that the problem of Arab national aspirations could not fail to be drawn into the orbit of European politics. The attitude of the Arabs was hence-forth a matter of immediate concern to the Allies and especially to Great Britain. Thanks to her hold on Syria and Iraq, Turkey was in a position to threaten British interests at two vital points: the Suez Canal, and the head of the Persian Gulf where lay the valuable oil-fields of the Anglo-Persian Company. Nor could the menace in the Arabian Peninsula itself be overlooked. The long Red Sea coast-line afforded the Turks numerous sheltered bases for laying mines or for sending emissaries across to Egypt, the Sudan and further into Africa to distribute arms and preach disaffection. In the Yaman, the Turkish garrison of two divisions was strong enough to threaten Aden. While in the political field, the proclamation of a holy war (*jihad*) by the sultan-caliph might, if it were to receive the endorsement of the Sharif of Mecca, turn the Hejaz into a hot-house of inflammatory propaganda to arouse not only the Arab countries but also the large non-Arab Moslem populations living under Allied rule or on the flank of Allied dependencies.

Of those dangers the most formidable was that involved in a call to holy war. It was a foregone conclusion that, if Turkey were to join the Central Powers, one of her first acts would be to rouse the Moslem world against the Allies. As Caliph and supreme Imam, the Sultan would declare that Turkey, the premier Islamic state and the seat of the caliphate, was at war with Christian Powers aiming at her destruction, that the Holy Places were in danger, and that it was incumbent upon all true believers to rally around the banner of the Faith. To what extent the call was likely to be obeyed it was not easy to tell beforehand. There had been no precedent in modern times for the proclamation of a *jihad* on a world-wide scale; and the fact that Turkey was herself in alliance with Christian Powers could only weaken the strength of her appeal. On the other hand, the sentiments of pan-Islamic solidarity which 'Abdul-Hamid had exerted himself to foster were a factor which could be neither accurately gauged nor safely ignored. At any rate, the Mahdist rebellion in the Sudan, and the resistance of the Moslem populations in Tunis, Morocco and Tripoli to European penetration, had shown not so very long ago that the invocation of a religious motive in a call to arms still retained something of its former incendiary power. Even a partially successful *jihad* might prove a serious threat to the Allies, which neither England with some seventy million Moslems in India and sixteen million in Egypt and the Sudan, nor France with her twenty million in Africa, nor Russia with a like number within her borders could afford to disregard.

By far the most serious danger was the threat to Egypt. In the outlying parts of the Moslem world, such as India or Morocco or the Caucasus, a successful call to *jihad* was expected to cause difficulties to Great Britian or France or

Russia, which, at the worst estimate, were not likely to exceed the dimensions of local rebellions; or, in the event of Afghanistan being drawn in, a local war on the north-west frontier of India. In Egypt, on the other hand, the threat had much more formidable implications, since the throttling of the Suez Canal would not merely have embarrassed England, but crippled her at a vital point. Thus the Moslem world in which *jihad* was to be preached fell into two distinct zones: an outer belt of countries inhabited by divers non-Arab nations, and an inner circle of countries which were Arab and whose geographical centre was Egypt. Land attacks on the Suez Canal could only be made across territories inhabited by Arabs, and one way of warding off that threat was to win the Arabs over to the Allied side. That is what Kitchener had immediately in mind when he sent his message to the Sharif, and that is how, with Turkey's entry into the War, the Arab question was automatically drawn into the European political orbit.

5.

The Turkish order for general mobilisation was issued on the 2nd of August and, under cover of it, although Turkey professed her neutrality, hostile preparations were pushed forward, which caused a good deal of disquiet in Cairo. Of the countries surrounding Egypt, Syria was the most important from the military point of view. Its garrison consisted of two army corps of three to four divisions each, amounting in normal conditions to a strength of sixty to seventy thousand men.[1] When Turkey entered the War, these groups were formed into an army, known as the Fourth Army, with headquarters at Damascus, whose principal objective, it was publicly announced, was to be an attack on Egypt. On the 25th of September, the British Agency in Cairo informed the Foreign Office that a concentration of

---

[1] The peace-time British garrison in Egypt amounted to less than six thousand men. The strength of the Egyptian army, of which far the greater part was stationed in the Sudan, was of approximately thirteen thousand men.

troops was being secretly made near the Egyptian frontier. Throughout October, the British Embassy in Constantinople kept telegraphing reports of disquieting movements of troops, of consignments of arms and gold intended to equip and subsidise the Beduin tribes of southern Syria and of Sinai for an attack on Egypt, of the activities of 600 preachers assembling in Aleppo and radiating thence to all parts of Syria and into Egypt to incite the Moslem population against Great Britain. Batches of German officers, headed by Colonel Kress von Kressenstein, had arrived in Syria to take up appointments on the staff of the Fourth Army; while others, belonging to the corps of engineers, were busy in the south of Syria with roads and railway-tracks pointing towards the Egyptian frontier. It also became known that the Turkish XIIth Army Corps, which included one division that was almost wholly Arab, was being moved from Mosul to Aleppo. On the 22nd of October, the Embassy telegraphed that a highly inflammatory manifesto, inciting the Moslem soldiers in Allied forces to mutiny in defence of Islam, was being circulated, and that several thousand copies were to be smuggled into Egypt through Syria.

On the western frontier of Egypt there was that unknown quantity, the Sanusi chief, who, although he professed friendship for Great Britain, was known to be in close relations wth the Turks and with the Sultan of Darfur. He was still engaged in hostilities with the Italians whom he had succeeded in keeping at bay in the narrow strip of coast-line where they maintained themselves with the aid of their naval artillery. Turkish emissaries were soon despatched to him with offers of money and honours, and with injunctions from the Caliph to preach *jihad* in his name.[1] The fact that Sayyed Ahmad commanded a large following of Moslem devotees, that he was influential with Moslem chiefs on the

---

[1] 'Then [i.e., about August 1915] there came accidentally into General Maxwell's hands a packet of letters addressed by the Sanusi to Moslem potentates and journalists all over Arabia and India, inciting them to a *jihad* and informing them that he was the representative of the Caliph in Northern Africa.' (Official History of the War, *Military Operations in Egypt and Palestine*, Vol. I, p. 105.)

borders of Egypt and the Sudan, and that he was well supplied with arms and ammunition meant another potential menace to Egypt.

In the Arabian Peninsula, the Turks kept a garrison of four divisions spaced out between the Hejaz, 'Asir and the Yaman. In the Hejaz the Sharif Husain had acquired enough hold over the tribes to be able, had he wished, to enrol a large force for a participation in the attack on Egypt. At a low estimate, he could raise a rifle-strength of 40,000 from among the tribesmen over whom the Turks, without his help, could exercise no influence whatsoever. The Turkish garrison in the Hejaz and 'Asir consisted of two divisions; but so unruly were the tribes that the troops seldom ventured out into the country, remaining for the most part ensconced within the walls of their forts and outposts. For a mobilisation of the tribal forces the Turks would have had first to secure the Sharif's co-operation. With it, they could have made free use of their own marooned garrison and armed a large force of tribesmen to swell the expeditionary force to the Suez Canal.

The military value of the Idrisi was only of local significance. He was in a position to harass the Turkish communications between the Hejaz and the Yaman, and to threaten the Turks in the rear in the event of their attacking Aden. His main usefulness to the Allies would be on the coast, where he could prevent the long seaboard of 'Asir from being used as a hostile base.

In the Yaman, the attitude of the Imam was primarily a matter of concern to Aden. The Turkish garrison of two divisions was largely composed of experienced and hardened troops who, unlike those in the Hejaz, were now on terms of outward friendliness with the inhabitants. An attack on Aden was probable, and its chances would be considerably strengthened by the Imam's acquiescence, let alone the participation of his followers.

On the Persian Gulf side, the attitude of Ibn Rashid in Shammar and Ibn Sa'ud in Najd were primarily governed by the feud between them. They were both, in sentiment, inimical to the Turks, and they had the advantage, which none of the chiefs in western Arabia enjoyed, of being masters in their own house, for they were both free of Turkish officials and garrisons. But the rulers of Shammar had, as we have seen, once called in the Turks to their help, and the alliance thus begun had never been denounced. It could safely be assumed that, once war had broken out, Ibn Rashid would definitely range himself on the side of the Turks.

6.

Among the statesmen of the Entente, no one perhaps was more alive to the dangers of the position in the Arab world than Kitchener; and it must remain to his credit and that of Ronald Storrs that they were the first to think of meeting them by the bold stroke of an alliance with Mecca. The criticism has often been made since, that that policy was a mistake, that it rested on an imperfect appreciation of conditions in Arabia, and that, in choosing the Sharif Husain as her main Arab ally against the Turks, in preference to the powerful Ibn Sa'ud, Great Britain had 'backed the wrong horse'. This criticism is not so much unfair as meaningless. For the great service which Husain rendered to the Allied cause in relation to the Holy War was one which no one else was in a position to render. And Kitchener's move in securing his goodwill before it was too late was nothing less than a master-stroke of acumen and foresight.

The Grand Sharif's position was indeed unique, as regards both the military contribution he could make and the political value of his intervention. Other chiefs in Arabia there were, whose ascendancy over their own followers was absolute and whose military resources were at least as promising as those of the Hejaz. But, from the Entente point of view, Husain had two outstanding assets which were not possessed by any of his neighbours. One was the strategic advantage of his position at the centre of the Turkish power in the Peninsula. The utmost that the Idrisi in 'Asir and the Imam Yahya in the Yaman could do was to reduce local garrisons to impotence; and as for Ibn Sa'ud, he was not in touch with Turkish forces. With the tribal contingents he might muster in the Hejaz, Husain could strike at the heart of the Ottoman power in Arabia and, by severing their communications with the north, isolate the garrisons in 'Asir and the Yaman. The other was the incomparable asset of his prestige in the Moslem world, which derived its force from his birth as well as from his office. Whereas the power of his neighbours was anyhow confined to their own dominions, he could appeal across frontiers to the immense populations of Islam. He was a descendant of the Prophet and Custodian of the Holy Places; and this dual claim to reverence placed him in a category of his own in which he had no rival, and on an eminence from which, on an issue involving the safety of the holy cities, he might challenge the authority of the Caliph himself. He was lord of Mecca, the metropolis and focus of Islam, to whose voice no devout Moslem – least of all an Arab Moslem – could remain deaf. To him, and to him alone, would it fall to endorse the Sultan's clamour that the Holy Places of Mecca and Madina were in danger. So that, on an issue like the call to *jihad*, his acquiescence was an important, if not the determining, factor; and would be eagerly canvassed by the Turks for the same reason as it was feared by the Entente. To say that Kitchener had hit upon the wrong candidate is to say something meaningless. There was no other candidate who, by withholding his endorsement, could rob the call to Holy War of its principal thunderbolt.

7.

The call was issued in three stages, in the first month of Turkey's entry into the War. First came the *fetva*[1] rendered by the Shaikh al-Islam on the 7th of November, in which that dignitary – the highest theological official in the Ottoman

---

[1] A *fetva* (in Arabic *fatwa*) is a formal pronouncement made by the appropriate theological authority on matters involving the interpretation of the canon Law.

Empire – declared it a sacred personal duty on all Moslems in the world, including those living under the rule of Great Britain, France or Russia, to unite against those three enemies of Islam; to take up arms against them and their allies; and to refuse in all circumstances, even when threatened with the death penalty, to assist the governments of the Entente in their attacks on the Ottoman Empire and its German and Austro-Hungarian defenders. Then came the Sultan's proclamation to the army and the fleet, issued on the 11th, in which he exhorted them to fight for the liberation of enslaved Islam as well as in defence of the threatened Empire, Lastly, there was the manifesto to the Moslem world, issued on the 23rd, over the signatures of the Shaikh al-Islam and of twenty-eight other religious dignitaries. It bore the Sultan's *imprimatur* in the following terms: 'I command that this manifesto be distributed in all the Moslem countries.' It called upon all the Moslems of the world, whether subjects of the Entente Powers or not, to obey the injunctions of the Holy Book as interpreted by the sacred *fetva*, and participate in the defence of Islam and the Holy Places.

Nor was this all. Those three formal utterances were followed by a spate of subsidiary literature, in the shape of leaflets, pamphlets, periodical reviews and every sort of printed matter specially composed to appeal to the masses who professed Islam. Their authorship was as often German as Turkish, and they appeared in all the languages of the Islamic world. They were broadcast by the million throughout the Ottoman Empire, and smuggled into Egypt, the Sudan, India, Persia, Afghanistan and beyond. They varied considerably in tone and contents, some of them advocating mass desertion from the ranks of the Entente armies, others the resort to assassination and other individual outrages. All harped on the tune that Islam was in peril through the greed of the Entente Powers, and that to take up arms in its defence was a God-ordained duty which no believer might shirk.

Missions were despatched to reinforce by word of mouth the cold appeal of print. Emissaries of all kinds – itinerant preachers, scholars, learned divines, professional agitators,

German orientalists – travelled in all directions open to
them, while a few succeeded in insinuating themselves into
Egypt, the Sudan and other parts of Africa which were under
Allied rule. Their main efforts were directed at winning
over to the Holy War the non-Turkish Moslem populations,
that is to say the Indians, the Afghans, the Persians and above
all the Arabs. The Moslems of Turkey, of whom the obed-
ient and deeply religious Anatolian peasantry formed the
backbone, stood scarcely in need of persuasion. But among
the Arabs, who were geographically best placed to harass the
Entente, the preaching of *jihad* was conducted with particular
vigour and with special emphasis on the duty devolving upon
all Moslems to defend the Holy Places.

8.

In Mecca, the Sharif was cautiously picking his way.
Kitchener's offer of the 31st of October, which had reached
him almost simultaneously with the issue of the call to *jihad*
had brought him definitely round to 'Abdullah's view as
against Faisal's. But it was still too early for him to act.
He had first to carry out some indispensable consultations,
with Arab nationalists in Syria and Iraq, and with his neighbours in Arabia, and elicit the degree of support he could
count upon. The distances involved and the care needed to
preserve secrecy would mean long months of patient schem-
ing. Meanwhile the Turks were pressing for his endorsement of *jihad* and for his active support. He was deluged
with letters and telegrams from Constantinople – from the
Grand Vizir, Enver, Tal'at and other personalities. And
now Jemal Pasha, commander-in-chief of the Fourth Army
in Syria, was urging him to declare himself openly for
a holy war, to send the Prophet's standard to Damascus,
and to raise an army among the tribes of the Hejaz.

In subtlety and resourcefulness, Husain was more than a
match for the Turks; and he acted with consummate dexter-
ity. To their solicitations that he should endorse the call to
jihad he returned enthusiastic replies couched in that diffuse

and nebulous prose of which he was a master. He would support the Holy War with all his heart, he wrote, and put his soul into praying for its success and giving it his silent blessing. But as for endorsing it openly, that was totally out of the question, for fear of enemy reprisals. The British navy was supreme in the Red Sea; Jedda and the long seaboard of the Hejaz were entirely at its mercy; if he were to associate himself openly with *jihad*, England would retaliate with a blockade, and maybe a bombardment, of the Hejaz ports; food supplies would cease to come by sea, and the population would soon be faced with shortage and, in course of time, famine. With all his heart would he support the Holy War, but not by a public endorsement of it, lest famine in the Hejaz should lead to a revolt of the tribes. He felt sure that the Sultan, in his infinite wisdom, would understand the position.

From that unassailable ground the Sharif never budged, and the Turks had perforce to swallow his pretext. Then, craftily, he made a show of zealous compliance with all their other requests, now and again suggesting refinements that had not occurred to them. He gave orders for the Prophet's standard, that is to say the cloth that went by that name, to be taken out in pomp from its repository in Madina and ceremoniously despatched to Damascus to bless the army about to invade Egypt. He took measures to raise a force of *mujahidin* (recruits for a holy war) from the tribes of the Hejaz, sending his sons to preside over the recruiting and give it an appearance of earnest. Meanwhile, in great secrecy, he despatched emissaries with letters to the Idrisi, the Imam Yahya, Ibn Sa'ud and Ibn Rashid to sound them on their attitude towards the Turks and explain why he was abstaining from endorsing the call to *jihad*.

During those months (January to March 1915), Husain had been receiving veiled encouragement from another British source, Sir Reginald Wingate, governor-general of the Sudan. In his thirty years of service in the Sudan, Wingate had acquired an intimate knowledge of the intricacies of local Islamic politics. On his own initiative, he had moved the principal Arab dignitary in the Sudan, Sayyed 'Ali al-Mirghani, to send the Sharif Husain a letter which, friendly and non-committal, was so worded as to invite a declaration of policy. Husain, guessing the source of the inquiry, returned a very cordial and not too cryptic reply: he spoke of the Turkish tyranny, his longing to be rid of it, the odds against him. Sayyed 'Ali answered with a positive proposal: the Sirdar[1] and I are friends, tell me of any way in which he might be of use and I will try my influence with him. The proposal was premature, since Husain had scarcely begun his consultations. He replied guardedly, adding in a postscript that he would be glad to receive any suggestions which 'your friend' might wish to make. To that, Sayyed 'Ali replied that, if only Husain would state his wants, the 'friend' might be able to help with money, arms and ammunition. Husain did not proceed to state his wants, but a few weeks later (in April) emissaries from him arrived to find out from Wingate what resources were available in the Sudan.

This correspondence, inconclusive though it was, encouraged the Sharif Husain greatly. It had shown that his policy had the support of the head of the Moslems in the Sudan; and the fact that, as he had guessed, the latter was acting in league with Wingate, had strengthened his confidence in the sincerity of Great Britain's desire for an alliance.

9.

By refusing to endorse the call to *jihad*, which was primarily intended to set the Arab world ablaze, the Sharif Husain had aroused the wrath of the Turks. The excuse he had given was unchallengeable, but that had made the Turks only angrier. Plans were made for his deposition and his replacement by a more amenable grand sharif, and orders were issued to the vali of the Hejaz to pave the way secretly for his arrest so as to effect it without causing a rising of the

---

[1] i.e. commander-in-chief of the Egyptian army, one of the functions of the governor-general of the Sudan.

tribes. At the same time, Husain was courteously invited to visit Damascus to confer with Jemal Pasha.

Every effort was being made in the meanwhile to deceive the Arab world into a belief that the call to holy war had received the blessing of the Sharif of Mecca. Sermons were by order preached, Friday after Friday, throughout the mosques of Syria and Iraq, in which the lie was unscrupulously trumpeted. The newspapers were made to play their part, and announcements appeared frequently that contained some fresh fabrication. A sample will serve as an illustration. In its issue of the 29th December, *al-Ittihad al-'Uthmani* (Bairut) published the following announcement:

> 'We announced yesterday, from official sources, that the Amir 'Abdullah, son of the Sharif of Mecca, had volunteered for service in the cause of *jihad* together with a large contingent of Hejaz tribesmen. We are now in a position to state that the Sharif of Mecca, in obedience to the will of the Caliph, has proclaimed the call to Holy War throughout the Hejaz, and that the tribes are everywhere answering the call with their full complements in arms.'

The newspapers of the period are replete with announcements in that sense. The story was also given out that the Sharif had accepted to visit Damascus, 'to confer with Jemal Pasha and manifest his loyalty to the Imperial Government'. But Husain had lived too long in Constantinople to have any doubts as to what a visit to Damascus might have held for him.

The same tactics were adopted in Iraq, where several Sunni and Shi'i dignitaries were instructed to issue circulars in exhortation to *jihad*. The ritual was performed of parading relics from the shrines of Najaf and Karbala, in an attempt to galvanise popular fervour: a sword said to have belonged thirteen centuries ago to the martyred Husain, son of the caliph 'Ali; and, of more doubtful authenticity still, a banner alleged to have been the standard of al-'Abbas, the Prophet's uncle. The newspapers, notably *Sada al-Islam*

(Baghdad), were used as vehicles for the same stories and admonitions as were appearing in Syria.

Emissaries to the Arab rulers were sent into the Peninsula with presents and blandishments. With Ibn Rashid, the negotiations bore fruit at once: he was eager to enter into alliance with the Turks, if only to gain their support against Ibn Sa'ud whom he feared. The same applied to the Imam Yahya who was showing every intention of remaining an ally. The Idrisi was hopelessly anti-Turk, and was ignored. So was Shaikh Mubarak ibn Sabah, ruler of Kuwait, who had been in treaty relations with Great Britain since 1899 and had, as soon as Turkey entered the War, concluded a treaty of active alliance with the British. As for Ibn Sa'ud, emissaries visited him but could obtain no definite promise from him. He gave as his pretext his fear that the British might attack his seaboard on the Persian Gulf. In actual fact, he was already in communication and practically in league with the Government of India; and when, earlier in the year, the Sharif Husain had written to inform him of his refusal to endorse the call to *jihad*, he had warmly commended Husain for his attitude. Thus, of the five principal potentates in Arabia, Ibn Rashid, and the Imam Yahya were actively standing by Turkey; while the Sharif, Ibn Sa'ud and the Idrisi, tempted by British overtures, were waiting for the overtures to materialise into bonds before breaking into open revolt.

The Turks did not confine their activities to Asia, but took measures to preach *jihad* in the Arab countries of Africa. Emissaries were smuggled into Egypt and the Sudan, who scoured the Nile Valley and whispered their messages of sedition. A mission was sent out to the Sanusi Chief in Cyrenaica at the head of which was a half-brother of Enver Pasha's, with presents of money and honours. How far the Turkish emissaries penetrated into central Africa is not known accurately, but traces of their activities were afterwards found in the Sudan and as far west as Darfur.

10.

The episode of the Prophet's standard occurred in December 1914, and was given the widest possible publicity. In a *communiqué* published in the newspapers of Syria on the 30th of November, it was announced that, as a result of the proclamation of a 'supreme *jihad*', a ceremony attended by 20,000 believers had been held at the Prophet's tomb in Madina and his standard reverently exalted for removal to Damascus 'to sanctify the valour of the armies'. The honour of carrying the banner fell to the aged *doyen* of the Prophet's descendants in Madina, the Sayyed 'Alawi ba-Faqih, and his three sons; and a telegram despatched by him to Jemal Pasha was prominently displayed in the press:

> 'Despite my more than seventy years, and in compliance with the God-ordained call to holy war . . . I advance with my three sons to *jihad* in the service of the Almighty, carrying in one hand the sacred banner of the Prophet, and in the other the Holy Book of God which decrees the *jihad* upon all believers. With the cheers and god-speeds of twenty thousand worshippers ringing in my ears, I proceed to Damascus to accomplish, in all eagerness and devotion, the supreme sacrifice of death for the word of God. . . . The land of Hejaz and all its Arab tribes are answering the call of our revered Caliph. . . .'

The standard and its convoy arrived in Damascus by train on the 15th of December, and were received with all the pomp of which the city was capable. At the railway-station, Jemal Pasha and his staff, the vali and his council, the principal religious heads, delegations from other parts of Syria, and an immense concourse of notabilities awaited the train's arrival. When it had drawn up and the standard had been raised on the platform, the guard of honour made up of senior Army officers presented arms, and Jemal saluted, knelt and kissed its hem; while the multitude shouted '*Allahu akbar!*' Then a procession was formed in which military units of all arms with their bands joined, special prominence being given to a handful of dusky soldiers who figured as deserters from the Egyptian army.[1]

The progress of the standard did not end at Damascus. It was borne with similar ceremonial to Jerusalem, the holiest city of Islam after Mecca and Madina. A halt was made at Nablus on the way, for the cortège to attend the Friday prayers, and to enable the aged standard-bearer to rest. The journey was wearing him out: he had not spoken idly in describing it as a supreme sacrifice. The standard reached Jerusalem on the 20th; and a ceremony, headed again by Jemal Pasha, was staged for its reception in the vast enclosure of the Dome of the Rock, and ended with prayers at the al-Aqsa mosque. There it was temporarily laid to rest against the day of its resuscitation when the army should set out on its advance into Egypt. Three days later, true to his promise, the Sayyed 'Alawi died; and preachers acting under instructions went forth among the people, praising his death as an example and magnifying it into a portent.

No effort had been spared to make the procession of the standard impressive and stimulating and, by a multitude of added touches, to give it the appearance of a symbol from Mecca. Few people were taken in: if the Sharif was really endorsing the call to *jihad* why had he not attended the procession? or, supposing that he was detained in Mecca, why had he not delegated one of his sons? A contemporary observer relates[2] that sceptics went so far as to whisper that the cloth was no standard at all, but a fragment of one of the palls that adorned the Prophet's tomb. The episode was, on the whole, a misfire; and its main historical interest is that it illustrates the importance which the Turks (and behind them the Germans) attached to the success of the call to *jihad* in the Arab countries.

[1] A fortnight before, this announcement had appeared in the Ottoman Press: 'Two Sudanese officers and twenty-three troops who had surrendered to the Ottoman command near al-'Arish have arrived in Damascus. They formed part of an advance party of the British forces, and surrendered because their religious feeling prevented them from taking part in the war against their fellow-Moslems.' In actual fact, these were troopers of the Egyptian Coastguard service who had deserted over to the Turks at a skirmish in the vicinity of Qantara on the 20th of November.

[2] *al-'Asr al-Damawi*, by Nasif Abu-Zaid (Damascus, 1923).

CHAPTER VIII

THE PLOT: 1915

I.

WHILE the Sharif Husain was finding his bearings, he received an emissary from *al-Fatat*, now centred in Damascus, in the person of Fauzi al-Bakri. This young member of a well-known Syrian family had recently been mobilised for service in the Turkish army and had obtained, ostensibly as the perquisite of a younger son, a decorative post in the bodyguard of the Grand Sharif. There was friendship of old standing between Husain and 'Ata Pasha, the head of the Bakri clan, and the appointment was without difficulty wangled from the Turks who were anxious to humour the Sharif.

Fauzi's elder brother, Nasib, was a member of *al-Fatat*, and it was he who, in agreement with the moving spirits of the society, had urged the appointment. No sooner had Fauzi received his orders to proceed to Mecca than he was taken into the society's secret, sworn in as a member, and given a message to take to the Sharif. The message, which was oral, was to this effect: the nationalist leaders in Syria and Iraq, including senior Arab officers in the Turkish army, favoured a revolt for the attainment of Arab independence; would the Sharif consent to lead it, and if so, would he receive a deputation in Mecca or delegate persons of trust to Damascus to concert measures?

Fauzi arrived in Mecca in the last week of January, and delivered his message in a whisper. The Sharif, too cautious to countenance a plot before a stranger, made no reply and asked nothing, but stared out of the window as though he had not heard. The opening held out to him in the message was of the very kind he had been seeking.

He had, however, to wait until the conclusion of an investigation he was then engaged upon. There had been a marked change lately in the attitude towards him of Vehib bey, the vali. Husain had reason to believe that the change was the result of mysterious instructions received by Vehib, and he had set his agents to watch him. Early in February, as the vali was travelling to Madina, a trunk disappeared from among his personal baggage. It contained documents which, when they were brought to Husain and examined, were found to reveal evidence of an officially-countenanced plot against his life.

Then Husain acted. He telegraphed to the Grand Vizir to say that he had grave representations to make, and asked to be authorised to send one of his sons to Constantinople to make them on his behalf. The desired permission was granted with alacrity, and Husain chose Faisal for the mission and spent long hours coaching him. Ostensibly, Faisal was bound for Constantinople to lay his father's arraignment of the vali before the Sultan and the Grand Vizir and supplement it with oral explanations; in reality, his task was to get in touch with the Arab leaders in Damascus and find out what their attitude would be towards England's proposal, how earnest they were and how far prepared.

2.

In Damascus, the Turk in authority was Ahmed Jemal Pasha. A leading member of the C.U.P. and Minister of Marine in the Ottoman cabinet, he had been chosen to direct the campaign for the liberation of Egypt and invested with functions which, under martial law, made him head of the government in Syria as well as commander-in-chief of the forces. He had arrived in Syria early in the preceding December, and made Damascus his headquarters.

Jemal was not a representative Young Turk of the C.U.P. stamp. He was an outspoken champion of Islam. Unlike the advocates of Pan-Turanianism, he professed, not without sincerity, a belief in the virtues and the future of an Ottoman nationalism based on Moslem solidarity. He was franco-phile by inclination and was known to dislike the Germans. As a soldier, his capacities were not yet proved; but there was that in the grandiloquence of his first utterances and of his proclamations to the army that betokened an inner futility. In his three years in Syria, he was to reveal himself a mediocre general but a keen and energetic administrator; a compla-cent and gullible politician; and, whenever his passions were aroused — which was often — , something of a ruffian.

The impression he made in Damascus on his arrival was not unfavourable. He had come with the intention of win-ning the Arab population over to loyal support of Turkey, and the Moslems to an active co-operation in the Holy War, and he went out of his way to allay fears and inspire confidence. He meant to play the *jihad* card for all it was worth, and it was only natural that he should turn to Mecca for support. There are letters in existence addressed by him and by Enver Pasha to the Sharif of Mecca, that reveal the lengths of forbearance and patience they were willing to go in their efforts to win Husain over. Shortly before his arrival, Turkish officials had raided the French consulates in Bairut and Damascus, and laid their hands on correspondence incriminating certain well-known Arab personalities. The seized documents contained evidence of activities that seemed indistinguishable from treason; but Jemal, bent on making a good impression, merely informed the Sharif of the discovery, locked the papers up in a drawer and turned his attention to the task of liberating Egypt.

Egypt had by that time been declared a British protector-ate. In proclamations issued under martial law, General Maxwell had decreed the abolition of Turkey's nominal suzerainty, the deposition of the Khedive Abbas II and the accession of Prince Husain Kamel to the throne with the title of Sultan of Egypt. Jemal launched his offensive on the Suez Canal on the night of the 2nd February 1915, with manifestly inadequate forces. He was counting on

provoking a rising in Egypt where the sentiment was none too
friendly to England.   But his attack was repulsed and Egypt
remained quiet; and, leaving small forces in Sinai to occupy
the British forces on the Canal with sporadic pin-pricks, he
withdrew the bulk of his army and returned to Damascus.
His proclamation to the troops before the advance had read:

> 'Soldiers!   Behind you stretch the empty deserts,
> before you stands the craven foe.
> Beyond the enemy is rich Egypt, avid to welcome you.
> If you falter, death only shall be your lot.
> Forward, for before you lies Paradise!'

But now he gave out that he had intended the advance all
along to be a movement of reconnaissance, to be followed in
due course by an offensive in earnest.

3.

Faisal arrived in Damascus on the 26th of March and
stayed four weeks before proceeding to Constantinople.   He
was warmly received by Jemal Pasha and invited to stay at
General Headquarters, but he was already under promise to
stay with the Bakri family and asked to be excused.

It was during that visit of his to Damascus that Faisal became initiated into Arab nationalist secrets.   In the first few
days, there was a constant stream of callers at the Bakri house;
but when the courtesy visits were over and the household
could look to a comparative privacy, the delicate business of
political consultations began.   First, the leading members of
al-Fatat.   It was some time before they spoke their mind
openly, for Faisal was a stranger to them and he was known
to favour co-operation with the Turks.   The exchanges proceeded warily until Faisal, uncovering a little more of his
mind, explained that his preference for the Turks came from
his fear of Europe.   The remark radically changed the
course of the conversations: it revealed an unsuspected
identity of sentiment between Faisal and his questioners, and
they promptly told him why.   At a meeting of the higher

committee of *al-Fatat*, held a few months previously, a resolution had been passed:

> 'In consequence of Turkey's entry into the War, the fate
> of the Arab provinces of the Ottoman Empire is seriously
> imperilled and every effort is to be made to secure their
> liberation and independence; it being also resolved that,
> in the event of European designs appearing to materialise,
> the society shall be bound to work on the side of Turkey in
> order to resist foreign penetration of whatever kind or form.'[1]

The discovery of a common basis to their opposite policies,
brought Faisal into closer communion with the members of
al-Fatat, and the talks slipped into intimacy. Faisal was let
into the secret of the society and sworn in as a member.
Then, through one who belonged to the two societies,
he saw members of *al-'Ahd*, the secret association of army
officers. He found there the same congenial attitude: desire
to break away from the Turks held in check by fear of French,
British, Italian and Russian designs.

These fears of European designs were not only real but
largely justified. France made no secret of her claims to
'rights' in Syria, and Russia was known to be a keen competitor. In the decade preceding the War, there had been
a showy recrudescence of French and Russian activity in
Syria: new schools inaugurated, appeals launched to subsidise existing ones, companies floated and a steadily growing intervention in ecclesiastical affairs. Care was taken to
emphasise that these activities had only cultural and economic aims; but it was universally believed, and with good
reason, that they served a political end as well. The particular friends of France were the Maronites in the Lebanon
and the Melchites, while Russia had her partisans in the
Orthodox community and England among her old friends
the Druzes. The rest of the population, that is to say, the
Moslems who formed the vast majority, had remained practically untouched by foreign political influence.

[1] I owe a good deal of the facts in this section to the late King Faisal to
whom my indebtedness for this and much other valuable information is
recorded elsewhere. I am also indebted to Dr. Ahmad Qadri, one of the
most active members of *al-Fatat*, who participated in the conversations here
recorded.

At one time, in 1912, the subject of European designs on Syria had become one of the main topics of daily conversation. The estrangement between the C.U.P. and the Arab leaders was growing, and the Powers who had ambitions to further were alertly watching its repercussions. France was suspicious of England, Russia envious of France. Then a trivial occurrence brought those suspicions into publicity. Certain members of the British diplomatic service had gone to Syria on a holiday; and one of them, who was then a secretary at the British Agency in Cairo, had chosen to spend a holiday on a ride from Haifa along the coast to Bairut and then up into the Lebanon. French agents reported the visits and persuaded their government that they concealed an ulterior objective. The French Government who, earlier in the year, had sent out M. Caillaux to Syria on a visit undoubtedly prompted by political motives, grasped the point and took the matter up with the British Foreign Office. Sir Edward Grey was able to give M. Poincaré a positive assurance that those visits had no political significance and that Great Britain had not and would never wish to put forward any claim to a political stake in Syria; and the French Premier, to make the assurance effective, announced it in the Chamber on the 21st December, 1912. His declaration showed plainly that France looked upon Syria as a French preserve and wanted it to be so regarded by others.

This declaration had been followed up by a fresh display of French activity and by the visits of personages (the Sultan of Morocco in 1913, M. Maurice Barrès in 1914) who spoke openly in the same sense. The Sultan of Morocco, visiting Syria under French *aegis*, was reported in the press as having declared at a public gathering that the occupation of Syria by France was 'necessary, inevitable and near'.

Nor were the fears of the Arab leaders confined to Syria. It was known that Italy had a forward policy of her own in regard to 'Asir and the Yaman, coveting as she did a sphere of influence and a base on the eastern shores of the Red Sea. Great Britain's policy of treaties with Arab Chiefs had given her what amounted to a protectorate in several of the coastal states of the Peninsula; and quite recently, public attention had been sharply exercised by the Aden boundary dispute in which Turkey had had formally to recognise a British protectorate over nine small states in the hinterland of Aden.

The cumulative effect of these various tendencies, in the years that followed the Italian occupation of Libya, had been to cause the Arab nationalist leaders serious alarm. Even among those who were quite free from anti-European bias – and they formed the majority of workers in the political field – the prospect of foreign rule was distasteful. A section of the Christian community in Syria, and more particularly the Maronites, were eager to come under French rule; others looked with favour on the prospect of a connexion with England, similar to the régime in Egypt. But they were essentially a minority formed of those who, as a result of Western education and clerical influence, had moved away from the spirit of the Arab movement. The rest of the population, including the preponderant Moslem element, although they were envious of the material benefits conferred upon Egypt by the British Occupation, looked sullenly at the threat of foreign domination; and, sharing their disinclination, the leaders asked themselves whether it were not better for them, if it did come to a choice, to continue bearing the Turkish rule they knew than fall under some other rule not less alien and infinitely more powerful.

As soon as it had become evident that Turkey was coming into the War, 'Aziz 'Ali had, from his retirement in Egypt, sent a peremptory message to the leading members of al-'Ahd: that they were on no account to be tempted into hostile action against Turkey, as the fact of her becoming belligerent would expose her Arab provinces to foreign conquest; until some effective guarantee against European designs were obtained, it was their duty to stand by Turkey. On their side and acting independently, the leaders of al-Fatat had passed their resolution, quoted above, which in substance said the same thing. The two societies were now of one mind, and their main concern became to explore the chances of their seizing the opportunity provided by the War to obtain valid guarantees of future Arab independence. They knew nothing at the time of Kitchener's correspondence with the Sharif.

They were in that frame of mind when Faisal came to Damascus and was sworn in to membership, first of the one society, then of the other. With the organisation of *al-'Ahd*, Faisal was greatly impressed. Its leaders had it in their power to provoke a revolt of the army at will. The Ottoman divisions stationed in Syria at the time were overwhelmingly Arab and their officers, most of whom were members of the society, would have marched with their men on a sign from the leaders. As Jemal Pasha wrote, in his memoirs[1] published after the War: 'If a revolt had broken out as the result of foreign intrigues there would have been no way of suppressing it, and the Government would have lost all its Arab territories.'

Yet the fear that a revolt might only result in the substitution of one domination for another was causing the leaders to refrain. And Faisal, whose own adherence to the Turks had been prompted by that very fear and by his underestimation of Arab preparedness, joined the two societies with the fervour of a convert. He told the leaders about Kitchener's offer, the divergence between 'Abdullah and himself, and his father's policy of caution. Then, leaving them to cogitate the problem in the light of these disclosures, he proceeded to Constantinople to carry out the ostensible half of his mission, arriving there on the 23rd of April.

4.

Faisal's stay in Constantinople lasted a little under a month. He was received with unusual deference and consideration, and given ample opportunity to state his father's case fully. He had several conversations with Prince Sa'id

[1] Jemal Pasha, *Memories of a Turkish Statesman* (translation), London, undated.

Halim (Grand Vizir), Tal'at bey (Minister for the Interior), Enver Pasha (Minister for War) and two audiences of the Sultan. His representations were listened to with a show of sympathy, but he was told that the remedy lay in his father's own hands. If only the Sharif were to declare himself openly in favour of the Holy War, the task of redressing the situation in the Hejaz in his favour would be simplified and he could then count on receiving the fullest satisfaction. Letters to that effect were addressed to the Sharif by the Grand Vizir, Enver and Tal'at. Enver's letter, dated the 8th of May, was the most fulsome of the three. He gave the Sharif a bombastic account of the position in the Dardanelles and of the Austro-German victory at Dunayetz on the Galician front; and, stressing the 'holy' aspect of the War, he pressed Husain to support it by giving his endorsement to *jihad*.

Faisal was back in Damascus on the 23rd of May, and found that his colleagues in *al-Fatat* and *al-'Ahd* had concerted a plan of action in his absence. They had drawn up a protocol defining the conditions on which the Arab leaders would be prepared to co-operate with Great Britain against Turkey, and their plan was that Faisal should take it to Mecca and ask his father to find out whether it was acceptable to the British Government as a basis for concerted action. The protocol is important enough to be quoted in full:

'The recognition by Great Britain of the independence of the Arab countries lying within the following frontiers:

North: The line Mersin-Adana to parallel 37° N. and thence along the line Birejik-Urfa-Mardin-Midiat-Jazirat(Ibn 'Umar)-Amadia to the Persian frontier;

East: The Persian frontier down to the Persian Gulf;

South: The Indian Ocean (with the exclusion of Aden, whose status was to be maintained);

West: The Red Sea and the Mediterranean Sea back to Mersin.

'The abolition of all exceptional privileges granted to foreigners under the Capitulations.

'The conclusion of a defensive alliance between Great Britain and the future independent Arab state.

'The grant of economic preference to Great Britain.'[1]

Such were the conditions on which the Arab leaders were prepared to support an Arab revolt to be proclaimed by the Sharif of Mecca, and to do everything in their power to help the Allied cause.

The Damascus Protocol is an extremely important text, not only for what it contains, but also on account of the use to which it was afterwards put by the Sharif Husain when, in the following July, he resumed his negotiations with Great Britain. Owing to the secrecy with which a document of that kind had to be handled, it was worded as concisely as the sense would allow, and had to take the form of a summary enunciation of principles. But on two fundamental points – Arab freedom and alliance with England – its meaning is self-evident; and perhaps its main value as an historical document is the light it throws on the Arab attitude towards the Powers of the West. The goal was independence, an independence secured against all foreign interference including that which went by the name of Capitulations; but if England were to undertake to recognise Arab independence, an alliance with her would be welcome.

In the discussions which followed his return, Faisal expressed doubts as to the likelihood of the conditions being accepted by the Allies of whose intentions he was profoundly suspicious; but he agreed that they were the minimum on which a call to revolt could be justified and undertook to hurry back to Mecca and submit them to his father's approval. An oath of allegiance was then taken by six of the principal leaders, by which they bound themselves to recognise the Sharif as the spokesman of the Arab race, and pledged themselves that, in the event of his securing an agreement with Great Britain on the basis of the Damascus Protocol, the Arab divisions in Syria would rise to a man. In token of this, Shaikh Badruddin al-Hasani, the leading

[1] The text as given above is my translation of the Arabic version lent to me by the late King Faisal.

dignitary in Damascus, gave Faisal his signet to hand to the Sharif as an earnest of Syria's confidence in him.

Time pressed. The Turks had already ordered the transfer to Gallipoli of one of the Arab divisions in Syria, and it was feared that others might be similarly transferred. But Faisal could not leave without seeing Jemal Pasha, and Jemal was away on a tour of inspection in the south of Syria.

Rather than wait for his return, Faisal travelled to Jerusalem, took his leave of Jemal and, returning to Damascus, caught the train for Madina. A copy of the Protocol, written out in lilliputian characters, had been sewn inside the lining of one of his retainers' boots. He arrived in Mecca on the 20th of June, gave his father a detailed report of his mission and an account of the process by which he had become converted, subject to the acceptance of those conditions, to the idea of a revolt. The Sharif, like the martinet he was with his sons, put him through a searching examination – 'one of the most difficult weeks of my life', Faisal would say in retrospect.

5.

In the interval, the British authorities in Egypt had taken what measures they could to parry the threat of *jihad*. At first the principal actors had been the Oriental Secretary at the British Agency (Mr. Ronald Storrs) and the Director of Military Intelligence in Cairo (Lieut.-Col. G. F. Clayton). In January 1915, Sir Henry McMahon took up his duties as High Commissioner for Egypt and the Sudan; and Sir Reginald Wingate was, as we have seen, Governor-General of the Sudan with his headquarters at Khartoum. Between them, the four did most of the spade-work.

Storrs and Clayton opened conversations with the Arab leaders domiciled in Egypt. One of the first to be approached was 'Aziz 'Ali; and, with him, Sayyed Rashid Rida, a far-famed theologian, politician and reformer, and a fervent exponent of Moslem-Arab regeneration. The conversations turned on the theme of Kitchener's messages to the Sharif, and were directed to persuading the Arabs that their future lay in an alliance with England. As the weeks went by, the circle of the consultations was extended until hardly a tendency or a school remained but had recorded or volunteered an opinion. But they did not lead to agreement, as indeed they could not. Those leaders who, like 'Aziz 'Ali and Rashid Rida, had enough influence to sway their followers in Syria and Iraq, asked for guarantees of Arab independence as an indispensable condition of a call to Arab revolt; and no one in Egypt was in a position to give the required assurance.

The conversations were not without result, however, for they opened the eyes of the British authorities to the futility of trying to win the Arabs over without definite pledges to them. On his side, Sir Reginald Wingate had come to the same conclusion. He had had consultations with Sayyed 'Ali al-Mirghani and other eminent Moslems in the Sudan; and, approaching the problem from the Moslem angle, found that it called for the immediate issue of a proclamation with definite assurances relating to the future of Arabia and the fate of the caliphate. As a result of his representations, which were powerfully backed by Kitchener, the Cabinet authorised McMahon to make a public declaration in the sense advocated by Wingate.

This declaration was intended to allay Moslem fears rather than satisfy Arab political aspirations. In it, Great Britain pledged herself to make it a condition of the conclusion of peace that the Arabian Peninsula should be recognised as an independent state exercising full sovereignty over the Holy Places of Islam; and it hinted at the readiness of the British Government to welcome the proclamation of an Arab caliphate. The declaration was published early in June. Leaflets were printed and distributed in large quantities throughout Egypt and the Sudan, and smuggled into Syria; and copies were scattered from British aeroplanes flying over Wajh, Yanbo, Rabegh and Jedda.

In authorising this declaration, the British Government were, in one direction, going a step beyond Kitchener's

THE EASTERN ARAB WORLD

❖

The shaded portion represents the area of Arab independence as defined in the Sharif Husain's note of July 14, 1915

assurances of the 31st of October 1914. He had promised the Sharif that Arabia would be defended against external aggression; the declaration went further in that it guaranteed the recognition and the security of an independent state in Arabia. But on the essential Arab demand that this guarantee should apply to Syria and Iraq as well as to the Peninsula, the declaration was silent; and the conversations begun by Storrs and Clayton in the autumn flagged and then suddenly wilted with the advent of summer.

The Government of India had been active in their field, and looked upon the Arabian Peninsula as their special concern. It was Delhi, not London, that normally controlled the politics of Aden and its hinterland, and of the Persian Gulf; and it was also Delhi that had directed the operations for the occupation of Basra in November 1914. Towards the end of the year, Captain J. R. Shakespear, of the Indian Political Service, had been delegated on a mission to Ibn Sa'ud, to try and secure his co-operation in the cause of the Allies. Ibn Sa'ud was not so well-disposed towards the Turks as to need seducing; and just as Turkey was entering the War, a member of al-'Ahd, deputed by 'Aziz 'Ali, had arrived at his capital to solicit his support for the nationalist cause, and had been well received. At the same time, his role as chief of the Wahhabis placed him in a delicate position in regard to the Holy War, and would have made it difficult for him to ignore it had the Grand Sharif endorsed the call. It was while Shakespear was with him, in January 1915, that emissaries arrived at Ibn Sa'ud's court carrying a sounding message from Husain.

As related above, Ibn Sa'ud had warmly supported the Sharif in his abstention from endorsing the call to *jihad*. He had also given Husain to understand that, so far as Najd was concerned, the Turks would expect help in vain. To Shakespear's overtures he had returned a friendly answer; and, before 1915 was out, he had concluded a treaty of alliance with the Viceroy of India.

An agreement was also concluded by the Government of India with the Idrisi in April. Like the subsequent treaty with Ibn Sa'ud, this agreement related to local interests only; and neither instrument contained any reference to the broad issues of the Arab national movement. Nor was the Idrisi, any more than Ibn Sa'ud, in a position to make a substantial military or moral contribution to the war against Turkey. The value of the agreements lay mainly in their negative results; they definitely shut out the prospect – at best, a dim one – of an alliance between Turkey and the two Chiefs, secured Ibn Sa'ud's help in preventing supplies from reaching the enemy through the Persian Gulf, and made it no longer possible for the Turks to use the seaboard of 'Asir as a hostile base against Allied shipping in the Red Sea.

As for Ibn Rashid and the Imam Yahya, they were left unsolicited and remained unseduced. The first had thrown in his lot with the Turks from the start; the second, with two Turkish divisions stationed about him, did not feel that whatever the Allies had to offer could outweigh the advantages of his good relations with the forces in occupation of his territory. He looked on while the Turks marched into the Aden Protectorate. Conversations were opened with him by the British Resident in Aden at a later stage, but to no effect; and he remained a passive spectator to the end.

When the Sharif resumed negotiations in July 1915, the War was going none too well for the Allies in the Near East. The operations in Gallipoli had been costly and unsuccessful. The Turkish attack on Egypt had been repulsed, but the threat remained and was immobilising large forces. The Sanusi Chief's intentions were still obscure, but enough was known of his dealings with the Turks to cause uneasiness; and, as things turned out later in the year, the uneasiness was justified. The Sultan of Darfur, still in close touch with the Sanusi, was showing signs of responding to the call of *jihad*. The Turkish forces in the Yaman had invaded the Aden Protectorate and, driving off the British troops sent to protect Lahaj, had moved to within a few miles of Aden. A brigade had to be hurriedly sent from Egypt to the rescue. Except for the campaign in southern Iraq, where the advance northwards from Basra was making good progress against heavy odds, the British forces in the Arab world were everywhere on the defensive.

It was while he was thus pre-occupied with the dangers still threatening Egypt that Sir Henry McMahon received a note from the Sharif Husain.

CHAPTER IX

GREAT BRITAIN'S PLEDGE: 1915

I.

THE Sharif's first note to Sir Henry McMahon was sent off about the middle of July, and reached Cairo on an unspecified date in August, carried in the greatest secrecy by an emissary in the Sharif's confidence, Shaikh Muhammad 'Aref ibn 'Uraifan. It bore no date and, as was customary in Arabia for prudence sake, no signature; but it was enclosed in a letter from 'Abdullah addressed personally to Storrs, and dated the 14th of July.

The note stated the Arab terms for intervention.[1] After a preamble stressing the determination of the Arab people to obtain their political independence, and their belief in the reciprocity of British and Arab interests, it enumerated the conditions on which the Sharif was prepared, on behalf of the Arab people, to enter into an alliance with Great Britain for the attainment of that end. It stated that the proposal would remain open for thirty days and asked that an explicit acceptance or rejection be returned within that period. The conditions put forward as the basis on which an alliance would be acceptable to the Arabs were those of the Damascus Protocol, with the addition of one relating to the caliphate: that, in the event of an Arab caliph being proclaimed, Great Britain would accord him recognition. There was also an addendum stipulating that the clauses relating to mutual assistance were to remain valid for fifteen years, or longer if desired by both parties.

[1] The texts of the note and of the letter, and of the notes subsequently exchanged between the Sharif Husain and Sir Henry McMahon will be found (in translation) in Appendix A.

Except for those two additions, the terms proposed in the note were those of the Damascus Protocol of which the first clause – that relating to the boundaries of the independent Arab territory – had been textually embodied in the note. In his preamble, the Sharif explained that, as time pressed, the Arabs had thought it preferable to confine themselves to fundamental questions, and to postpone the discussion of secondary matters to a more leisurely occasion.

In his letter to Storrs, 'Abdullah did not discuss the conditions contained in his father's note, but requested its transmission to the proper quarter, and suggested that, since the Arabs had made up their minds, there was no need to continue the distribution of propaganda leaflets in Arabia. He stressed the importance of care and secrecy in the exchange of correspondence. His only concrete demand related to the presents of grain which Egypt donated annually, on the occasion of the pilgrimage, out of charitable endowments for distribution among the poor in Mecca and Madina. The War had caused an interruption of the pilgrimage from Egypt, and 'Abdullah urged that the bounties which went customarily with it be despatched by some appropriate means to the Hejaz where they would make more satisfying propaganda than leaflets.

2.

Sir Henry McMahon's reply, dated the 30th of August, is a curious example of official evasiveness. Acting presumably on instructions from the Foreign Office, he abstained from saying either yes or no. He reiterated the general assurances previously given to the Sharif in Lord Kitchener's name both as regards Arab independence and the Arab caliphate. But when it came to specifying the meaning of those assurances and to defining the area of that Arab independence, he declared that a discussion seemed to him inopportune because, he argued, it appeared a waste of time to discuss such things under the stress of war;

and, even more naïvely, because the Turks were still in occupation of portions of the Arab countries. And this, in reply to a proposal occasioned by the stress of war, and of which the point was that its adoption would enable the Arabs to rise and help the Allies to put an end to the Turkish occupation! A third reason he gave – and it is perhaps the most astonishing of the three – was that certain Arab subjects of the Sultan, in regions still held by the Turks, were serving in the armies of the Sultan. He concluded his note with a declaration of his readiness to despatch the Egyptian bounties of grain for the poor.

The note makes foolish reading, not only on account of its palpable insincerity but also because it tried to reconcile two irreconcilables: to win the Sharif over to an effective alliance and at the same time deny him the only means by which he could make that alliance effective. Its inconsistency is largely to be accounted for by the fact that, even at that stage, McMahon and his advisers were still very imperfectly acquainted with the underground forces at work. They had not been informed of the tenor of Faisàl's conversations in Damascus, knew nothing of *al-Fatat*, and had only the vaguest inkling of the existence of *al-'Ahd*. They believed that the Sharif Husain was speaking for himself and perhaps working for his own ends, and that he could be won over by a promise to recognise him as caliph and by an undefined prospect of Arab independence. Knowledge was to come to them accidentally a month later, but at the end of August they had not the remotest idea of what lay behind the Sharif's proposal.

McMahon's first note, like all his subsequent ones, was in Arabic. The text of each note had of course been drawn up in English and then translated at the British Agency and issued in Arabic; and the quotations which appear in this narrative, as well as the texts printed in the Appendix, are from my own rendering of the Arabic version. The style varies from one note to the other, as though a different translator had been employed on each. But they all reveal their English origin unmistakably, save for the array of fulsome compliments and honorifics that are not English or Arabic, but a medley of Turco-Persian toadyisms, which someone on McMahon's staff had thought appropriate.[1] This flummery served only to annoy Husain, who showed his irritation in his reply. In every way, McMahon's note of the 30th of August 1915, was bound to be distasteful to Husain.

3.

The Sharif wrote back very promptly, for his second note is dated the 9th of September, and is much longer than the first.

Husain's style, too, had its peculiarities. His notes to McMahon were all composed by himself in that cumbrous idiom of Turkish-ridden Arabic which he had acquired in Constantinople in the Hamidian days, when it was often safer for a man, if he had to speak his mind, to speak it unintelligibly. Being by nature outspoken and direct, he had had, in self-protection, to cultivate caution in his utterances, and the result was a mode of expression in which his native directness was enveloped in a tight network of parentheses, incidentals, allusions, saws and apophthegms, woven together by a process of literary orchestration into a sonorous rigmarole, by the side of which the style of *Euphues* seems Attic. He had become a master of protective verbiage, and this habit had gone on so long that, in the end, the verbiage had almost mastered him. In the notes he sent to Cairo, he alternates between terseness and complexity; and although his meaning is always unmistakable, it often lies hidden under a jungle of verbal creepers and has to be patiently disentangled: a task which, difficult enough when one reads him, must make the despair of translators.

[1] For example, the High Commissioner's first note opens thus: 'To the excellent and well-born Sayyed, the descendant of Sharifs, the Crown of the Proud, Scion of Muhammad's Tree and Branch of the Quraishite Trunk, him of the Exalted Presence and of the Lofty Rank, Sayyed son of Sayyed, Sharif son of Sharif, the Venerable, Honoured Sayyed, his Excellency the Sharif Husain, Lord of the Many, Amir of Mecca the Blessed, the lodestar of the Faithful and the cynosure of all devout Believers, may his Blessing descend upon the people in their multitudes!'

In his reply, Husain's single-mindedness stands out in sharp contrast to the evasiveness of McMahon's note. He had seen through its artifice and interpreted it as being merely due to ignorance; and, making a shrewd guess at the misconceptions which had prompted it, tries to remove them. He expresses surprise at the 'lukewarmth and hesitancy' with which his proposals for fixing the boundaries of Arab independence had been received, and is at pains to explain that those proposals had not originated with himself but had been put forward by 'our people' as an essential condition. He is irritated with McMahon for harping on the caliphate as though it were all that mattered, and blurts out that he regards it as a dead institution; and in the same paragraph gives McMahon a little rap on account of his lavish use of titles and compliments:

> 'For our aim, O respected Minister, is to ensure that the conditions which are essential to our future shall be secured on a foundation of reality, and not on highly-decorated phrases and titles.'[1]

He goes on to say that the question of frontiers must be treated as fundamental, for it is so regarded by all the people on whose behalf he speaks, including those whom circumstances were compelling to serve their Turkish rulers. He makes it clear that the issue of his negotiations with McMahon 'depends solely upon whether you will reject or admit the proposed frontiers'.

4.

The choice before McMahon was now perfectly clear, and equally clear was it to him that his answer, this time, would have to be either yes or no.

In the interval, he and his advisers had had information which had served to increase their knowledge of Arab affairs, and modify their attitude in regard to Husain's pro-

---

[1] The snub was either not understood or deliberately ignored, and Sir Henry McMahon's subsequent notes are all preceded by a long preamble of fulsome adjectives.

posals. A young Arab officer in the Turkish army had arrived in Cairo early in October, as a prisoner of war from the Gallipoli front. He had deliberately crossed over to the British lines and, stating that he had important intelligence to disclose, had surrendered and asked to be taken to Egypt. He turned out to be a member of *al-'Ahd* and a keen worker in the cause of Arab emancipation. He was a Moslem from Iraq, and his name was Muhammad Sharif al-Faruqi.

The information disclosed by Faruqi had a decisive influence on the attitude of McMahon and his advisers. He was not, in fact, an accredited emissary of *al-'Ahd*; but he was well acquainted with the organisation and aims of the society and those of *al-Fatat*, its civilian sister, and had a good deal to say on the sentiments animating their members. His statements were carefully sifted and checked, and passed the test so well that he came to be regarded not only as a sincere and well-intentioned informer, which he undoubtedly was, but also as the authorised spokesman of *al-'Ahd* and *al-Fatat,* which it was afterwards discovered he was not. However, his knowledge was reliable so far as it went, and he told the authorities much that was new to them about the real state of feeling among Arab nationalists in Syria and Iraq. So that when the Sharif's second note arrived, McMahon and his advisers had enough knowledge of the background to read it with a fuller understanding.

The note which McMahon despatched in reply is by far the most important in the whole correspondence, and may perhaps be regarded as the most important international document in the history of the Arab national movement. It contains the pledges which brought the Arabs into the War, openly on the side of the Allies. In the years that followed the War, it became an outstanding bone of contention; and, down to the present day, is still invoked as the main piece of evidence on which the Arabs accuse Great Britain of having broken faith with them.

The note is dated the 24th of October 1915. In it, McMahon begins by assuring the Sharif that his previous unwillingness to discuss frontiers meant only that he did not

think the time had come yet for discussing such a subject con-
clusively; but that, since the Sharif had represented the
matter as fundamental and urgent, he (McMahon) had been
authorised by the British Government to give on their behalf
certain assurances to the Arabs. He went on to state what
those assurances were. They amounted to a pledge on Great
Britain's part to recognise and uphold the independence of
the Arabs in the area contained within the frontiers proposed
by the Sharif, with the exception of certain parts of Asia
Minor and of Syria. A reservation was also made in regard
to those territories within that same area, in which Great
Britain was in treaty relations with various Arab Chiefs.

The paragraphs in McMahon's note which define the
pledge and its accompanying reservations ran as follows:

> 'The districts of Mersin and Alexandretta, and portions of
> Syria lying to the west of the districts of Damascus, Homs,
> Hama and Aleppo, cannot be said to be purely Arab, and
> must on that account be excepted from the proposed de-
> limitation.
>
> 'Subject to that modification, and without prejudice to
> the treaties concluded between us and certain Arab Chiefs,
> we accept that delimitation.
>
> 'As for the regions lying within the proposed frontiers, in
> which Great Britain is free to act without detriment to the
> interests of her ally France, I am authorised to give you the
> following pledges on behalf of the Government of Great
> Britain, and to reply as follows to your note:
>
> 'THAT, SUBJECT TO THE MODIFICATIONS STATED ABOVE, GREAT
> BRITAIN IS PREPARED TO RECOGNISE AND UPHOLD THE INDE-
> PENDENCE OF THE ARABS IN ALL THE REGIONS LYING WITHIN
> THE FRONTIERS PROPOSED BY THE SHARIF OF MECCA.'

The note contains four other stipulations, on questions
other than that of frontiers. In the first, Great Britain guarantees that the Holy Places shall be secured against external
aggression. In the second, she expresses her readiness to
assist the Arabs in the setting up of suitable systems of administration in the area of future Arab independence. The
third stipulates that the Arabs shall have recourse to England
only, for the recruitment of the foreign advisers and officials

they might need. The fourth provides that, in view of Great Britain's special interests in Iraq, a particular form of administration will have to be devised for the provinces of Basra and Baghdad, on a basis which is unspecified, but which implies a measure of Anglo-Arab partnership in that part of the independent Arab State.

In his concluding paragraphs, McMahon expresses the hope that these assurances will result in a lasting alliance between Great Britain and the Arabs, and that an early result of the alliance will be the expulsion of the Turks from the Arab countries and the liberation of the Arab peoples. He abstains from making any reference to the question of the caliphate which Husain had testily brushed aside; but, in spite of the Sharif's tart remark about titles and compliments, he goes on showering them by the bucketful, incorrigibly.

5.

The reply which the Sharif returned in answer to McMahon's second note shows him at his best as a far-sighted diplomat and at his worst as a writer of despatches. Two or three of its paragraphs almost defy translation. One of them – that which relates to the provinces of Iraq – is a long, prickly affair of clauses and sub-clauses, dashes and digressions, growing out of each other like the expansions of a cactus plant, and must be read over and over again, and with faith in its author's lucidity, before the sense can be unravelled. Once this is done, the sentence loses its terrors and the meaning emerges all the richer for the complexity of its texture.

This (third) note of the Sharif's is dated the 5th of November. Husain begins by defining his attitude on the question of the frontiers. He consents at once to the exclusion of the Vilayet of Adana (which included the port of Mersin) from the area of Arab independence; but he refuses to accept the exclusion of 'portions of Syria lying to the west of the districts of Damascus, Homs, Hama and Aleppo', on the ground that, unlike Mersin and Adana, they were purely Arab regions; nor does he admit the exclusion of Alexandretta. He accepts the reservation about those Arab Chiefs with whom Great Britain had treaty relations, but in such terms as to make it appear possible that his concurrence applied only to chiefs in the neighbourhood of Basra. With regard to the proposed Anglo-Arab partnership in the provinces of Iraq, he does not accept McMahon's proposal in its entirety, but consents to a British post-War occupation of those parts of Iraq which were then (November 1915) in British hands, on the understanding that the occupation would be temporary, that it would not be regarded as implying any alienation of Arab territory, and that, in return, a subsidy to be agreed upon should be paid by Great Britain to the future Arab State as a contribution towards its budgetary resources in the years of its infancy.

The outstanding divergence, then, was still on the question of frontiers, and it related to the coastal regions of northern Syria. In consenting to the exclusion of the Vilayet of Adana, the Sharif had conceded more and less than McMahon had asked. What McMahon had asked was the exclusion of the districts of Mersin and Alexandretta. The Sharif had agreed to Mersin and had volunteered the exclusion of the entire Vilayet of Adana into the bargain. But he had not consented to the exclusion of Alexandretta which lay in the Vilayet of Aleppo, any more than he would accept McMahon's reservation of any other part of Syria.

Then he raises a new point – that of a guarantee against a separate peace – and asks for a positive assurance that the Arabs would not, in any event, be left alone to face the united forces of Germany and Turkey. He also mentions the possibility of the Arabs being treated as 'informal' belligerents at the peace conference, and seeks to obtain a guarantee from Great Britain in the form of an assurance that she would stand by them and advocate their case in the peace negotiations. He is unwilling to proclaim the revolt at once, without some further preparation, but in any case he must have those guarantees before he can make any move at all.

6.

The British reply to the Sharif's third note took some time in coming. It is dated the 13th of December and its style – at any rate in the Arabic in which it issued – oscillates between vagueness and precision.

In it, McMahon expresses his satisfaction at the exclusion of the Vilayet of Adana, but maintains his reservation of the coastal regions of northern Syria, no longer on the plea that they were not purely Arab, but solely on the ground that French interests were involved. On the subject of the existing treaties with Arab Chiefs, he notifies the Sharif that his acquiescence is taken to apply to the Arabian Peninsula as well as to Iraq. But when he comes to deal with Husain's specific proposal for Anglo-Arab partnership in the future administration of portions of Iraq, he becomes vague, and, in studiedly diffuse phrases, tells Husain that the proper safeguarding of British interests would necessitate some such arrangement as he had outlined, but that it called for more detailed consideration than was possible at the time.

The note expresses McMahon's approval of the Sharif's caution, but urges him to do his best, pending the proclamation of a revolt, to dissuade Arabs from aiding the enemy. It concludes with an assurance that Great Britain would not conclude peace on any terms that did not provide for 'the freedom of the Arab peoples'.

7.

To that note from McMahon, the Sharif replied with a note – his fourth – dated the 1st of January 1916. By that time, he had received a long report from Faruqi about the conversations which he had had with McMahon and his advisers in Cairo, and he begins his note by expressing his satisfaction at hearing that that officer's evidence had borne out all that he (Husain) had said.

On the subject of the future administration of Iraq, he

confidently interprets McMahon's loose acquiescence as conveying a definite acceptance of his own proposals, and declares that he is prepared to leave the assessment of the monetary compensation to Great Britain's 'wisdom and sense of fair play'.

He then reverts to the subject of the coastal regions of northern Syria; and it is clear that he finds himself in a dilemma. On the one hand, he is anxious to clinch a negotiation which had been going on virtually since October 1914, so as to begin active preparations for the revolt; and on the other, the proposal to exclude any part of Syria from the area of Arab independence was one on which he was not at liberty to compromise, let alone to yield. His way out of the dilemma is neither a compromise nor an acquiescence, but a postponement. He tells McMahon that he is anxious to avoid disturbing the concord between France and Great Britain, and that he will therefore shelve the matter for the duration of the War. But he gives him in the plainest language to understand that it would remain out of the question that France or any other Power should be conceded 'a single square foot of territory in those parts', and that he would seize the earliest opportunity after the conclusion of the War to vindicate the Arab claim to the whole of Syria.

He does not ask for an answer to any of his observations, but writes as one who considers that the bargain is concluded; and the note ends with a reiteration of his resolve to proclaim a revolt at the earliest moment, and with an intimation that he would inform McMahon in due course of his requirements in arms, ammunition and supplies.

Husain's willingness to postpone the question of the coastal regions of northern Syria may seem inconsistent with his former insistence on a prompt and full acquiescence in his terms in advance. The explanation is a psychological one: it lies in the profound belief he had in British integrity – a belief widely held in the Arab world at the time. In the years he had spent in Constantinople he had watched the moves on the diplomatic chess-board with a detached and critical eye, and had become attracted to the representatives of Great Britain as being the cleanest players in the game. He had entered into cordial relations with the British Embassy, so far as prudence allowed, and had encountered friendliness and an absence of guile which, to one living in the atmosphere of Hamidian tortuosity, must have seemed to pertain to the realm of the supernatural. And he had learnt that his elevation to the Grand Sharifate in 1908 had had England's secret backing.

This combination of admiration and gratitude had begotten in him a deep regard for certain individual Englishmen and a solid belief in English standards of honourable dealing. Having secured McMahon's positive assurances on the fundamental question of the area of Arab independence, he was willing to let secondary definitions bide their time; and he had such faith in the strength of the Arab claim to the whole of Syria and in the fairness with which Great Britain would deal with it in due time, that he confidently left the question of France's interests in the coastal regions, together with the arrangements to be made for the administration of Iraq, remain over for future settlement.

8.

Sir Henry McMahon replied in a note dated the 30th of January, which is mainly a repetition of previous utterances. He praises the Sharif for his desire to avoid anything which might embarrass Great Britain in her relations with France, but hints that it would be vain to expect a relaxation of Anglo-French solidarity after the War. The hint appears to have been intended to mean, in effect, that, in the event of France maintaining her claims, Great Britain could not hold out any guarantee that those portions of Syria which had been excepted from the Arab area in the note of the 24th of October, 1915, would be included in the territories in which she had pledged herself to recognise and uphold Arab independence.

9.

With that, the negotiations came to a close and both sides regarded the bargain as concluded. Other notes were subsequently exchanged between the Sharif Husain and Sir Henry McMahon, but they related to the preparations for the revolt and added nothing beyond fresh protestations of mutual fidelity to the terms of the Anglo-Arab engagement. The eight notes summarised in this chapter are the only ones that bear on the provisions of the agreement and form the whole of what is known as the McMahon Correspondence.

The terms of the agreement, in its essential provisions, may be summed up quite briefly. The obligations incurred by each side with regard to military performance were not explicitly stated, for they had been debated orally with the Sharif's messenger. But it was understood all along (and the Sharif never questioned) that he would bring all his power and influence, with all the material resources he could muster, to bear on the task of defeating Turkey; and similarly understood that Great Britain would help him by supplementing his deficient material resources, in arms, equipment and money. On the political side, the Sharif had committed himself to the proclamation of an Arab revolt and to an open denunciation of the Turks as enemies of Islam, while Great Britain had explicitly incurred two distinct obligations: to recognise the Arab caliphate if one were proclaimed; to recognise and uphold Arab independence in a certain area.

How much of the Arab territory was included in that area became a subject of controversy in the years that followed the War, and the controversy became particularly acute in regard to that part of Syria which is now the mandated territory of Palestine. The Arab view is that Palestine did fall within the area of promised Arab independence. The British Government maintain the contrary. The two opposite assertions remain confronted to the present day, and the only way in which a judgment can be arrived at is to examine

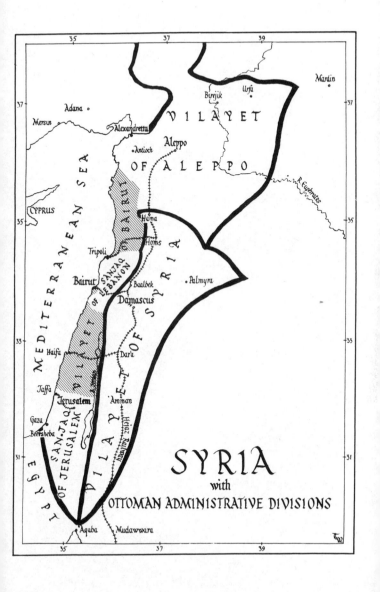

35 37 39

Mardin

37   37

V I L A Y E T

Adana   Birejik   Urfa

Mersin
          Alexandretta   OF A L E P P O
                        Antioch   Aleppo

                                              R. Euphrates

35   35
CYPRUS   Hama

                    Tripoli   Homs

                          Baalbek   Palmyra
              Bairut

                        Damascus

33   33
          Haifa   Dara

      Jaffa
      Jerusalem   Amman

      Gaza
      Beersheba

31   31

      EGYPT   SYRIA
                        with
                  OTTOMAN ADMINISTRATIVE DIVISIONS

          Aqaba   Mudawwara

35 37 39

Labels within map:
MEDITERRANEAN SEA

SANJAQ OF LEBANON

VILAYET OF BAIRUT

VILAYET OF SYRIA

SANJAQ OF JERUSALEM

VILAYET OF

the McMahon Correspondence, now, for the first time, available in English in full.

10.

It should be noticed at the outset that Sir Henry McMahon never defines in his own words the area of Arab independence. What he does is to accept *en bloc*, save for certain reservations, the frontiers proposed by the Sharif Husain. It follows, therefore, that, unless Palestine or any other part of the area defined by the Sharif was specifically mentioned in the reservations, it must be held to have formed part of the territory accepted by Great Britain as the area of Arab independence.

The first point that strikes one is that nowhere in the texts before us is there any mention of Palestine. While certain portions of the Arab area are specifically, if somewhat loosely, singled out as calling for special treatment, no mention is made anywhere of that part of Syria which was known, in Ottoman administrative parlance, as the Sanjaq of Jerusalem. The territory of Palestine in its present frontiers is made up of the former Sanjaq of Jerusalem with the addition of a portion of the former Vilayet of Bairut which was contiguous with it. And the fact that Sir Henry McMahon, who is at pains throughout the correspondence to enumerate by name each of the provinces affected by his reservations, does not mention the Sanjaq of Jerusalem, even indirectly, disposes at once of the legend that the present territory of Palestine was specifically excluded from the area in which Great Britain pledged herself to recognise and uphold an independent Arab government.

The British Government's contention is that Palestine was excluded by implication, when Sir Henry McMahon notified the Sharif that 'portions of Syria lying to the west of the districts of Damascus, Homs, Hama and Aleppo' were to be excluded from the area of Arab independence. This contention was publicly sponsored by Mr. Winston Churchill in 1922 when, speaking as a responsible Minister of the Crown, he tried to argue that the word *districts* in that phrase was to be read as equivalent to *vilayets*; and that, since the 'Vilayet of Damascus' included that part of Syria – now known as Transjordan – which lay to the east of the River Jordan, it followed that that part of Syria – now known as Palestine – which lay to the west of the Jordan was one of the portions of territory reserved in Sir Henry McMahon's phrase.

An examination of the text shows that the British Government's argument is untenable. In the first place, the word *districts* in Sir Henry McMahon's phrase could not have been intended as the equivalent of *vilayets*, because there were no such things as the 'Vilayet of Damascus', the 'Vilayet of Homs' and the 'Vilayet of Hama'. There was one single Vilayet of Syria of which Damascus was the capital, and two smaller administrative divisions of which Homs and Hama were the principal towns. Sir Henry McMahon's phrase can only make sense if we take his *districts* as meaning 'districts' in the current use of the word, that is to say, the regions adjacent to the four cities, and his reservation as applying to that part of Syria – roughly from Sidon to Alexandretta – which lies to the west of the continuous line formed by those four cities and the districts immediately adjoining them.

Two parallels will serve to show the absurdity of the attempts made to put a different interpretation on that phrase. If it had run: the districts of Lincoln, Gainsborough, Doncaster and York, no one would interpret the word *districts* as meaning *counties*, or the area covered by the phrase as embracing the entire counties of Lincolnshire and Yorkshire. Or supposing that the phrase had said: the districts of New York, Newark, New Brunswick and Trenton, would anyone read the word *districts* as equivalent to *states*, and the phrase as covering the entire States of New York and New Jersey? Yet that is precisely what the British Government tried to plead in their unconvincing attempt to justify the exclusion of Palestine from the area of Arab independence.[1]

[1] Throughout the correspondence, both the Sharif Husain and Sir Henry McMahon use the word *vilayet* in its general sense of 'district' or 'region', as well as in its technical connotation of Turkish administrative division. Examples of the indiscriminate use of the term will be found in the footnotes to the texts published in Appendix A.

Again, in his third note dated the 13th of December, Sir Henry McMahon refers to the regions which he wished to exclude as being in 'the two Vilayets of Aleppo and Bairut'. Had he had Palestine in mind, he would certainly have added 'and the Sanjaq of Jerusalem'. The fact that he did not goes to confirm the conclusion that the only portions of Syria which it was proposed at the time to reserve in favour of France were the coastal regions of northern Syria.

Lastly, in giving the pledge contained in his second note, Sir Henry McMahon stated that Great Britain recognised as the area of Arab independence all the regions lying within the frontiers proposed by the Sharif of Mecca in which she was 'free to act without detriment to the interests of her ally France'. Both in that note and in his subsequent note of the 13th of December, he justified his exclusion of certain parts of Syria on the grounds of Great Britain's regard for French interests. If, then, Great Britain were to find herself at the end of the War free to act in respect of any portion of Syria which she had felt bound to reserve in favour of France, the reservation loses its justification and indeed whatever force it may have had when it was originally made; and that portion of Syria which was no longer destined to be included in the sphere of French interests – as was eventually the case with Palestine – must, in default of any specific agreement to the contrary, necessarily remain within the area of Arab independence proposed by the Sharif and accepted by Great Britain.

11

The controversy is still going on, and eminent people in and out of Government circles are still loudly maintaining – in some cases, quite genuinely – that Palestine was in fact excluded by Sir Henry McMahon from the area of Arab independence.

No one who has had the text of the McMahon Correspondence before him can legitimately hold such a view, and it is only because the full text has not hitherto been available in any language other than Arabic that such an untenable contention could with impunity be advanced. Although they were repeatedly pressed to issue an authoritative English version, successive British governments have refused to publish the full text, on the plea that it would be contrary to the public interest to disclose it. The plea might have had some force had the notes exchanged between the Sharif Husain and Sir Henry McMahon not been available in any form, and had their contents remained a real as well as an official secret.

In actual fact, the terms of the McMahon Correspondence are known all over the Arab world. Extracts have from time to time been officially published in Mecca by the Sharif Husain himself, and several of the notes have appeared *verbatim* and in full in Arabic books and newspapers. It is open to any person with a knowledge of Arabic, who can obtain access to the files of defunct Arabic newspapers, to piece the whole of the McMahon notes together; and that work I have done in four years of travel and research, from Cairo to Baghdad and from Aleppo to Jedda.

What the British Government had in mind when they invoked the public interest as their justification for refusing to publish the McMahon Correspondence remains a mystery. I have felt bound, in the course of my researches, to investigate that aspect of the problem before assuming the responsibilities implied in my duty as a historian. But by the time I had collated the available versions of the McMahon notes and drawn up the full and final text, it became manifest that there was nothing in the correspondence that was not already a matter of public knowledge throughout the Arab world. It also became apparent that the British Government's interpretation of the meaning and scope of their own pledges was inconsistent with both the letter and the spirit of the texts. It seemed a matter of public duty to make the Arabic texts known, for this reason if for no other, that the divergence between the British and the Arab interpretations of the pledges has been the underlying cause of a great deal of avoidable waste, suffering and bloodshed already, and will continue to cause waste, suffering and bloodshed in the future so long as the present misunderstanding remains. Far from its being contrary to the public interest, the publication of the texts is urgently needed in the interests of all the parties concerned, and the Royal Commission on Palestine have already set the example by reproducing the whole of Sir Henry McMahon's note of October 24th, 1915, in Chapter II of their Report.[1]

Nor is that merely an individual opinion. Both in Great Britain and in the Arab world, responsible public men have repeatedly urged that the complete texts be made known. A host of letters on this subject from students, historians and statesmen is to be found in the columns of the British Press over the last eighteen years. The official reports of debates in the House of Lords and the House of Commons are strewn with utterances made by eminent members urging, on the highest moral and political grounds, the desirability of making the texts available in an authoritative form. Some of the speakers had held ministerial office in one or other of the War Cabinets, and made their plea in the light of the inside knowledge they possessed. One of them was the late Sir Edward Grey (afterwards Viscount Grey of Fallodon), whose opinion should carry more weight, perhaps, than that of any other statesman, since he was the responsible minister on whose instructions the McMahon notes were issued. Speaking in the House of Lords on the 27th of March 1923, he said:

'A considerable number of these engagements, or some of them, which have not been officially made public by the Government, have become public through other sources. Whether all have become public I do not know, but I seriously suggest to the Government that the best way of clearing our honour in this matter is officially to publish the whole of the engagements relating to the matter, which we entered into during the War. . . . I am sure that we cannot redeem our honour by covering up our engagements and pretending that there is no inconsistency, if there really is inconsistency. I am sure that the most honourable course will be to let it

[1] Cmd. 5479, 1937.

be known what the engagements are, and, if there is inconsistency, then to admit it frankly, and, admitting that fact,
and, having enabled people to judge exactly what is the
amount of the inconsistency, to consider what is the most fair
and honourable way out of the *impasse* into which the engagements may have led us. . . .'

These are the words of the very statesman who, as Secretary of State for Foreign Affairs, was responsible for the
engagements made in the McMahon Correspondence. Similar views were expressed by the late Earl of Oxford and
by Mr. Lloyd George in a debate in the House of Commons
on the 20th of March 1923, when the two veteran statesmen
vied with each other in pressing the prime minister of the
day to make the documents public. Other public figures
representing each of the different political parties have from
time to time added their voices to those of Grey, Asquith and
Lloyd George.

12.

The idea of carrying out the necessary research to piece
together the text of the McMahon Correspondence was suggested to me in 1931 by the late King Husain in 'Amman, a
few months before his death. In contrast with his former
reticence, he was now loquacious in his eagerness to make
the whole truth known. He showed me the original drafts
of his notes to McMahon and allowed me to examine and
copy them out, while he looked on in silence, breaking it only
to answer my questions. I can never forget him as he sat
there, ill at ease, in an arm-chair far too large for his small
frame, shrunken with paralysis, his beautiful face blanched
by the pallor of death, his eyes suddenly glowing from the
vacancy of resignation to flashes of controlled passion. He
was as alert and lucid as when I had first seen him, at the
height of his vigour, seven years previously; but, this time,
his mind seemed less flexible and the mannerisms of expression which were a feature of his conversation obtruded themselves with greater frequency, as though habit had begun

to steal upon reasoning. His old craving for self-justification had become an obsession. As he pressed me to write the story of the Arab Revolt, he would point to the papers before me and say: 'Here are the premises of our revolt, and my justification. I say my justification.' The phrase may have recurred as often as eight or ten times, in the course of my first hour with him.

By that time – this was in the spring of 1931 – Husain had been in exile for six years. He had lost his throne and been forced out of his country, in circumstances which will be related presently, and was now a sick, old man, anxious only to explain himself. In his bitterness, he ascribed all his misfortunes to the non-fulfilment of the promises made to him by Sir Henry McMahon, which he plaintively represented as the sole cause of his present plight. He kept mentioning Kitchener, whom he had never met, but only to lament his death, and spoke scathingly of 'Luweed Jurj', as though Mr. Lloyd George had been the villain of the piece; and his strictures lost none of their force for being clad in the comic finery of Hamidian etiquette: 'The English, my son, are an honourable kind, in word and in deed, in fortune and in adversity. I say honourable. Only his Excellency the estimable, energetic Luweed Jurj is something of an acrobat and a fox. I say a fox, saving your presence. God have mercy on the soul of his Excellency Kitchener!'

CHAPTER X

THE REVOLT: JUNE 1916

1.

IT was, as a matter of coincidence, on the very day of Kitchener's death – on Monday, the 5th of June 1916 – that the Arab Revolt began, and it began on a much smaller scale than the Sharif had originally planned. His first project had been to provoke risings in Syria and in the Hejaz simultaneously, to time them to synchronise with a landing of Allied troops at some point near Alexandretta, and in that way to take the Turks between two fires and paralyse their forces between Aleppo and Mecca; then, carrying the rebellion eastward, to strike at them in Iraq. But, owing to its rejection by the Allies, he had had to renounce that plan and content himself with a revolt in the Hejaz as the prelude to an attack on the Turkish position in Syria.

2.

Sir Henry McMahon's fourth note had arrived in Mecca on the 12th of February; and, from that moment, the Sharif began his final preparations.

Caution was more necessary and called for more artfulness than ever. The Turks were becoming increasingly suspicious. Besides, strengthened by the Allied abandonment of Gallipoli and by the prospect of an impending British surrender at Kut al-Amara, they had been furbishing up their old plans for the conquest of Egypt and were pressing Husain to levy recruits for it in the Hejaz. He had had to send Faisal back to Damascus, just before the turn of the year, in response to Jemal Pasha's insistent requests; and his task now was to resist other demands and push his preparations forward under the nose of the Turks but without going so far as to goad them into a retaliatory arrest of his son, for that would have jeopardised the success of the Syrian uprising. His eldest son, 'Ali, he deputed to Madina to watch the Turkish governor and instruct the neighbouring tribal chiefs who were to be let into the secret. 'Abdullah remained at his father's side, to help in those convolutions of the plot that had to be wound in Mecca. The fourth son, the Amir Zaid, scarcely yet grown to manhood, was kept in readiness for occasional duty.

There was one factor in the situation, however, that seemed likely to ruin the Sharif's plans, both in his expectations of a rebellion in Syria and in his efforts to avoid a premature rupture with the Turks. This was Jemal Pasha's new policy in Syria.

3.

Jemal had made a point, as we have seen, of trying to win the Syrian population, and more particularly the Moslems, over to a whole-hearted participation in the War which he declared (and perhaps held) to be a war in defence of Islam. His immediate task on taking over the command of the Fourth Army had been to organise the attack on Egypt, and as the troops at his disposal were mainly Arab he had thought it prudent to avoid giving them any grounds for disaffection. He had arrived in Syria knowing little or nothing of the existence of secret nationalist societies; and, upon being shown the documents seized in the French consulates at Bairut and Damascus, had decided to ignore them, especially as the incriminated persons included Moslems of standing. The only political prosecution he had approved was that of Nakhla Mutran Pasha, a well-known Christian, who was found guilty of trying to enlist the support of the French consul in a scheme for the annexation of Baalbek to the Lebanon, sentenced to exile for life, exhibited in the streets of

Damascus, and who subsequently died, not without State assistance, on his way to exile.

When the Egyptian campaign had failed, largely owing to Jemal's miscalculations, he had returned from the Sinai front inwardly humiliated and, as is usual with frustrated mediocrity, shorter in the temper. Papers were placed before him incriminating one Yusuf Hayek, a Maronite priest from the Lebanon, with having exchanged treasonable correspondence with M. Deschanel, then president of the French Chamber. Jemal signed the death-warrant unhesitatingly, and the unfortunate priest who was a fervent francophile was publicly hanged in Damascus (March 22, 1915).

Then, gradually, reports came in, with an increasing tale of proof, of underground nationalist activities: that the army was honeycombed with revolutionary cells, that England and France had agents in the country to provoke a revolt, that an Allied landing on the Syrian coast was impending, that Arab officers in the army had promised to abet the landing. Military Intelligence is seldom at its best in following up political clues, and the General Staff of the Fourth Army was no exception: while it had an ear for rumours, its nose failed to pick up their scent. The information was substantially true, but it could not be traced home to any of the plotters, and Jemal was disturbed by it and made anxious and vindictive but bewildered. Like Polyphemus, he wanted to strike but did not know at whom. Just then (June 1915), Enver asked him to release troops for the Gallipoli front, and he sent the 25th Division which was entirely Arab and formed one of the mainstays of *al-'Ahd's* plans for a revolt. And subsequently, whenever an opportunity arose, he would displace Arab units from Syria and replace them by battalions manned by Turks.

Then, turning to civilian organisations, he decided to prosecute the persons incriminated in the documents seized at the French consulates. A large number of people were arrested, brought before a military court of sinister fame at 'Aley in the Lebanon, interrogated, tortured and tried. Thirteen of those were sentenced to death; forty-five others who were abroad or had escaped, to the same sentence in absence, and a number to varying terms of imprisonment and deportation – all of them men of standing, and some of them personalities famed throughout the Arab world.

Of the thirteen who were present to hear their death-sentence, two were reprieved and the rest executed at dawn on the 21st of August 1915. Eleven gallows had been erected in Bairut's principal square which, strangely enough, went by the name of Liberty Square. Ten of the victims were Moslems, the other a Christian. They came from different parts of Syria – Bairut, Baalbek, Hama, Damascus, Jenin; and most of them were young and died well, leaving it to their horror-stricken compatriots to exalt their last words at the gallows into a stirring message of patriotic faith. Amongst them was Muhammad Mihmisani, a brilliant graduate of the school of law in Paris and one of the founders of *al-Fatat*, who, regardless of torture and of offers of pardon in return for a confession, died without divulging the existence of the society.

The two reprieved persons were Hafez bey al-Sa'id (Jaffa) and Shaikh Sa'id al-Karmi (Tulkarm), who, on account of their advanced years, had their sentences commuted to imprisonment for life. The former died in prison. One man, Hasan Hammad (Nablus) had a miraculous escape. Owing to a delay in the service of the summons, he had not appeared for trial but had gone on innocently discharging his duties as head of the Land Registry Office in his native town. He was sentenced to death in absence, but meanwhile the summons had reached him and he had started on his way to attend the military court at 'Aley. On arrival at the local hotel, he happened to pick up a newspaper which gave the news of the sentence passed on him. Seizing his suit-case, he boarded the train for Damascus where he went into hiding, grew a beard, married the daughter of his protector and begat two children whom he brought back safely to Nablus at the end of the War.

Thus had begun Jemal Pasha's new Arab policy – a modest beginning in relation to what was to come.

4.

When Faisal arrived in Damascus, early in the following January, he found conditions changed beyond recognition. He had come with the settled purpose of fomenting a revolt of the Arab divisions in the Turkish army and a mass rising of the population, on a signal from his father. Accompanying him were a picked retinue of some forty determined men, several of them members of the Sharif's clan, who were to form his personal bodyguard and who, like him, were carrying their life in their hands. To Jemal, he justified their presence by representing them as an advance-guard of the force which the Sharif had been asked to raise in the Hejaz, and the pretext had been taken at its face-value and welcomed. Banquets and receptions were held in his honour and in celebration of the arrival of the advance-guard. But when the festivities were over and Faisal had had time to look around and take stock, he found himself in the strangest surroundings.

The last remaining Arab divisions had been transferred with most of his friends from *al-'Ahd*, and their place taken by battalions manned by Turks. Prominent civilians had been deported by the hundred, to distant places in Anatolia. The famine which was afterwards to take an appalling toll of lives had already begun; and the population, impoverished by army requisitions, currency depreciation and shortage of food, were mainly pre-occupied with their fight against hunger. It added to the general apprehension that another and larger batch of Moslem and Christian notables had been arrested on charges of treason and were awaiting their trial at 'Aley.

Among these were some of the best known and most influential names in Syria, whose arrest seemed to show that Jemal had done with his tactics of politic forbearance. The trial lasted several months and was conducted with calculated severity to the accompaniment of minatory ill-treatment and torture. The Sharif Husain intervened, with telegrams to Jemal, to the Grand Vizir and to the Sultan, urging that, if any of the accused were found guilty, punishment be limited to life-sentences: otherwise, added Husain darkly, blood will cry for blood. Faisal pleaded with Jemal in person. But their intervention was in vain.

The first victim was Joseph Hani, a well-known Christian resident of Bairut, who was publicly hanged on the 5th of April. A month later, twenty-one others were similarly executed, seven in Damascus, fourteen in Bairut. Amongst them were the senator 'Abdul-Hamid al-Zahrawi (of Homs), who had presided over the Arab Congress in Paris; three of the deputies for Damascus, Shafiq al-Muayyad, Shukri al-'Asali and Rushdi al-Sham'a; Salim al-Jaza'iri, an able and gallant officer in the Turkish army; Saifuddin al-Khatib (of Haifa), a magistrate; the Amir 'Aref al-Shehabi (of Hasbayya), a young barrister of great promise; Ahmad Tabbara (of Bairut), a newspaper proprietor and writer who had been one of the delegates at the Arab Congress in Paris; 'Ali 'Umar Nashashibi (of Jerusalem), Muhammad Shanti (of Jaffa), and George Haddad (of the Lebanon), all three young men of wide repute and popularity; and the Amir 'Umar Jazairi (of Damascus), a descendant of the celebrated Algerian Amir 'Abdul-Qader. Seventeen were Moslems and the rest Christians.

The sentences had not been announced beforehand. . On the eve of the execution, a gaoler had entered the hall of the prison at 'Aley and read out the names of twenty-one of the accused, bidding them dress and follow him. Those for Damascus were taken by train and, on arrival there, marched to the Marjeh – the main square – where seven gallows stood in readiness. The others were driven down to Bairut in carriages and, guessing their fate, whiled the hours of darkness away with hymns to Arab freedom, one cab-load answering another, until, as dawn was breaking, the convoy came to a halt in Liberty Square. By six o'clock that morning – the 6th of May – the holocaust was over, and within two hours a special number of al-Sharq[1] was being distributed free, in

---

[1] A daily Arabic newspaper founded in 1915 in Damascus under official auspices, to serve Jemal Pasha's policy.

which the charges, the trials, the sentences and the executions were announced in the same breath. The charges were defined as 'treasonable participation in activities of which the aims were to separate Syria, Palestine and Iraq from the Ottoman Sultanate and to constitute them into an independent State'.

A shudder shook the country. No one, even among those who knew the savagery latent in Jemal's nature, had expected such severity. The sentences were all the more appalling as they had fallen on innocent and guilty alike, since many of the victims were known to have kept aloof from anything approaching treason. On the population at large the immediate effect was one of terror. The few leaders who had remained undetected were horror-stricken: not in their wildest moments of apprehension had they imagined such a toll of their confederates; and, realising their own powerlessness, they turned with heavy hearts to the contemplation of their strangled liberties and to the task of securing freedom, no longer for its own sake alone but as a means to vengeance as well. Faisal was deeply affected. He had gone beyond the bounds of prudence in pleading with Jemal for the lives of the Arab patriots. Whatever doubts may have lingered in his mind as to the wisdom of breaking with the Turks were now swept away in a passionate revulsion of feeling, and the cry which escaped him on hearing the news of the executions became the battle-cry of the Arab Revolt.

5.

On the day of the executions, the Amir Faisal was staying with the Bakris in their farm-house at Qabun, five miles out of Damascus. He and his hosts were breakfasting in the garden when a runner came with the news and gave them the special number of *al-Sharq* which carried the hideous tale. One of the Bakris read it out aloud, and mournfully the twenty-one names rang out, to the mounting horror of the listeners, and lingered like the notes of a dirge in the still air of that spring morning in the orchards of Damascus. Long minutes passed in silence broken only by a prayer uttered in a low voice or a sighed invocation for the repose of the dead. One of the company recited the opening verse of the Qoran. Then, like one suddenly demented, Faisal leapt to his feet and, tearing his *kufiya* from his head, flung it down and trampled it savagely with a cry: '*Tab al-maut va 'arab!*'[1]

6.

The news of the executions drove the Sharif Husain to act at once. He had been pushing his preparations as actively as he could, especially since Jemal had informed him, in the first week of April, that a force of 3,500 men was on the point of marching through the Hejaz on its way to the Yaman. The force, under the command of one Khairy bey, was composed of picked and specially-equipped troops and was to act in co-operation with a German field mission led by Baron Othmar von Stotzingen. Husain, not relishing the thought of such an addition to the Turkish garrison in Arabia, was trying to forestall its arrival.

He had already prepared the tribes by taking the chiefs into his confidence and securing their co-operation. The bulk of the tribesmen, however, were ill-equipped and Husain was in correspondence with Sir Henry McMahon over the despatch of money, rifles and ammunition. He had asked that the consignments be sent to Port-Sudan whence, on a sign from him, they could be shipped in dows to some discreet anchorage on the Hejaz coast. In order to put indirect pressure on the merchants and other townsfolk who were politically lukewarm, he asked for a blockade of the ports of the Hejaz by British warships. He was still working for risings to take place in Syria simultaneously with the proclamation of his own revolt in the Hejaz, and was pressing

[1] A phrase which I find it beyond me to render adequately by mere translation. Literally, it is equivalent to: 'Death has become sweet, O Arabs!' But the Arabic is much richer in meaning and amounts to an appeal to all Arabs to take up arms, at the risk of their lives, to avenge the executions in blood.

McMahon to arrange for a landing of British troops on the Syrian coast to interrupt the Turkish communications with Asia Minor, or at any rate to cause a diversion.

On this point, the Sharif's advice was not taken. The question of a landing at Alexandretta had first been debated in Allied circles as far back as the end of 1914. It had come up again for more detailed consideration a year later when Lord Kitchener had arrived in the Eastern Mediterranean to study the problem of the evacuation of Gallipoli. He had been converted to the plan and, convinced that it could lead to the severance of communications between Turkey and Iraq as well as between Turkey and Syria, had strongly recommended it to the War Cabinet. But the proposal had been vetoed, partly on military grounds and partly owing to political objections held by the French Government who, having no troops to spare, did not relish the thought of a landing in Syria being carried out by other than French troops. That the abandonment of the scheme was justifiable on purely military grounds is open to question, although it seems probable that the weight of opinion at the War Office and the Admiralty was against its adoption. But it was strongly supported by the experts on the spot – Lord Kitchener, Sir Charles Monro, Sir John Maxwell and Sir Henry McMahon – and there is a school of military historians who still hold that the plan was feasible and that its execution would probably have caused Turkey to collapse a good deal sooner than she did.

However that may be, the Sharif's advice was rejected, and not even the demonstration he had asked for was approved. In after years, he used to say that he had never understood why his advice was rejected. On one of my visits to him at Shunat Nimrin in Transjordan in the spring of 1924, I heard him expound his strategy in retrospect. His approach to the problem was essentially psychological, and he reasoned in terms of character, morale and spirit as though they were the all-important variables, while guns and shells were to be regarded as mere constants, common to both sides, and therefore cancelling each other out. The Turk was a born stonewaller – it was wasteful to attack him frontally, as at Gallipoli, with whatever superiority. Turkish units fought best on ground of their own choosing, with familiar bases to fall back upon – it paid to render their tracks insecure. The Turkish soldier shrank from adventure, enslaved himself to habit and was easily bewildered by the unexpected – take him by surprise with an attack in the rear, a threat on his flank, and a flare of risings on every side of him, and he was doomed. Thus argued Husain who was no soldier but who understood the Turks as well as the Arabs; and one virtue in his plan was that it rested on a strategy which was suited to Arab methods of warfare and, at the same time, was designed to put the Turks to their greatest disadvantage. But it did not commend itself to the mandarins on the Allied general staffs, and his only course was to recall his son from Syria.

7.

Faisal received the order to return a few days after the executions of the 6th of May. It was so worded, in the code he had agreed upon with his father, as to convey that the revolt was imminent. His problem now was how to travel back to Mecca and arrange for the departure of his body-guard without arousing Turkish suspicions.

He played his cards with consummate skill. He sought an audience with Jemal Pasha and engaged the conversation on the subject of the recruits from the Hejaz. He said news had reached him that a considerable body of recruits raised by his father had assembled in Madina and were ready to proceed to Damascus: did not the Pasha agree that it would add to the solemnity of their arrival if the Sharif were to send one of his sons at their head? The Pasha fell into the trap. He not only agreed, but he was of opinion that Faisal himself should be the son to lead the recruits in the Sharif's name. Faisal carried the comedy a step further by objecting, pointing out that there were two brothers older than himself who should take precedence over him and who, being in the Hejaz at the moment, could bring a retinue of Hejaz notabilities and religious dignitaries in their suite. To which Jemal replied: 'I beg of you to go, all the same. Let one of your brothers come too, if he can, but it is essential that you should proceed to Madina to expedite the preparations. You shall have your own retinue.'

Faisal arranged for his bodyguard to remain at Qabun, as guests of the Bakris, while Nasib al-Bakri was to travel to Madina with him and return with specific instructions as to the time and the mode of their departure.

On the 16th of May, accompanied by Nasib and three or four other notables delegated by Jemal, Faisal left for Madina. His brother 'Ali had been in constant communication with their father and knew that the revolt was imminent. It might even break out sooner than the Sharif had planned, for the special force under Khairy bey had arrived in Madina, and 'Ali had had instructions that it was to be prevented, at all costs, from marching on to Mecca. The German complement of the force – the von Stotzingen mission – had had to leave the train at al-'Ala, beyond which non-Moslems were not allowed to proceed, and make their way westward in the direction of Wajh whence they could pursue their journey along the coast to Jedda and Qunfida.

On the 24th,' Ali received fresh instructions from his father. Now that Faisal was back, there was no cause for further delay, and 'Ali was to fix a day for the rising in Madina and notify his father of it in good time. He was also to inform the more important tribal chiefs. The two brothers conferred, and decided upon Monday, the 5th of June. They sent a message to their father and, on Faisal's suggestion, pressed him to ask again for a military demonstration to be made by Allied forces on the Syrian coast. Then 'Ali sent out emissaries to the tribal chiefs; while Faisal despatched Nasib al-Bakri post-haste to Damascus to arrange for the flight of the bodyguard.

At sunrise on the 5th of June, the two brothers rode out to the tomb of Hamza where the 1,500 recruits raised by the Sharif were in camp, and proclaimed the independence of the Arabs from Turkish rule, in the name of the Sharif

Husain, Lord of Mecca. Then they galloped away, followed by the recruits, and joined the tribesmen at the appointed place to the south-east of Madina.

The Arab Revolt had begun.

8.

In Mecca, the revolt was fixed for the following Saturday, the 10th of June. The city was then occupied by a fraction only – amounting to about 1,400 men – of its normal garrison, for with the onset of the hot weather the governor-general and the bulk of the troops had moved to Taif, the summer station of the Hejaz. The signal was given by the Sharif at dawn, when the several Turkish barracks and garrison-posts were simultaneously attacked with rifle-fire, for the Arab forces had no artillery. For three days a fierce duel raged, until the smaller Turkish posts surrendered. The main barracks and the fort of Jiad being equipped with heavier artillery, resisted for another three weeks. By that time, two artillery companies of the Egyptian Army in the Sudan had been rushed across by Sir Reginald Wingate, and two guns had been brought up to Mecca, which decided the remaining Turkish forces to surrender.

The best account I have been able to find of the fall of Mecca is that which appeared in *al-Qibla*, the newspaper which shortly afterwards began to appear in Mecca. Here is my own translation, made from the numbers dated Shawwal 15–18, 1334 (August 14–17, 1916):

'At 3.30 a.m., just before daybreak on Saturday, the 9th Sha'ban [June 10], a sustained rifle-fire was opened on the barracks in Mecca and on the Hamidiya building in which are housed the offices of the Government; and a siege was laid on all the Turkish troops in their several strongholds. The fort of Jiad, which stands on the summit of an inexpugnable mountain[1] and overlooks every quarter of the city, opened and kept up a continuous artillery-fire on the refuges of the Beduin and their entrenchments, on all

---

[1] On the southernmost outskirts of Mecca.

dwellings, and more particularly on the Sharifian Palace at which they aimed most of their shells. Thus both parties remained exchanging rifle-shots, to the accompaniment of shell-firing from the fort, until 9 a.m.

'Thereupon, the officers in command of the garrison at the Jirwal barracks[1] telephoned to the Sharifian Palace to ask for the cessation of hostilities and to request that the local civil officer be sent across to explain the causes of the outbreak and discuss the measures to be taken for putting it down and avoiding further loss of life and bloodshed.[2] The request was complied with, and the civil officer deputed to the officers to whom he stated that the country had declared its independence and that the conflict would end only upon their evacuating the barracks and surrendering the whole of their armoury to the Arab commander. The officers would not listen to this proposal, but decided to offer resistance and defend themselves; and they gave orders to the commander of the fort to resume the firing of shells on the people with renewed intensity. On being informed of this by the civil officer, the Sharif ordered the renewal of hostilities which were resumed on a more awesome scale than before the negotiations and went on till nightfall, when the fighting slackened. . . . The losses of the Turks in the course of the operations are estimated at 150 killed or wounded, while the casualties (killed and wounded) suffered by the Arabs amounted to eight.

'Fighting was resumed shortly after dawn on the morning of Sunday, [June 11], accompanied by rifle- and artillery-fire around all the posts held by the garrison. At 11 a.m., the forces of the Sharif attacked the post of Bash-Karakol[3] which

[1] The main barracks, at the western extremity of Mecca, guarding the roads to Jedda and Madina.

[2] According to popular report, the officer in command of the garrison, when he telephoned to the Sharif Husain, said: 'The Arabs are in revolt, and it is said that they have declared their complete independence. Will you do what you can about it.' The Sharif is reported to have dryly replied: 'I have also heard that they want their independence. I shall certainly do all I can about it.'

[3] The main guard-house, situated outside the south-eastern corner of the Great Mosque.

is situated near al-Safa, and seized it by storm, capturing its garrison.

'The fighting on the Monday, [June 12,] followed the lines of the two preceding days, but was more particularly intense around the Government offices in the Hamidiya, in which the Deputy Governor-General, himself an army officer, had entrenched himself with a garrison and had been keeping up a reckless and indiscriminate rifle-fire aimed at all passers-by, regardless of whether they were old or infirm or women or worshippers in the Holy Mosque. A detachment of Sharifian forces made a determined attack and succeeded in storming the place and forcing its garrison into surrender. They were then marched together with the Deputy Governor-General, and all the officers under him, with due military honours, to the Sharifian Palace where they were quartered in the apartment reserved for prisoners of war and were treated with the best courtesy and consideration accorded to people in their station. . . . When the Deputy Governor-General arrived at the Palace with the rest of the prisoners and became acquainted with the facts, causes and objects of the revolt, he wrote with his own hand to each of the commanders of the main barracks and of the fort, to inform them of his plight and advise them to surrender. But his letters seemed to have had no effect: the barracks adopted tactics of delay and procrastination; while the fort, linking its fate with that of the barracks, took to firing bullets and shells on the people and the houses and on the Holy Mosque, in such a way that divine worship was completely interrupted and it became impossible for people to enter the Mosque for the rite of circumambulation or for prayer, either individually or in congregation, and even to come near the precincts of the ancient Sanctuary. . . . The audacity of the garrison did not stop at that, but they went so far as to fire two shells on the Sacred Ka'ba itself and a third on the shrine of Abraham. Whereupon thousands of worshippers rushed, under a deluge of bullets and fragments from bursting shells, to extinguish the fire which had set the pall of the Sacred Ka'ba ablaze. . . .

'And thus things dragged for many a long day, as regards both the main barracks and the fort, for on the one hand the Arabs had no artillery with which to storm the heavily-entrenched Turks; and on the other the Turks did not dare sally forth the least distance from their fortified positions. Eventually, guns and artillerymen[1] arrived from Jedda, and started shelling the fort until they opened a breach in one side of it. Whereupon the Arabs, taking advantage of the opening thus afforded, stormed the fort with conspicuous bravery, under a fire of bullets and shells, and took it by assault, killing two Turkish officers and one private, while the only casualty which the attacking force suffered was one man wounded.

'Thus fell the fort of Jiad, on the morning of Tuesday, Ramadan 4, [July 4,] to the Sharifian forces, who also captured two big guns, three small guns, approximately 8,000 rifles of different patterns, obsolete and modern, and a very large amount of ammunition and war-material. Altogether the siege of the fort lasted twenty-five days, during which the garrison had thought fit to commit the outrage we have related.

'When our guns had silenced the batteries in the fort and brought about its surrender, they repaired to the Jirwal barracks and, taking up their stand alongside the investing forces, they started letting off their shells and so aiming them as to open a breach for an assault. The Turkish garrison, whenever things became too hot for them, tried to deceive the Sharifian forces by raising the white flag and asking for a parley with the commanding officer. At length they surrendered in earnest. A group of officers bearing a white flag advanced to the midst of the Arab encampment to meet and parley with the commander. They were marched back to their barracks and made to surrender all their arms, ammunition and equipment; in fact, everything to be found in the barracks except the personal belongings of the officers

---

[1] These were part of the two artillery companies of the Egyptian army in the Sudan, which were hurried across to Jedda by Sir Reginald Wingate as soon as the news of the revolt was known.

and men, that is to say, their money and baggage and even their horses, for the orders were that they were to be allowed to keep these.

'In such manner did the main barracks surrender to the forces of the Sharif on the evening of Sunday, Ramadan 9, [July 9,] after dark. The losses of the Turks in the siege are estimated at twenty-one killed and seventy-six wounded, exclusive of their losses in the first phase of the operations. The survivors were marched off to the billets allotted to them, partly in Shuhada[1] and partly in various houses within the city. Their number was thirty officers and 1,120 other ranks. The booty of arms was considerable. The fall of the barracks meant the end of Turkish power in Mecca, as it enabled the forces of the Sharif to occupy all the garrison posts, guard-rooms and Government offices, as well as all the official quarters and buildings in the city.'

Jedda was attacked on the day of the outbreak in Mecca, but from the outside. A force of some 3,500 tribesmen belonging to the great Harb confederation and led by the Sharif Muhsin attempted to force an entry into the town; but here again the lack of artillery put them to disadvantage in face of the superior equipment of the Turkish garrison, which was 1,500 strong, and they had to content themselves with siege tactics. Faruqi who had been sent over from Cairo took part in the siege. British warships shelled the external Turkish positions, and seaplanes dropped bombs outside the perimeter of the walled city. Within a few days word had come from the Turkish commander in Mecca that no reinforcements could be expected, and the garrison surrendered on the 16th of June.

Meanwhile, a force under the command of the Amir 'Abdullah had invested Taif, while another had gone northwards and succeeded in capturing Rabegh and Yanbo. Qunfida was captured with the help of the British navy. The siege of Taif was a longer operation. Although he had the Egyptian batteries with him, 'Abdullah was not minded to take the place by assault, knowing that the end was not in doubt; and

[1] One of the outlying quarters of Mecca.

he wisely waited, refusing all Turkish proposals for a truce until the garrison surrendered unconditionally on the 21st of September, with the Governor-General of the Hejaz, Ghalib Pasha, as the chief prize.

By that date the Revolt had asserted itself, with some 6,000 prisoners and a fair booty of war material to its credit, and with the principal towns of the Hejaz in the hands of the Sharif, save for Madina.

CHAPTER XI

IMMEDIATE EFFECTS

I.

THE news of the Revolt caused stupor in Turkey and in Germany, and was screened from the public for several weeks. As late as the 26th June, Turkish *communiqués* were still being issued to deny that there had been any revolt in the Hejaz. On the 29th, the first admission – it if can be called one – was made in an announcement published in Damascus, in the official *al-Sharq* of that date, to say that 'certain tribal sections had attacked a few posts in the neighbourhood of Madina', but making no mention of the capture of Mecca and Jedda, or of the Sharif. The earliest reference to him was made on the 2nd of July when an Imperial Decree announced his dismissal, without giving reasons, and the appointment, to be Amir of Mecca in his stead, of the Sharif 'Ali Haidar. It was not until the 26th of July that an account of the rising, giving a distorted and belittling version of the facts, was allowed to appear in *Tanin* (Constantinople) of that date; and, for several months, the Press continued to describe the Sharif Husain's movement as an act of personal insubordination, provoked by British intrigue, and one which was in process of being crushed with the help of the population and tribesmen of the Hejaz who had remained loyal to 'the caliphate and the Prophet's injunctions regarding the sacred duty of *jihad*'.

In Syria, the Turks took particular pains to discredit and belittle the Sharif's rising. The columns of *al-Sharq*, after the silence of the first few weeks, are full of inspired articles and fabricated news. In its issue of the 19th of September, it published a report alleged to have been received from the Turkish commander-in-chief in Madina, to the effect that large numbers of the tribesmen of the Hejaz had offered their submission, that Faisal had been defeated and taken refuge on a British warship and that his brother 'Ali was 'wandering about, lost and bewildered'. On the 24th, three days after the fall of Taif, it printed a *communiqué* announcing that 'all was quiet in Taif . . . where certain Beduin led by the Amir 'Abdullah had been repulsed with heavy losses'. Nothing else was allowed to appear in the Press.

Jemal Pasha's rage knew no bounds and was savagely vented on the few Arab leaders who had hitherto escaped his severity. He issued orders for wholesale arrests; and his military police, casting their net more or less at random, laid hands, in Damascus alone, on some forty of the principal residents left, threw them into prison and subjected them to various forms of atrocious torture. The aged and venerable Shukri Pasha al-Ayyubi was flogged day after day to within an inch of his life. 'Abdul-Hamid Pasha Qaltaqji, a briga-dier in the Turkish army, Zaki bey al-'Azmeh, another officer of high rank, and Fares Khuri, one of the Christian deputies in the Ottoman Chamber, were put into solitary confinement, beaten and starved. Not one of them con-fessed or gave away any of the secrets of the Arab movement. Shukri al-Quwwatli, one of the younger and most spirited members of *al-Fatat*, was so lacerated by the flogging that he tried to commit suicide by cutting open one of his arteries with a blunt table-knife, for fear that he might be reduced to making an unwitting confession regarding the society. Meanwhile evidence was being fabricated to give a sem-blance of justification to the imposition of death-sentences, and there is little doubt that many would have suffered that fate had it not been for Faisal's timely intervention. He wrote to Jemal Pasha to warn him that, in the event of any of the accused being executed or dying under ill-treatment, he would order reprisals on the Turkish officers captured at Mecca and Taif, and that he would unhesitatingly shoot ten officers for each Arab victim of Jemal's terrorism. The threat had its effect, and the accused were released and placed under stringent police supervision.

In the interval, 120 other Arab notables from all over Syria had been arrested and deported to Anatolia. The severity of martial law was intensified by fresh measures of repression. In October, the special privileges of autonomy which had been granted to the Lebanon in 1864 were finally abolished, and the province placed under undisguised Turkish administration, with all the rigours which that implied.

To make matters worse, famine had begun to ravage the country. There had been a visitation of locusts in the spring of 1915, which had destroyed the crops and created a scarcity. The shortage was made more serious by maladministration, defective transport services, the depreciation of the currency; and, above all, by profiteering and a dastardly collusion, for which no epithet would seem too strong, between Turkish officials and certain Syrian merchants. The poorer people were starving. Three extracts from reports by eyewitnesses will suffice to give a picture of the famine at that stage.

In a despatch to his Government, dated the 15th of July 1916, the American Consul-General wrote:

> 'The condition of the poor here is deplorable. The streets are filled with starving women and children. . . . The government is absolutely callous to the sufferings of these poor people, nor will it allow the American Red Cross to assist them. In my early evening walks I frequently see people lying dead in the gutter. . . .'

In an article contributed to *The Times* of the 12th of August by 'A neutral correspondent', who had just left Syria the following passage occurs:

> 'The state of the people of Syria is past all belief. . . . There is a new terrorisation of the Arabic-speaking Moslems. It is estimated that from 60,000 to 80,000 have died of starvation in Northern Syria. . . .'

An American lady who lived in Bairut and had left the

country that summer wrote in *The Times* of the 15th September:

> 'Towards spring, cases of starvation began to be known. People were found in the streets unconscious, and were carried to the hospitals. We passed women and children lying by the roadside with closed eyes and ghastly, pale faces. It was a common thing to find people searching the garbage heaps for orange peel, old bones, or other refuse, and eating them greedily when found. Everywhere women could be seen seeking eatable weeds among the grass along the roads. . . .

This was taking place in a country which normally produced a great deal more of staple food supplies than was needed for her own consumption.

And yet worse was to come.

2.

Nor was there any immediate, visible reaction to the Revolt in any of the other Arab countries. Iraq, or at any rate that part of it which was still held by the Turks, was also in the grip of a stringent military autocracy and was similarly terrorised, though not to the same extent, by a system of internment, deportation and executions. So far as leadership was concerned, Iraq differed from Syria in that most of her nationalist workers were army officers serving in units stationed in other parts of the Ottoman Empire. It was they who formed the backbone of *al-'Ahd* and afterwards the mainstay of the Arab campaign that developed out of the Revolt, in which they played by far the most distinguished part.

The effect of the Sharif's rising in Iraq, and more particularly in those tracts which were already under British occupation, was mainly conditioned by the reaction of the Government of India to it. Two factors governed that reaction. One was the deep sentiment of attachment to the caliphate prevailing among the Moslems of India; the other was that the Government of India had designs upon Iraq which they regarded as a field for future colonisation. Their attitude to the Arab movement was fundamentally determined by those two factors; and this gave their foreign policy a parochial and acquisitive outlook which made it inimical to the idea of an Arab revolt. The Moslems of India, amongst whom Sultan 'Abdul-Hamid had successfully propagated his doctrine of the supremacy of the caliph, and to whom the Arab national movement made no appeal, regarded the Revolt as an insurgence against the authority of Islam and an onslaught upon its unity. They were also suspicious of British designs on Arabia and genuinely alarmed for the safety of the Holy Places. Public meetings were held, notably at Lucknow on the 27th of June, at which the action of the Sharif was reviled in no measured terms; and the fact that the feeling was based on fears that were unfounded was of poor consolation to the Government of India. Hence their acute embarrassment to which was added their concern for the future of Iraq as an outlet for their surplus population. It was largely owing to this concern that little, if anything, was done to win the Arabs of Iraq to an active participation in the Sharif's movement.

In the Arabian Peninsula, the news of the rising had a profound effect. It did not win over the two Arab Rulers – Ibn Rashid and the Imam of the Yaman – who had already cast their lot in with the Turks; but it caused them seriously to re-consider their position, and it deprived them of the help of certain important tribal Chiefs – such as the heads of the Hashed and Bakil clans – whose support of the Turks they had been trying to secure. All the other rulers in the Peninsula hailed the Revolt with an approval which found its open expression in a durbar held on the 20th of November at Kuwait. It was attended by Ibn Sa'ud, the Amir of Kuwait, the Shaikh of Muhammara and over 150 other persons amongst whom were powerful minor chieftains. Ibn Sa'ud summed up the position in an eloquent speech which gave rise to a remarkable display of enthusiasm, in which he urged all Arabs to join the standard of the Revolt and spare no effort to further the common cause of England and the

Arabs. Reports of the meeting and Ibn Sa'ud's stirring words swept the Peninsula like wild-fire, the newsbearers quoting whole passages of his speech, as newsbearers in Arabia will.

In Egypt and the Sudan the news of the Sharif's rising came at a particularly opportune moment. For some months, the British forces had been engaged in hostilities with the Sanusi on the western flank of Egypt and with 'Ali Dinar, the Sultan of Darfur, on the western borders of the Sudan. The two campaigns, although they had local underlying causes, were the direct outcome of the call to *jihad*. . Aided by Turkish officers and troops and by German submarines operating near the coast, Sayyed Ahmad al-Sanusi had over-run Egyptian territory in November 1915 and forced the withdrawal of the garrisons manning Sallum and the frontier posts back to Marsa Matruh, some 130 miles to the east. A special force, averaging between two and three brigades in strength, was assembled at Marsa Matruh, and an arduous campaign began which ended in the re-occupation of Sallum in March and the expulsion of the Sanusi forces. One notable result of the campaign was the capture of Ja'far Pasha al-'Askari, an Iraqi Arab officer who had shown ability and gallantry in leading the Turkish attack on Egypt, and who was destined in course of time to play a distinguished part in command of the 'regular' forces in the Revolt.

Farther south, a campaign had been initiated early in the year against the Sultan of Darfur who had taken up the cause of *jihad* and was inflaming his followers and neighbouring tribes for an attack on the Sudan. At several points in Upper Egypt, operations were being conducted to repel incursions into the Nile valley by devotees of the Sanusi order.

None of these miniature wars ever developed into nationwide hostilities; but, taken together, they immobilised a considerable number of British troops and caused the defenders of Egypt and the Sudan a good deal of trouble and anxiety, especially as the political feeling in Egypt was far from friendly to the Allied cause. The Arab Revolt took place at a time when those anxieties were more than ever justified, and when the effervescence created by the Sanusi Chief's open adhesion to the Holy War might still have developed into a conflagration.

At first, the news of the Sharif's rising made little impression in Egypt. In those circles which were friendly to Turkey, it was unfavourably received, and attempts were made to discredit it by minimising its importance. There was a stringent censorship of the press, which prevented any open condemnation; but the hostility was real and scarcely veiled -- although it was by no means general -- and derived its strength from anti-British as much as from pro-Turkish sentiment. Among the Syrian and Iraqi communities the Revolt was hailed with universal enthusiasm, and Syrian influence in the newspapers of Cairo and Khartoum gave it a good press. By the time the Sharif had distributed his first proclamation in July, and still more after the fall of Taif in September and the celebration of the pilgrimage which, that year, fell in the first week of October and had a good attendance from Egypt, the Revolt was being regarded by thoughtful opinion in Cairo as the most serious blow that had yet been inflicted on Turkey.

3.

In that first and most important of his proclamations, the Sharif explained his action and appealed to all Moslems to follow his example. He took his stand on the two platforms of religion and nationalism, but spoke as one who was primarily concerned with the welfare of Islam. The proclamation denounced the anti-Moslem practices of the C.U.P., of which it enumerated instances, and the arbitrary tyranny of the Enver-Jemal-Tal'at clique whom it held responsible for the executions and terrorism in Syria and for other crimes against Islam and the Arabs. It represented the Revolt as a religious and national duty, and as a God-given opportunity for the attainment of independence. It ended by calling upon all Moslems throughout the world to follow his example, in discharge of their obligations to him, as Sharif of Mecca, and to the cause of Islamic solidarity.

The significance of the proclamation, however, lay not so much in its apologia of the Revolt as in its appeal to Moslem insurgence against Turkey. So far, at any rate, as the Arab world was concerned it was the last nail in the coffin of *jihad*.

4.

Jemal Pasha admitted as much, in a speech he delivered in Damascus a few months later at a banquet held in honour of the president of the Ottoman Council of State. The text of the speech appeared in *al-Sharq* (January 23, 1917), and shows Jemal in a fine frenzy of bombast and wrath:

> 'Unfortunately, the course of the holy *jihad* has been blocked by a mean individual who, in the very heart of the Holy Land of Islam, has allied himself to those Christian Powers whose object is to despoil the world of Islam and purloin Constantinople, its capital. That vile individual, who is not ashamed to call himself a descendant of the Prophet – God's peace and blessings be upon him! – has compelled the Ottoman Empire to despatch forces against him, which should have been defeating the British on the Canal and capturing Cairo. The act of that traitor has been primarily to render a service to the British. But it will not prevent the ultimate triumph of Islam or stop our soldiers – those heroes who defended Constantinople – from crossing the Canal, annihilating the British and cutting off the head of that scoundrel in Mecca. . . .'

5.

One of the first military consequences of the Revolt was that it disposed of the German expedition under Baron von Stotzingen.

This mission, consisting of four officers, two wireless operators and a few attendants, had been sent out to Arabia to act in combination with Khairy bey's picked force of troops for the Yaman. Together, they were intended to strengthen Turkish domination in the Peninsula, and to open a new sphere of operations against the Allies. From papers afterwards seized in a German officer's kit, it was learnt that their first objective was to install a wireless post in Southern Arabia for the purpose of establishing communication with General von Lettow-Vorbeck's command in German East Africa and link it up with Berlin. They were then to organize a propaganda service for Somaliland, Abyssinia, the Sudan and possibly India. A third objective seems to have been Aden, to reinforce the three battalions holding the approaches to the fortress. And lastly, as von Stotzingen had confided to Faisal in Damascus, they were to arrange for the despatch of arms and ammunition across the Red Sea into Abyssinia for the purpose of fomenting revolts in Eritrea, Somaliland and the Sudan.

The German mission had journeyed down on the Hejaz Railway as far south as al-'Ala, the southernmost station to which non-Moslems were allowed to travel. The main Turkish force had gone on to Madina, but the Germans had had to leave the train and make for the coast, on the understanding that they were to form up with Khairy bey at Qunfida and thence march down to the Yaman. They were at Yanbo when the Revolt broke out, and fled for their lives, throwing most of their equipment into the sea. Three members of the mission disappeared and were never heard of again, but von Stotzingen and the other officers managed to escape and return safely to Damascus. As for Khairy bey's force, it was immobilised in Madina where it remained until the city surrendered to the Sharif after the conclusion of the War.

It was the arrival of this Turco-German expedition that had decided the Sharif to proclaim the rising when he did. He had not intended to do so until the following August, by which time he could have completed his preparations. His sons had pressed him to hold his hand and await at least the arrival of a sufficient supply of arms and munitions. But he, having weighed the alternatives, had decided in favour of immediate action, in the belief that the Turco-German expedition constituted a more formidable danger than was implied in a temporary deficiency in guns. It is not easy for a layman to hazard, with any confidence, a judgment on

the soundness of the Sharif's military previsions; but, from
what the experts say, he appears to have been right.   This is
what they say.

First, the official historian:

> 'It is hard to over-estimate the importance of the Turco-
> German expedition, which might even have taken Aden by
> surprise. With these reinforcements the Idrisi might have
> been crushed and the Imam left triumphant in the south.
> Of not less importance would have been its influence across
> the Red Sea, had Stotzingen obtained touch with German
> agents.   It might have been able to give material assistance
> to the 'Mad' Mullah of Somaliland, who had designs upon
> Italian Eritrea, where the white garrison did not exceed two
> thousand. . . .   All these plans and possibilities were brought
> to naught by the Arab Revolt.'[1]

Then there is the opinion of Général Brémond who headed
the French military mission in the Hejaz. He writes that
the Turco-German expedition to the Yaman was such as to

> 'expose the Allies to a great danger: had the enterprise suc-
> ceeded, it might have blocked up the Red Sea and opened up
> the Indian Ocean to German operations. . . .   Fortunately,
> the Hejaz Revolt frustrated the expedition; and by so doing,
> it undoubtedly rendered a very great service to the Allied
> cause.'[2]

And lastly, the verdict of the late Dr. D. G. Hogarth, the
eminent scholar, who had spent the years of the War in
Cairo, on the staff of the Arab Bureau, and who, writing in
The Century (July 1920), declared that:

> 'Had the Revolt never done anything else than frustrate
> that combined march of Turks and Germans to Southern
> Arabia in 1916, we should owe it more than we have paid
> to this day.'

6.

It took the Sharif six anxious months to consolidate his
gains.   He had failed to capture Madina; but, otherwise, his

[1] Official History of the War: *Military Operations in Egypt and Palestine*
(1928), Vol. I, p. 230.
[2] *Marins à Chameau* (Paris, 1935).

immediate military objectives had all been attained with the
fall of Taif in the latter half of September.

The three months that followed were the darkest in the
history of the Arab campaign. The Turks whose garrison
in Madina, with the addition of Khairy bey's force, amounted
to some 14,000 troops well equipped with artillery were
making frequent sorties; and, in one of their sallies, the roar
of their guns had set the rifle-armed Arabs on the run. It
looked as though the enemy might possibly re-capture
Rabegh and march on to Mecca. A long controversy arose,
in which everyone with a stake in the Revolt took part, as to
whether a brigade of Allied troops should be landed at
Rabegh to straddle the road leading to Mecca against a
Turkish attempt. The proposal was wisely abandoned and
the threat never materialised. All danger of a march on
Mecca was finally dispelled in the following January, when
one of the Sharif's armies, led by the Amir Faisal, moved
northwards and, with the help of the British navy, occupied
the port of Wajh.

It was during those months that British and French
missions established themselves in Jedda. The first
to arrive was Lieut.-Colonel C. C. Wilson, of the Sudan
Political Service, who came as British Agent accredited to
the Sharif, and became the principal intermediary between
him and the British authorities in the Sudan and in Egypt.
In September a French mission under Colonel E. Brémond
landed in Jedda. Other officers came later, on various
specific duties, save for one, T. E. Lawrence who arrived in
October on a visit of curiosity and stayed on, as everybody
knows, to arouse by his acts the curiosity of the world. The
duties of those officers were intended to be advisory; and, in
order to co-ordinate their activities, Sir Reginald Wingate
was made commander-in-chief of operations in the Hejaz.
The appointment did not mean that Wingate assumed control of the Sharif's forces, but that he became responsible for
the proper discharge of all British assistance, whether for
advice or in the way of supplies, rendered to the Arabs in the
War. And when, at the end of the year, Wingate succeeded

Sir Henry McMahon as High Commissioner in Cairo, he assumed responsibility for the political as well as the military aspects of Anglo-Arab co-operation.

The actual control of Arab military operations was at first entrusted – and to no one else could it more worthily have been entrusted – to 'Aziz 'Ali, who had volunteered for the task. 'Aziz had been watching events closely and biding his time. It will be remembered that, shortly after Turkey's entry into the War, he had been approached by the British authorities in Cairo and that, on discovering that Great Britain was not yet prepared to give an explicit and specific pledge in favour of Arab independence, he had broken off the conversations and gone back to his retirement. He had subsequently been informed in confidence of the tenor of the McMahon Correspondence and, on that, had swung round to the side of Anglo-Arab co-operation and offered his services.

'Aziz 'Ali arrived in Jedda in September to assume command. With his customary energy, he set about the thankless task of creating the nucleus of a trained army out of a population that had little sense of organisation or discipline. But he did not hold his command for long: the Sharif was a difficult master for one of 'Aziz 'Ali's unyielding love of efficiency, and there was friction. He left, and was eventually succeeded by Ja'far al-'Askari who, as we have seen, had been taken prisoner in the operations against the Sanusi.

Ja'far, too, had at first been unwilling to join the Revolt, until news was brought to him in his internment of the executions of the 6th of May. He was profoundly affected by the news and, uttering a curse on all Arabs who continued to serve the Turks after such savagery, volunteered for service with the Sharif. Meanwhile, on Faruqi's initiative, the prisoners-of-war camps in Egypt and India had been combed for Arab officers and other ranks, and offers made to them to join in the war for Arab liberation. A number of officers and men who were thus released from internment arrived in Yanbo or in Wajh and attached themselves to the trained army which was in process of formation. Amongst these were Nuri al-Sa'id and Maulud Mukhlis, both of them Iraqis and both of them members of *al-'Ahd,* who were afterwards to serve with outstanding distinction in the Arab campaign.

7.

On the 2nd of November, it was announced that the Sharif Husain had been proclaimed King. An assembly of religious and secular notabilities had gathered together in the morning, doubtless under Sharifian inspiration, and had acclaimed him as 'King of the Arab Countries' and performed the ceremony of the *bai'a,* the traditional Arab custom in which the investiture is accompanied by a formal declaration of allegiance. The news was at once telegraphed by the Amir 'Abdullah, acting as his father's Foreign Minister, to the principal Allied and neutral governments, with a request for their recognition of the new title. The news caused a flutter, especially in British and French circles. It was regarded as an untimely and injudicious step – as indeed it was – and one which, if it were to be recognised, would involve them in complications of various kinds. In choosing the title of King of the Arab Countries, the Sharif was trespassing, or appearing to trespass, on the acquired position of other Arab rulers; and, so far as that objection went, the Allies were wise in withholding their recognition of it. Eventually a formula was devised by them, whereby the Sharif was recognised as King of the Hejaz, and formal notification of this was addressed to him on the 3rd of January 1917, in identical British and French notes.

8.

The chapter which had opened with the rising in Madina on the 5th of June closed with the capture of Wajh on the 25th of January. The Revolt had found its feet. The efforts made by the Turks to re-capture Mecca had been in vain and, with the Arabs in Wajh, the project could scarcely be contemplated. They were reduced to holding their ground in Madina, as well they might so long as trains could run to and from Damascus. But that would mean a large garrison immobilised in Madina itself, and smaller ones strung like beads on the long thread of the Hejaz Railway. The Sharif 'Ali Haidar, nominated by the Sultan to succeed 'that scoundrel in Mecca', was also in Madina, whither he had arrived in July with a large retinue and bags of gold with which to win his entry into Mecca after its re-capture. But shortly after the fall of Wajh, he asked the Sultan's permission to return and was allowed to go to the Lebanon, where he remained in secluded retirement to the end of the War.

9.

The forces of the Revolt had, by that time, sorted themselves out into three main groups, each of which was led by one of the Sharif's sons. 'Ali's force stood facing Madina, less to operate against the city than to remind its commander that the revolt was a living reality. 'Abdullah moved up to Wadi 'Ais, mainly in order to harass the Turkish communications and intercept food and other supplies. Faisal had marched into Wajh and made it his base for the larger operations that were to follow. It is difficult to arrive at an exact estimate of the numerical strength of the forces. Not only did they fluctuate between wide limits: but at that stage their numerical strength did not correspond to their rifle-strength. Three weeks after the outbreak of the revolt, the Arab forces amounted to anything between 30,000 and 40,000, but with barely 10,000 rifles between them, and with no guns or machine-guns of their own. By the time Wajh was captured, the numbers of tribesmen enrolled had risen to 70,000 and of serviceable rifles to 28,000.

But for all the poverty of their equipment and the laxity of their discipline, the forces had already accomplished remarkable results. Besides the 6,000 prisoners actually taken, they had locked up a garrison of 14,000 Turks in Madina and another 5,000 whose base was at Tabuk; and, by their threats to the communications between Damascus and Madina, they had compelled the enemy to increase the garrison in Ma'an to over 7,000. To say nothing of the three Turkish divisions – one in 'Asir and two in the Yaman – whose communications with their home bases were now completely severed.

From the point of view of Allied strategy, the Revolt had barred the road to the Red Sea and the Indian Ocean, and had interposed an obstacle to Turco-German southward expansion. With Ibn Sa'ud allied to Great Britain, an unbroken Arab belt now stretched from the Red Sea to the Persian Gulf, making those two waterways safe for Allied traffic. Further to the north, Sir Archibald Murray was preparing his advance into Palestine, and had the satisfaction of knowing that the Revolt was seriously embarrassing the enemy facing him. At first he had not taken kindly to the idea of an Arab rising, which he had regarded somewhat contemptuously as a side-show and a possible nuisance. But by the time Faisal's force had reached Wajh, General Murray's attitude had changed, having, as T. E. Lawrence puts it, 'realised with a sudden shock that more Turkish troops were fighting the Arabs than were fighting him'.

CHAPTER XII

THE ARABS IN THE WAR: 1916–18

I.

As the occupation of Wajh on the 25th of January, 1917, had brought the first phase of the Revolt to a close, so the capture of 'Aqaba in the following July marks the beginning of the last and most spectacular phase – the Arab drive towards Damascus. The intervening months were a period of sporadic military activity in each of the three Arab camps, and of intense political preparation for the advance to the north.

As the months went by and the supply of equipment increased, the Arab grip on the beleaguered Turks tightened. Although the Allies were still niggardly with guns, they had made handsome contributions in rifles and ammunition, and had sent competent officers to act as instructors. Raids on the Hejaz Railway became frequent and more effective, although they did not reach the high standard of destructiveness which they were later to attain, thanks to Lawrence's diabolical skill. At this stage, the raiders were usually tearing up the line and destroying bridges and culverts: later, they learnt to blow up trains and engines. At times, they would attack one of the stations on the railway and capture its garrison, or raid a passing enemy convoy. The damage to the line was never so serious as to put it permanently out of use, but it made it difficult and costly for the Turks to keep pace with the frequent demolitions. They realised the futility of attempting to take the offensive, and remained glued to their outposts on the line, venturing out in large parties now and again to re-lay a section of the line or shore up a bridge as best they could.

The success of those raids was largely due to the skill and gallantry of a handful of officers who had been lent to the Sharif as instructors and who did far more than instruct. So much limelight has been projected on Lawrence that his colleagues have remained in comparative obscurity. It was not merely that they trained the Arabs in the arts of modern warfare and taught them the use of explosives and the technique of demolitions: but their devotion to the task in hand, which was read as devotion to the Arab cause, and the powers of endurance and daring they exhibited among a people whose own standards in those qualities were high enough, were the real foundations of Anglo-Arab co-operation in the campaign. On more than one occasion in the years that followed the War, have I heard the late King Faisal declare that, with the exception of Lawrence whose genius entitled him to a place of his own, the claims of Colonel S. F. Newcombe or of Major P. C. Joyce to Arab gratitude were not less strong than those of any other Englishman.

The time had now passed when the Turks could make sorties. 'Abdullah had moved to Wadi 'Ais, to the north-west of Madina, while 'Ali, leaving his base at Rabegh and fighting his way successfully against the enemy outposts on the road to Madina, had pitched his camp within sixty miles of the city, to the south-west of it. Between them, the two brothers harassed the Turks, each for what he could do with the resources at his disposal, and each supplementing the other in the common task of reducing the Turkish commander to impotence. For a time, the Amir Zaid, the youngest of the Sharif's sons, with a force of his own, took a share in the siege of Madina. All three groups had also been lent instructors, mainly by the French, in the persons of Moroccan and Algerian officers. And while Faisal at Wajh was busy preparing the Arab advance into Syria, the three Amirs in the south drew a ring round the holy city, and, being precluded by its sanctity from bombarding it, had to content themselves with the tactics of a siege which they maintained until the end of the War. Theirs was the less spectacular part, but one without which Faisal's triumph could perhaps not have been.

There were two important captures. Early in January the Amir 'Abdullah's force encountered a Turkish mission, led by one Eshref bey, on their way to the Yaman to open up the communications which the Revolt had interrupted. The troops accompanying the mission were well-armed and, having bags of gold in their keeping and a resolute desperado at their head, fought like tigers. Those who, like Eshref bey, escaped death, were captured, and the bags of gold with the papers of the mission were seized. In April, a bigger feat was carried out by a force led by the Amir Zaid. A large convoy of supplies sent by the Turks to Ibn Rashid was surprised and routed at Hanakiya, about eighty miles to the north-east of Madina, and the enemy made poorer by 3,000 camels laden with food and clothing, to say nothing of the rest of the booty and 250 prisoners. What made the victory more significant still was that it brought about a rift between Ibn Rashid and the Turks, for he took to badgering them for a replacement of the losses and, failing to get it, sulked and lost heart in his solidarity with them.

2.

In his camp at Wajh, Faisal worked unremittingly at the hardest task of all – to induce the tribes to sink their differences in the pursuit of a common aim.

The attribute of disunion, as between one tribe and another, was inherent in the structure of the Arabian society with its clannish organisation and numerous divisions and fractions. Within each clan, there reigned the very opposite of disunity: a strong sense of solidarity and a passionate, unquestioning devotion to the interests of the clan and its good name, beside which the conventional notion of patriotism seems a cold, mental affair. But no such bond united one tribe to the other, and the resulting dissociation was rendered still more pronounced by the stringent codes governing blood-feuds, the laws of retaliation and the rights of way. With his mind focused on Damascus, Faisal could see before him an interminable jungle of feuds and antagonisms, of old scores still to be paid, of debts to be written off in blood.

It had not mattered before, in the static days of the camp outside Madina; but now that the Revolt was about to turn into a war of movement, to win Damascus 600 miles away, those barriers had to be overthrown. The problem was to find the means. Gold he had in plenty, thanks to his British allies; but effective though it had been as an inducement to military service and as a lubricant to reduce friction, gold was powerless against the ramparts of pride and tradition; and Faisal, who had spent his early youth in a chieftain's tent, knew the desert code too well to rely solely on money for a solvent. His personal ascendancy was considerable, being grounded not only in his birth but in the wide fame of his valour, and he used it wisely, so far as it could be used with effect. But one power there is which alone can move Arabia to forgo the prerogatives of her proud individualism, and that power is faith. Faisal's main task was one of political proselytisation: to preach the gospel of Arab emancipation and fire the minds of the tribes with the glow of his own fervour.

With those three levers – gold, influence and a message – he set to work on the task of converting the chiefs. He went patiently through the history of their feuds, listening to every man's grievance, never refusing a hearing to anyone however lowly or prolix. Whenever a dispute could be composed by payment, he assessed the amount of the compensation owed, and paid it. In cases where tribal honour was not redeemable with money, he would invoke the Arab tradition of mediation and intervene as the disinterested arbitrator whose warrant was the destiny of the Arab race. While he was still busy with the tribes of the Hejaz, he despatched emissaries to the chieftains in Southern Syria, the heads of the Bani 'Atiya, the Huwaitat and the Ruala confederations. Some came in person to Wajh, others sent their kinsmen. To all, Faisal appealed in the name of the Sharif, urging the magnificence of the opportunity which presented itself for gaining for ever, with the help of England's might, the liberty that would be theirs to hand down to posterity.

Le Bédouin est l'homme le plus libre de la terre,[1] and the gospel which Faisal preached found ears attuned to its music. By his own faith sustained, he worked indefatigably, month after month, until the barriers were removed, the reconciliations effected, and the inveterate enemies of several generations, infected with his faith, had taken an oath to serve as brothers in arms under him for the liberation of all Arabs, and to 'hold independence dearer than family, property or life itself'.

3.

Among the chieftains who had come to Wajh in answer to Faisal's summons was 'Auda Abu Tayeh, the head of the Tawayha section of the Huwaitat confederation whose roaming-ground was the south-eastern corner of Syria. 'Auda was not only the leader of a very warlike tribe, but also, as the saying went, a tribe all to himself, as easily supreme in the council-tent as on the field. He seldom took advice and, in a life packed with hazards, had proved that he was generally better off without it. He was then a man of fifty-five still vigorous and agile, and was accounted the doughtiest fighter in the country. In appearance he reminded one of an eagle: a nose like a quadrant, a head tilted back and eyes large and sleepy, with a haughty, far-off look. His arrival sent a thrill through the camp, but no one was more delighted than Faisal, who knew what efforts the Turks had been making to seduce 'Auda to their allegiance.

With him Faisal reached a quick understanding. They had not met before, but each sized the other up at the first interview and never had cause to revise his judgment, 'Auda was at feud with almost every other chieftain within his reach: he gave Faisal a sweeping promise that, for his part, his only feud now was with the Turks; and, in the same breath

[1] R. Dozy, *Histoire des Musulmans d'Espagne.*

he proposed an attack on 'Aqaba which, he boasted, he and his tribesmen could capture unaided. The proposal fell in with Faisal's own plans and was adopted. So 'Auda was to return whence he had come, to muster his followers and storm the Turkish posts guarding 'Aqaba.

At the time, Faisal was about to send a mission into Syria to preach insurrection and lay the foundations of future concerted action. He chose one of his cousins, the Sharif Naser, to lead the expedition as his personal representative, and Nasib al-Bakri to act as its political officer. Lawrence asked to be allowed to go, offering his services as an emissary to the Arab leaders in Damascus. On the 9th of May, the mission set out from Wajh, with 'Auda and an escort of some thirty-five riders. After a time, the party broke up and scattered in different directions: 'Auda went to collect his tribesmen; the Sharif Naser pitched his camp near Kaf in the Wadi Serhan; Nasib made his way to the Jabal Druze; and Lawrence went off alone on one of the most original and daring expeditions of his career and one which, for some unknown reason, is passed over in silence in all his published writings. He rode northwards to Palmyra, visited the chiefs of the Wuld 'Ali and Kawakiba tribes, and, having enrolled thirty-five tribesmen of the former, rode across to Baalbek and dynamited a small bridge on the railway-line from Rayyaq. Then he rode to within five miles of Damascus and went into hiding at Qabun, the property of the Bakris, where Faisal had often stayed. He sent one of the retainers on the estate with a message to Rida Pasha Rikabi, an Arab general in the Turkish army, and one of the leading members of al-'Ahd. It was no small risk for Rikabi who, as general officer commanding the city, was very much in the public eye; but, hearing that he was wanted by an emissary of the Amir Faisal's, he came out surreptitiously to Qabun and met Lawrence who gave him the message he was bearing. This was that Faisal had decided to advance into Syria in stages, that the next stage was 'Aqaba, and that all he wanted for the present was that the leaders in Damascus should do everything possible to encourage Arab troops serving in the Turkish army to desert and join his forces at 'Aqaba. He did not want any rising to take place yet.

This meeting took place on the 13th of June, and by the 18th, Lawrence was back at Kaf in the Sharif Naser's camp. On his way back, he had met a few other chieftains, amongst whom were the Druze leader, Husain al-Atrash, and Nuri Sha'lan the paramount chief of the great Ruala confederation, and had given them the same message from Faisal and sounded them as to their resources. Naser and Lawrence then went on another round of visits to various tribal chieftains, which occupied ten days. At last, the march on 'Aqaba began.

'Auda had assembled 500 of his tribesmen at Bair,[1] and was overtaken there by Naser and Lawrence. On the 30th, the force set out southwards past al-Jafr[1] and then, turning westwards, crossed the Hejaz Railway, stopping long enough to blow up a few bridges and damage a whole kilometre of line. On the 2nd of July, they attacked the Turkish force guarding the post of Abul-Ithl on the Ma'an-'Aqaba road. The garrison which consisted of a battalion 600 strong was routed and almost every man in it either killed or taken prisoner. The victory was typical of 'Auda's methods:

> 'At sunset 'Auda collected fifty horsemen in a hollow valley 200 yards from the Turkish position and suddenly charged. The Turks broke, whereupon the rest of the Arab force dashed down the hill on their camels. The fight was over in five minutes. Captain Lawrence counted 300 dead Turks on the field; by his exertions and those of Sharif Naser 160 were saved from death and taken prisoner. The loss of the Arabs was two killed and a few wounded.'[2]

The Arabs were short of food, the heat was unusually severe, and a clamour arose of weary bodies asking for a respite; but 'Auda would not hear of a rest, arguing that a delay might mean starvation, and he pressed his men on inflexibly.

---

[1] A well in the desert east of the Hejaz Railway between 'Amman and Ma'an.
[2] Official History of the War: *Military Operations in Egypt and Palestine*, Vol. I, p. 240.

There remained four Turkish posts between Abul-Ithl and 'Aqaba: they were captured in as many days, and the toll of enemy dead rose to 600 while the prisoners totalled 700. On the 6th of July, the Arab force marched into 'Aqaba thirsty, underfed, and exhausted, and driving before it a rabble of prisoners larger than itself.

4·

The capture of 'Aqaba marks a turning-point. Hitherto, the Revolt had had the Hejaz for a theatre and the forces supplied by the tribes for its fighting element. Now the scene had shifted to Syria, and the function and composition of Faisal's army underwent a transformation. It became the right wing of the Egyptian Expeditionary Force, with a small army of trained 'regular' troops, and its task henceforth was to carry the war into Syria in conformity with General Allenby's plans.

For nearly a year, Sir Archibald Murray had been slowly driving the Turks back across the Sinai Peninsula and, by the beginning of 1917, had reached the confines of Palestine. Then, in March and April, he had delivered two attacks on Gaza which had failed disastrously. He had been recalled and replaced by Sir Edmund Allenby who had arrived in Cairo towards the end of June to take up his command; and the news of the fall of 'Aqaba was the first news of military significance that had greeted the new commander-in-chief on his arrival.

Allenby was quick to grasp the importance of the move to 'Aqaba and the use that might be made of an Arab flying wing in his forthcoming thrust. He made it known that Faisal could count upon him for help, and he kept his promise handsomely. Faisal came up to 'Aqaba in August, and presently the tiny hamlet took on the aspect of a large and variegated military beehive with wireless stations and an aerodrome, and jetties for the landing of supplies. The nucleus of a 'regular' army was provided by the Arab units which had been formed in Wajh, to which was subsequently added some 600 men of the Arab Legion raised in Egypt from among volunteers in the prisoners-of-war camps. As 'Aqaba lay outside the historical limits of the Moslem holy land, non-Moslems could have access to it without restriction. A number of British and French officers arrived to serve as advisers to the Arab command or as heads of special contingents of armoured-car, aeroplane, and camel corps unit. In the Hejaz proper, Faisal's brothers were to continue their operations in the vicinity of Madina until the end of the War, with the single exception of the Amir Zaid who, in the following year, moved northwards to the Syrian theatre.

For the first six months after the capture of 'Aqaba, Faisal was mainly engaged on the double task of getting his forces into fighting trim and of extending the range of his tribal alliances. He was now within 150 miles of Allenby's advanced posts, and in easy communication by air and telegraph with the headquarters of the Egyptian Expeditionary Force. The largest enemy concentration facing him was at Ma'an which became his immediate military objective. By the end of the year he had carried his work of tribal pacification so far as to include all the tribes in the Ma'an area; and his trained army had expanded from a nucleus of two battalions to a well-equipped force consisting of one infantry brigade and two mounted (camel and mule) battalions.

While Faisal was thus engrossed in military and political preparation, the Sharif Naser, 'Auda and Lawrence were out on various expeditions to raid the railway, demolish the track, bridges and culverts, and inflict a multitude of small but telling blows on the enemy. These raids took place throughout the autumn, before and after Allenby began his northward drive into Palestine at the end of October. In one of them – near Mudawwara, about the end of September – a party led by Lawrence blew up a train in which seventy Turkish soldiers lost their lives. Three weeks later the same party captured a large consignment of supplies destined, this time again, for the unlucky Ibn Rashid. In the last days of December, the Sharif Naser carried out a daring raid at Jurf al-Darawish in which he captured over 200 prisoners. Then he occupied Tafila – an important village in the wheat-growing district – and when a column of 800 Turks advanced to recapture it, they were driven back in disorder, losing some 300 killed and 200 prisoners.

In its military implications, the move to 'Aqaba caused serious embarrassment to the Turco-German command in Syria at a time when every available man and gun were needed to oppose the British advance on Jerusalem. But its political consequences, although less apparent at first, were more damaging still. 'Aqaba became the tangible embodiment of the Revolt and a base for the political undermining as well as the military undoing of the Turkish power in Syria.

5.

The political action manifested itself in a variety of ways, all of them tending to weaken Turkey by winning the Arabs of Syria over to the Allied side. The principal weapon of propaganda employed was that, thanks to the agreement concluded between Sir Henry McMahon and the Sharif (now King) Husain, the Allied cause had become identical with the cause of Arab independence; and that the triumph of Allied arms would bring freedom to the Arab peoples.

An active campaign in that sense had been organised by the political officers of the Egyptian Expeditionary Force in the months that followed the outbreak of the Revolt. As the British forces advanced eastwards from the Suez Canal in the summer of 1916, secret emissaries were despatched to the chiefs of tribes in southern Palestine to induce them to withhold their support from the Turks. Colonel A. C. Parker whose service in the Sinai Peninsula had earned him widespread respect and confidence invited Shaikh Furaih abu Meddain, the paramount chief of the Beersheba tribes, to a conference at al-'Arish and handed him an autograph letter from King Husain calling upon all Arabs to aid the efforts of the British forces who were working for Arab liberation.

Aeroplanes flew over the Turkish lines and rained copies of King Husain's letter, on the back of which was printed an appeal from the British command asking Arab officers and men in the Turkish army to desert and cross over to the British lines to meet delegates from the Sharif of Mecca. These delegates had been sent over by Husain at the request of his British allies. At their head was one of Husain's cousins, the Sharif 'Abdullah Hamza, and their mission was to bring home to the chieftains in Southern Syria the terms and the objects of Anglo-Arab co-operation, and to induce them to abstain from serving the Turks and facilitate the progress of the British advance into Palestine.

On his side, Faisal was not less active in promoting the defection of those chieftains who were within his reach. His emissaries travelled far into the interior of Syria and established communication with the heads of the semi-nomadic populations in the regions on either side of the Jordan. He was still unwilling to provoke a mass rising in Syria, since his military preparations were far from complete and his immediate objects were primarily to come to a secret understanding with the important chiefs and to encourage the desertion of Arabs serving in the Turkish army.

This propaganda bore fruit in both directions. Its full effects can never be exactly ascertained in view of the precautions which had to be taken for fear of reprisals on the relatives and dependants of the men who obeyed the call. But enough is known, both from direct evidence and indirectly from the countermeasures taken by the Turco-German command, to show that the campaign met with a considerable and increasing measure of success. The tribes in the Beersheba district who had fought on the Turkish side in the spring of 1917 melted away on a word from Furaih abu Meddain and re-appeared further south on the right flank of the British forces advancing on Gaza. As a result of this defection, the Turks decided to evacuate al-'Arish which was thereupon occupied by a British cavalry division. The enemy tried to make a stand at Maghdaba but were compelled to retreat and eventually to surrender when the Arab soldiers in their ranks deserted over to the enemy in a body. Throughout Allenby's advance on Jerusalem in the autumn of 1917, Arabs deserted from the Turkish ranks in large numbers. A few crossed over to the British lines and gave themselves up, others went to 'Aqaba to join the Arab colours, the largest number disappeared into the countryside.

Realising the serious effects of the Anglo-Arab propaganda, the German command concerted measures to counter it. An Arab Bureau was founded at Damascus in October of that year, with a picked staff of German experts in Arab affairs and a handsome budget for expenditure on counter-propaganda. The penalties for desertion were made more stringent and an order by Jemal Pasha was circulated making it a capital offence for anyone, soldier or civilian, to retain in his keeping any of the leaflets which were being dropped from British aeroplanes in the Gaza-Beersheba sector.[1] The Germans who had never had much confidence in Jemal's political sense now intervened to undo some of the effects of his policy, and Marshal von Falkenhayn – newly appointed to the supreme military command in this theatre – brought pressure to bear at Constantinople. This resulted in the issue, on the 14th of November, of a public appeal signed by Jemal to all Arabs who had taken up arms for the King of the Hejaz in which he offered those of them who would give themselves up within thirty days a free and unconditional pardon.

But, notwithstanding this offer and the other measures, desertions continued and disaffection increased until, as Liman von Sanders expressed it, the British forces advancing towards Jerusalem found themselves fighting in a friendly country, while the Turks who were defending their own territory found themselves fighting in the midst of a decidedly hostile population.[2] The same appreciation was expressed to me by General Mehemed Jemal Pasha[3] at a conversation

---

[1] Text in *al-Balagh*, January 29. 1917. and other Syrian newspapers.
[2] Liman von Sanders, *Fünf Jahre Türkei*.
[3] Not to be confused with his namesake Ahmed Jemal Pasha. Mehemed Jemal was serving as G.O.C. VIIIth Army Corps (headquarters at Ma'an) throughout the War until the beginning of 1918 when he succeeded Ahmed Jemal as G.O.C. Fourth Army and took up his headquarters in Damascus.

I had with him in Constantinople in the spring of 1936. In his view, the disaffection spread in Syria by the Anglo-Arab propaganda turned out to have been even more detrimental to the Turkish hold on the country than the military losses caused directly by the entry of the Arabs into the War.

There is a good deal of first-hand and otherwise reliable evidence that goes to support beyond all doubt the views expressed by Mehemed Jemal Pasha and Liman von Sanders.

6.

The political consequences of this phase of the Anglo-Arab partnership are important not only from an historical point of view, but also for the sake of their bearing upon the controversies which raged in the years following the War.

As we shall see, those controversies affected the fate of all the Arab territories that lie outside the Arabian Peninsula, and everywhere in those regions protests accompanied by violence taking the form of armed insurrections were made against the settlement devised by the Allies. In course of time, these protests led to radical revisions of the original settlement, with the single exception of that portion of Syria which is now known as the mandated territory of Palestine, that is to say that very region in which the fact and the terms of the Anglo-Arab alliance were first used as a weapon for the immediate furtherance of the progress of British arms.

In an earlier chapter, an analysis of the text of the Mc-Mahon Correspondence revealed that Palestine had not been excluded from the area in which Great Britain had pledged herself to recognise and uphold an independent Arab state. The point to be noticed now is that the political campaign initiated in 1916 by the British command was in itself a positive indication that, in the minds of British and Arab alike, Palestine was regarded as falling within that area. The efforts made to win the population over to the Allied side were made in the name of King Husain and of Arab freedom not only in Palestine but everywhere else in Syria, with the single exception of the Lebanon where Husain's name was never mentioned and the emphasis in the propaganda was exclusively placed upon the particular concern of France for the welfare of the Lebanon. This differentiation was altogether consistent with the reservations made on behalf of France in the McMahon Correspondence and is historically important as showing that, as late as the spring of 1917 at any rate, Palestine was treated on a footing with those other parts of Syria in which Great Britain had pledged herself, without reservation, to recognise and uphold an independent Arab state.

7.

The attack launched by General Allenby at the end of October led to the capture of Jerusalem on the 9th of December. The cities of Gaza, Hebron, Jaffa and Bethlehem had fallen earlier, in a campaign as remarkable for the care with which it had been planned as for the daring and gallantry brought to its execution. Minor operations were then carried out to consolidate the gains. By the end of 1917, the British forces were in secure occupation of practically the whole of that part of Syria that formed the Sanjaq of Jerusalem.

The progress of the British armies had been rendered particularly arduous by the difficult nature of the terrain and the advent of an unusually inclement autumn; and the only way in which it may be said to have been favoured was in the friendly attitude of the civilian population. The troops were greeted as liberators and allies, with spontaneous offers of help. Arab officers and men serving in the Turkish army crossed over to the British lines and volunteered information which proved valuable about the plans and tactical dispositions of the enemy. In Jerusalem, the victors met with a genuine, if subdued, welcome from a population shrunken to half its size by hunger, exile and deportation. Yet when the British command established a recruiting-office for volunteers to serve in Faisal's army, local enthusiasm outran the scarcity of able-bodied men. A young member of one of the leading Arab families, Amin al-Husaini,[1] toured the occupied country, set on foot a movement of enlistment and took an active part in the organisation of the force. The contingent thus raised was a small one, amounting to some 2,000 men; but the remarkable thing was that, in the stricken state of the country, it was raised at all.

In the following January (1918), Allenby struck out to the east of Jordan in an effort to capture 'Amman, and was to have been seconded by tribal contingents acting under Faisal's orders. But the junction was never effected: the Arabs failed to carry out their part of the plan in the allotted time, while the British forces were unable to consolidate their positions and fell back to the west bank of the Jordan. Realising that a junction with his British allies was not yet feasible, Faisal confined his operations to the Ma'an region and tried to isolate that town with a view to its ultimate capture. An unusually severe winter had set in, accompanied by a prolonged fall of snow to which the Beduin were not accustomed.

That period of the campaign was marked by a vigorous recrudescence of political and military activity on the part of the Turco-German command. The garrison at Ma'an was reinforced. The German Arab Bureau whose establishment in Damascus has already been mentioned sent out agents with a plentiful supply of gold to spread disaffection among Faisal's followers. Herr Niedermayr, one of the ablest of a band of Germans specially picked for political work in Eastern countries, arrived in 'Amman with a retinue of subordinates to supervise the propaganda in person. Peace overtures, of which an account will be given later, were made to Faisal by the Turkish command with the explicit backing of the German Government. So far as the political propaganda went, those efforts came to nothing. As for military activity, the measures taken by the Turks served only to increase the toll of their losses.

At Sail al-Hasa on the 26th of January, a force of 800 Turks

---

[1] who afterwards became Mufti of Jerusalem and President of the Supreme Moslem Council in Palestine.

was routed, of whom barely fifty escaped. There were over 500 killed and some 200 captured. In March, a strong column sallied out of Ma'an and drove the Arabs out of Tafila, but only to lose it again after an engagement lasting several days. The Arab pressure on Ma'an was tightening and the attacks on the Hejaz Railway were becoming so frequent that traffic on it was reduced to one train a week, and the journey from Damascus to Madina was taking five days as against a normal schedule of eighteen hours. The Turks decided to evacuate Madina. Hitherto, they had retained it for political rather than military reasons. They had lost Mecca and Jerusalem – two of the three holiest cities of Islam – and had clung tenaciously on to the third from motives of prestige. But that was proving too costly.

The Arab rising had already resulted in greater losses than Turkey could afford. It may be reckoned at a conservative estimate that, by the end of March 1918, the Turks had lost 4,800 killed, 1,600 wounded and 8,000 captured, in Turco-Arab engagements alone. These figures do not include Arab desertions from the Turkish ranks. In addition, there were garrisons of 12,000 at Madina, 7,000 at Ma'an and some 3,000 at various points on the intervening sections of the railway, who were immobilised by the action of the Arabs. In all, the number of Turks killed, captured or contained by the Arab Revolt amounted already to some 35,000. And the pressure was tightening, while the problem of supplying and equipping the beleaguered garrisons was becoming increasingly difficult.

News of the decision to evacuate Madina reached Faisal about the middle of March and prompted him to quick action. It became apparent to him that the intention of the Turco-German command was, first, to secure the safe withdrawal of the main Madina garrison and of the subsidiary garrisons on the Hejaz Railway line and bring them into Ma'an; then, having done that, to use them either for immediate offensive purposes against his own forces or for reinforcing the armies barring the road to Damascus against a British-Arab northward push. After consultation with Joyce and Lawrence, and with the concurrence and help of Allenby, Faisal drew up a plan for an immediate offensive with the object of isolating Ma'an, severing its communications with Madina and frustrating the Turkish scheme.

Faisal's plan was to divide his available forces into three columns, variously composed, and send them to attack the railway simultaneously in three different sectors. Making judicious use of the armoured cars and of a detachment of the Egyptian Camel Corps lent to him by the authorities in Cairo, he provided each column with the personnel and the equipment best suited to its particular task. The attacks began in the first week of April: the northern column destroyed the railway-line between Ma'an and 'Amman; the southern column, under Lieutenant-Colonel Alan Dawnay, operated in the sector south of Ma'an as far as Mudawwara and wrecked the line beyond repair; the central column, under Ja'far Pasha, occupied the outer defences of Ma'an and demolished the line immediately to the north and south of it. By the 20th of April, Ma'an was isolated. In ten days the three columns had destroyed over fifty bridges and culverts and 3,000 rails, and captured 450 prisoners and large supplies of ammunition, The Turks launched several heavy counter-attacks against Semna which was held by the central column; but Ja'far with his Arab regulars held his ground and the Turkish plan of evacuating Madina became an impossibility.

Farther south, the Amirs 'Ali and 'Abdullah were renewing their activities, and carried out extensive demolitions throughout May and June. Another defeat was inflicted on Ibn Rashid by 'Abdullah near Taima; and when, in July, the Turks sent a strong detachment of infantry and cavalry by an inland route from Madina to reinforce their ally, the Amir 'Abdullah fell upon them and every man in the force was either killed or captured.

An idea of the scale of the Arab operations in the Ma'an sector may be gained by a comparison in effectives. Apart from the garrisons based on Ma'an, which were known as the II Corps, three Turkish armies were opposing the British and Arab forces on both sides of the Jordan. To the west of it, the British were face-to-face with two distinct groups – the Seventh and Eighth Armies – and commanded respectively, by Mustafa Kemal Pasha (the future President of the Kemalist Republic) and Jevad Pasha; to the east, the Arabs were opposed by the Fourth Army with its head-quarters at 'Amman. The two armies facing the British amounted to a rifle-strength of 17,000. The forces engaged by the Arabs in the area to the east of Jordan amounted to 14,000.[1] These figures include the Turkish II Corps based on Ma'an but not the 12,000 effectives contained by the Arabs in Madina and on the railway between it and Mudawwara.

Thus, in estimating the military value of the Arab campaign, it is important to bear in mind that Faisal's forces alone were engaging approximately the same number of Turkish effectives as were the British forces to the west of Jordan; that, by occupying the area to the east of Ma'an, Faisal was covering the right flank of the British army in Palestine and protecting its long line of communications from Turkish raids in the neighbourhood of Hebron and Beersheba; and that, in addition to Faisal, 'Ali and 'Abdullah were containing and harassing a large enemy force which, in the words of the Official Historian, 'would have been invaluable to Liman[2] either at the moment of Sir Edmund Allenby's greatest embarrassment or that of the final offensive.' As in 1917, there were more Turkish troops fighting the Arabs in the Ma'an area and the Hejaz than there were in Palestine to resist the British northward advance.

8.

As the summer advanced, Allenby's plans were maturing for the final offensive. He had originally intended to launch

---

[1] These figures, which represent rifle- and sabre-strength as opposed to ration-strength, are those given in General Allenby's despatches, and are taken from A. P. Wavell, *The Palestine Campaigns*, to which I am indebted for other information used in this chapter.

[2] On March 1, 1918, Liman von Sanders had succeeded von Falkenhayn as commander-in-chief of the Turco-German forces and had established his headquarters in Nazareth.

it in the spring, but the great German thrust on the Western front in March had compelled him to detach two of his seven divisions for service in France, and he had had to await the arrival of substitutes from India and Mesopotamia and to carry out a radical re-organisation of his forces. By September, he had completed his preparations. His plan, which he put to execution on the 19th, was a masterpiece of tactical skill and was brilliantly carried out; and the combined British-Arab offensive swept the Turks out of Syria like thistledown before the wind.

The plan was entirely the work of Allenby and his staff, and is regarded by competent critics as a classic in the history of strategy and a testimony to his military genius. There were, as we have seen, two Turkish armies – the Eighth and the Seventh – before him, and a third – the Fourth – opposing the Arabs. Behind those, was a fourth Turkish force – the Second Army – garrisoning the north of Syria between Aleppo and Damascus. Allenby's own forces amounted to eight infantry and four cavalry divisions, amongst whom were a French brigade and a small Italian contingent, and were formed into two groups – the XX Corps and the XXI Corps – and a corps of cavalry. This gave him a superiority of over two to one in fighting strength. But even when allowance is made for the disparity, Allenby's victory still ranks as a brilliant feat, not only for the skilful use he made of his initial advantage, but also for the speed and the finality with which he crushed the enemy at a comparatively trifling cost to himself.

It was part of Allenby's plan to sever the Turkish communications between Damascus and the south before launching his offensive, and for that he had to have recourse to the Arabs. The vital point in the enemy's communications was Dar'a, a station on the Hejaz Railway, where the branch line to Haifa bifurcated from the main line to Madina. If Dar'a were to be isolated, the possibility of the Turks hurrying reinforcements by train to Palestine would be eliminated, the working of their rear services paralysed, and their quickest mode of retreat from the combined British-Arab offensive cut off. Moreover, a threat to the railway at Dar'a might cause – as, in fact, it did cause – Liman von Sanders to despatch some of his reserves from the Nazareth area to protect the junction, thus weakening the resistance which he might otherwise have opposed to the British advance.

When he was made privy to this plan, Faisal played up with spirit. By that time his forces had improved considerably in training and equipment. His regular army numbered now close upon 8,000 men, brought up to a fair pitch of efficiency by the untiring exertions of Ja'far Pasha and his fellow-officers, and strengthened by the British contingents of armoured-car, machine-gun and signals detachments. He had also increased the vast resources of man-power provided by the tribes, for he had in the course of 1918 so extended his propaganda as to have secured the adhesion to the Revolt of all the remaining chieftains between the Gulf of 'Aqaba and the Euphrates. Nuri Sha'lan, the paramount shaikh of the Ruala confederation had actually mobilised his followers for the final offensive, and the chieftains of the Hauran and the Jabal Druze had secretly undertaken to bring about a rising of the countryside to synchronise with the launching of the offensive. Of equal importance with the growth of the forces at Faisal's disposal was the change in their composition. The Hejazi element had almost entirely dropped out; and his present troops, regular as well as tribal, were for the most part formed of the inhabitants of Syria, Palestine and Iraq, that is to say of men who had a direct stake and, in many instances, a home in the country they were about to enter.

Early in September, Faisal moved his base to Azraq, some fifty miles to the east of 'Amman, which he had chosen to be the centre of his concentration. The first attack was made on the 16th, three days before the start of the British offensive. In compliance with Allenby's plan, the railway was cut between Dar'a and 'Amman, severely enough to interrupt all traffic between the two places. On the following day, other Arab parties destroyed the railway at points to the north and to the west of Dar'a, and were about to storm the town when the arrival of strong German reinforcements made them pause. Liman von Sanders had walked into the trap set for him, and the Arabs continued their threatening demonstrations in the hope of drawing off a further contingent from the Nazareth area. On the 18th, they carried out more demolitions on the railway, with the result that, by the evening of that day, Dar'a was effectively isolated on every side. Early in the following morning the British offensive was launched on the Palestine front.

Allenby's operations began with a feint designed to lead the Turks to expect the brunt of his attack to fall on their left wing, northwards against their Seventh Army which was based on Nablus, and eastwards against their Fourth Army based on 'Amman. Having previously misled them into strengthening their concentration at the centre of their line, he followed the stratagem up by directing his XX Corps to make a sharp attack against the Seventh Army. But this was only a feint. The real attack was delivered by the XXI Corps against the Turkish right wing, that is to say against the Eighth Army holding the ground between the coast and the foothills of Samaria, and was delivered with such force as to compel the enemy commander to fall back in a disorderly pivotal movement, leaving the coastal plain undefended. Then Allenby hurled his cavalry along the gap thus opened. In less than twenty-four hours, a mounted brigade had reached the outskirts of Nazareth and all but captured Liman von Sanders and his staff who were still as much pre-occupied with meeting the Arab attack around Dar'a as with Allenby's advance of which they had not yet realised the gravity. A few hours later, another brigade occupied 'Affuleh, a station on the Haifa-Dar'a-Damascus Railway, and in the afternoon of the same day – September 20 – a division entered Baisan. Thus by sunset on the second day, Allenby's forces were holding the three sides of a rectangle within which were trapped the entire Turkish Eighth and Seventh Armies. Their only avenues of escape lay to the east across the Jordan; but these were fast being closed to

them by divisions of the XX Corps who were advancing
northwards towards Nablus and eastwards in the direction
of 'Amman. While in the hilly region beyond the Jordan,
the Arab forces, having surrounded Dar'a, were closing in
on the II Corps in Ma'an. To make matters worse for the
demoralised Turks, the whole countryside had risen on a
signal from Faisal.

Seldom had a victory been so complete. The Eighth Army
was no more: with the exception of a German unit and a
rabble of stragglers, its manhood was either killed or captured. Of the Seventh Army, only a few scattered battalions
were able to retreat towards Dar'a. There remained the
Fourth Army on the other side of Jordan, the II Corps in
Ma'an and the Second Army in the north, all of whom were
to meet with a similar fate in the days that followed.

9.

The story of the days that followed is the tale of the consummation of the Turkish rout and of the capture of
Damascus and, later, of Aleppo.

First, came the retreat of the troops in 'Amman and
Ma'an, which began on the 22nd; and, as soon as it had
begun, a British mounted brigade crossed the Jordan and
advanced on 'Amman which it occupied on the 25th. The
Fourth Army had to make its retreat on foot as the railway-
line to Dar'a had been destroyed, and was left to go to its
doom while the British commanding officer remained in
'Amman to secure the surrender of the Turkish II Corps
retreating from Ma'an which the Arabs had occupied on the
23rd. Further north, the Arabs were closing in on Dar'a
which they occupied on the 27th, while other contingents led
by 'Auda and Nuri Sha'lan captured Edra' and Ghazaleh,
making a haul of 3,500 prisoners in two days. Meanwhile,
British cavalry had forced their way across the Jordan to the
south and north of the Sea of Galilee and were riding at a
gallop, fighting their way stubbornly towards Damascus.
The Arab regulars covered their right flank, dogging the steps

of the Fourth Army; while the tribal hosts, always at their deadliest in a war of movement, charged wildly at the retreating Turks, galloping and fighting as they went, in a mad race towards the goal of the Revolt.

The first to arrive were the Sharif Naser and Nuri Sha'lan with their forces who, having ridden seventy miles in twenty-four hours, fighting part of the way, reached the outskirts of Damascus on the evening of the 30th of September; but, in deference to the wishes expressed by the commander-in-chief, they abstained from entering it that night and contented themselves with sending in a strong contingent to carry the tidings to the population and a message enjoining the setting up of an Arab government. This had already been done, and Naser's messengers, as they reached the main square, beheld the Arab flag flying. Four hundred years of Ottoman domination had passed into history.

Early on the following day – the 1st of October – a detachment of British cavalry entered the town, closely followed by the Sharif Naser, Nuri Sha'lan and their retinues. Two days later, Allenby drove in from Jerusalem just as Faisal, attended by some 1,200 retainers, was making his entry on horseback at full gallop into the former capital of the Arab Empire.

Damascus was in a frenzy of joy and gave itself over wholly to its emotion. I must leave it to other pens than mine to describe the scenes of enthusiasm with which the arrival of the victors, British and Arab alike, were greeted. Those who were present say that they were unforgettable and that a population famed for the vigour of its impulses outdid itself in a riot of delirious thanksgiving. It seemed as though the sufferings of the four hideous years, sharpening the city's capacity to feel, had intensified its passion; and that the nightmare of Jemal's tyranny had quickened its instincts. The climax occurred when Faisal entered the city and appeared as the embodiment of freedom to a people to whom freedom meant, not merely an escape, but also a long-dreamt fulfilment.

10.

The rest of Syria was occupied before October was out, as the result of two distinct operations. One line of advance was along the coast through Tyre and Sidon to Bairut and Tripoli; the other followed an inland course through Homs, Hama and Aleppo. The Arabs played no part in the first, but had a considerable share in the second.

The coastal advance began on the 3rd from Haifa and Acre which had been occupied soon after Allenby's breakthrough. A British division set out along the historic and beautiful highway leading northwards from Acre, and occupied Tyre on the 4th and Sidon on the 6th. The march was in the nature of a military promenade, for no enemy resistance was encountered, and the troops were everywhere received with demonstrations of welcome. They entered Bairut on the 8th, and a detachment continued the march on to Tripoli which was occupied five days later.

Meanwhile, Allenby had issued orders for a northward advance from Damascus to Aleppo, which seemed a more difficult undertaking. The British forces were feeling the strain of the hard campaign, made worse by an alarming outbreak of sickness and by the difficulty of ensuring supplies at that distance from the base. Moreover, there were considerable bodies of the enemy at different points on the route, and it was believed that a strong concentration was being formed in the north to defend Aleppo. All those obstacles were overcome, and, here again, success was achieved by British and Arab forces acting in combination.

As a British division was moving along the main road, a brigade of Arab regulars was covering its right flank, while the Sharif Naser at the head of a force of irregulars went to attack Homs from the east. He reached it on the 15th, one day ahead of the British advance column, and found that the Turks had withdrawn. Two days later, he occupied Hama, again without opposition. But a stiff resistance was encountered on the outskirts of Aleppo. Mustafa Pasha

Kemal was in command, at the head of a strong and well-equipped corps of two divisions. A plan was drawn up for a concerted attack by the British cavalry and the Arab regulars to take place on the 26th. But during the afternoon of the 25th, Arab tribal forces penetrated into the city and fell on the garrison with such vigour that they compelled its commander to withdraw and to order the retirement of the two divisions guarding Aleppo on the south; and both the British cavalry and the Arab regulars marched in on the morning of the 26th, while an Indian cavalry brigade was gallantly repelling a determined attack by Mustafa Pasha Kemal a few miles to the north of the city. On the 29th, a detachment of the Sharif Naser's forces occupied the junction at Muslemiya where the railway from Constantinople divides into its Syrian and Mesopotamian branches, and its occupation marked the northernmost limit of the Allied advance, for, on the following day, Turkey signed the Mudros Armistice.

11.

The occupation of Bairut and Aleppo and almost every other town in Syria gave rise to similar scenes of rejoicing as had greeted the liberators in Damascus. And, as in Damascus, the emotion aroused by the prospect of political freedom was raised to a delirium of joy at the deliverance from suffering. If the rejoicing seemed less exuberant in Bairut and the Lebanon, this was only because, in point of deprivation and famine, they had had by far the greatest share.

Statistics give only a partial picture where the sufferings of individuals are concerned, yet there is that in the census of deaths in certain parts of Syria that reveals something of the horrors that had to be endured. The conditions depicted in an earlier chapter relate to the famine of 1916, and it is not an exaggeration to say that the ravages caused by starvation had increased tenfold in the two years that followed. Estimates vary between wide limits. Certainly not less than

300.000 people died of hunger or of diseases due to malnutrition.

In the Lebanon which had the worst of the visitation whole villages perished; others had their population reduced to less than one half, and cases were known of villagers tramping the countryside to die out of sight of their starving womenfolk and children. One quotation will suffice: it is from a report written by an American resident of standing.[1]

> 'During a two-day journey through the Lebanon with the chairman of the American Red Cross in Bairut we made house-to-house visits in several villages. The scenes were indescribable, whole families writhing in agony on the bare floor of their miserable huts, whose moans could be heard a block away. Every piece of their household effects had been sold to buy bread, and in many cases the tiles of the roofs had shared the same fate. Hundreds of houses whose owners had died were empty and were rapidly falling to pieces. It is conservatively estimated that not less than 120,000 persons have died of actual starvation during the last two years in the Lebanon alone. . . .'

This was written in July 1917. Between that date and the occupation of Bairut fifteen months later, conditions became infinitely worse. One shrinks from a recital of particular cases, and there is at any rate this virtue in statistics, that there is no place in them for the portrayal of the agony of a human being. That 300,000 died of starvation in Syria during the War is not open to doubt. The actual figure may be as high as 350,000. Some 3,000 persons were sent into detention or exile, of whom many died under ill-treatment. Taking into account losses due to military service, Syria's contribution to the holocaust of the War must have been not far short of half a million lives out of a total population of considerably under four million – a higher percentage, probably, than that of any other belligerent.

[1] The United States was not technically at war with Turkey. Diplomatic relations between the two governments were severed, but there was no declaration of war on either side. American residents were allowed unmolested in Syria, and a great deal of valuable relief work was carried out by them, and particularly by the American community in Bairut.

The sufferings endured by the population were not un-connected with their political aspirations and, more particu-larly, with their sympathies with the cause of the Allies. As we have seen, it was the discovery of incriminating docu-ments in the archives of the French consulates that had led to the trial and execution of a number of prominent citizens, and the deportation into exile of hundreds of others; and, in the vast majority of cases, sentence had been passed on the ground of some actual or presumed transaction with one or other of the Allied Powers, or of supposed sympathy with their cause. The famine, it will be remembered, was due to a variety of causes; but behind those causes there lay a deliberate motive which was vindictive. On instructions from Jemal Pasha, facilities for the purchase of corn were granted or withheld on political grounds. In the Lebanon where whole sections of the population were known to be disaffected and were suspected of being in sympathy, if not in active league, with the Allies, the discrimination was applied wholesale and with a dastardly indifference to its consequences.

The effects of these visitations were only too visible when the British forces entered Bairut, and a tribute is owed them for the speed and the efficacy with which they distributed food and clothing from their own stores of supplies. The crews of the French destroyers who had entered Bairut harbour on the eve of the arrival of the British were equally helpful. Still more creditable were the efforts made in the months that followed, to provide necessities on a larger scale to the destitute population in the inland districts, when French, British and American relief agencies sprang up, that vied with each other in a humane and honourable competition.

CHAPTER XIII

PLEDGES AND COUNTER-PLEDGES

I.

As the War proceeded, the Entente Powers became increasingly concerned with the prospect of Turkey's disruption. Hitherto, in spite of the considerable shrinkage of its territory, the Ottoman Empire had maintained its essential integrity largely owing to the jealousies amongst the Powers. The old slogan of the European Concert, so vehemently championed by Palmerston, had been adopted as the basis of an agreed policy for preventing the break-up of the Sultan's empire; and that policy had prevailed throughout the nineteenth century and up to the outbreak of the War. It had all the advantages of a self-denying ordinance without any of its drawbacks, since it had substantially achieved its professed object and yet allowed each of the Powers in turn to rob the Sultan of one or other of his coveted dominions. In the twoscore years that had elapsed between 'Adbul-Hamid's accession and the War of 1914, the Sultan had had to surrender several rich provinces in Asia Minor to Russia, Cyprus and Egypt to Great Britain, Tunisia to France, Libya to Italy, and Bosnia-Herzegovina to Austria. To say nothing of those Balkan provinces which, with the help of Russia, had succeeded in casting off the Turkish yoke.

Now that Turkey was in the War, a host of pent-up desires began to sniff their way towards gratification. Russia wanted Constantinople and the Straits; France claimed Syria; Great Britain was beginning to feel the need of an overland route to the East and of whatever else might be necessary to neutralise France's and Russia's gains; Italy had designs on Asia Minor; and the Government of India turned hungry eyes towards Iraq. Negotiations were opened early in 1915, and presently a series of secret agreements were concluded at various dates in the first three years of the War, in which the four Allies helped themselves handsomely to slices of the Ottoman Empire.

In the course of carving up the Sultan's dominions, Great Britain found herself driven to contract certain fresh obligations, some of which conflicted with, while others confirmed, the pledges she had given in 1915 through Sir Henry McMahon to the Arabs.

2.

The first of those commitments – the Sykes-Picot Agreement, as it is generally called – was entered into by Great Britain with France and Russia, in the spring of 1916. No sooner had Sir Henry McMahon clinched his bargain with the Sharif Husain than conversations were opened in London by the Foreign Office with the French Government, of which the object was to come to some arrangement whereby France's pretensions with regard to Syria might be made to square with the British pledges to the Arabs. For various reasons, the Foreign Office chose to withhold from the French the terms, and perhaps even the fact, of the compact made with the Sharif Husain; and this lack of candour, which was afterwards deeply – and rightly – resented by the French, gave from the very start a false basis to the negotiations. When the preliminaries were over, each of the two governments delegated a representative to confer with one another. The French delegate was Monsieur F. Georges-Picot who had served in Syria as consul-general in Bairut in the years preceding the War. His British colleague was Sir Mark Sykes whose fame as a student of Eastern affairs had been established by his extensive travels in the highways and byways of the Ottoman Empire as well as by his writings.

The two delegates together drew up a scheme for the disposal of those parts of the Ottoman Empire which were coveted by Great Britain and France. They were then instructed to proceed to Petrograd in order to discuss their proposals with the Russian Government. Negotiations were opened there about the middle of March 1916, and resulted in a three-cornered understanding expressed in draft notes to be exchanged between the three governments; and presently the notes were formally exchanged on various dates in April and May of that year. In them were defined the Ottoman territories which each of the three Powers desired the other two to recognise as its sphere of influence, and they contained, besides, miscellaneous provisions for safeguarding the interests of each Power in the areas allocated to the other two.

So far as the allocation of territory went, the three Powers had helped themselves to generous slices of the Sultan's dominions. Russia earmarked Constantinople with a few miles of hinterland on either side of the Bosporus for herself, as well as a large portion of Eastern Anatolia comprising practically the whole of the four vilayets which adjoined the Turco-Russian frontier. France reserved to herself the greater part of Syria, a considerable portion of Southern Anatolia and the Mosul district in Iraq [shown Blue on the map]. Great Britain's share [shown Red on the map] was made up of a band of territory running from the southernmost extremity of Syria across to Iraq where it opened out fanwise to include Baghdad and Basra and the whole of the country between the Persian Gulf and the area assigned to France; it also comprised the ports of Haifa and Acre with a small strip of hinterland. Yet another area [shown Brown on the map] comprising a portion of what is now known as Palestine was reserved for a special international régime of its own.

With the spheres earmarked for Russia we are not directly concerned, since they fell outside the regions peopled by Arabs. The French and British spheres and the international Brown area, on the other hand, comprised the whole of Syria and Iraq which, according to the Agreement,[1] were to be placed under some form of European tutelage. Each of the French and British areas was to be regarded as consisting of two parts, differentiated from each other according to the form of government which it was intended they should have. France's share was divided into the 'Blue' and the 'A' areas, Great Britain's into the 'Red' and the 'B' areas. In the Blue and Red areas, France and Great Britain were to be free to establish an administration of their own. The Agreement did not expressly provide for annexation, nor did it exclude it, but left it open to the Powers to annex any part or the whole of the Blue and Red areas if they wished. In each of the A and B areas, the Agreement provided for an administration under Arab suzerainty to be recognised and upheld by the Power concerned, and reserved to France or Great Britain, as the case might be, priority in economic enterprise and the exclusive right to supply the future Arab administration with whatever foreign officials and advisers it might need.

The special provisions made for the Brown (Palestine) area were the outcome of a conflict of aims between the three Powers. France had pressed her desire to have the whole of Syria (including Palestine) placed in her sphere. Great Britain had opposed that, for two main reasons: one was that she desired to have under her own control in the Haifa-Acre bay a port to serve as an outlet from Iraq to the Mediterranean; the other was that she did not relish the prospect of France or any other Great Power establishing herself in immediate proximity to the Suez Canal.

This attitude was the outcome of a new trend in Great Britain's Eastern policy, and was prompted by a growing recognition of the strategic significance of overland communications in the Imperial scheme. During his term of office in Egypt, Kitchener had made frequent representations to Whitehall about the geographical importance of Southern

---

[1] The text of the Agreement, in so far as it relates to the Arab provinces of the Ottoman Empire, will be found in Appendix B. It has often been published before, but is reproduced at the end of this book for convenience of reference.

Syria (from the Haifa-Acre bay on the Mediterranean to the Gulf of 'Aqaba on the Red Sea) both as a bulwark to the Suez Canal and as an overland highway to the East; and there is reason to believe that the survey of the Sinai Peninsula which Colonel S. F. Newcombe of the Royal Engineers carried out in 1914 was undertaken at Kitchener's instigation. In any case, the results of the survey had confirmed him in his views and enabled him to press them home with greater force when, after the outbreak of the War, he occupied a seat in the Cabinet. His views gained ground and were substantially adopted by an official committee appointed by the Prime Minister to consider France's and Russia's claims to portions of the Ottoman Empire in the light of British interests. In June 1915, the Committee had reported that, in their view, the French claim might be conceded only in respect of Northern Syria, and that the southern part, roughly corresponding to Palestine, should be excluded from the area of French influence and reserved for special treatment. It was probably in pursuance of that recommendation that Sir Henry McMahon was instructed, in his negotiations with the Sharif Husain, to reserve only the coastal regions of Northern Syria in favour of France, and not Palestine as well.

The argument used to oppose the French claim to Palestine was that the existence of the Holy Places in and around Jerusalem would call for a special régime. The French countered by proposing that Jerusalem and Bethlehem with their immediate surroundings should form a separate enclave to be subjected to a special régime of international control to suit its sacred character, but that the rest of Palestine should continue to form an integral part of Syria.

But when the discussions were resumed in Petrograd, Russia put forward claims of her own. She had schools and convents and holy sites in her care all over the Holy Land, notably in Nazareth, Nablus and Hebron, far beyond the limits of the small enclave proposed by France. At first she attempted to stake a claim to a Russian protectorate over the Holy Land, but that was resisted by both Great Britain and France. Then, seeing the wisdom of dropping that claim

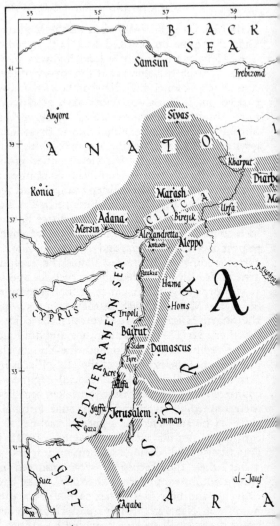

THE PARTITION
AS DEVISED IN THE 1916

BLUE AREA

SYRIA AND IRAQ
("SYKES-PICOT") AGREEMENT.

AREA ⧄ (See page 249)

for the time being, she declared her willingness to consent to a régime of international control provided it applied to the whole of the Holy Land in such a way as to include all the Russian establishments and sites within the zone of international administration. This proposal brought Great Britain round to Russia's side, and France had to give way. And so the Brown area came into being.

3.

The Sykes-Picot Agreement is a shocking document. It is not only the product of greed at its worst, that is to say, of greed allied to suspicion and so leading to stupidity: it also stands out as a startling piece of double-dealing.

A glance at the map will reveal the faults of its basic provisions. Taken together, Syria and Iraq with the sparsely inhabited or desert regions between them form a rough rectangle of which three sides – the north, the east and the south sides – are land-bound, while the fourth is formed by the Mediterranean seaboard on the west. The population inhabiting it is made up of Arabic-speaking communities who had reached different stages of development, those occupying the eastern and western extremities of the rectangle (that is to say, the coastal regions of the Mediterranean seaboard and the lower basins of the Tigris and the Euphrates) being intellectually more advanced and politically more developed than those, mainly nomadic, who lived in the inland regions. In spite of various social and confessional differences, the population was, in its broader characteristics, homogeneous. The fact of a common language and culture made for unity, and the growth of the national consciousness had already made its influence felt.

What the Sykes-Picot Agreement did was, first, to cut up the Arab Rectangle in such a manner as to place artificial obstacles in the way of unity. That may have been the deliberate intention of its authors – an unconscious echo perhaps of Palmerston's hostility to the idea of a stable Arab state planting itself across the overland route to India; but it was none the less retrograde and in conflict with the natural forces at work. An awakening had taken place since Palmerston's days, and the national movement was now a force with the plank of Arab unity as well as independence in the forefront of its aims. Whatever gains the Allied Powers may have hoped to derive from the partition of that territory, it showed a lack of perspicacity on their part to have imagined that it could make for a peaceful or a lasting settlement.

Another peculiarity of the Agreement was that it provided for a topsy-turvy political structure in which the first were to come last and the last first. The inhabitants of Syria and Iraq were politically more developed and mature than the inhabitants of the inland regions. Yet the Agreement provided that the greater part of Syria and Iraq might be placed under a régime of direct foreign administration, while the inland regions were in any case to form independent Arab States. The absurdity of these provisions is particularly evident in the case of the regions destined to form the British sphere of influence. The Red area, comprising Baghdad and Basra, the two centres of politically-minded activity in Iraq, was to be placed under tutelage and denied even the outward forms of self-government; whereas area B, which is as to two thirds of its extent a semi-desert steppe and whose population lagged far behind in point of political experience and maturity, was recognised as being entitled to independent status. It was like putting the adults to school and sending the pupils of the elementary classes out into the world.

But more serious even than those errors of judgment was the breach of faith. The Agreement had been negotiated and concluded without the knowledge of the Sharif Husain, and it contained provisions which were in direct conflict with the terms of Sir Henry McMahon's compact with him. Worse still, the fact of its conclusion was dishonestly concealed from him because it was realised that, were he to have been apprised of it, he would have unhesitatingly denounced his alliance with Great Britain. He only heard of the existence of the Agreement some eighteen months later, in circumstances which will be related presently.

One of the most puzzling facts about the Agreement is that Sir Mark Sykes was a party to it. No one who knew Sykes would think of associating his name with anything approaching stupidity or duplicity. Among his outstanding traits were an unmistakable genuineness and an infectious enthusiasm for the causes he had at heart. And as for knowledge, he was probably better acquainted with the Arab problem than any of the diplomats with whom he collaborated. The process by which he may have persuaded himself to believe in the soundness, let alone the honesty, of the Sykes-Picot Agreement remains a mystery.

The explanation is partly psychological. His mind was both perceptive and quick, and at the same time strangely inattentive and undiscerning; and, in his nature, he had something of the improvidence as well as all the warmth of the enthusiast. He knew a good deal about the Arabs at first hand, but his knowledge was as remarkable for its gaps as for its range, and his judgments alternated between perspicacity and incomprehension, as though his mental vision were patterned like a chess-board in which the white squares stood for insight and the black for the obscurities and the uncertainties of knowledge acquired in haste. This placed him at a disadvantage in the game of diplomatic bargaining, especially when there were ideas to champion as well as interests to serve; and when he found himself pitted against Picot and Sazonoff, both of whom were single-minded in their determination to grab all that they could, he gradually drifted out of the world of his own ideas into the fool's paradise invented by the greed and the jealousies of the three Powers.

As the War proceeded and Sykes saw more of the forces at work in the Arab world, he moved away from the position he had drifted into in 1916; and already in the autumn of 1917, he was known to be entertaining doubts as to the practical and perhaps the moral validity of the Sykes-Picot Agreement. He had gone out to the East again, paid a visit to King Husain at Jedda, and had conversations with the Arab leaders in Cairo. The strength of the desire for independence and for unity began to dawn on him and, with it, the injustice and the folly of the partition envisaged in the Agreement. He continued to believe that the maintenance of the Anglo-French entente should be the cornerstone of British policy in the East; but, now that a few of the black squares in his mental chess-board had turned to white, his moral and political senses rebelled against the strangling of a movement which he had discovered to be stronger and more coherent than he had reckoned. A year later still, he had moved even further from the narrow conceptions of the Agreement, and in a letter he wrote to Lord Robert Cecil in October 1918, he urged that, for the sake of general world interests, Great Britain should do all in her power 'to foster and revive Arab civilisation and promote Arab unity with a view of preparing them [sc. the Arabic-speaking peoples of Asia] for ultimate independence'.[1]

4.

This evolution had probably not begun to take place in Sir Mark Sykes's mind in May 1917, when he went to Jedda to confer with King Husain. M. Picot had arrived in Cairo at the head of a mission whose task was to further the cause of French interests in Syria by means of political action among the Arab leaders in Egypt. The arrival of the mission and the rumours which began to circulate in connexion with its activities had aroused King Husain's apprehensions, and he asked Sir Reginald Wingate (who had succeeded Sir Henry McMahon as High Commissioner) for assurances as to the mission's intentions. At Wingate's suggestion, the Foreign Office instructed Sykes to travel to Jedda to try and allay the King's anxieties as best he might, and to pave the way for the visit which the French Government wished Picot to pay him.

Here was an opportunity for putting the whole position

[1] Shane Leslie, *Mark Sykes: His Life and Letters*, (London, 1923).

candidly before Husain, in consideration – if for no other reason – of the loyalty with which he was carrying out his share of the Anglo-Arab compact. But it was not taken. Sykes went to Jedda early in May, saw the King and, about a fortnight later, returned with Picot for further interviews. They had a long audience of the King on May 19, and another on the following day, at which the future of the Arab countries and its relation to British and French interests was lengthily discussed. What passed at those interviews has never been fully made public; but this much is certain, that the two delegates left Jedda without disclosing to King Husain the terms of the Sykes-Picot Agreement. Subsequent events show that they did not even mention its existence except by general allusions to Anglo-French understanding and solidarity.

In the years that followed the War, Husain used to assert in the most emphatic terms that no mention of an Allied pact relating to Arab territories had been made at those or any other interviews, and that the first inkling he had had of it was when its existence was revealed to him by the Turks. He maintained that the Jedda discussions in May 1917 had turned mainly on the question of whether the Arabs would accept to recognise a French sphere of influence in the coastal regions of northern Syria, that is to say in the Lebanon. His attitude appears to have been that he was precluded, by his position as the authorised spokesman of the national movement, from acquiescing in any infringement of Arab sovereignty, and that the furthest he would go was to undertake to consult the leaders of the Movement and try to induce them to consent to some arrangement with France in the Lebanon, similar to that made with Great Britain in regard to Iraq in the McMahon Correspondence, that is to say to a partnership between France and an Arab administration in the Lebanon, limited to a fixed period of years during which France would aid the administration with a subsidy and promote her interests within the framework of Arab sovereignty.

It was not until six months later, that is to say in December 1917, that Husain heard of the existence and the terms of the Sykes-Picot Agreement, and the information which reached him came from enemy sources. The Bolshevik party had seized power in Russia a month previously, and one of their first acts had been to publish certain secret documents from the archives of the Imperial Ministry of Foreign Affairs. Amongst those were the texts of the Agreement of 1916, which the Turks lost no time in forwarding to Husain with an offer for a Turco-Arab separate peace.

5.

This offer emanated from Jemal Pasha in the last weeks of his tenure of office in Syria, and was represented by him as an overture made on behalf of the Ottoman Government and endorsed by their German allies. In the last week of November 1917, Jemal despatched a secret emissary to 'Aqaba carrying a letter from him to the Amir Faisal and another to Ja'far Pasha. The letters were dated November 26. The tone and the contents of each were skilfully designed to appeal to the personality of the addressee; but their purport was the same.

The letter addressed to Faisal was worded as an appeal from one serious-minded Moslem to another: that it was the duty of those who cared for the glory of Islam to dedicate their energies, and if need be their lives, to its service; that Faisal and his father had been misled by promises of Arab independence into rebelling against the supreme authority in Islam; that those promises had now been shown to have been utterly mendacious since the true intentions of the Allies were to partition the Arab countries and place them under foreign masters: French in Syria, British in Iraq and International in Palestine; and that the only course left for the Arabs to take was to return to the Ottoman fold and secure their legitimate rights by coming to an understanding with the Turks. The letter concluded with an invitation to Faisal to come in person to Damascus under promise of a

253

safe-conduct, in order to open negotiations. It also contained on a separate sheet an outline of the terms on which the Turks were prepared to negotiate. These terms envisaged the grant of the fullest autonomy to all the Arab provinces of the Empire, in which their nationalist aspirations would be fully met; and there was a clause to say that, in the event of the negotiations resulting in an agreement, as there was every reason to believe they should, the validity of its terms would be secured not only by the Sultan's ratification, but also by a collateral guarantee from the German Government.

Both in his letter to Faisal and in his shorter communication to Ja'far, Jemal Pasha stressed the significance of the Sykes-Picot Agreement as proving that the Arabs had suffered themselves to be duped by the Allies. He went so far as to say that, had Great Britain's promises meant what they said, he might have seen some sense, albeit misguided, in the Arab Revolt, and possibly even excused it. But since it was now proved beyond all doubt that the Allies harboured secret designs which were the very negation of Arab independence, then it behoved the Arab leaders to undeceive themselves and realise that their co-operation with the Allies which they fondly imagined would gain them independence, was in reality leading to the enslavement of the Arab countries to France, Great Britain and Russia.

So anxious were the Turkish Government and their German allies to ensure the success of their overtures to the Arabs that they caused a public announcement to be made. On the 4th of December, at a command banquet held in Bairut in his honour, Jemal Pasha delivered a speech in which he stated openly that he had made overtures to the Sharif Husain. The speech – by far the most revealing ever made by Jemal in Syria – created a profound impression. In addition to a review of the military situation, which was intended as an apologia for his own failure, Jemal gave his hearers an account of the harm wrought by the Arab Revolt, not only to the unity of Islam, but also to those very interests which the leaders of the Revolt professed to serve.

Delivered as it was a few days before the fall of Jerusalem, at a time when Jemal knew that his own recall was imminent, the speech was a mixture of self-justification and propaganda, and parts of it deserve to be reproduced for the light they throw on the Turkish concern for a reconciliation with the Arabs:[1]

' .... I have been at pains to discover the process by which the British had won over the Sharif Husain. The terms of the secret Agreement just published in Petrograd, and certain information brought by recent comers, have thrown light on the facts. The facts are that, in the early part of 1916, Great Britain, France, Russia and Italy[2] entered into a secret compact in which they envisaged the establishment of an independent Arab State composed of all the Arab provinces of the Ottoman Empire, to be placed under the tutelage and protectorate of those Powers. . . . In reality, the Agreement was a device for bringing about an Arab revolt to suit the designs of the British who, needing tools and catspaws to serve their own ends, encouraged certain Arabs to rebel by giving them mendacious promises and hoodwinking them with false hopes. . . .

'Eventually, the unfortunate Sharif Husain fell into the trap laid for him by the British, allowed himself to be ensnared by their cajoleries, and committed his offence against the unity and the majesty of Islam. And the British, having received his assurance that he would revolt, then decided to secure the defence of the Suez Canal by advancing in the Sinai Peninsula. In fact, it was only after they had made certain of the Sharif's defection that they crossed the Canal. That they are outside the gates of Jerusalem to-day is the direct outcome of the Sharif's revolt in Mecca.

'Were not the liberation promised to the Sharif Husain by the British a mirage and a delusion, had there been some prospect, however remote, of his dreams of independence being realised, I might have conceded some speck of reason to the revolt in the Hejaz. But, the real intentions of the

---

[1] The text of the speech is given in full in *al-Sharq*, nos. 464–5, from which the extracts given above are taken.

[2] In actual fact, Italy was not a party to the Agreement of 1916, the existence of which was not divulged to her by the three other Powers. It was not until the spring of 1917 that the Italian Government, having discovered the existence of the Agreement, staked a claim to a portion of Asia Minor and had her claim formally recognised by France and Great Britain at the conference of St. Jean-de-Maurienne.

British are now known: it has not taken them so very long to come to light. And thus will the Sharif Husain who, as I say, is responsible for the enemy's arrival at the ramparts of Jerusalem be made to suffer the humiliation, which he has brought upon himself, of having bartered the dignity conferred upon him by the Caliph of Islam for a state of enslavement to the British. . . .

'I have recently addressed a letter to the Sharif, in which I depicted the facts in their true light and represented to him the gravity and the dangers of the present situation. If he is a true Moslem and has the qualities and sentiments of a real Arab, he will turn against the British and return to the fold of the Caliph and of Islam. In thus writing to him, I have performed what I regard as my duty to our Faith, and I pray God that He may inspire the Sharif to follow the way of wisdom, truth and divine guidance. . . .'

The speech was delivered in Turkish and a careful translation read out in Arabic by the Mufti of the Fourth Army. All newspapers in Syria were enjoined to print the full text, and copies were sent to Madina whence they were smuggled into Mecca. The evidence of contemporary witnesses, as well as that of the speech itself, shows that the Turkish expectations of success for these peace overtures were pitched very high.

6.

Faisal returned no answer, but contented himself with forwarding the letters post-haste to his father; and Husain, although gravely perturbed, refused to have any truck with the enemy. He instructed Faisal to send Jemal a curt rejection of his peace overtures and, having done that, forwarded the whole correspondence to the High Commissioner in Egypt with a request for an explanation regarding the secret Agreement mentioned by Jemal.

Sir Reginald Wingate, much embarrassed, referred the matter to the Foreign Office. Here was an opportunity presenting itself to the British Government for extricating themselves from a false position by the simple process of dealing as loyally with their ally as he was dealing with them; but they did not take it. And this is what they did. They telegraphed the text of a message from the Foreign Secretary (Mr. Balfour) to King Husain, of which the least that can be said is that it was a piece of deliberate equivocation. They did not admit or deny the authenticity of the Petrograd disclosures, but gave a misleading presentation of the character and scope of the Agreement in terms implying that Husain should regard Jemal's version as another instance of Turkish intrigue. The message was conveyed to Husain in a telegram to him from Wingate, followed up by a formal note from the acting British Agent at Jedda to the King of the Hejaz.

The telegram from Wingate was to the following effect:[1]

> Documents found by Bolsheviki in Petrograd Foreign Ministry do not constitute an actually concluded agreement but consist of records of provisional exchanges and conversations between Great Britain, France and Russia, which were held in the early days of the War, and before the Arab Revolt, with a view to avoiding difficulties between the Powers in the prosecution of the war with Turkey.
>
> Whether from ignorance or from malice Jemal Pasha has distorted the original purpose of the understanding between the Powers and overlooked its stipulations regarding the consent of the populations concerned and the safeguarding of their interests. He has also ignored the fact that the subsequent outbreak and the striking success of the Arab Revolt, as well as the withdrawal of Russia, had long ago created an altogether different situation.

The text of the note, which is dated the 8th of February 1918, is also available in the original Arabic in which it reached Husain, and a translation of it is given in Appendix C. It opens with a tribute to the Arab King for having loyally informed his allies of the peace offer made to him, and for his wisdom in rejecting it. It makes no mention of the Agreement of 1916 which had furnished the Turks with a pretext for their overtures of peace, but tries to set Husain's

---

[1] The text given here is my translation of the Arabic version which appeared in an article by ‘Auni bey ‘Abdul-Hadi in *al-Jami‘a al-Islamiya* (Jaffa), September 14, 1934.

mind at ease by representing Jemal's offer as a mere Turkish device designed to sow dissension between the Arabs and the Allies. It concludes with an emphatic assurance that Great Britain, in accordance with her former pledge, would stand by the Arabs in their struggle for liberation and assist them in obtaining their freedom.

In the light of the facts so far as they are now known, the message sent out in Mr. Balfour's name was a dishonest communication. The Turkish peace offer had raised doubts in King Husain's mind, and he had sought to verify his doubts in the only way open to an honest man – that of placing them before his allies. The reply he received was obviously designed to deceive him, for it not only evaded the issue, namely, that of whether or not it was true that the Allied Powers had concluded secret agreements affecting the future disposal of the Arab countries, but it clothed the evasion in language which implied that no such agreements had been concluded. And Husain, with his faith in British standards of fair dealing still unshaken, took the disingenuous message at its face value and set his mind at rest.

7.

Meanwhile, after several months of close negotiation with Jewish leaders in England, the British Government had entered into yet another commitment which conflicted with their previous pledges to the Arabs. This was the famous Balfour Declaration; and this is, briefly, how it came to be issued.

Shortly after the outbreak of the War, a group of Zionist leaders in England set to work to enlist the sympathy of the Government to their cause. Hitherto, Zionist effort in the political field had mainly concentrated on persuading the rulers of Turkey, by a variety of means, to permit an increased Jewish colonisation of Palestine. The effort had not met with success: 'Abdul-Hamid had discouraged it point-blank; while the Young Turks who, in view of the strong Jewish influence in the counsels of the C.U.P., were

inclined at first to listen to Zionist proposals, found it prudent
eventually to reject them, especially after an angry scene in
the Ottoman Chamber in the autumn of 1912 when Arab
deputies had protested against the acquisition by Jews of a
large area of arable land in the Plain of Esdraelon and the
threatened dispossession of the Arab peasants. The centre
of Zionist activity, at the outbreak of war, was in Berlin.
When Turkey joined the Central Powers, Zionist leaders
found it expedient to cultivate the Allied side as well, so that,
in the event of the War resulting in a disruption of the Ottoman Empire, the Zionist cause might be ensured a sympathetic hearing.

The task which the Zionists in England, led by Dr. Chaim
Weizmann, had set themselves, was no easy one. The
majority of influential English Jews were opposed to Zionism
or, more exactly, to the nationalistic idea inherent in political
Zionism. Outside the ranks of Jewry, the Zionist cause had
one powerful supporter in C. P. Scott, then editor of the
Manchester Guardian, and another in A. J. Balfour; but no
other known partisans of any eminence until Mr. Lloyd
George, on being approached by Dr. Weizmann, gave his
prompt adhesion to the movement. An effort was then
made to secure the goodwill of the Cabinet. Mr. Herbert
(now Lord) Samuel, who was a member of the Asquith Government, approached the Prime Minister and some of his
colleagues. But Asquith turned out to be unsympathetic,
and the effort led to no positive result.[1] It was only some
two years later, when Mr. Lloyd George had succeeded
Asquith as Prime Minister, with Balfour as his Foreign Secretary, that negotiations were for the first time opened between the Zionist leaders and an authorised representative
of the Government.

By that time, much had happened that tied the hands of

[1] Mr. Herbert Samuel's representations were embodied in a memorandum
in which he strongly urged the annexation of Palestine by Great Britain,
with a view to settling some three or four million Jews. Mr. Asquith, to
use his own phrase, was 'not attracted' by the proposal. Ten years later,
after a visit to Palestine, he wrote: 'The talk of making Palestine into a
Jewish "National Home" seems to me as fantastic as it always has done.'
Memories and Reflections, 1928, Vol. II.

the British Government in their freedom of decision with regard to the future of Palestine. In the first place, the bargain concluded with the Sharif Husain in 1915 committed Great Britain to recognising and upholding an independent Arab State in an area from which, as we have seen, Palestine had not been excluded. In the second place, the provisions of the Sykes-Picot Agreement envisaged the placing of the Holy Land under some form of international administration in the setting up of which not only France and Russia and the other Allies, but also the Sharif of Mecca, were to have their say. Thirdly, the hostility of an influential section of Anglo-Jewry had hardened to such a pitch that they had declared their irrevocable opposition to the establishment of the Jewish State which the Zionists were advocating; and a campaign had begun, led by the Board of Deputies of British Jews and the Anglo-Jewish Association – the two most representative bodies in English Jewry – of which the object was to dissuade the Government from acceding to the wishes of the Zionists.[1] The views voiced by those two bodies had a spokesman in the Cabinet itself, in the person of the late Edwin Montagu, then Secretary of State for India.

Undeterred, however, by those obstacles, Mr. Lloyd George appointed Sir Mark Sykes to open negotiations with the Zionists. What his motives were in wishing to come to an understanding with the Zionist leaders, and what the considerations were which induced the British Government eventually to issue the Balfour Declaration are questions to which the answers have been obscured by a smoke-screen of legend and propaganda. It is alleged, for instance, that the Jews used their financial and political influence to bring the United States into the War on the side of the Entente and that the Balfour Declaration was a reward for actual services rendered. All the published evidence goes to disprove that allegation, and one can only infer either that it does not rest on any foundation or, if it does, that the services rendered by

[1] More detailed information on this point is available in *Reports of the Executive of the Zionist Organisation to the XIIth Zionist Congress*, I. Political Report (National Labour Press, London, 1921), to which I am indebted for material used in this chapter.

international Jewry in that connexion were of so occult a nature that they have hitherto escaped the scrutiny of all the historians of America's intervention. Again, it is often stated that the Balfour Declaration was issued in return for promises pledging large subscriptions from Jewish sources to war-loan funds; but that, too, may safely be discounted. The available evidence is too fragmentary to be of value and, so far as it goes, tends to show that the most substantial purchases of British war-loan stock that can be traced to Jewish sources in 1917 and 1918 were made in the name of Jews who were opposed to the policy foreshadowed in the Balfour Declaration. Yet another legend is that which attributes the genesis of the Declaration to a desire on the part of the British Government to reward Dr. Weizmann for his timely invention of a new explosive.

In actual fact, the British Government were moved mainly by two considerations. One was political: to win over the powerful Zionist elements in Germany and Austria, who were actually in negotiation with the Central Powers for the issue of a Turkish 'Balfour Declaration', by providing them with a positive interest in an Entente victory; and, at the same time, to mitigate the hostility of Jews in Allied countries towards Russia and give those Jews, who had been so active in overthrowing the Tsarist régime, an incentive to keep Russia in the War. The other was the imperialistic motive, first propounded by Kitchener, of securing Palestine or a portion of it as a bulwark to the British position in Egypt and an overland link with the East. This motive was the dominant one, and whatever part other considerations – financial, political, religious or humanitarian – may have played, there is no doubt that it sufficed by itself to bring about the Balfour Declaration. And it may legitimately be assumed that had they not come to an agreement with the Zionists, the British Government would have tried every means open to them of concluding such other bargains as would have ensured the reversion of Palestine to Great Britain as her share of the spoils of war.

The significance of Palestine in the Imperial scheme had

become much clearer as the War proceeded. Its importance lay primarily in its proximity to Egypt, from which it was separated by the practically desert Sinai Peninsula. It had been an axiom of military science, in the days before the War, that a desert bulwark was equivalent to a fortified frontier; and since the Turco-Egyptian boundary lay across the eastern extremity of Sinai, Egypt was safe enough. But the experience of the War had profoundly shaken that belief. In 1915, a sizable and well-equipped Turkish force had crossed the desert and reached the banks of the Suez Canal. In the summer of the following year, Sir Archibald Murray had crossed Sinai with a large army and, laying a railway and a pipeline as he advanced, had occupied al-'Arish and was about to attack Gaza. The old axiom was no longer true; modern science had conquered the desert, and the Suez Canal was demonstrably less secure. Even were Turkey to remain mistress of Palestine, there would be cause for concern. But now that France was claiming Syria as her preserve and had given her allies unmistakably to understand that Palestine was included in her claim, it became imperative for Great Britain, from the point of view of safety if from no other, to interpose a buffer between her position on the Suez Canal and the future French position in Syria, some more reliable buffer than the international Brown area of the Sykes-Picot Agreement; if possible, a British buffer. Hence the Balfour Declaration. It prepared the ground for the claim which was afterwards to be preferred, in the fulness of victory, that, since England had given a solemn undertaking to the Zionists in regard to a national home in Palestine, it was only fitting that the task of governing Palestine for the fulfilment of that undertaking be assumed by England.

8.

The first step was for the British Government to satisfy themselves that, in the event of their making a declaration in favour of Zionist aspirations, the Zionists would welcome and work for the establishment of British rule in Palestine. When Mr. Lloyd George came to power in December 1916, there was in existence a plan drawn up by the leaders of the Zionist movement, in which a programme was outlined for the administration of Palestine in the event of an Entente victory. The plan was based on the assumption that, after the War, the administration of Palestine would be taken over either by France or by Great Britain or by both acting jointly in a condominium. The Zionist leaders were then unaware of the existence of the Sykes-Picot Agreement, and had naturally assumed that France might be successful in pressing her claim to Palestine as being part of Syria. As it stood, the Zionist programme, with its equal regard for French and British designs on Palestine, did not altogether suit Mr. Lloyd George's book. But when the issue was discussed in exploratory conversations between British statesmen and Zionist leaders, the latter, taking the hint, decided with alacrity to eliminate France altogether from their scheme and to plump for an exclusively British Palestine. It was then that Mr. Lloyd George authorised Sir Mark Sykes to enter into negotiations with the Zionists; and accordingly, the first conference was held on the 7th of February 1917, in London. At that conference, the Zionist leaders gave Sykes a formal assurance that they were irrevocably opposed to any internationalisation of the Holy Land, even under an Anglo-French condominium; and that, provided Great Britain would support them in their national aspirations, they would henceforth work for the establishment of a British protectorate in Palestine. That was the basis of the bargain which led to the issue of the Balfour Declaration nine months later when the cry went forth that Mr. Lloyd George and his colleagues, by their bold espousal of the cause of persecuted Jewry, had furnished the world with another proof of the humanitarian idealism with which they were inspired.

In recent years, statements have been made by both Mr. Lloyd George and Dr. Weizmann, purporting to give a different account of the motives which had prompted the issue of the Balfour Declaration. In an address he gave at the

Royal Institute of International Affairs in London on June 9, 1936, Dr. Weizmann said:

> 'The suggestion that is often heard that the Balfour Declaration was made . . . for Imperialist or any other similar vulgar reason is entirely false. I think one fact may disprove this legend. When the British Government agreed to issue the famous Balfour Declaration, it agreed on one condition: that Palestine should not be the charge of Great Britain.'

This statement is not in accordance with the facts or even with the very condensed version given in the report published in 1921 by the Executive of the Zionist Organisation,[1] in which it is stated that considerations of the strategic value of Palestine to the British Empire had weighed with the promoters of the Balfour Declaration, and that, at their very first formal conference with Sir Mark Sykes, the Zionist leaders had made it clear to him that their objectives envisaged the establishment of a British protectorate in Palestine. Dr. Weizmann was present at that conference. Nor does his statement tally with the account published by Asquith of the representations that were made to him as Prime Minister, as far back as the beginning of 1915. Among those representations was, as we have seen, a memorandum by Mr. Herbert Samuel advocating the annexation of Palestine by Great Britain with a view to settling some three or four million Jews in it – a proposal which had already found favour with Mr. Lloyd George, but which had been rejected by Mr. Asquith. This is what Asquith wrote, under an entry dated March 13, 1915:

> ' . . . . I have already referred to Herbert Samuel's dithyrambic memorandum, urging that in the carving up of the Turks' Asiatic dominion we should take Palestine, into which the scattered Jews would in time swarm back from all quarters of the globe, and in due course obtain Home Rule. Curiously enough, the only other partisan of this proposal is Lloyd George who, I need not say, does not care a damn for the Jews or their past or their future, but thinks it will be an outrage to let the Holy Places pass into the possession or under the protectorate of "agnostic, atheistic France".'[2]

[1] v. footnote on page 260 above.
[2] *Memories and Reflections*, by the Earl of Oxford and Asquith, 1928.

The Declaration might have appeared sooner had it not been for certain political difficulties. One was the opposition of the non-Zionist Jews who were seriously alarmed at the nationalistic implications of political Zionism, and who gave publicity to their opposition in a remarkable statement, remarkable alike for its sincerity and, as has been amply shown in the event, for its foresight. The statement appeared in *The Times* of May 24, 1917, over the signatures of David L. Alexander, president of the Board of Deputies of British Jews, and Claude G. Montefiore, president of the Anglo-Jewish Association. In it, the signatories stressed their fidelity to *cultural* Zionism of which the aim was to make Palestine a Jewish spiritual centre in which the Jewish genius might find an opportunity of developing on lines of its own. They entered a strong and earnest protest against the idea of *political* Zionism which claimed that the Jewish settlements in Palestine should be recognised as possessing a national character in a political sense, and that the settlers should be invested with certain special rights on a basis of political privileges and economic preferences. They prophesied that the establishment of a Jewish nationality in Palestine was bound to 'have the effect throughout the world of stamping the Jews as strangers in their native lands, and of undermining their hard-won position as citizens and nationals of those lands'. Events have proved that those fears were only too well grounded, for it cannot be denied that the development of Zionism in the post-War period has been one of the main psychological factors in the deplorable growth of anti-Semitism.

Another difficulty lay in the reluctance of the French Government to give up their pretensions with regard to Palestine. There were powerful groups in French political life, in business and banking circles, and in the ecclesiastical world, to whom the proposal of excluding Palestine from the sphere of French influence would have been abhorrent; and the French Cabinet, at whose head was the cautious Ribot, could scarcely be expected to countenance any such proposal. It was clear to the British Government and to the Zionist leaders that they would have to act with infinite circumspection. The tactics they employed aimed at obtaining the assent of the French Government to the principle of a Zionist establishment in the Holy Land, without specific reference to the question of future sovereignty in Palestine. At the first approach, the attitude of the French Government was far from encouraging. Then it was that the Zionist leaders heard for the first time, through an accidental leakage, of the existence of the Sykes-Picot Agreement and of its provisions regarding the internationalisation of Palestine; and, feeling that they were being duped, they protested angrily to the British Government who, however, appear to have succeeded in reassuring them, for the negotiations proceeded as though the Sykes-Picot Agreement had not existed.

At last, after protracted negotiations, the assent of the French Government was secured to the principle of a declaration in favour of Zionism. In the United States, Mr. Justice Brandeis, making a very able use of his influence at the White House, obtained President Wilson's approval of the terms of the proposed Declaration. For a time, the progress of the negotiations was impeded by a division of opinion among the members of the British Cabinet and by the vigorous opposition of Edwin Montagu, the only Jew in the Cabinet. There was also a fundamental divergence as to the character of the future Jewish establishment in Palestine. The Zionists were pressing for a statement of policy accepting the principle 'of recognising Palestine as *the* national home of the Jewish people'. The British Government, unwilling to commit themselves to so far-reaching a policy, refused to promise anything more than that they would view with favour 'the establishment in Palestine of *a* national home for the Jewish people'. The difference was one between a limited Jewish national home in Palestine and an unlimited one. In the end, the Zionists gave way and agreed to the text which was finally drawn up in the following terms:

'His Majesty's Government view with favour the establishment in Palestine of a national home for the Jewish people and will use their best endeavours to facilitate the achievement of this object, it being clearly understood that nothing shall be done which may prejudice the civil and religious rights of existing non-Jewish communities in Palestine, or the rights and political status enjoyed by Jews in any other country.'

The Balfour Declaration, as it came to be universally known, was issued from the Foreign Office on the 2nd of November 1917, and made public a few days later, that is to say, two years after the issue of Sir Henry McMahon's note of the 24th of October 1915, and eighteen months after the outbreak of the Arab Revolt, when the Sharif Husain, relying on England's pledges of Arab independence, which he had every reason to believe applied to Palestine, had thrown in his lot openly with the Allies.

9.

In those parts of the Arab world which were in direct touch with the Allies, the Balfour Declaration created bewilderment and dismay, even among those who were not aware of the exact nature of the British pledges to the Arabs. It was taken to imply a denial of Arab political freedom in Palestine. The news reached Egypt first, where it soon provoked a wave of protest on the part of the Arab leaders congregated in Cairo; and, for a time, the British authorities there, aided by a strict censorship and an active propaganda service, had much to do to allay Arab apprehensions and prevent a collapse of the Revolt. In the occupied part of Palestine, the British command did their best to conceal the news, as though they had a bad conscience about it.

When the news reached King Husain, he was greatly disturbed by it and asked for a definition of the meaning and scope of the Declaration. His request was met by the despatch of Commander Hogarth,[1] one of the heads of the Arab

---

[1] The late David George Hogarth, scholar and archaeologist, sometime Keeper of the Ashmolean Museum, and one of the greatest authorities of his time on Arabian history.

Bureau in Cairo, who arrived in Jedda in the first week of January 1918, and had two interviews with the King.

The message which Hogarth had been instructed to deliver had the effect of setting Husain's mind completely at rest, and this was important from the standpoint of the morale of the Revolt. But what is equally important from the point of view of the historian is that the message he gave the King, on behalf of the British Government, was an explicit assurance that 'Jewish settlement in Palestine would only be allowed in so far as would be consistent with *the political and economic freedom of the Arab population*'. The message was delivered orally, but Husain took it down, and the quotation I have just given is my own rendering of the note made by him in Arabic at the time. The phrase I have italicised represents a fundamental departure from the text of the Balfour Declaration which purports to guarantee only *the civil and religious rights* of the Arab population. In that difference lay the difference between a peaceful and willing Arab-Jew co-operation in Palestine and the abominable duel of the last twenty years. For it is beyond all reasonable doubt certain that, had the Balfour Declaration in fact safeguarded the political and economic freedom of the Arabs, as Hogarth solemnly assured King Husain it would, there would have been no Arab opposition, but indeed Arab welcome, to a humanitarian and judicious settlement of Jews in Palestine.

In his reply, Husain was quite explicit. He said to Hogarth that in so far as the aim of the Balfour Declaration was to provide a refuge to Jews from persecution, he would use all his influence to further that aim. He would also assent to any arrangement that might be found suitable for the safeguard and control of the Holy Places by the adherents of each of the creeds who had sanctuaries in Palestine. But he made it plain that there could be no question of surrendering the Arab claim to sovereignty, although he would willingly consider when the time came, whatever measures might seem advisable to supply the future Arab government in Syria (including Palestine) with expert administrative and technical guidance.

In the months that followed, Husain gave ample proof of the sincerity of his attitude. He sent out messages to his principal followers in Egypt and in the forces of the Revolt to inform them that he had had assurances from the British Government that the settlement of Jews in Palestine would not conflict with Arab independence in that territory; and to urge them to continue to have faith in Great Britain's pledge and their own efforts to achieve their freedom. He ordered his sons to do what they could to allay the apprehensions caused by the Balfour Declaration among their followers. He despatched an emissary to Faisal at 'Aqaba with similar instructions. He caused an article to be published in his official mouthpiece,[1] calling upon the Arab population in Palestine to bear in mind that their sacred books and their traditions enjoined upon them the duties of hospitality and tolerance, and exhorting them to welcome the Jews as brethren and co-operate with them for the common welfare. The article appears to have been written by Husain himself and is historically valuable not only as an instance of his freedom from religious prejudice or fanaticism, but also as reflecting the general Arab attitude towards Jewry prior to the appearance of political Zionism on the scene.

In Egypt, the efforts of the British authorities to explain away the political implications of the Balfour Declaration had met with some success. In March, a Zionist commission headed by Dr. Weizmann arrived in Cairo on their way to Palestine; and they, too, went to no little trouble to allay Arab apprehensions. Dr. Weizmann, with his great gift of persuasion, scored a temporary success in interviews he had with several Arab personalities, and in this he was ably and zealously seconded by Major the Hon. W. Ormsby-Gore,[2] who was accompanying the commission as political officer delegated by the Foreign Office. They gave their hearers such a comforting account of Zionist aims and dispositions

[1] *al-Qibla* (Mecca), no. 183, March 23, 1918.
[2] Now Lord Harlech.

as dispelled their fears and brought them to a state of acquiescence in the idea of Zionist-Arab co-operation. Meetings were arranged and held between Zionist and Arab leaders. The proprietor of an influential newspaper in Cairo[1] was so far impressed with Dr. Weizmann's and Major Ormsby-Gore's assurances that he made use of the weighty columns of his journal to dispel Arab fears about their political future and advocate an understanding between the two races.

10.

In the spring of 1918, when the feeling aroused by the appearance of the Balfour Declaration and the disclosure of the Sykes-Picot Agreement was working havoc with the Anglo-Arab alliance, seven Arabs domiciled in Cairo formed themselves into a group to concert action. They were all of them men of standing and influence, who had been made privy to the terms of the Husain-McMahon compact at the time and had worked with zeal ever since on the furtherance of the Revolt. But now, in view of the dangerous uneasiness prevailing in Arab circles, and with their own confidence in the good faith of the Allies profoundly shaken, they were assailed by grave doubts and apprehensions. Eventually, they drew up a statement in the form of a memorial to the British Government, in which they depicted the situation as it presented itself to them, in both its internal and external aspects, and begged for a clear and comprehensive definition of Great Britain's policy with regard to the future of the Arab countries as a whole. In particular, the memorial reflected the concern of its authors as to the form and character of the Arab governments to be set up in Syria, Palestine and Iraq after the War. Statements made by persons in King Husain's entourage had given rise to a belief that he intended, in the event of victory over the Turks, to set up his

[1] Dr. Faris Nimr Pasha, one of the founders of *al-Muqattam*, the well-known Arabic daily published in Cairo. Dr. Nimr, it may be recalled, was one of the original members of the Bairut secret society (v. Chapter V, Section 2 *supra*).

own administrations in those countries and make them answerable to himself in Mecca. One of the objects of the memorial was to elucidate what the attitude of Great Britain and the Allies was towards the scheme attributed (and, as it turned out, wrongly attributed) to Husain.

The memorial was handed in to the Arab Bureau in Cairo for transmission to London; and, in handing it, its authors asked that their identity be not disclosed until the time should come when their memorial and the answer to it might be made public simultaneously. Their identity is now known, and it is also known that their motive for desiring anonymity was fear lest Husain might have taken umbrage at the comparison which they had drawn between the Hejaz and the northern Arab countries to the detriment of the former.

In course of time, on the 16th of June 1918, a reply was returned by the Foreign Office, and it proved to be extremely important, both for what it contained and for the effect it had. It was delivered with some formality by one of the senior members of the Intelligence Service – Mr. Walrond by name – to the authors of the memorial at a meeting specially convened at Army Headquarters for the purpose. The Arab leaders present were also informed that a copy of the Declaration to the Seven (as the Foreign Office statement was familiarly named) had been communicated to King Husain. It was read out in English, and an Arabic translation was afterwards made by one of those present for the benefit of those others who did not understand English. A translation of the Arabic version will be found in Appendix D; and this, so far as I am aware, is the first occasion on which the full text has appeared in an English rendering or in any language other than Arabic.

The Declaration to the Seven is by far the most important statement of policy publicly made by Great Britain in connexion with the Arab Revolt; and yet, strangely enough, it has remained one of the least known outside the Arab world. Its significance lies in this, that it confirms England's previous pledges to the Arabs in plainer language than in any former public utterance, and, more valuable still, provides an authoritative enunciation of the principles on which those pledges rested.

In their statement, the Foreign Office dealt with the whole of the region claimed by the Sharif Husain as the area of legitimate Arab independence, and defined the British Government's policy with regard to the future of that area. For the purposes of that definition they regarded the area as falling into four categories determined by the military situation at the time.

The first two categories comprised (i) the Arab territories which were free and independent before the War, and (ii) the territories liberated from Turkish rule by the action of the Arabs themselves. In those two categories, comprising the Arabian Peninsula from Aden to 'Aqaba,[1] the British Government recognised 'the complete and sovereign independence of the Arabs inhabiting those territories'.

The third category comprised (iii) the Arab territories liberated from Turkish rule by the action of the Allied armies. In that category, comprising Iraq from the Persian Gulf to a line some distance north of Baghdad, and Palestine from the Egyptian frontier to a line some distance north of Jerusalem and Jaffa, the British Government stated that their policy towards the inhabitants of those territories was 'that the future government of those territories should be based upon the principle of the consent of the governed'. The statement emphasised that that policy would always be that of the British Government.

The fourth category comprised (iv) the Arab territories that were then still under Turkish rule. In that category, comprising the greater part of Syria and the province of Mosul in Iraq, the statement asserted that it was the British Government's desire 'that the oppressed peoples in those territories should obtain their freedom and independence', and that British policy was to continue to work for the achievement of that object.

---

[1] With the exclusion of the former, and the inclusion of the latter which had, at that time, already been liberated by the action of the Arabs themselves.

In so far as it referred to Syria, Palestine and Iraq, the Declaration to the Seven contained two assurances of fundamental importance. One was that Great Britain had been working and would continue to work not only for the liberation of those countries from Turkish rule but also for their freedom and independence. The other, that she pledged herself to ensure that no régime would be set up in any of them that was not acceptable to their populations. The fact that such assurances were given after the disclosure of the Sykes-Picot Agreement and the issue of the Balfour Declaration added greatly to their significance and to the effect they had upon the minds of the Arab leaders and upon the fervour of the Arab participation in the final offensive. They were regarded as the natural corollary of the doctrine of self-determination, which President Wilson had enunciated a few months previously, and were hailed as proof that Great Britain was determined that that doctrine should prevail in the post-War settlement in Turkey's Arab provinces.

A wave of jubilation swept the Arab world as the contents of the Foreign Office statement became known. Copies of it were received by the Amir Faisal at his camp in 'Aqaba, and the despondency that had settled upon the forces of the Revolt gave place to a fresh outburst of enthusiasm. In one sense, the Declaration to the Seven was more decisive still than the Husain-McMahon compact; it was more comprehensive, free from any territorial reservations, and it had the added merit of being a public utterance. In the following month, a few weeks after it was published, the news came of President Wilson's Mount Vernon address of the 4th of July 1918, of which the Second Point upheld the same principle as had been enunciated in the Declaration to the Seven, namely that the post-War settlement would be based upon 'the free acceptance of that settlement by the people immediately concerned'. Taken together, the British and the American utterances had a decisive effect in dispelling the doubts and apprehensions aroused by the Sykes-Picot Agreement and the Balfour Declaration; and the forces of the Revolt, refreshed by these new earnests of freedom, turned with renewed vigour to their task, and, when Allenby's call for the supreme effort came, were not found hesitant or wanting.

11.

Lastly, there appeared a few days before the Armistice yet another declaration, issued jointly by Great Britain and France this time, in which pledges were made to the Arabs in regard to the future of the northern Arab countries.

On the 7th of November 1918, an official *communiqué* was given out to the press in Palestine, Syria and Iraq by the British military commands in those territories. It contained the text of a statement of policy, in which the aims pursued by the French and British Governments in regard to those countries were broadly outlined. The widest possible distribution was made: not only were copies given to every newspaper with injunctions to display it prominently, but various other means were resorted to for its dissemination among the rural as well as the urban centres, such as placarding on the notice-boards and hoardings. Where the population was mainly illiterate it was read out to them in Arabic by Arab civilians employed in the military administration.

The text of the statement, universally known as the Anglo-French Declaration, will be found in Appendix E. It announces the identity of French and British war-aims in the East, which it defines as the complete and final liberation of the populations living under the Turkish yoke, and the setting up of national governments chosen by the people themselves in the free exercise of the popular will. It goes on to say that the two Powers were in agreement in their desire to see such governments set up, to assist in their establishment and to grant them recognition as soon as they became established. It ends with a self-righteous paragraph in which the two Powers stress the purity of their motives and depict themselves as aspiring only to be the disinterested mentors of the future self-determined and self-governing Arab States.

The issue of the Anglo-French Declaration was brought about by the critical situation which had suddenly arisen in the Arab territories occupied by the Allies. The initial cause of it had been the incident of the Arab flag in Bairut.

On the 3rd of October, several days before the entry of the first British or French troops, Arab sovereignty had been proclaimed and the Arab flag hoisted in Bairut by Shukri Pasha al-Ayyubi in the name of the Amir Faisal. To this act, the French took strong exception, and, as a result of their representations, General Allenby ordered the flag to be removed. Its removal had caused violent effervescence in Damascus and Faisal had been hard put to it to quell an incipient mutiny in the ranks of his army.

The ebullition caused by this incident was hardly lessened when it became known that Bairut and the other ports of the Syrian littoral were to be placed under French occupation. The activities of the Zionists in Palestine became known in Damascus and added to the general ferment. The capture of Damascus and Aleppo had brought the Syrian and Iraqi leaders who had fought in the ranks of the Revolt into direct touch with their fellow-patriots who had had to remain at home or in exile under the weight of the Turkish terrorism; and this contact had provided an opportunity for a free interchange of views. The stay-at-homes had had much information from Turkish sources to impart, that had given the newcomers food for thought about the sincerity of Allied professions.

A wave of suspicion and apprehension as to the hidden motives of the Allied Governments swept the country. Faisal protested to Allenby, declaring that he could no longer keep the Arab forces in control unless an authoritative and unequivocal definition of Allied intentions were immediately proclaimed. It seemed probable that the feeling would lead to an explosion. The Anglo-French Declaration was hurriedly issued. It had an instantaneous effect, and within a few days the effervescence had died down. Like the Declaration to the Seven, it proclaimed the principle of the consent of the governed; and, for the same reason, had staved off the danger, at a critical time, of a rupture between Great Britain and her Arab allies.

CHAPTER XIV

THE POST-WAR SETTLEMENT

I.

THE War was won, and for the first time in its history the Arab national movement stood abreast of its destiny. Victory had carried its standard as far north as it had dreamed, to the very confines of its kingdom. Syria had been freed, from Sinai to the Taurus; so had Iraq, up to Mosul; while in the Peninsula itself all that remained of the Turkish power were a few helpless garrisons doomed to surrender. All the Arabic-speaking provinces of the Ottoman Empire in Asia were at last rid of the alien yoke that had lain on them for four stifling centuries. It seemed as though the war-god himself, in homage to the role of the language in the history of the Movement, had stayed the northward advance on the very watershed of speech, just where Arabic ceased and Turkish began. The area of the Turk's defeat was precisely the area of Arab aspirations, and its frontiers coincided exactly with those defined by the Sharif Husain as the natural limits of Arab independence.

It added to the exultation of the people and their leaders that the Revolt had signally helped the common victory. Save for Aden where their contribution had been indirect though by no means negligible, and Iraq where the expulsion of the Turks had been entirely accomplished by British arms, the forces of the Revolt had everywhere else played their assigned part – and more – in the enemy's defeat. They had not only fought the Turk, but also those of their own kin who had been actively siding with him. The leaders felt that they had amply fulfilled their share of the bargain concluded between Sir Henry McMahon and the Sharif Husain, and they confidently looked to Great Britain to fulfil hers.

But when it came to a reckoning at the Peace Conference, there was a wide divergence between what the Arabs claimed and what Great Britain was willing to recognise as her share of the bargain. Why the dispute arose, what its subjects of contention were, and how it led, in less than two years after the Armistice, to the first of a series of sanguinary conflicts between the Arabs and their former British and French allies will be told in the present chapter. It is an unedifying and unsavoury story.

As we shall see, Great Britain and France imposed upon the Arabs a 'settlement' which violated both the promises specifically made to them and the principles which the Allies had enunciated as the foundations of the future Peace. In face of what afterwards happened, it is tempting to speculate upon the course which events might have taken had Great Britain and France chosen, at the Peace deliberations, to live up to their pledges and principles. As a rule, such speculations are valid rather as mental exercises than as contributions to history. But in this case, it is beyond all doubt certain that the post-War handling of the Arab question led directly and inevitably to explosions which would not have happened but for that so-called settlement. Thousands of lives, millions of treasure and incalculable moral suffering and damage would have been avoided. The Iraq rising of 1920, the Syrian rebellion of 1925 and the repeated outbreaks in Palestine would not have occurred. For they were all the direct outcome of the various régimes which were wrongfully and forcibly imposed upon the Arabs in Iraq, Syria and Palestine in violation of the pledges which had brought them into the War. Whatever part subsidiary causes may have played, the underlying cause of all those upheavals, and of a good deal else that has clouded the natural friendliness of Arab to Englishman and Englishman to Arab, is to be sought in the bitterness and the revulsion of feeling which the post-War provisions engendered – and nowhere else. The Arabs felt that they had been betrayed, and betrayed by their best friend.

2.

When the Amir Faisal arrived in Paris in January 1919, as head of the Hejaz Delegation to the Peace Conference, he encountered three main influences at work in opposition to the fulfilment of Arab hopes. One was the British imperialistic interest in Iraq and Palestine; the second, the French imperialistic interest in Syria; the third, in league with the first, the Zionist nationalistic interest in Palestine. The divergence which emerged at the Conference was over the disposal of those northern Arab territories. The Arabian Peninsula proper remained outside the controversy: for, although Great Britain had a stake in the maintenance of her protectorates and spheres of influence, and Italy was angling for a base on the eastern seaboard of the Red Sea, the impenetrability of the Peninsula to foreign colonisation was never seriously questioned. And the wrangle in Paris had as its sole bone of contention the fate of that rectangle of Arab land lying between the Mediterranean and Persia, which comprises Syria, Palestine and Iraq, in which both Great Britain and France had acquisitive imperialistic aims.

In 1919, the status of that whole area was still that of an 'Occupied Enemy Territory' provisionally subject to military law pending its ultimate disposal at the conclusion of peace. Administrations deriving their immediate authority from the British commander-in-chief had been set up throughout the area, but there were certain significant differences in regard to the form, structure and personnel of the machinery set up in Iraq and its counterparts in Syria and Palestine.

In Iraq, the country had been treated as one unit and placed under a single administration, with a British civil commissioner at its head, whose personnel was preponderantly British in the higher ranks and largely Indian in the lower ranks. As for Syria-Palestine, the country had been divided into three zones each of which had been placed under a separate administration totally distinct from the other two, the first, known as *Occupied Enemy Territory Administration* South – *O.E.T.A.* South, for short – comprised Palestine in approximately its present frontiers and was British; the second, known as *O.E.T.A.* East, comprised the interior of Syria from 'Aqaba to Aleppo and was Arab; the third, known as *O.E.T.A.* West, comprised the Lebanon and the Syrian seaboard from Tyre to the confines of Cilicia and was French.[1]

As for the Arabian Peninsula, it had been left *in statu quo*. In the Hejaz, King Husain was the titular sovereign of what had formerly been a province of the Ottoman Empire and was now an independent Arab State; and his position, secure so far as recognition by the Allied Powers went, was only threatened by the perils of the dissension between him and Ibn Saud. The latter, as sultan of Najd with his capital at Riad, was the undisputed master of Central Arabia from the Hejaz border in the west to the Persian Gulf in the east. North of his dominions lay the territory of Shammar, stretching as far as the Iraq border, and still under the rule of Ibn Rashid whose power and prestige had been seriously weakened by the Turkish defeat. In the south, were the Idrisi and the Imam Yahya, the first maintaining his sway over the territory of 'Asir, and the second making good his claim – now that the Turks had surrendered to the British command at Aden – to sovereignty over the Yaman. The positions of the smaller rulers of Kuwait, Masqat and the Hadramaut remained to all practical purposes unaffected save for the final severance of their ties with Turkey. In the Peninsula as a whole, the status of each ruler was but the confirmation of the position he had made or kept for himself in the War.

These differences were significant in that they provided an index to the ulterior motives of the Allies. So far as the interior of Arabia went, the possibility of foreign penetration was ruled out by practical as well as political considerations, and the Peninsula was largely left to itself. But in the

---

[1] Another French administration, known as *O.E.T.A.* North, had been set up in Cilicia, but this lay outside the Arab Rectangle.

northern Arab territories, on which Great Britain and France had acquisitive designs, the administrative arrangements which we have just described seemed to foreshadow the ultimate settlement which the Allies were secretly envisaging, although they had been fulsomely represented as provisional and as being in no way prejudicial to the issue which only the Peace Conference could pronounce upon finally.

These measures, temporary though they were represented to be, had contributed to the unrest which led to the issue of the Anglo-French Declaration of November 7, 1918. In answer to Faisal's protest against the partition of Syria, even as a temporary measure of so-called administrative convenience, General Allenby assured him that the future of Syria would be determined in accordance with the wishes of the population. There can be no doubt that Allenby, who was the soul of honour, did believe in the validity of the assurances he was instructed to give to Faisal; and, as was his way when convinced, he gave them in tones that inspired confidence. What with that and with the assurances contained in the Anglo-French Declaration, Faisal had assented to, and persuaded his followers to cease agitating against, the administrative partition of Syria for the time being. And he had started for London, some two weeks after the issue of the Anglo-French Declaration, to press home the case for Arab unity and independence, and with a mandate from his father to represent him at the Peace Conference.

3.

In one aspect, this first visit of Faisal's to Europe was an adventure in bewilderment. He arrived in Marseilles on the 26th of November, on board H.M.S. *Gloucester*, and was met by two French officers of high rank who gave him his first inkling of the official French attitude towards him. They informed him that the Government welcomed him in France as a visitor but could not regard him as having a representative or any official capacity. He was politely invited to go on a tour of the battlefields on the Western front, which he accepted with an equal show of politeness. He arrived in London on the 10th of December.

In London, he found a cordial and flattering welcome, but this was more than offset by certain disagreeable surprises. He learnt that the Petrograd disclosures of secret compacts among the Allies were no figment of a malicious Bolshevik imagination and that the Sykes-Picot Agreement was a hard fact over which Clemenceau and Lloyd George were just then having one of their bitter-sweet tussles. He was informed that the French Government had taken strong exception to his having been nominated to be head of the administration in *O.E.T.A.* East, and that they were now objecting to the proposal that he should represent the Hejaz at the Peace Conference. He found himself the target of a determined offensive on the subject of Palestine. To a man in his middle thirties, who scarcely understood either English or French, had never been to England before, and had had no previous experience of the seamy side of European diplomacy, the cumulative effect of those three weeks in London was bewildering and depressing.[1]

The Sykes-Picot Agreement was at that time one of the topics of the day. Clemenceau had been in London and had had a tussle with Mr. Lloyd George on the question of whether or not the Agreement was still valid. Lloyd George wanted it annulled, on the plea that Russia – one of the three parties to it – had denounced it; Clemenceau held that it was none the less binding on the two other parties.

In the period that had elapsed since the conclusion of the Agreement, the divergence between France's and Great Britain's aims and interests in the Arab countries had become more apparent to the statesmen of both Powers. The British view now was that the Agreement was not only in practice unworkable, but that, so far as it could be applied at all, it ran counter to British interests in two important

---

[1] During my stay in Baghdad in the spring of 1933, the late King Faisal allowed me to consult a diary in which were recorded in his own hand the events and impressions of this visit to Europe, including his sojourn in Paris during the Peace Conference. Part of the information used in this chapter is drawn from material contained in that diary.

respects: one was that it assigned the Vilayet of Mosul with its rich oil-fields to France; the other, that it placed Palestine under an international administration of a kind that would necessarily preclude or at any rate interfere with the establishment of that measure of British control which Mr. Lloyd George was bent upon securing. The French view was that the Agreement was the only deed in which France's share of the Ottoman spoils had been clearly and specifically recognised by Great Britain; and, being both ill-disposed towards the Arab awakening in general[1] and suspicious of England's patronage of the Arabs, the Quai d'Orsay felt that their safest course was to uphold the validity of the Agreement as a whole, subject only to such modifications as they might find it profitable to consent to in barter for other gains.

Finding Clemenceau obdurate, Mr. Lloyd George had changed his tactics and asked him specifically to consent to Mosul and Palestine being placed within the British sphere, in return for a *quid pro quo* compensation which would include the assignment of a substantial share of the Mosul oil to France. Clemenceau had agreed to consider the offer, but had returned to Paris without committing himself to an acceptance. Two months later, in a note dated the 15th of February, the offer was formally accepted by the French Government; and Great Britain then found herself, to use Sir Henry McMahon's phrase,[2] 'free to act without detriment to the interests of her ally France' in respect of Palestine and of the Vilayet of Mosul.

During his stay in London, Faisal was informed of the general trend, though not of the whole scope, of the Anglo-French conversations and was subjected to a good deal of pressure on the part of the British Government to give his assent in principle to the objects they had in view. They

[1] Not only from a desire to exercise power more freely in the spheres assigned to France in Syria and Iraq, but also from concern about the probable repercussions of a successful awakening in the eastern Arab world on the Arab populations in her North African Empire.
[2] In his second note to the Sharif Husain, dated the 24th of October 1915 (Appendix A).

were particularly insistent on the subject of Palestine, and instructed Lawrence to use his influence – which was then considerable – with Faisal to induce him to give formal recognition, on behalf of the Arabs he represented, to Zionist aspirations in Palestine. On their side, the Zionists were equally active in their efforts to get Faisal to put his name to a formal Agreement to be concluded between him, acting on behalf of the King of the Hejaz, and Dr. Weizmann on that of the Zionist Organisation, with a view to making that recognition final and binding.

Faisal found himself placed in a difficult position. The proposals which his friends in Whitehall were pressing him to endorse were not only extraneous to the terms of his mission, which amounted to a few lines of summary instructions issued by his father, but also in conflict with the general and somewhat inflamed feeling in the northern Arab countries. He tried to obtain specific directions from King Husain, but all he could elicit from his autocratic and single-minded father was an order to accept nothing less than the fulfilment of the pledges made by Great Britain with regard to Arab independence. The order gave him no latitude whatever.

On the other hand, the pressure to which he was being subjected in London was telling on him. He felt keenly the insufficiency of his equipment, his ignorance of English, his unfamiliarity with the methods of European diplomacy, and, above all, the limitations imposed upon his usefulness by his father's refusal to grant him full powers. It added to his sense of weakness and isolation that he knew the French to be hostile to his person and to his mission: apart from the scant courtesy with which he had been treated on his passage through France, he had had a multitude of signs to show him that his own distrust of the French was unfeignedly reciprocated. He allowed himself to be persuaded that his chances of neutralising the hostility of the French would be greater if he could see his way to meeting Great Britain's wishes to the fullest possible extent. The only friends he had in Europe were English – most of them men who had served

with the Arab forces and proved their devotion to the
common cause. He naturally turned to them for advice,
and more particularly to Lawrence.

Faisal would have stayed his hand until the Peace Conference had actually assembled, both with regard to the Sykes-
Picot Agreement as a whole and to the specific problems
which the revelation of its existence had created for the
spokesman of the Arabs. But there was the question of
Palestine about which the Foreign Office, acting partly under
Zionist pressure and partly from a desire to face the Peace
Conference with a *fait accompli*, were badgering him for an
immediate answer. They wanted him to commit himself to
an agreement with the Zionists in anticipation of the decisions of the Peace Conference. Faisal saw the impropriety
of their manœuvres and, with an equal eye, measured the
dangers of accepting the proposed Agreement (or any agreement) before reference to his father and the risks of indispos-
ing the British Government against him. He did not feel
strong enough to return a point-blank refusal. The friends
he consulted used the same arguments as the Foreign Office,
while Lawrence was showing uncommon zeal in persuading
him that there was no harm in his concluding the proposed
Agreement with the Zionists subject to the Arab claims to
independence being fully recognised.

Faisal's views about the future of Palestine did not differ
from those of his father and were identical with those held
then by the great majority of politically-minded Arabs. The
representative Arab view was substantially that which King
Husain had expressed to the British Government through the
medium of Commander Hogarth at the interview they had
had in Jedda in January 1918.[1] In the Arab view, Palestine
was an Arab territory forming an integral part of Syria and,
as such, was bound to remain in the area of Arab independence. The fact that it was held in veneration by three of the
world's religions, together with the existence of the holy sites
and sanctuaries, gave it a special character which the Arabs
were anxious to see respected and adequately safeguarded on

[1] v. Chapter XIII, Section 9, *supra*.

a basis to be agreed upon by all the creeds concerned. Jewish settlement and colonisation would be welcomed on humanitarian grounds, subject to the limitations imposed by a proper regard for the welfare and the political and economic rights of the existing population. Such was, in brief, the view most widely held in Arab circles.

In Faisal's mind, this view had gradually developed into a positive belief in the possibility of Arab-Jewish co-operation in Palestine. He had been informed at the time of Hogarth's assurances to King Husain, and had been influenced by the confident messages he had received from his father at his camp in 'Aqaba in the spring of 1918. Later in the year, he had met Dr. Weizmann, to whom he had granted an audience at the request of the British Government. The interview had taken place in the first week of June, in Faisal's camp, which was then pitched on a hillock some few miles north of 'Aqaba, and in the course of it Weizmann had given him an assurance that the Zionists had no intention of working for the establishment of a Jewish government in Palestine, but that all they wished to do was to help in the development of the country so far as that would be possible without damage to legitimate Arab interests. The combined effect of those assurances had been to induce in him a belief that there was nothing either in the Zionist aspirations as such or in the policy professed by the British Government in regard to their fulfilment that would interfere with Arab political and economic freedom in Palestine.

In that frame of mind, torn as he was between his reluctance to commit his father without previous consultation and his desire to placate the Foreign Office, he took the only course that in the circumstances he felt was open to him. He consented to sign the Agreement, but made his consent conditional upon the fulfilment by Great Britain of her pledges respecting Arab independence. The stipulation was inscribed by him on the text of the Agreement which he signed. It was couched in such sweeping and categorical terms as to leave the main issue untouched; and, since the condition which he attached was not fulfilled, the Agreement never acquired validity. Its main interest is in the evidence it affords of the lengths to which Faisal was prepared to go in the sense of Arab-Jewish co-operation so long as that did not conflict with Arab independence.[1]

4.

About the middle of January, Faisal moved to Paris and found that the French Government were resolved to deny him the status of a delegate at the Peace Conference, on the plea that the Hejaz was not officially recognised as one of the Allied belligerent states. But on the intervention of the Foreign Office, the Quai d'Orsay had to give way, and the Hejaz Delegation were granted not one seat but two at the Conference. The hostility remained unabated, however, and for the next three months, until he sailed for Syria at the end of April, Faisal encountered a resolute opposition on the part of the French to the cause which he had come to Paris to vindicate.

The first hearing of the Arab case took place at the Quai d'Orsay on the 6th of February, when the Hejaz Delegation were invited to attend a formal meeting of the conference. A few days previously, Faisal had submitted a statement to the Conference, in which he had briefly defined the Arab claim to independence. The statement, dated January 29, 1919, read as follows:

> 'As representing my father who, by request of Britain and France, led the Arab rebellion against the Turks, I have come to ask that the Arabic-speaking peoples of Asia, from the line Alexandretta-Diarbekr southward to the Indian Ocean, be recognised as independent sovereign peoples, under the guarantee of the League of Nations. The Hejaz, which is already a sovereign State, and Aden, which is a British dependency[2] are excluded from the Arab demand. The confirmation of the States already existing in the area, the adjustment of their boundaries with one another, with

---

[1] For the texts of the Faisal-Weizmann Agreement and of Faisal's stipulation see Appendix F.
[2] Aden had been excluded by the Sharif Husain from the very start.

the Hejaz, and with the British at Aden, and the formation of such new States as are required, and their boundaries, are matters of arrangement between us, after the wishes of their respective inhabitants have been ascertained. Detailed suggestions in these smaller points will be put forward by my Government when the time comes. I base my request on the principles enunciated by President Wilson (attached)[1] and am confident that the Powers will attach more importance to the bodies and souls of the Arabic-speaking peoples than to their own material interests.[2]'

The address which Faisal gave at the meeting on the 6th of February was a reasoned amplification of that statement. He stressed the claims of the Arabic-speaking peoples of Asia to independence and unity, laying special emphasis on the cultural, geographical and economic factors that made for cohesion amongst them. He mentioned the part played by the Arabs in the War and the sacrifices they had made. In courteous but outspoken language, he expressed his condemnation of the Sykes-Picot Agreement. He concluded by thanking Great Britain and France for the help they had given the Arabs in their struggle for freedom, and by asking for the fulfilment of the promises made to them.

In the discussion which followed his address, Faisal made a proposal which could only have come from one who believed in the justice of his own case. This was that steps be taken to ascertain the wishes of the populations concerned, so that a fair and lasting settlement might be arrived at. Both in his statement of January 29 and in his address before the Conference, he had laid emphasis on the principle of 'the consent of the governed' and taken his stand on the platform of the Mount Vernon Address and the Anglo-French Declaration rather than on the McMahon pledges. His proposal was that a commission of inquiry be appointed by the Peace Conference to visit Syria and Palestine and ascertain the wishes of the population by an exhaustive investigation on the spot.

---

[1] The text attached to the statement was that of the Second Point of Wilson's Mount Vernon address, of July 4, 1918.
[2] David Hunter Miller, *My Diary at the Conference of Paris*, Vol. IV.

The proposal appealed to President Wilson and received his immediate support. Mr. Lloyd George was scarcely favourable to it, but began by accepting it with good grace. M. Clemenceau received it with hostility and did his best to discredit it. It was not, however, until the 20th of March that the proposal was formally debated and Wilson's championship of it endorsed. At a secret conference held in Mr. Lloyd George's flat in the Rue Nitot on that date, of which the minutes have been published by Mr. R. S. Baker,[1] Wilson suggested that a commission of inquiry consisting of French, British, Italian and American members in equal numbers should be appointed to go to Syria, and if need be to the neighbouring territories, in order to investigate the facts and report to the Peace Conference. The suggestion was carried through at that sitting and Wilson undertook to draft the terms of reference for the future commission.

At another meeting of the Council of Four, held on the 25th of March, the proposal was formally adopted and the instructions drawn up by Wilson for the guidance of the commission approved. It was also decided that each of the four Powers concerned were to appoint two members to serve on the commission. Wilson's choice fell on Dr. Henry C. King, President of Oberlin College, and Mr. Charles R. Crane, whose wide experience and independence of judgment made him eminently fitted for the task. The British Government appointed Sir Henry McMahon and Commander D. G. Hogarth. The French Government showed no precipitancy in selecting their commissioners.

It is related that when news of the decision reached Faisal's ears he drank champagne for the first time, and drank it as though it were water. Then he went for a drive past the headquarters of the American and British Delegations and threw cushions at the Crillon, the Majestic and the Quai d'Orsay, saying that, as he had no bombs, he could only express his feelings in that way.

In the last week of April, he sailed for Syria to resume con-

[1] Ray Stannard Baker, *Woodrow Wilson and World Settlement*, Vol. III.

trol of affairs at Damascus pending the arrival of the inter-Allied Commission.

5.

The French Government's dislike of the proposal was due to their knowledge that the consensus of opinion in Syria as a whole was unfavourable to them. They were also profoundly suspicious of their British Allies, and the fact that Allenby's triumph had raised British prestige enormously added to their apprehensions. The more ardent spirits at the Quai d'Orsay went so far as to believe that the proposal to hold an inquiry on the spot was nothing less than a piece of Foreign Office intrigue calculated to eliminate the claims of France to a protectorate – or, to use the newly-introduced term, a Mandate – over Syria.

The British Government's attitude was somewhat different. Although there was a strong current of opinion in British circles, especially among those who had seen conditions in the East at first hand, in favour of buying out the French interest in Syria, Great Britain's stake was hardly compelling enough to cause her to make an issue; and there is no doubt whatever that the British professions of disinterestedness which were repeatedly given to the French at the time were genuine. On the other hand, there seemed to be some probability that an inquiry on the spot would reveal a determined opposition to the British Government's desire to establish a mandate in Iraq and Palestine. And, without going to the lengths of an open opposition, the Foreign Office were, to say the least, lukewarm about the proposal.

The divergence between the two Powers can best be gauged by an examination of the minutes of the secret conference held on the 20th of March. At one stage in the discussion, Mr. Lloyd George defined the British attitude in the following terms as recorded in the minutes:

'Mr. LLOYD GEORGE said that M. Pichon had opened as though the question of the mandate for Syria was one between Great Britain and France. There was, in fact, no such question as far as Great Britain was concerned. He wished to say at once that just as we had disinterested ourselves in 1912,[1] so we now disinterested ourselves in 1919. If the Conference asked us to take Syria, we should reply in the negative. . . . The British Government definitely intended to have nothing to do with Syria. The question of the extent to which Great Britain and France were concerned was cleared up in the interview he had had with M. Clemenceau in London, and at which he had said that he wanted Mosul with adjacent regions and Palestine. . . .

' . . . . M. CLEMENCEAU said he adhered in principle to an inquiry, but it was necessary to have certain guarantees. The inquiry must not confine itself to Syria. Mandates were required for Palestine, Mesopotamia and Armenia, and other parts of the Turkish Empire, as well as Syria. . . .

' . . . . Mr. LLOYD GEORGE said he had no objection to an inquiry into Palestine and Mesopotamia, which were the regions in which the British Empire were principally concerned. Neither would he object to an inquiry into Armenia, in which they were not so closely concerned.'

Later in the discussion Mr. Lloyd George revealed something of his fears when he said that 'he supposed that if the evidence were so overwhelming that, for example, the British Empire was ruled out of Mesopotamia, they would be free to consider whether they could take a mandate elsewhere in Turkey'. It is not clear what other morsel of the Ottoman Empire, if any in particular, he had in mind when he spoke; but in any case it was not Syria.

The proposed inquiry was also causing apprehension among the Zionists and their partisans, lest it should bring to light the impossibility of fulfilling their hopes without a resort to force in Palestine. Sir Mark Sykes had returned to Paris early in February from a tour of over two months in Palestine and Syria, and had brought disquieting news. What he had observed on that journey had opened his eyes to realities that had hitherto escaped him. He had been particularly affected by his own discovery of the gap between what he had previously understood Zionism to be and what he had just seen of Zionism in the making in Palestine and of its effects on the minds of the Arabs.

[1] See Chapter VIII, Section 3, *supra*.

' .... From being the evangelist of Zionism during the War he had returned to Paris with feelings shocked by the intense bitterness which had been provoked in the Holy Land. Matters had reached a stage beyond his conception of what Zionism would be. His last journey to Palestine had raised many doubts, which were not set at rest by a visit to Rome. To Cardinal Gasquet he admitted the change of his views on Zionism, and that he was determined to qualify, guide and, if possible, save the dangerous situation which was rapidly arising.'[1]

Sykes's views about the Sykes-Picot Agreement had undergone a similar revulsion: he had become convinced of its inadaptability to actual conditions and of the futility of trying to execute it. And, although he was feeling worn out with the exertions of his tour, he had hurried back to Paris bent upon doing all he could to correct false hopes and put a brake upon ambitions which now seemed to him insensate. But within a few days of his return he fell ill and died: and it is perhaps not an exaggeration to say that, for Jews, Arabs and British alike, to say nothing of the French, his death at that juncture was little short of a calamity. Without going so far as to suppose that one individual, however genuine, talented and forceful, could have infected the Versailles peacemakers with his own sense of justice, there is little doubt that, had he lived, his recital of facts and his forecast of consequences might have filled the minds of the politicians with those anxieties which are often, in politics, the beginning of wisdom.

In those few days of activity before his fatal illness, Sykes had seen Lloyd George, Balfour and several of his French and Zionist friends, and had begun the campaign for a return to sanity upon which he had set his heart. What effect his warnings may have had at the time is not known. But when, a few weeks after Sykes's death, Faisal's proposal for an inquiry on the spot began to be seriously considered, the prevalent sentiment in British, French and Zionist political circles was one of still greater discomfort. And Balfour went to the lengths of addressing a memorandum to his

[1] Shane Leslie, *Mark Sykes: His Life and Letters*, 1923.

chief, in which he urged that Palestine be altogether excluded from the purview of the inquiry, while Clemenceau
kept insisting that France could not consent to its being held
unless it were to cover Iraq and Palestine as well as Syria.

6.

On his return to Damascus early in May, Faisal had found
that restlessness and anxiety about the future were still in the
ascendant. He was subjected to a great deal of solicitation
on the part of the political societies and leaders, and urged
to make a public pronouncement and tell the country exactly
how matters stood with regard to the fulfilment of the national aspirations. He adopted a cautious attitude, con-
fiding his disillusionment and fears only to a small circle of
his immediate collaborators; while in his public utterances,
he laid the emphasis on the prospects opened out by the impending arrival of the inter-Allied commission of inquiry.

Nevertheless, a feeling of alarm got abroad, and an agitation began for an organised insurgence against what was
freely described as being an inexplicable and therefore suspect reticence on Faisal's part. Then, a group of responsible leaders came forward with a proposal for the formation
of a national assembly. In this, the initiative was taken by
members of a recently-formed party: the Arab Independence
Party (*Hizb al-Istiqlal al-'Arabi*), which was none other than
the former society *al-Fatat* in a new guise.[1] Faisal gave his
support to the movement and tried to direct it into the
channel of orderly constitutional procedure. Elections were
held, necessarily in haste,[2] which were not confined to that

---

[1] In Damascus on the 5th of February, 1919, the committee of *al-Fatat*,
deeming that the need for secrecy no longer remained, had publicly revealed its existence and announced that it would continue its political
activities in the open under the name of *Hizb al-Istiqlal al-'Arabi*. The
membership rose enormously in the months that followed this announcement, and the society became active and influential in Iraq as well as in
Palestine and Syria. Its adherents are often referred to as *Istiqlalist* (i.e.,
Independentist), to distinguish between them and the members of other
societies founded for similar aims.

[2] The hurry had been prompted by a belief on the part of Faisal that the
visit of the inter-Allied Commission of inquiry would not be delayed.

portion of Syria which was under Arab administration (*O.E.T.A.* East), but embraced the French-administered *O.E.T.A.* West, and the British-administered *O.E.T.A.* South; and on the 2nd of July, the assembly henceforth known as the General Syrian Congress met in Damascus.

The Congress was nominally composed of a uniform number of delegates from all parts of Syria, but some of the representatives elected in *O.E.T.A.* West had been prevented by the French authorities from proceeding to Damascus. The opening session was attended by sixty-nine out of a total of eighty-five elected delegates representing Syria and Palestine, and including Christians in a higher proportion than their numerical strength in the country. The deliberations of the Congress resulted in a set of resolutions defining the national aims in regard to Syria, Palestine and Iraq being passed with practically unqualified unanimity.

The text of the Resolutions will be found in Appendix G. Its importance is that it contains an authoritative statement of the Arab attitude towards the issues of the day. Although the Congress had had to be elected in some haste and the customary routine of electoral procedure not fully observed everywhere, there is no doubt – as subsequent events amply confirmed – that it was a representative assembly in the true sense of the word, that its deliberations did reflect the fears and hopes of the vast majority of the population, and that the resolutions it passed may safely be taken as expressing those views and sentiments that were most widely held. Thus the text of the Resolutions is a reliable standard by which to measure the chasm between Arab aspirations and Allied designs as they had begun to manifest themselves in Paris.

The Resolutions were expressed in ten clauses and contained demands which may briefly be summarised as follows:

(a) recognition of the independence of Syria including Palestine as a sovereign state with the Amir Faisal as King; recognition of the independence of Iraq;

(b) repudiation of the Sykes-Picot Agreement and the Balfour Declaration and of any plan for the partition of

293

Syria or the creation of a Jewish Commonwealth in
Palestine;

(c) rejection of the political tutelage implied in the proposed
mandatory systems; but acceptance of foreign assistance
for a limited period provided it did not conflict with
national independence and unity, preference being given
to American or – failing America – to British assistance;

(d) rejection of French assistance in any form.

The Resolutions were passed amidst an impressive display
of patriotic fervour. The only dissentient voices heard were
those of a group of delegates who objected to the insertion of
the clause accepting foreign assistance. On all the other
clauses there was complete unanimity. And the wishes expressed by the Congress were echoed throughout the country;
for, as the Resolutions became known, mass demonstrations
were held in all those portions of Syria in which the French
held no sway, and delegations flocked to the capital to cheer
the Amir Faisal and acclaim the Congress.

7.

The proposal to send out a commission of inquiry representing all the four Powers never materialised. In the
weeks following the decision taken on the 25th of March,
it was subjected to a campaign of denigration and intrigue
which succeeded in wrecking the original scheme. The lead
in the campaign was taken by the Quai d'Orsay; and the
British Government, who were more lukewarm than ever now
that it had been decided to extend the inquiry to Iraq and
Palestine, found a pretext in the French and Zionist hostility
to it for backing out. Italy, having no direct stake, was indifferent. President Wilson alone held his ground. Certain
members of the United States Delegation were opposed to
the inquiry, not from any motive of national interest, but in
the belief that enough material for ascertaining the facts
was (or could be made) available in Paris, and that the
arrival of such a commission in Syria might add to the effervescence and arouse greater hopes than could ultimately be

fulfilled. But Wilson remained bent upon carrying out an investigation on the spot, even if that would mean sending out the American contingent by themselves.

The two commissioners whom he had selected were instructed to form their staff and hold themselves in readiness to start. Their official designation was 'American Section of the International Commission on Mandates in Turkey', but they came to be generally known as the King-Crane Commission, and will be so referred to hereafter.[1]

The Commission arrived in Jaffa on the 10th of June and spent six weeks visiting Palestine and Syria. They carried out as extensive an inquiry as they found possible in the time, interviewed a large number of delegations in some forty towns and rural centres, and received a total of over 1,800 petitions. They made a point of making themselves accessible to every shade of opinion without restriction. After a brief visit to Cilicia, they went to Constantinople where they drew up their report, and were back in Paris in the last week of August. On the 28th of that month, they deposited a copy of their report with the secretariat of the United States Delegation. Shortly after, Dr. King sailed for New York where he arranged for the report to be transmitted to President Wilson by the quickest means.

The King-Crane Report is now public property. At first, it was treated as a confidential document by everyone concerned, including the President. What action he may have taken beyond communicating its text to the Allied Governments concerned is not known. When Dr. King arrived in New York and caused the Report to be handed in at Washington about the middle of September, Wilson had already started on the speaking tour which culminated in his serious illness. It is doubtful whether he ever read the whole text; but he was aware of its general drift from the summary of findings which the two commissioners had previously telegraphed to him. On being approached in 1922 for permission

[1] The Commission was composed of two commissioners (Dr. Henry C. King and Mr. Charles R. Crane), three advisers (Professor Albert H. Lybyer, Dr. George R. Montgomery and Captain William Yale), and a secretary-treasurer (Captain Donald M. Brodie).

to make its contents known, he readily authorised publication, and the text of the Report appeared in full in at least one American journal.[1]

The King-Crane Report is a document of outstanding importance. It is the only source to which the historian can turn for a disinterested and wholly objective analysis of the state of feeling in Arab political circles in the period immediately following the War. The investigation carried out by the American·commissioners was the only attempt made on behalf of the Peace Conference to establish the facts relating to Arab aspirations by actual ascertainment on the spot: in that alone, their findings merit special attention. But it added greatly to the value of the inquiry that it was undertaken by a body with no national ambitions to promote, who approached their task with open minds, and that it was conducted by two men of recognised independence of judgment, in whom the qualities of insight and sanity were remarkably combined. Of that, the Report bears ample evidence throughout: perhaps its most outstanding characteristics are the shrewdness of its findings and the unmistakable honesty of its recommendations.[2]

The commissioners expressed themselves in favour of the mandatory system for Syria-Palestine and Iraq, but on condition that the mandate be for a limited term and that it should definitely aim at bringing the mandated countries to independent status as rapidly as conditions would allow. They recommended that Iraq be treated as one country and that the unity of Syria (including Palestine) be similarly preserved, subject to the maintenance of Lebanese autonomy within the framework of Syrian unity; that there be one Mandate for the whole of Iraq and one for Syria-Palestine; and that the form of government in each be that of a constitutional monarchy, with the Amir Faisal as King in Syria and

[1] The text I have consulted is that which appeared in *Editor and Publisher* (New York), issue dated December 2, 1922, of which the authenticity has never been questioned.
[2] The text of the recommendations, so far as they relate to Syria-Palestine and Iraq, will be found in Appendix H. Although the commissioners did not go to Iraq their Report contains recommendations for its future, based on data collected in Syria.

another Arab sovereign, to be chosen by plebiscite, to rule over Iraq.

On the subject of the choice of mandatories, the commissioners found that the consensus of opinion in Syria, while repudiating the 'mandated' form of tutelage, was overwhelmingly in favour of 'assistance' being provided by the United States or, failing her, by Great Britain, but on no account by France. After a reasoned analysis of their findings, they recommended that the United States be asked to undertake the single Mandate for all Syria and Great Britain to undertake one for Iraq. They added that if the Syrian mandate could not be assumed by the United States it should be assigned to Great Britain. They found themselves unable to recommend a French mandate, on the grounds that the attempt to establish one might precipitate war between the Arabs and the French, and force a dangerous alternative upon Great Britain.

The commissioners devoted a good deal of space to an analysis of the Zionist problem. They described themselves as having begun their study of it with minds predisposed in its favour; but that the facts of the situation they had found in Palestine had driven them to recommend a limitation of Zionist ambitions. The statements made to them by Jewish representatives had convinced them that the Zionists looked forward to a practically complete dispossession of the non-Jewish inhabitants of Palestine by various forms of purchase; and they expressed the opinion that such a consummation, even if it were achieved within the forms of law, would be a gross violation of the rights of the people and of the principles proclaimed by the Allies and by President Wilson. Not one of the British officers whom they had consulted believed that the Zionist programme could be carried out except by force of arms. They felt bound to recommend that the Zionist programme be greatly reduced, that Jewish immigration be definitely limited and that the idea of making Palestine into a Jewish Commonwealth be abandoned.

It was only to be expected that so candid and forceful a statement would make extremely disagreeable reading for the Versailles peacemakers, as indeed it did. The Report was pigeon-holed and ignored, and was not acted upon even in Washington. In the three years that elapsed before it became public property, Great Britain and France had devised and imposed a 'settlement' of their own making, in which the advice of the King-Crane Commission had been totally and, as it turned out, unwisely disregarded.

8.

In August, the Amir Faisal was invited by Mr. Lloyd George to visit Europe again. The tension in Anglo-French relations over the Arab question was becoming dangerously strained. On the French side, the campaign engineered by politicians of the 'colonial' school had rallied an influential section of opinion, and the Press had embarked on a noisy and sometimes virulent denunciation of what was represented to the public as the nefarious intrigues of the British in Syria. In July, an article had appeared in the *Bulletin de l'Asie Française* over the signature of M. Robert de Caix, a well-known publicist and an authority on French colonial policy, which was a passionate indictment of Great Britain. The article created a stir out of all proportion to its merits: it was couched in language of the kind that inflames, and the fact that it revealed knowledge as well as fervour gave it added weight. The author's line of attack was that Great Britain was trying to evade her obligations under the Sykes-Picot Agreement by a variety of devious means of which one was to encourage the Arabs to oppose French 'rights' in Syria.

The campaign had not been ignored on the other side of the Channel, and had even led to a certain amount of retaliation in the English Press. But there was another factor at work: the mounting cost of the British garrisons in Syria and Cilicia. Neither of these regions came within the category of Turkish possessions coveted by Great Britain, and she had nothing to gain by leaving her garrisons there until peace was actually concluded. Then it was that Mr. Lloyd George, with his flair for opportunity, decided to act. He made a proposal to Clemenceau which had the double merit of placating France and reducing Great Britain's expenditure.

There was only one way of placating the French Government in relation to Syria and that was to give them their pound of flesh as defined in the Sykes-Picot Agreement. In his article, M. de Caix had stated the issue plainly: although he regarded the Sykes-Picot Agreement as a fraudulent document, since its provisions conflicted with Sir Henry McMahon's earlier compact with the Sharif Husain, yet the 'rights' acquired by France to a mandate in Syria were the outcome of a long tradition and were therefore unchallengeable; and it was, in the French view, a condition of Anglo-French harmony that Great Britain should recognise that claim. The proposal put forward by Mr. Lloyd George did not necessarily imply that the claim was fully recognised, but was designed to meet it half-way as well as to lighten the British tax-payer's burden. It remained to be seen whether it would commend itself to the Arabs, and thus Faisal was invited to come to Europe.

The main provision in the proposal was that the British garrisons in Syria and Cilicia were to be withdrawn and replaced in Cilicia (*O.E.T.A.* North) and western Syria (*O.E.T.A.* West) by French troops, and in Eastern Syria (*O.E.T.A.* East) by Arab troops. This gave the Arabs the exclusive garrisoning of the towns and districts of 'Aqaba, 'Amman, Damascus, Homs, Hama and Aleppo, and placed the French in occupation of all the Syrian littoral west of the Sykes-Picot line (Blue Area in the map). The withdrawal was to begin on the 1st of November. Palestine west of the Jordan (*O.E.T.A.* South) was to remain garrisoned by the British. There was also a provision reserving to the British Government the right to construct a railway and a pipe-line of their own to connect Iraq with the Mediterranean at Haifa 'in accordance with the principles of the Sykes-Picot Agreement'.[1]

---

[1] The text of the British aide-mémoire in which the provisions of Mr. Lloyd George's proposal were set forth is given in David Hunter Miller, *My Diary at the Conference of Paris*, Vol. XVI.

At a meeting of the Supreme Council held in Paris on the 15th of September, Mr. Lloyd George explained his proposal and it was readily assented to by Clemenceau, but only in so far as it provided for the substitution of French for British troops, and on the understanding that his acceptance would not prejudice the ultimate settlement of mandates or boundaries. What Clemenceau meant by making his acceptance a limited one was that the French Government desired eventually to obtain a mandate for Eastern Syria as well and were far from reconciled to the idea of its becoming an Arab State independent of French control.

Faisal reached London on the 19th, was received by the Prime Minister and the acting Foreign Secretary on that day and informed of what had taken place in Paris. He took great exception to Lloyd George's proposal; and, after a series of inconclusive conferences with him and other ministers, addressed a formal protest to the Prime Minister. It was in the form of a note, dated October 11, and stated the reasons why the Arabs could not consent to the measures set forth in the British aide-mémoire.

In that note,[1] Faisal pointed out that when, shortly after the Armistice, he had withdrawn his troops to the interior of Syria, he had done so only on Allenby's explicit assurance that the country would remain garrisoned by British troops until the final settlement by the Peace Conference. He protested not only against the proposed measures in themselves, but also against their being put forward as a natural corollary to the Sykes-Picot Agreement to which the Arabs had not been a party. Taking his stand on the assurances contained in the Declaration to the Seven (June 16, 1918) and in the Anglo-French Declaration (November 7, 1918), he stated his inability to accept the British proposal and made a strong plea for the summoning of a conference of the three Powers (Great Britain, France and the United States) to discuss and settle the future of the Arab countries on the basis

---

[1] The text of the note has frequently appeared in the Arabic Press, and notably in the issue dated September 14, 1934 of *al-Jami'a al-Islamiya* (Jaffa).

of the pledges made and the principles proclaimed by the Allies.

The note formed a temperate and cogent protest, and the case it presented was one that the British Government knew to be, in its essentials, unanswerable. It added to their embarrassment that they had grounds for believing that it was the intention of the French eventually to occupy Eastern Syria, and with that knowledge in their minds, they put pressure on Faisal to enter into direct negotiations with Clemenceau. They hoped that a Franco-Arab agreement, if one could be concluded, would not only relieve them of an embarrassing obligation, but also allay the suspicions of their French allies.

Faisal did come to an agreement with the French. Finding that his plea for an immediate conference of the Powers was falling on deaf ears, he yielded to the British Government's pressure and went to Paris. On the 27th of November, he had an interview with Clemenceau at which the conditions of a provisional Franco-Arab arrangement were discussed and agreed upon. It stipulated that the occupation by France of the Lebanon and the rest of the coastal regions of Syria as far north as Alexandretta would be respected by the Arab Government in the interior, but that that occupation would not extend to the region of the Biqa'[1], which was to become a neutral zone between the French and the Arab administrations. It also stipulated that the Arab State should henceforth turn to France for any assistance it might require. The arrangement was to be regarded as provisional pending final settlement by the Peace Conference.

In consenting to this arrangement, Faisal appeared to be surrendering ground which it was not in his power to give away. For, quite apart from his father's instructions, the feeling in the Arab world was strongly against the dismemberment of Syria and the imposition of any form of foreign tutelage. Of that, he was well aware. But to him the understanding with Clemenceau seemed the only alternative

---

[1] The plain of Coele-Syria between the Lebanon and Ante-Lebanon ranges, in which Baalbek stands.

to a breach with the Allies and it had, in his eyes, the saving grace of being a provisional arrangement which, with the support he still expected from the British Government and from the United States, could not fail to be modified when the Arab question would come up for final settlement.

Faisal has often been accused of weakness by admirers as well as by detractors; and his critics point to the compromise with Clemenceau as an outstanding instance. The criticism is to this extent severe, that it does not take into account his temperamental preference for peaceful solutions or that astonishing credulity which, in the days when he was still unversed in the ways and shifts of European diplomacy, was his. So deeply imbued was he with the strength and the justice of the Arab case that he had persuaded himself that all that was needed for its vindication was a fair hearing by a tribunal of the Powers with the United States among the judges. The British Government's decision to begin evacuating Syria meant that a collision between French and Arab forces could not be avoided unless some provisional understanding were arrived at to ensure a truce until the advent of the lasting Peace. Faisal was wise enough to set his will against an outbreak of hostilities; and when account is taken of that queer combination of sagacity and credulity, the bald charge of weakness loses much of its weight.

He remained in Europe in the belief that a conference of the Powers was about to be convened at last. As for his responsibilities in Syria, he tried to discharge them as best he could by keeping in constant communication with his younger brother, the Amir Zaid, whom he had left in charge at Damascus.

9.

Preparations for the British withdrawal began in the first week of November. As was to be expected, they were regarded in Syria as the prelude to the handing over of the Lebanon and the coastal regions to the north of it to France for permanent occupation; and it was not long before the discontent was to find its expression in acts of hostility. When news came of Faisal's agreement with Clemenceau it was greeted with disapproval and, later, with open condemnation. It was widely felt that Faisal had sold the country to the French. Incidents broke out in various places: minor clashes which presently led to hostilities of a more serious character between French and Arab forces, notably near Tripoli, at Baalbek and further south in the regions of Marj 'Uyun and the Upper Jordan.

Faisal decided to pay a quick visit to Syria, to try and relieve the tension and obtain a specific mandate from the National Congress for the prosecution of his negotiations in Paris. He arrived in Bairut on the 14th of January 1920, and went on to Damascus where he met with a somewhat chilly reception. Aleppo, which he visited a fortnight later, turned out to be scarcely less frigid. He found the majority of the leaders in a state of dismay at the prospect which his understanding with Clemenceau had opened out; and the mass demonstrations which paraded the streets with cries of 'Unity' and 'Independence' gave substance to the disapproval expressed by the leaders. He used all his powers of persuasion to obtain their assent to his returning to Paris with a delegation of their own number. But however patient his negotiations with them and however ingenious his arguments, the retort came up again and again that, since the Paris conversations had envisaged the dismemberment of Syria (into Palestine, the Lebanon and Eastern Syria) and the occupation of parts of it by foreign troops, they could not be regarded as offering a basis for discussion.

Never before had the desire for Arab unity, which was implicit in the very origins of the national movement, expressed itself with such vigour; and it was all the more vigorous as it was voiced by those who had taken an active part in the Revolt. The city of Damascus – the heart of the Arab world – was then harbouring a great number of political leaders, army officers and students from Palestine and Iraq, as well as from all parts of Syria. Taken together, they represented the views and feelings of the vast majority in

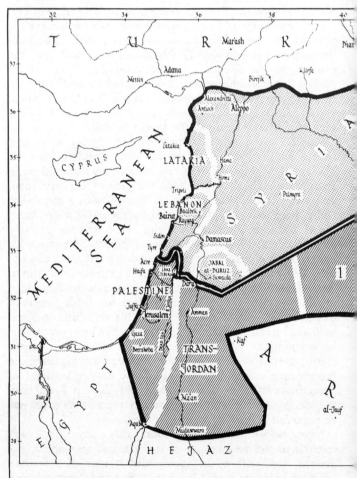

THE BRITISH ▨ AND ▨
IN SYRIA-PAL

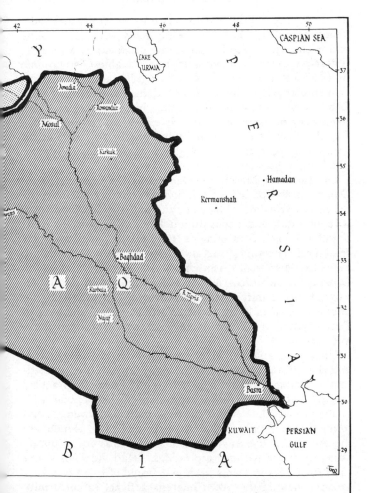

42   44   46   48   50

Y

Amadia

Rowanduz

Mosul

Kirkuk

·Hamadan

Kermanshah
·

LAKE
URMIA

P
E
R
S
I
A

A

Q

Baghdad

Karbala

R. Tigris

Najaf

Basra

KUWAIT

PERSIAN
GULF

B   I   A

57
56
55
54
53
32
31
30
29

NCH MANDATES
NE AND IRAQ

those countries on the two dominant issues: Unity and Independence. And while there were many who were willing and even eager to see Independence qualified by a recourse to foreign assistance, none were for the slightest compromise on the doctrine of Unity. In vain did Faisal argue that the dismemberment of Syria envisaged in his agreement with Clemenceau was not final, and that, in consenting to it as a temporary measure, he had only bowed to the inevitable. But the weeks and then the months went by, without his succeeding in forming a delegation to accompany him or obtaining a mandate for himself.

On the 8th of March, the General Syrian Congress sat in Damascus and passed a resolution proclaiming the independence of Syria (including Palestine and the Lebanon) as a sovereign state and a constitutional monarchy with the Amir Faisal as King. A meeting of Iraqi leaders passed a similar resolution concerning Iraq and chose the Amir 'Abdullah to be its first monarch. A proviso was added reserving to the Lebanon its acquired right to autonomy within the framework of Syrian unity. It was also provided that the structure of government in Syria and Iraq would rest on the basis of Decentralisation – the old bone of contention between Turks and Arabs.

Since Iraq and Palestine were under British occupation and the coastal regions of Syria under French, the proceedings at Damascus could have led to no immediate practical result. But they were an expression of the popular will, giving voice to the tenets of the Arab national movement and to the wishes of the populations concerned; and, as such, left the authors of the Anglo-French Declaration in no uncertainty as to the national aspirations. Had the French and the British Governments been in a frame of mind to take a broader view of their own interests and act in conformity with the terms of the Declaration, they could not have ignored that manifestation of the popular will. Instead of which they announced that they would not recognise any validity to the proceedings at Damascus, and took steps to convene an early conference of the Supreme Council. They also invited Faisal to return to Europe. But their action in denouncing the proceedings of the Congress was not only a short-sighted breach of their own promises: it was also a blunder, in that it made it harder than ever for Faisal to obtain a mandate for his mission from the national delegates.

The Supreme Council met at San Remo and took its decisions on the 25th of April. The whole of the Arab Rectangle lying between the Mediterranean and the Persian frontier was to be placed under mandatory rule. Syria was to be broken up into three separate fractions: Palestine, the Lebanon, and a reduced 'Syria' consisting of what was left. Iraq was to remain undivided. As for the mandates, they were so distributed as to suit the ambitions of each Power. Syria and the Lebanon were to be placed under a single mandate to be entrusted to France; Great Britain was to hold a mandate for Iraq and another for Palestine. A rider was added to the effect that the mandate for Palestine would carry with it an obligation to apply the Balfour Declaration. Nothing was said about the glaring contradiction between those decisions and the declared wishes of the peoples concerned.

The decisions taken at San Remo were made public on the 5th of May, and their promulgation gave birth to a new sentiment in the Arab world – that of contempt for the Powers of the West. It was not only the denial of the two cherished goals of independence and unity that provoked the revulsion of feeling, but also, and more profoundly, the breach of faith. The distinction is an important one: it foreshadows the subsequent transition from disappointment to despair, and in it lies the key to the upheavals that followed. In the eyes of the Arabs, the San Remo decisions were nothing short of a betrayal, and the fact that they violated a compact sealed in blood made the betrayal more hateful and despicable.

There is little doubt that the verdict of history will substantially endorse the Arab view. Whatever else may be said of the San Remo decisions, they did violate the general principles proclaimed and the specific promises made by the

Allies, and more particularly by Great Britain. The purport of the pledges given in secret is now known: what with that and the assurances made publicly, the student has all the relevant material for a judgment. It was on the strength of those promises that the Arabs had come into the War and made their contribution and their sacrifices; and that fact alone sufficed to turn the corresponding obligation into a debt of honour. What the San Remo conference did was, in effect, to ignore the debt and come to decisions which, on all the essential points, ran counter to the wishes of the peoples concerned.

10.

No sooner was the San Remo conference over than the relations between French and Arabs in Syria turned for the worse. The Mandate which had been assigned to France gave her what some of her politicians and bureaucrats had long desired: a free hand to impose her will on Faisal. The Arabs, on their side, goaded into despair by the San Remo decisions, began to put pressure on him to declare war upon the French.

Torn as he was between Général Gouraud's[1] hectoring messages and the heated entreaties of his followers, Faisal vacillated and temporised. He refused to declare war upon the French, but winked (and possibly even connived) at the attacks conducted by certain youthful Arab officers on the French positions near the Lebanese border. When, on the other hand, it was reported to him that the French had sent bands into the Arab zone to stir up trouble, he contented himself with making representations to Gouraud, while the feeling among his followers mounted to fever-pitch. Although his confidence had been severely shaken by the San Remo decisions, he had not lost all hope of securing a fair hearing before a conference of France, Great Britain and the United States. He did not realise at the time the full

[1] He had been appointed in November 1919 to be commander-in-chief and, later, high commissioner in the territories under French mandate.

significance of the change in American sentiment towards the politics of the Old World, and he still longed for an opportunity to visit Europe again at the earliest possible time.

In July, matters came to a head. When Faisal wrote to Gouraud early in the month to announce his decision to sail for Europe at last, the latter informed him that he was about to send him an important communication from his Government. This communication was eventually despatched on the 14th of July and reached Faisal later in the day. It was an ultimatum amounting to a summons on five counts, which had to be complied with in four days, failing which the French Government threatened 'to resume its full liberty of action'.

The text of the ultimatum is known.[1] It enumerated a series of allegations against the Arab administration in Damascus, some of which related to measures taken by that government in the exercise of its authority, others to the anti-French propaganda and acts of hostility carried out under its aegis. This was followed by a statement of the five conditions which the Arab administration were required to comply with: the handing over of the Rayyaq-Aleppo Railway to French military control, which was to entail the occupation by French forces of the city of Aleppo and the stations at Rayyaq, Baalbek, Homs and Hama; the abolition of conscription and the reduction of the Arab army strength; an unqualified acceptance of the French mandate; the adoption of the currency system imposed by the French administration; and the punishment of persons notoriously implicated in acts of anti-French hostility. The text of the communication bore evidence of ulterior motives, in the manner of the Austro-Hungarian ultimatum to Servia in July 1914.

In the light of the text and of what afterwards happened, it is clear beyond all doubt that the French had made up their minds in any case to extend their military occupation to the rest of Syria, and that the ultimatum was no more than a tactical move to that end. To the surprise and then the anger of his followers, Faisal decided to accept all the conditions

[1] A full translation has appeared in *al-Nahar* (Bairut).

without discussion. In doing that, he was exposing himself to the gravest kind of unpopularity, and he knew it. But he felt that, in view of the obvious French determination, a rejection of the ultimatum would be invoked as a pretext for the occupation of Damascus; and that, taking the long view, his wisest course was to yield on the immediate issue and proceed at once to London and raise the whole question in a different atmosphere. His reliance on the British Government was still a factor in his policy, and the fact that a telegram had just reached him from Lord Curzon advising him to avoid hostilities at all costs, had strengthened him in his decision.

Although the ultimatum was formally accepted and a beginning had been made to execute its conditions, French columns advanced on Damascus and entered the city on the tenth day following its presentation. Not all Faisal's pliability, nor his surrender of pride for the sake of ultimate freedom, nor the courage with which he faced the anger of his followers had sufficed. The whole population of his capital rose at the news of the French advance, and the measures which he found it necessary to take to restore order cost the lives of over one hundred of his subjects shot by his police in the streets of Damascus. Others were killed in a gallant attempt to stem the advance of the columns. As the French were nearing the Maisalun Pass, a body of some 2,000 patriots rushed out in defiance of Faisal's orders and joined the small regular force guarding the pass. The heroic stand they made proved futile against the aeroplanes and the superior numbers and equipment of the French, and their ranks were decimated. The young Minister of War, Yusuf-al-'Azmeh, was killed leading a handful of the regular forces against the French machine-guns. The bulk of the army garrisoning the city had already been demobilised by Faisal, in compliance with the ultimatum. The road to Damascus lay open, and there was no further resistance.

There is no need to go into a detailed recital of the events of those ten days. They were so crowded with incidents occurring in quick succession, and the evidence is so conflicting, that only after a patient and meticulous examination can the truth in general outline be unravelled. The partisans of each side have produced evidence to satisfy themselves that it was some act committed by the other that brought about all the rest: the sequence of events is so tangled as to provide material for several theories. All that we need concern ourselves with here is that the occupation of Damascus was not an effect of incidental causes, but of a pre-conceived plan, that the ultimatum was no more than a tactical prelude to the fulfilment of that plan, and that the only way in which Faisal could have hindered or prevented its execution was to have declared war upon the French and raised the country and the tribes against them. This is not the view taken by the apologists of the French, who represent the occupation of Damascus and the rest of Syria as an act of self-defence, in much the same vein as Japanese spokesmen have described the occupation of Shanghai and Nanking as a measure of self-preservation forced upon them by the dangerous menace of Chinese aggression.

One of the first acts of the French in Damascus was to invite Faisal to leave the country, which he did on the 28th of July in company with a number of his closest associates. He went by train to Dar'a, crossing that plain of the Upper Hauran along which the forces of the Revolt and their British allies had swept in their triumphant gallop towards Damascus, and then to Haifa whence he sailed for Italy. There he remained in a retreat on the shores of Lake Maggiore until the following December when he arrived in London, in response to an invitation from the British Government.

II.

Faisal's belief in the friendly sentiments of the British towards him was no delusion. The accusation, often made in Arab circles, that Great Britain, having used the Arabs to her ends, deliberately turned against them when the War was won requires qualification. Both in the ranks of the

Government and outside it there were those who felt that
an obligation had been incurred and were anxious to see
it honourably met. There was also genuines sympathy
for Faisal and the cause he represented. Save for the
Americans who, although sympathetic, remained platonic, it
is true to say that the British were the only friends the Arabs
had at Versailles. And if Faisal repeatedly resorted to them
for help, despite the advice of many of his own followers, it
was because he knew, what they did not, that in England he
could count upon a measure of support which no other Power
was likely to give, not only to him personally but also to the
Arab cause in general.

On the subject of Syria in particular, the British Government had, at any rate during the Peace Conference, stoutly
championed the Arab claim to independence. The retort
might be made that that was because Great Britain had no
stake in Syria and had nothing to lose; but the fact remains
that, in the early months of 1919, her Prime Minister was
acting as though he would join issue with the French over
Syria. There is a passage in the minutes of the secret conference of the Big Four, held on the 20th of March 1919,
in Paris[1] which is of great importance for the light it throws
on the contrast between the French and British attitudes:

' . . . .Mr. LLOYD GEORGE said that the agreement
[i.e., between the Sharif Husain and Sir H. McMahon] might
have been made by England alone, but it was England who
had organised the whole of the Syrian campaign. There
would have been no question of Syria but for England.
Great Britain had put from 900,000 to 1,000,000 men into
the field against Turkey, but Arab help had been essential;
that was a point on which General Allenby could speak.

'GENERAL ALLENBY said it had been invaluable.

'Mr. LLOYD GEORGE, continuing, said that it was on the
basis of the above-quoted letter [i.e., Sir H. McMahon's note of
October 24, 1915] that King Husain had put all his resources
into the field, which had helped us most materially to win
the victory. France had for practical purposes accepted
our undertaking to King Husain in signing the 1916 [Sykes-
Picot] agreement. This had not been M. Pichon, but his

[1] Ray Stannard Baker, *Wilson and World Settlement*, Vol. III.

310

predecessors. He was bound to say that if the British Government now agreed that Damascus, Homs, Hama and Aleppo should be included in the sphere of direct French influence, they would be breaking faith with the Arabs, and they could not face this. He was particularly anxious for M. Clemenceau to follow this. The agreement of 1916 had been signed subsequent to the letter to King Husain. In the following extract from the agreement of 1916 France recognised Arab independence:

> "It is accordingly understood between the French and British Governments: (1) That France and Great Britain are prepared to recognise and uphold an independent Arab State or Confederation of Arab States in the areas A and B marked on the annexed map[1] under the suzerainty of an Arab Chief."

'Hence France, by this act, practically recognised our agreement with King Husain by excluding Damascus, Homs, Hama and Aleppo from the Blue zone of direct administration, for the map attached to the agreement showed that Damascus, Homs, Hama and Aleppo were included, not in the zone of direct administration, but in the independent Arab State.

'M. PICHON said that this had never been contested, but how could France be bound by an agreement the very existence of which was unknown to her at the time when the 1916 agreement was signed? In the 1916 agreement, France had not in any way recognised the Hejaz.[2] She had undertaken to uphold "an independent Arab State or Confederation of Arab States," but not the King of the Hejaz. If France was promised a mandate for Syria, she would undertake to do nothing except in agreement with the Arab State or Confederation of States. This is the role which France demanded in Syria. If Great Britain would only promise her good offices, he believed that France could reach an understanding with Faisal.'

Mr. Lloyd George's attitude at that meeting shows that the British Government did recognise the justice of the Arab

---

[1] v. map facing p. 244.

[2] This assertion does not tally with the facts. In actual fact, the authority of the Sharif of Mecca was recognised in Article 3 of the Sykes-Picot Agreement as having a say in the disposal of the Arab countries, with special reference to the future of Palestine. Moreover, France had formally recognised the Sharif Husain as King of the Hejaz (v. p. 213 *supra*).

claim to independence in Syria and that they gave it their unequivocal support at the Peace Conference. It disposes of the allegation that Great Britain made no effort to fulfil her promises to the Arabs outside the Arabian Peninsula. But it also shows that she was aware that the desire of the French to occupy the regions of Damascus, Homs, Hama and Aleppo was incompatible with her own obligations to the Arabs. In words of unmistakable meaning, Mr. Lloyd George declared that, if the British Government were to agree to the inclusion of the four towns in the sphere of direct French influence, they would be breaking faith with the Arabs, and he added that 'they could not face this'. That is where the betrayal occurred: the French occupied the four towns and brought them into the sphere of their direct influence, while the British Government looked on and assented. Thus the charge that history will level at Great Britain is not that she made no effort at the Peace Conference to redeem any of her pledges, but that the only effort she made to fulfil them was in regard to Syria – as distinct from Palestine and Iraq – and that, even in the case of Syria, she ended by consenting to an act of spoliation which constituted, on the admission of her Prime Minister, a breach of faith with the Arabs.

12.

What with the decisions of the San Remo conference, the occupation of the whole of Syria by the French, the consolidation of British control in Iraq on a basis which denied even the outward forms of self-government, and the emergence of a policy of intensive Zionist development in Palestine, the year 1920 has an evil name in Arab annals: it is referred to as the Year of Catastrophe ('*Am al-Nakba*). It saw the first armed risings that occurred in protest against the post-War settlement imposed by the Allies on the Arab countries. In that year, serious outbreaks took place in Syria, Palestine and Iraq. There came a time when practically the whole of the Arab Rectangle was seething with discontent expressing itself in acts of violence.

The first of those outbreaks occurred in Palestine at Easter, when the Arab population of Jerusalem, taking alarm at the activities and utterances of the Zionist leaders, made an onslaught upon the Jews. The causes of the outbreak have never been officially explained. A commission of inquiry, appointed by the British commander-in-chief, did investigate and report upon the disturbances; but its report was never published and remains a secret to the present day, save for the generally accepted conclusion that, in the opinion of the commission, the causes of the outbreak were political and had their roots in the fears felt by the Arab population for the future of the country.

In Syria, the occasional clashes which had taken place in the first half of the year were followed, after the entry of the French into Damascus, by a series of organised attacks in different parts of the country. In the region between Aleppo and Antioch, a group of leaders succeeded in raising a considerable body of volunteers and fought several engagements with French columns sent out against them. The insurgent forces could not get the better of the large reinforcements which the French had brought into the country, and were mastered almost everywhere before the year was out. But their failure, far from reconciling the population to its lot, made the French mandate appear still more hateful and served to increase the disaffection and strengthen the spirit of resistance.

By far the most serious rising occurred in Iraq. Throughout the spring, the discontent against the régime of direct British rule had found its expression in a movement of spontaneous agitation. It was not an anti-British movement in the sense that it was inspired by mere hostility to Great Britain, but an insurgence against the denial of independence and the arbitrary imposition of the mandatory system. Instead of enjoying Arab rule with a measure of British assistance, the people found themselves subjected to British rule with nominal Arab assistance. It added to the intensity of the agitation that it was furthered and encouraged by the Iraqi leaders in Damascus and, more particularly, by the

Iraqi branch of *al-'Ahd*, the pre-War secret society of Arab officers in the Ottoman army,[1] most of whom had served in the Revolt. The agitation had been met by ill-advised measures of repression carried out with single-minded severity and determination by Colonel A. T. Wilson, the acting Civil Commissioner, who, in his fervent belief in the virtues of good government, remained impervious to the manifestations of the Arab fervour for self-government. Wholesale arrests of leaders, accompanied by acts of summary punishment and deportation took place which, as they did not remove the real causes of the discontent, served mainly to inflame it.

The announcement of the San Remo decisions came as the crowning provocation; and, from that moment, the feeling hardened into a determination to revolt. The committee of *al-'Ahd* issued a proclamation denouncing the decisions and calling upon the people of Iraq to resist the dictation of the Allied Powers by force. On the 17th of June, it was announced that the British Government had authorised the calling of a General Elective Assembly for the purpose of drawing up an organic law for Iraq, but the announcement had come too late to have a pacifying effect, and in any case it left the San Remo decisions as they stood. Towards the end of June, an incident brought matters to a head, and the tribes of the middle Euphrates rose.

The story of the rebellion has often been told, but perhaps the most reliable account is to be found in a recent work of outstanding scholarly merit.[2] It is a distressing tale of warfare between friends, of which the horror is exceeded only by the folly which brought it about. It lasted from July to October at the end of which the toll of losses had risen to some 10,000 casualties. The number of Arabs killed is not known with any certainty: it may have been as high as 4,000. Over 400 British lives were lost, apart from 1,800

---

[1] v. Chapter VI, Section 6, *supra*.
[2] Philip Willard Ireland, *Iraq: A Study in Political Development*, 1937, a work of admirable fairness and accuracy, so far as the chronicling of events goes, to which I am indebted for certain facts concerning the rebellion in Iraq.

other casualties. The cost to the British exchequer was over £40,000,000, which was more than three times the total amount of the subsidies paid by Great Britain – in gold, arms and supplies – for the furtherance of the Arab Revolt from beginning to end. The damage to property and to the sources of revenue in the country was immense.

What added to the gravity of the rebellion was that it took on the character of a religious crusade. At first, during the greater part of July, it had been directed mainly by tribal chiefs and by ex-officers of the Arab Revolt. As the weeks went by and the rebels gained ground, the religious leaders of the Shi'a joined the movement openly in the hope of giving it the intensity of a holy war. By the end of July, when news had come of the French occupation of Damascus, the leaders of the insurgence felt that the moment had come for a supreme effort. It took the form of a general call to *jihad*, which was first proclaimed early in August in Najaf and Karbala, the two holiest cities of the Shi'a in Iraq, and later throughout the whole countryside of the middle and lower Euphrates. The rebellion spread to parts of the country which had not yet stirred, and the conflagration became general. The time came when, for several weeks in August and September, the rebels were masters everywhere except for the three principal cities of Baghdad, Basra and Mosul. In the countryside, the Administration had lost its authority, and control of affairs was assumed by provisional governments proclaimed in various centres by the local leaders.

Early in October, Sir Percy Cox arrived in Iraq to resume office as Civil Commissioner. By that time, the back of the rebellion had been broken but the country was still far from peaceful. He took immediate steps to implement the British Government's decision, announced in the preceding June, to bring about the preparation of an organic law by a representative Iraqi body. A provisional Arab government was formed. It was known as the Council of State and consisted of Iraqi personalities serving as ministers, with British advisers attached to each department. Ultimate control was vested in the hands of Sir Percy Cox, who now assumed the title of High Commissioner. This government was, in effect, British with an Arab façade. Its appointment did nothing to allay the feeling against the mandate or reconcile the population of Iraq to an acceptance of mandatory rule. But it served as a bridge between the British authority and the disaffected population, and paved the way to a series of developments which, in course of time, were to lead to the abolition of the mandate and the grant to Iraq of its political independence.

13.

The losses occasioned by the rebellion in Iraq caused an intensification of the campaign in England for the reduction of expenditure on commitments abroad. The need for economy drove the British Government to act. On the initiative of Mr. Winston Churchill, Secretary of State for the Colonies, a conference was called in Cairo in March 1921, to examine the position in the Arab countries and devise measures for remedying it. Decisions were taken at the conference, which led to a radical change of policy in Iraq, and to changes of a different order of importance in that part of Southern Syria which lies to the east of Jordan.

In the weeks preceding the conference, Faisal had had numerous conversations in London with personalities in and out of the Government, and in particular with Mr. Churchill and Colonel Lawrence who was then serving as personal adviser on Arab affairs to the Colonial Secretary. Those conversations had resulted in an understanding of which the upshot was that the British Government would hand over the administration in Iraq to an Arab government, use their influence to secure the nomination of Faisal to be King of Iraq and enter into negotiations with him for the conclusion of a treaty of alliance to replace the mandate.

The conference assembled in Cairo on the 12th of March. It was entirely composed of British officials and soldiers, among whom were the High Commissioner for Iraq (Sir

Percy Cox) and the High Commissioner for Palestine (Sir Herbert Samuel). The conference decided to recommend that effect be given at the earliest time to the understanding arrived at in London between Faisal and Churchill. It was proposed that Faisal should proceed to Iraq as a candidate for the throne, to be proclaimed King by a plebiscite of the people. The hope was entertained that, by establishing an Arab government in Iraq to pave the way for the abolition of the mandate, it would become possible for the British Government to reduce their garrisons considerably and effect a large economy. For the rebellion of 1920 had brought it home to them that one of the ways of avoiding wasteful expenditure was to keep the promises they had made. It was a policy of *Economy with Honour*.

On the 24th of March, Mr. Churchill arrived in Jerusalem, and there again his main problem was to devise measures for the reduction of commitments. The problem did not affect Palestine directly except in so far as the situation which had arisen east of the Jordan constituted a menace to the security of the territory under British mandate in which the experiment of establishing a National Home for Jews was in process of execution. The Amir 'Abdullah had un-expectedly appeared in Ma'an in November 1920 at the head of a body of retainers and tribesmen, and was credited with the intention of raising a larger force to invade Syria and avenge his brother's expulsion from Damascus. He had done nothing in the intervening months to give effect to that intention, yet the authorities in Palestine were disquieted by the fact of his presence and the possibilities latent in the general state of disaffection. The regions east of Jordan had formed part of the Arab administration set up under the Amir Faisal, but had not come under French occupation; and Great Britain had persuaded France to agree to their inclusion in the area of the British mandate. Mr. Churchill invited the Amir 'Abdullah to confer with him in Jerusalem and a series of conversations took place, also attended by Lawrence, at which a provisional arrangement was arrived at.

The arrangement with 'Abdullah had to be provisional as he was unable to agree to anything in the nature of a final settlement without previous consultation with his father. His claim for the constitution of Palestine and Transjordan (as the regions east of the Jordan from a point below Dar'a to 'Aqaba came to be known) into a single Arab state was rejected on the grounds that it would conflict with Great Britain's promises to the Jews; and as none of the alternatives which 'Abdullah put forward, such as the incorporation of Transjordan with Iraq, commended itself to Churchill, it was provisionally agreed that Great Britain should use her good offices with France to secure the restoration of an Arab administration in Syria with the Amir 'Abdullah at its head; and that, in the meanwhile, he should remain in Transjordan, check all movement of hostility on the part of the disaffected population and thus pave the way to a reconciliation with the French. The arrangement was for six months during which 'Abdullah was to receive financial assistance from the British Government to enable him to create and maintain an Arab force to be recruited locally for the preservation of order in Transjordan.

It has been said of the Cairo Conference that it resulted in a substantial fulfilment of the promises made to the Arabs in the War. The claim is valid only in regard to Iraq, since the policy outlined in Cairo in 1921 did lead to the recognition of the country's independence in the following year and, eventually, to the replacement of the Mandate by a treaty of alliance between Great Britain and the independent state of Iraq. But so far as the western half of the Arab Rectangle was concerned, the breach of faith remained unredressed, and the denial of freedom to Syria as a whole was made worse by the consecration of the country's dismemberment: northern Syria being left to her fate under French occupation; Palestine remaining under direct British administration; and the new state of Transjordan, carved out of the former *O.E.T.A.* East, becoming absorbed into the area of British mandatory control. It is difficult to find a parallel for such flagrant disregard of promises made, and the claim which is sometimes advanced on behalf of the Cairo Conference does not bear investigation, even when it is pùt forward with the weight of T. E. Lawrence's backing.

In a footnote to p. 276 of *Seven Pillars of Wisdom* (1935) Lawrence wrote: –

> '. . . Mr. Winston Churchill was entrusted by our harassed Cabinet with the settlement of the Middle East; and in a few weeks, at his conference in Cairo, he made straight all the tangle, finding solutions fulfilling (I think) our promises in letter and spirit (where humanly possible) without sacrificing any interest of our Empire or any interest of the·people concerned. So we were quit of the war-time Eastern adventure, with clean hands, but three years too late to earn the gratitude which peoples, if not states, can pay.'

The claims made in that footnote are so palpably untenable as to cast serious doubts on Lawrence's understanding of the issues involved. For, in actual fact, Mr. Churchill's solutions – with the exception of Iraq – fulfilled neither the letter nor the spirit of the promises; while the failure of his efforts at 'making straight all the tangle' is only too apparent in the light of the measures of coercion which were subsequently resorted to in vain by France in Syria and by Great Britain in Palestine to force the mandates through upon an unwilling population. Stranger still is the claim that those solutions did not sacrifice any interest of the people concerned. Yet there is this of value in Lawrence's observation that it illustrates one aspect of his connexion with the Arab problem, which must not be overlooked when the time comes for an historical assessment of his contribution to the Arab national movement.

14.

The time has not come when that assessment can be made with any finality. The available evidence is still overwhelmingly one-sided, since it rests mainly on Lawrence's own revelations and on the testimony of his British friends and admirers. The relevant evidence from other sources, and more particularly from Arab sources, is still for the most part unknown: until it is made accessible and confronted with the material at present available, our estimate of Lawrence's share in the shaping of Arab destinies can only be tentative and provisional. The admiration which his exploits have aroused is as great and as well-grounded as the fame achieved by his book. But both the book and the deeds require to be weighed in the calm balance of historical appraisal; and the pages of *Seven Pillars of Wisdom* itself show that there is need for more light.

In the course of my researches, I acquired new material from Arab sources which I have used in the preceding chapters of this narrative. The material is not so complete in respect of Lawrence's contribution as to permit of a final summing-up. But there is enough to reveal divergences between the Arab estimate and the picture which is now before the world. There is much in common between the two views: Lawrence's genius in guerrilla warfare, the skill and daring of his feats, his remarkable powers of endurance, and the greatness of his military services are almost everywhere recognised. As against that, there is much in the reliable portions of the Arab evidence that conflicts with the accepted view and with the picture which Lawrence himself saw and showed.

One fact that emerges is that Lawrence's understanding of the forces at work in the earlier history of the Arab national movement is both incomplete and faulty. Not that there was anything so remote or so complex in the outward tendencies of the movement as to elude his grasp; and his mind was sensitive and quick. But the barriers of language and temperament being what they were, sensitiveness and intelligence could not alone give him insight, if he lacked the background of knowledge; and Lawrence's deficiency in this respect may be traced, in the first place, to the inadequacy of his knowledge of Arabic and of his acquaintance with the historical background of the Arab Revolt. Like all highly perceptive people, he was generally right, but was apt to place too much reliance on his intuition. The errors of fact and of interpretation in *Seven Pillars of Wisdom* show how far he still was, after two years of close association with Arabs, from a correct interpretation of the genesis of the Revolt and of the events that had led up to it. His knowledge makes an impressive display at first sight; but when examined and tested, it is found to be often incomplete and faulty.

It is doubtful whether Lawrence was fully conscious of the extent of his limitations, though he frequently alluded to them in speech or in his writings. He was aware, for instance, that his knowledge of Arabic was far from perfect, yet he believed that he was sufficiently fluent in it to pass for an Arab in conversation with Arabs. In that, he showed more self-confidence than powers of observation, as anyone could tell who had heard his pronunciation. It is conceivable that, now and again, in casual encounters, he may have escaped detection. But neither his accent nor his use of words – to say nothing of his appearance – could have deceived anyone in Arabia for long; and an episode in *Seven Pillars of Wisdom*, in which he tried to pass for an Arab under the scrutiny and cross-examination of a suspicious stranger, shows the lengths to which he could go in deluding himself. At my first meeting with him in September 1921, he volunteered a sweeping belittlement of his knowledge of Arabic; but the confession had an air of being dragged in, as an act of homage to the virtue of modesty, and was in any case considerably watered down in his subsequent remarks. On that occasion, we talked for some three hours. His conversation was lively and entertaining on a variety of subjects, except when it came to the topic of the Arab campaign on which he would answer my questions dully, not so much with reluctance as with apathy, as though he had exhausted his interest in the subject. But I was struck with the self-assurance with which he passed judgment on certain issues, and by the startling inconsistency between the professed weakness of his Arabic and the uses to which he kept putting it.

It may be that the key to much that is baffling in Lawrence lies in that very inconsistency which pervades his revelations and causes him to appear unreal, now as a man of vision and then as a victim of self-delusion, alternating between candour and affectation, towering above the vulgarities of self-advertisement and yet obsessed with the desire to shine. The day may come when some qualified historian will give the world a critical edition of *Seven Pillars of Wisdom*, which shall take into account the all-important Arabic sources and bring Lawrence's work into truer perspective. An analysis of the book will not suffice, but it is an indispensable preliminary. There are errors and misfits in it, which cannot be disposed of as mere lapses or defects of knowledge or memory and which point rather to some constant psychological peculiarities. It seems as though Lawrence, with his aptitude to see life as a succession of images, had felt the need to connect and rationalise his experiences into a pattern; and, in doing so, had allowed sensations to impinge upon facts, and predilections to colour both. This hankering after a pattern seems to have been a dominant trait and one which governed his vision more masterfully in thought than in action, and perhaps most masterfully of all when the time came for him to narrate his experiences in a form dictated by his craving for literary creativeness.

An instance in point is his account of the capture of 'Aqaba and of his share in the plan and its execution. His summing-up is that " 'Aqaba had been taken on my plan by my effort" – a claim which will perplex the historian, for there is on the Arab side what appears to be equally reliable evidence to the contrary. The Arab evidence is that the plan was first suggested to Faisal by 'Auda Abu Tayeh at their first meeting in Wajh; that Lawrence was not made privy to it until Faisal had given his assent; and that it was carried into execution by 'Auda and his Huwaitat tribesmen independently of all outside help, for no help was needed in that kind of warfare which was of the traditional kind and one in which Arabs excel. Both the Sharif Naser and Lawrence had accompanied the expedition and taken some part in the fighting, but neither as leaders nor advisers, Naser attending as Faisal's personal representative and

Lawrence as a trusted friend and companion-in-arms who, once the plan had been decided upon in Wajh, had manifested a desire to be present. Yet afterwards he came to regard and describe himself as the prime mover and real leader of the expedition.

Other instances are to be found in the chapters dealing with the antecedents of the Revolt. The account given in Chapter IV of the Arab secret societies contains obvious errors of interpretation as well as of fact. In Chapter V, the narrative gives a totally false idea of the genesis of the negotiations that led eventually to the Revolt. It makes no mention of Kitchener's overtures to the Sharif of Mecca or of their effect on Husain's course of action; it gives a confused and chronologically impossible account of the Anglo-Arab negotiations and of Faisal's mission in Syria; it represents him as having been a member, and indeed the president, of one of the secret societies before the War – an assertion which is not only unfounded but also ignores the change which Faisal's attitude underwent in 1915, and the significance of that change in that it decided his father to resume the suspended negotiations. Such errors do not necessarily prove carelessness on Lawrence's part: he had acquired his information in the heat of war, at a time when the evidence was still fragmentary and the opportunities for checking the little that was available practically non-existent. At the same time, the fact must be faced that his knowledge as revealed in his book was in some important respects faulty, and his conception of the play of forces in the background of the Revolt palpably defective.

Lawrence's contribution to the fortunes of the Arab national movement was twofold: military and political. On the military side, his services are spoken of with unfeigned admiration and gratitude throughout the Arab world. On the political side, the value of his contribution is questioned. The criticisms bear mainly on his share in the post-War settlement. He is accused of having countenanced and even advocated measures which amounted to a denial of his own former preaching and ran counter to the true interests of the peoples concerned; and of having acquiesced in the dismemberment and subjection of certain of the Arab territories, after having repeatedly assured his Arab friends during the War that that would never be their lot. The explanation usually offered is that Lawrence's views and beliefs were not grounded on fixed principles but were swayed by the surroundings and the personalities of the moment: in Arabia he had encouraged, because he genuinely shared, the Arab hopes; in Whitehall, the boom of imperial interests silenced all other sounds, and he fastened his hopes upon Mr. Churchill. The criticisms are not without substance, but the explanation is thin and unconvincing. It ignores the efforts made by Lawrence at the Peace Conference to obtain a fair hearing for the Arab case, and the decisive part he played in bringing about the change of policy in Iraq. It takes no account of the factor of uncertainty that was at the root of Lawrence's beliefs, the strain on his mind after two years of relentless effort, the injury caused to his spirit by the sordidness of the bickerings at Versailles. Nor does it allow for the fact that, as time went, his interest in the Arab problem waned to a point approaching exhaustion, and that, when he attended the Cairo Conference in 1921, he was already longing to be 'quit of the war-time Eastern adventure'. One may infer that there was mutual incomprehension: just as Lawrence had formed and to the end retained an incondite picture of the underlying political issues, so his Arab companions in the Revolt never understood his searchings of heart about what he termed the Fraud, or the vacillation of his doubts and uncertainties, or even the weariness of spirit that caused him, after the bitter experience of Versailles, to adapt himself to the close horizon of the Cairo Conference and find solace in its decisions.

CHAPTER XV

THE PENINSULA AFTER THE WAR

I.

THE post-War history of the Arab countries will not be told in detail here. Apart from considerations of space, the fact that the last twenty years have seen the birth in the Arab world of new forces and tendencies which were not inherent in the trends of the national movement would alone carry this narrative far beyond its natural scope. Nor will an attempt be made to survey the ground covered by the movement of ideas in the western half of the Arabic-speaking world, that is to say in the chain of countries stretching from Egypt to the shores of the Atlantic Ocean. Our narrative must remain primarily concerned with the eastern half of the Arab world, and confined to a review in outline of those developments alone that were the characteristic outcome of the Arab awakening of the nineteenth century, and of the forces which it set into motion in the main theatre of its expansion.

One difficulty confronts us at once. Hitherto the whole of the eastern Arab world – save for certain territories on the coastal fringe of the Peninsula – had formed part of the Ottoman Empire and, being constituted into a system of provinces which were equally dependent on the central administration, had enjoyed a uniform political status. After the War, with the passing of the Ottoman suzerainty, new states and régimes had come into being, whose political status ranged from that of complete independence to that of virtual subjection to a foreign Power; and this diversity was bound to bring in its train a corresponding variation in the aims and the tactics of nationalist activity in each territory.   The problem which confronts us in the concluding chapters of this narrative is how to keep track of the significant manifestations of nationalist effort in each of the new states without losing sight of the progress achieved in the entire Arab area by the Movement as a whole.

We have seen that the states formed immediately after the War fell into two broad categories, namely those of the Arabian Peninsula proper and those lying in the Arab Rectangle to the north of it; and that the freedom of self-government allowed to the former was in marked contrast with the status of subjection to British or French rule imposed upon the latter.   There were factors, such as differences in social structure and political maturity, which in themselves militated against the adoption of a uniform system throughout the Arab world.   But the determining factor in the differentiation made by the Allies was that the Peninsula, unlike the Arab Rectangle, was regarded by them as too inhospitable and in any case unprofitable to foreign penetration.

It will be convenient if, in tracing the course of developments in the post-War period, we were to take each of those two categories in turn rather than adhere strictly to the chronological sequence of events in the area as a whole.

2.

In the Peninsula, the essential change was the replacement of Ottoman suzerainty by Arab sovereignty.   Five new states came into being, in which former vassals of the Sultan of Turkey assumed in fact the prerogatives of independent rule: the kingdom of the Hejaz (King Husain), the sultanate of Najd and its Dependencies (Sultan 'Abdul-'Aziz Ibn Sa'ud), the imamate of the Yaman (Imam Yahya), the territory of 'Asir (the Idrisi Muhammad), and the principality of Shammar (Ibn Rashid).   These five states between them covered the whole of the inhabited area of the Peninsula, with the exception of the smaller principalities on the seaboard of the Persian Gulf and the Indian Ocean; and each of the five rulers regarded himself as sovereign in his territory.

The emergence of these independent states opened a new chapter in the history of the Peninsula and one which was destined to be the prelude to a series of other changes. Apart from the ties which some of them had formed with Great Britain, there were thorny problems to be settled, which concerned their relations with each other. The feud between the Houses of Ibn Rashid and Ibn Saʻud was more than ever a live issue; the Imam Yahya looked askance at his neighbour the Idrisi whose presence in ʻAsir he regarded as an intrusion and an encroachment on his own domain; and, more significant still, the dissensions between Husain and Ibn Saʻud over the ownership of a strip of border territory threatened to lead to a serious trial of strength between the acknowledged leader of the Arab Revolt and a chieftain whose ability and determination had revived the Wahhabi movement and endowed it with military power. Whatever blessings the advent of the Peace may have brought to Arabia, it was clear that peace was not among them.

In that network of dissensions, Husain was at some disadvantage. His dual position as ruler of the Holy Land of Islam and spokesman of the Arab national aspirations gave him prestige and precedence, but it also saddled him with responsibilities of a particularly thankless and embarrassing kind. On the one hand he had to face the unabated hostility of the Moslems of India, who had not forgiven him his insurgence against the caliph and were now agitating to mobilise opinion in favour of maintaining the sultan of Turkey as the only acknowledged head of Islam. On the other hand, he had committed himself, by the mere fact of the Revolt, to the final disseverance of the Turkish connexion with the Holy Land. The success of the Revolt had deprived the sultan-caliph of one of the prerogatives which were regarded as essential attributes of the caliphate – over-lordship of Mecca and Madina – and on that score alone, Husain was bound to find himself in conflict not only with his co-religionaries in India but also with those Arab Moslems whose conservatism, as was the case with the Wahhabis of Najd, had not yet been affected by the national aspirations of which he was the spokesman, or at any rate not so affected as to reconcile them to a non-Wahhabi régime in the Holy Cities.

Another source of embarrassment to Husain sprang from his responsibilities as spokesman for the Arab claims. To him it fell to press for the fulfilment of the Allied pledges, and the more evident it became that Great Britain and France were bent upon a dishonest interpretation of their own promises the more difficult did his position become in regard to his relations both with his fellow-Arabs and his British allies. He found himself driven to the invidious and sterile course of having to badger the British Government for what he felt to be his due, without any of the resources of strength that are indispensable to success in diplomacy. Husain's only strength was the moral force inherent in the justice of his case, but that, by itself, could scarcely prevail in the atmosphere of Versailles or San Remo. It added to his embarrassment that he knew his fighting resources to be inferior to those of Ibn Sa'ud, and that he had to lean on Great Britain for support in case it should come to a trial of strength between the Hejaz and Najd. In his dealings with the British Government he was bound on the one hand to make himself importunate in the process of claiming his due, and on the other to confess weakness by soliciting their help in his quarrel with his Wahhabi neighbour— a stultifying inconsistency which he was not able to overcome and which led eventually to his downfall in 1924.

Had Husain succeeded in composing his differences with Ibn Sa'ud he would in all probability have averted the catastrophe. But, for all the ability and far-sightedness he had shown in the preparation of the Revolt, he revealed himself wanting in the attributes of real statesmanship when it came to building up a new order in the Peninsula. His first mistake had been to assume that his sponsorship of the Revolt entitled him to political authority over his neighbours.

328

Both the Idrisi and Ibn Sa'ud had welcomed his alliance with Great Britain and his rupture with Turkey, and they had readily accepted that he should lead the Arab insurgence; but they had no thought of placing themselves in vassalage to him or of abating their claims to full sovereignty in their own dominions. That is why they had resented Husain's assumption of the title of King of the Arab Countries[1], with its implication of all-embracing sovereignty. In the case of Ibn Sa'ud, the position was made worse by the fact that he was the head of a vigorous Wahhabi revival with missionary activities reaching out beyond the confines of Najd and into territories regarded by Husain as owing allegiance to him. This had given rise to a boundary dispute between them, which Husain had attempted during the War to settle in his favour by somewhat high-handed methods, and with a show of studied condescension and even discourtesy towards Ibn Sa'ud. In that, he showed a lack of perspicacity and political wisdom. For, whatever grounds he may have had for crediting his neighbour with acquisitive designs, he should have foreseen the provocative effect of his attitude on the ruler of Najd who had a far more powerful army at his disposal than Husain possessed or could muster.

The first serious clash occurred on the 19th of May, 1919, near Turaba on the eastern border of the Hejaz, when Ibn Sa'ud's forces fell upon a column under the command of the Amir 'Abdullah and all but annihilated it. The victory was so complete that the Wahhabi hosts might have advanced into the Hejaz unopposed. But, on that occasion, the British Government came to the aid of Husain by warning Ibn Sa'ud that they would view any further breach of the peace with disapproval; and Ibn Sa'ud who was then, like Husain, receiving a subsidy from Great Britain desisted. The episode had no immediate consequences, but it rankled

[1] See Chapter XI, Section 7, *supra*. Although the Allies had recognised him only as *King of the Hejaz* and advised him to abandon the more ambitious designation, Husain had continued to style himself *King of the Arab Countries* or *King of the Arabs*, in his dealings with his neighbours and his own subjects.

in the minds of Husain and his son and opened their eyes to the inadequacy of their military resources. The wise course, and one which the British Government had done their best to encourage, would have been for Husain to make his peace with Ibn Sa'ud, even at some sacrifice of pride and of territory. But he was wanting in that kind of sagacity and fell back, instead, upon a futile policy of alliance with Ibn Rashid – Ibn Sa'ud's hereditary foe – and with certain tribal chieftains on the outer fringe of Najd. He also tried to enter into friendly relations with the Imam Yahya of the Yaman.

The ruler of the Yaman was still at feud with the Idrisi of 'Asir, and presently events were to take a turn which made that feud still more acute. In January 1921, the British had evacuated the port of Hudaida on the Red Sea, which they had occupied at the end of the War after the surrender of the Turkish forces in the Yaman, and allowed the Idrisi to enter it and annex it to his dominions. Hudaida had been the seaport of the Yaman in the days of the Ottoman rule, and its capture by the Idrisi deprived the trade of that province of a natural and indispensable outlet which had been in use for generations. Its annexation to 'Asir created another piece of irredentism in Arabia and one in which Husain, in pursuit of his policy of alliances against Ibn Sa'ud and the Idrisi, felt bound to support the claims of the Imam Yahya.

In the autumn of that year, there came an abrupt change in the balance of forces in the Peninsula, when Ibn Sa'ud brought his old feud with the dynasty of Ibn Rashid to an end by making himself master, after a daring campaign, of all their hereditary domain. The annexation to Najd of the whole territory of Shammar brought Ibn Sa'ud's frontier to the confines of Iraq. It also meant the disappearance of a dynasty whose goodwill Husain had secured as political allies against a neighbour whom he had failed to conciliate and whose genius for generalship and good government was becoming a byword in Arabia.

3.

In the summer of 1921, some four months after the close of the Cairo Conference, the British Government opened negotiations with King Husain for the conclusion of a treaty of which the professed object was to settle all questions outstanding between them and place their alliance upon a formal and satisfactory basis. The emissary was T. E. Lawrence who arrived in Jedda at the end of August and tried to persuade Husain to accept the treaty which he had brought in draft. No one who knew the realities of the problem could have expected that Husain or any other responsible Arab would conclude a treaty on the terms that were offered. For, apart from certain highly unpalatable clauses restricting the sovereignty of the King of the Hejaz in his own territory, there was one, put forward by the British Government as a *sine qua non*, which was in itself sufficient to render the treaty unacceptable. This was the clause by which the King of the Hejaz was required to recognise what was loosely described as the 'special position' of Great Britain in Iraq and Palestine, that is to say in plain English, to acknowledge the mandates conferred by the San Remo Conference and thereby condone the British Government's breach of faith in respect of those two territories. It seems hardly credible that the Foreign Office could have been so naïve as to expect the clause to pass. But they knew the decisions of the San Remo Conference to be morally indefensible and, having a bad conscience, were trying to buy out Arab opposition by dangling before Husain a formal treaty of alliance securing the Hejaz against aggression, with the offer of an indefinite continuation of the subsidy paid to him out of the British treasury. Husain's refusal was downright; and, feeling incensed with what he regarded as a childish manœuvre, he departed from his usual courtesy and was somewhat curt with Lawrence.

The episode affected Husain profoundly. It came as a shock to him to find that the British Government could in all seriousness put before him such a travesty of their own promises; and the impact of this discovery on his mind was all the more telling as it gave meaning to former signs which, in the simplicity of his belief in the British word, he had not cared to read. He had had occasion in the past to take his allies to task over some inconsistency or other in their war-time engagements. But the assurances he had on each occasion received had set his mind so well at rest that even when he had doubted the wisdom of the British Government he had not questioned their integrity. His faith in British standards of fair dealing was primarily the result of individual contacts, and he held it unquestioningly and uncritically, without ever suspecting that the practices of British politicians might fall short of the standards observed by individual Englishmen. It was also an axiom in his political creed that the Arabs and the British were natural allies in a psychological as well as a geographical sense, that they had interests in common and that those interests could best be served by the creation of a system of independent Arab states closely united to each other and to Great Britain. The treaty presented to him by Lawrence was as incompatible with his beliefs as with his expectations. It shook his faith in British standards of fair dealing and in the destiny of the Anglo-Arab alliance. It re-kindled the alarm he had felt in 1917 in face of the Sykes-Picot Agreement and the Balfour Declaration. It also opened up a vista of frustrated hopes, of invidious recrimination with his allies and of turmoil with his own people; and, as is usual when a cherished belief is shaken, the process brought not enlightenment but pain and bewilderment. In passing judgment on the mistakes he afterwards made, allowance must be made for the ravages wrought by that discovery on his mental composure.

In the spring of 1923, negotiations were opened again for the conclusion of an Anglo-Hejaz treaty. The negotiations dragged on through 1923 and into the summer of 1924 without leading to an agreement; and, as in 1921, the main stumbling-block was the question of the pledges, with this difference, however, that this time, the only point at issue was the fate of Palestine. Iraq and Transjordan were not in question, since they had both been recognised as independent Arab states; and, although their independence was not yet a fact, Husain was willing for the time being to content himself with the principle. Syria, being under French jurisdiction, was not specifically mentioned. Some difficulty arose over Husain's unwillingness to recognise Ibn Sa'ud's conquest of Shammar or the Idrisi's annexation of Hudaida. But the main obstacle was Palestine; and, as the negotiations progressed and all other differences were being disposed of, the divergence became a deadlock and one which threw the British and the Arab attitudes towards the problem of Zionism into sharp relief.

The divergence turned on a question of safeguards. The British Government's desire was that King Husain should recognise the mandate in Palestine and the policy outlined in the Balfour Declaration in which the only safeguard for Arab rights in Palestine was the clause relating to *civil and religious* rights. Husain asked that the safeguard be extended to include *political and economic* rights as well. His attitude was still that which he had defined to Commander Hogarth at Jedda in January 1918: [1] while not opposed, but indeed agreeable, to a regulated Jewish colonisation on humanitarian grounds, he could only consent to it on the clear understanding that all legitimate Arab rights would be respected. In his counter-draft, he proposed that Palestine be constituted into an independent state with a national government representing all the inhabitants, including the Jews; that it be expressly allowed the faculty of joining a federation of Arab states; and that its 'political and economic freedom' must in no sense or degree fall short of that of the other Arab states. It is interesting to note that the wording of the safeguards in the British draft and the Hejaz counter-draft respectively reproduced in their *ipsissima verba* the terms, on the one hand, of the Balfour Declaration and,

[1] See Chapter XIII, Section 9, *supra*.

on the other, of Hogarth's oral assurance to King Husain. The difference between the two was fundamental, for it spelt a choice between Arab co-operation and Arab resistance, that is to say between peace and strife in the Holy Land. And Husain, who was in close communication with the people of Palestine and realised the genuineness and the depth of their fears for the future, exerted himself in vain to convince the British Government of the futility of trying to allay those fears with inadequate safeguards.

With a tenacity which ended by grating on Foreign Office nerves, he kept protesting in message after message that he was not moved by narrow or selfish motives, that his attitude was dictated solely by the conviction that there could be no peace for the British, Jews or Arabs in Palestine so long as the latter had cause to suspect that the ultimate aim of Zionism was to establish a Jewish state in their midst and at the expense of their national aspirations. He begged for an explicit guarantee of all legitimate Arab rights, not in the ambiguous wording of the Balfour Declaration but in the terms of the positive assurance given to him in January 1918 through the medium of Commander Hogarth. But the deadlock was never surmounted. Whether it was that they made light of Husain's forecast of trouble, or that they were more deeply pledged to the Zionists than they cared to divulge, or that they wished as a matter of policy to keep both Zionists and Arabs in dependence upon Great Britain's favour, the British Government rejected King Husain's plea. And they clothed their rejection in a tissue of ambiguous assurances which were scarcely relevant to the point of his representations and which in any case did not meet it.

Such was the state of the negotiations when the catastrophe came. Husain's last contribution before his downfall was in a personal letter to the Prime Minister (Ramsay MacDonald), dated the 4th of August, 1924, in which he appealed once more for the putting into effect of the promises made in the War. But to that letter he never received a reply, for before the month was out the Wahhabi

hosts were marching on the Hejaz, and by the beginning
of October he had ceased to be king.

4.

When the blow fell, Husain found himself almost without
a friend, and for that he was largely to blame. As a ruler,
he had shown himself unequal to the task of laying the
foundations of good government, and had created much
discontent not only among his own subjects but also among
the multitudes of pilgrims who flocked annually to the Hejaz.
As a neighbour, he had acted with singular tactlessness in
his dealings with the Egyptian Government, with the
Idrisi and with Ibn Sa'ud, each of whom had in turn severed
relations with him. He had done nothing to placate the
Moslems of India; on the contrary, the tales of profiteering
and of vexatious treatment which the pilgrims were wont
to carry home had done much to swell his unpopularity.
Perhaps one of his worst mistakes was when, in March 1924,
immediately after the abolition of the caliphate in Turkey,
he lent himself to a hastily improvised proclamation of
himself as Caliph by Moslem bodies in the Hejaz, Palestine,
Syria and Iraq, without a prior ascertainment of opinion
in the Moslem world at large. His assumption of the dignity
was not only repudiated by the unanimous consensus of the
rest of Islam; it also gave Ibn Sa'ud and the Indian Moslems
a handy weapon with which to impugn his motives and
discredit him. The cry went forth that his real designs
had at last revealed themselves: to serve his personal ambition at the expense of Islam and its unity. The accusation was essentially unfair, as Husain was above all a
man with deep convictions and as pious a believer as any
of his detractors; but his acceptance of the caliphate,
although hesitant and half-hearted, gave an appearance of
reality to the charge and wrought havoc with his name.

In his isolation, he turned to England but found no response. By that time, the feeling in Whitehall was distinctly
inimical to him, and he was regarded as an object of ridicule

and a nuisance. The fashion had been started of circulating funny stories about the old man's idiosyncrasies – some of which were undoubtedly laughable – and as the stories went round they begat others and created a demand for more, as funny stories will. A time came when the British Agent's periodical reports on the situation in the Hejaz would arrive packed with material for official laughter, to be circulated more widely than usual in Whitehall on account of their comic value. Husain became a laughing-stock. He was no longer taken seriously by the civil servants; and when the negotiations were resumed in 1923, the attitude of the officials towards him was one, at first of amused tolerance, then of bored longanimity, and finally, as the months went by and he stuck unflinchingly to his point, of irritation and surfeit.

The Wahhabi forces began their advance in the last week of August; and when news came that they had entered Taif unopposed and committed a massacre, a panic arose in the Hejaz and a deputation of the leading citizens implored the King to abdicate, in the hope that this might placate Ibn Sa'ud. In vain did Husain urge on the British Government to restrain the invader as they had done in the past. They declared that they regarded the conflict as a religious dispute in which they could not intervene unless they were specifically asked to do so as arbitrators by the two parties to the dispute. Knowing that victory was bound to be his, Ibn Sa'ud wanted no mediation, and, notwithstanding Husain's abdication in favour of 'Ali, his eldest son, he pressed his advance and occupied Mecca on October 13. For over a year, King 'Ali who had moved to Jedda kept up a precarious defensive, while Ibn Sa'ud bided his time. He could have broken through the Hejazi defences without much difficulty, but preferred to wait for the inevitable surrender. This took place in December 1925. 'Ali capitulated and left for Baghdad to live in exile at his brother's court; and on the 8th January, 1926, Ibn Sa'ud was formally proclaimed King of the Hejaz by a general consensus of the citizens of the principal towns.

As for Husain, he had sailed away a few days after his abdication and taken refuge in 'Aqaba until the following June when he was informed by the British Government that his presence in that port to which Ibn Sa'ud had been objecting, would no longer be tolerated. He elected to go to Cyprus where he remained until 1930. A stroke which afflicted him at the end of that year – he was then in his seventy-fifth year – seemed to presage his end, and he was allowed to go to 'Amman to end his days near his sons. He died in the following June, an embittered but still unwavering old man whom posterity may judge more kindly than his contemporaries, when the facts come to light. For despite his limitations and his defects, he had that strength of the spirit and that integrity of character that betoken greatness; and, if the standard is that a man's moral worth must signify more than the measure of his failure, then Husain deserves our admiration as well as our sympathy. Whatever the other causes, one cause of his downfall lay in the tenacity with which he stuck to his hopes and beliefs, while another can be traced directly to his refusal to lend himself to what he regarded as a betrayal. There is little doubt that, had he accepted to sign the treaty on the terms arrived at in the later stages of the negotiations, he would have retained his throne and probably ended his days in possession and security. But, true to his convictions and his conscience, he held out on a point of justice to the people he represented, and estranged his allies in the process, so that, when the blow fell, he found himself isolated and friendless, and alone to reap the whirlwind.

5.

The conquest of the Hejaz brought Ibn Sa'ud into the foreground of the Arabian scene, and the history of the Peninsula is henceforth dominated by the part he plays in its evolution. The change meant far more than a change of régime. It brought about a radical transformation in the life of Western Arabia, in both its private and public aspects.

It introduced a system of government and a conception of civic duties which, in a few years, were to supersede practices in vogue for centuries. It re-established the ascendancy of Moslem ethics and Arab traditions, in the conduct of public affairs as well as in the code of collective and individual behaviour. It is probably the most profound, and it may yet prove to be the most beneficial, change that has supervened in Arabia since the preaching of Islam; and, as in the seventh century, the new order thus brought into being, while fashioned to some extent by the social and economic forces of the day, owes its existence in the first place to the efforts of one man of genius.

The problems facing Ibn Sa'ud in the Hejaz were numerous and complex, and he tackled them with that combination of boldness and sagacity which form an attractive feature of his personality. They involved not only tasks of domestic import but also pressing questions of international significance. Of these, the most urgent were that of his status as *de facto* ruler of the Holy Land of Islam in relation to the rest of the Moslem world, and the cognate problem created by the impact of Wahhabi tenets on the other schools of religious thought. Another was that of the definition of the territorial limits of his conquest, which concerned both his neighbours in the Peninsula and the Powers holding mandates in the Arab Rectangle. A third was the question of his relations with Great Britain and with the other foreign Powers.

Such were his main external problems at the start. Internally, he had to grapple with the thorny task created by the coming of his Wahhabi followers, with their ardent religious zeal, into contact with the lax and self-indulgent Hejazis; to strive to moderate and modify the fundamentalism of the Wahhabi divines in regard not only to religious observances but also to the use of modern means of communication such as the telephone and the wireless which, in their ignorance of electro-magnetic science, they were inclined to condemn as heretical contraptions of the devil; and, not least, to relieve the distress and the starvation brought about by the campaign, by the falling-off in the revenues derived from the pilgrimage, and by the vagaries of Husain's rule. On all these tasks, as well as on the other tasks of government, Ibn Sa'ud brought a calm and balanced mind and a will of iron to bear, and in their solution achieved a remarkable measure of success.

In his relations with the external Moslem world, Ibn Sa'ud had at first to face a good deal of criticism, partly on account of the intransigent attitude of his followers and partly because he had accepted the throne of the Hejaz without prior reference to the wishes of Islam at large. The criticisms were not unmerited, more particularly as he had repeatedly declared, before the conclusion of the campaign, that the choice of the future ruler of the Hejaz would be left to the decision of the Moslem world as a whole. He had made those declarations with the apparent intention of abiding by them, but, when it came to the point, he announced that the divergence between the Wahhabi school and the other schools of orthodox Islam was too wide to allow of an immediate beginning in equal co-operation, and that he felt called upon to retain control in his own hands and convene a congress of all Islam to confer on other questions affecting the administration of the Hejaz. The congress assembled in June 1926. It was far from completely representative of all Islam, and its deliberations did not cover all the questions on which there was disagreement, but, in so far as it brought the Wahhabi doctors into direct contact with the views of the rest of Islam, it was exceedingly useful, for that contact gave Ibn Sa'ud an opportunity to start on the task of reconciling the two views. He made wise use of his opportunity and followed it up so that, as the years went by, the divergence gradually lost its acerbity and has practically ceased to make itself heard.

6.

With his neighbours in the Peninsula, Ibn Sa'ud's policy evolved itself in stages. His initial problem was confined to the delimitation of frontiers and the establishment of friendly relations with them, and more particularly with the rulers of 'Asir and the Yaman. Acquisitive designs he had none, but it was not long before he found himself driven to action by the vicissitudes of the conflict between those two states. 'Asir had fallen on bad days since the death, early in 1923, of Sayyed Muhammad, the founder and mainstay of the Idrisi dynasty. Dissensions had arisen between his heir and other members of the family, civil war had broken out and, in the prevailing disorder, the Imam of the Yaman had occupied the southern regions and a good deal of the coast, including the port of Hudaida. When Ibn Sa'ud came upon the scene, his help was solicited by the ruling Idrisi on terms which would have given him virtual control in 'Asir. But he had wisely refrained from intervening. As the conflict progressed, however, and the Imam seemed on the way to annexing the whole of southern 'Asir to his dominions, Ibn Sa'ud stepped in and concluded an agreement[1] with the Idrisi, by which 'Asir placed itself voluntarily under what amounted to a protectorate to be exercised by the King of the Hejaz. This proved to be but the first step towards final absorption. Sayyed Muhammad's successors, lacking his ability and prestige, were powerless to stay the disintegration which had begun after his death or to defend their territory against the Imam's relentless pressure. The choice before the ruler of 'Asir soon became one between submission to the Imam of the Yaman and vassalage to the King of the Hejaz. For a variety of reasons, he chose the latter course and eventually, in 1930, he concluded another agreement by which 'Asir was formally placed under Ibn Sa'ud's protection and became to all intents and purposes a dependency of his kingdom. This meant that there were only two independent Powers of any consequence left in the Peninsula, and that Ibn Sa'ud and the Imam Yahya, whose empires were now co-terminous with each other all the way from the Red Sea in the west to the furthest limits of human habitation in the east, would

[1] *Treaty of Mecca*, October 22, 1926.

need to settle between themselves the exact lie of the common frontier.

It was scarcely to be expected that such a settlement would be arrived at without friction. The Imam Yahya, who was then in his middle sixties, had spent a life-time on the task of securing to the Yaman, first its independence, and then its aggrandisement to what he and his followers claimed to be its historic domain. In that domain he included large portions of 'Asir. He had already redeemed Hudaida, the lowlands of the Tihama and an expanse of hilly country and seaboard previously occupied by the Idrisi, and he was in process of continuing his irredentist expansion when the Idrisi of the day took cover under the protectorate of his Wahhabi neighbour who undertook to defend 'Asir against any further encroachment. This meant that the Imam found himself faced with two alternatives: to content himself with his gains or make war upon Ibn Sa'ud; and of the two, the second alternative appeared all the more likely to materialise as it was nourished, independently of the tension over 'Asir, by a controversy over the ownership of certain other regions lying at the extremity of the still undelimited frontier. It seemed as though a conflict was bound to occur sooner or later, although the two rulers were genuinely endeavouring to settle their differences by negotiation.

In 1934, after three years of parleying, hostilities did break out, which resulted, after a campaign lasting barely two months, in a signal victory for the Wahhabis. They swept across the plains of the Tihama and occupied Hudaida. The Imam sued for peace, and Ibn Sa'ud who had repeatedly declared that he had accepted to place 'Asir under his protectorate not with a view to reconquering what it had lost but in order to protect what was left, showed his sincerity and his statesmanship by granting an armistice on the same terms as he had proposed before the resort to arms. He claimed no indemnity, no reparations and no surrender of arms or territory. Although the Imam had tried his patience to exhaustion and taken the initiative in breaking off negotiations and resorting to force, Ibn Sa'ud treated with nim as though there had been no aggression and no war. The treaty they concluded (*Treaty of Taif*, May 20, 1934) bears the impress of Ibn Sa'ud's moderation and sanity; and, being altogether free from vindictiveness, false righteousness or cupidity, has brought Arabia the blessings of real peace.

7.

The delimitation of Ibn Sa'ud's northern frontier was a matter for negotiation with Great Britain who held the mandates for the territories bordering upon his post-War acquisitions. Shortly after his annexation of the Jabal Shammar, the frontier between that territory and the mandated state of Iraq was fixed in an agreement concluded in 1922.[1] In the following two years, Ibn Sa'ud had extended his sway over the greater part of the Wadi Sirhan which ran from al-Jauf in a roughly north-westerly direction to the confines of the British and French mandates in Transjordan and Syria. What with that and with the serious tribal conflicts which had been occurring in consequence of the shifts of allegiance, the British Government decided to open negotiations with Ibn Sa'ud without waiting for the conclusion of his campaign against the Hejaz, and delegated Sir Gilbert Clayton who, after a brief stay in the Sultan of Najd's camp near Bahra (half-way between Jedda and Mecca), concluded two agreements with him. In one of these (the *Hadda Agreement*, November 2, 1925), the frontier between Najd and Transjordan was so fixed as to leave the greater part of the Wadi Sirhan to Ibn Sa'ud and interpose a belt of British mandated territory between him and the area under French mandate. In the other (the *Bahra Agreement*, November 1, 1925), provisions were made for regulating tribal migrations from Najd into Iraq and Transjordan and *vice-versa*, to such effect as to bring about a general appeasement in the relations between the tribes in those territories. The settlement of the frontier between

[1] *The Muhammara Agreement.*

the Hejaz and Transjordan had to be left over, pending the conclusion of hostilities between Najd and the Hejaz.

Hardly had the agreement fixing his northern frontier been concluded than Ibn Sa'ud raised the question of his treaty relations with Great Britain. Those relations were still governed by the agreement which he had concluded with the Government of India in December 1915,[1] and which placed him in a position of semi-vassalage to the British. No term had been set to that agreement, and Ibn Sa'ud was anxious to negotiate for its replacement by some other instrument more in consonance with the status of real independence to which he aspired. The British Government waited until Ibn Sa'ud had completed his conquest of the Hejaz and securely established his rule, and in November 1926 opened negotiations which led to the conclusion in the following spring of the *Treaty of Jedda* (May 20, 1927), in which the King of the Hejaz and of Najd and its Dependencies, as Ibn Sa'ud then styled himself, was formally recognised as a sovereign and independent ruler. The treaty was subsequently ratified and published. It differs in several respects from the draft treaties formerly presented to Husain, but the most significant point of difference is that the clause relating to Great Britain's 'special position' in the territories under her mandate and to the application of the Balfour Declaration in Palestine, which the British Government had made a *sine qua non* of agreement with Husain, does not figure in the *Treaty of Jedda*. The treaty was for a term of seven years, renewable by mutual consent, and was in fact so renewed with certain minor amendments in 1934. It has proved a wise and workable instrument, and its success is a signal tribute to the constructive statesmanship of the late Sir Gilbert Clayton whose work it largely was.

Having placed his relations with Great Britain upon a new and satisfactory basis, Ibn Sa'ud proceeded to strengthen his international position by the conclusion of treaties with

[1] See Chapter VIII, Section 5, *supra*.

those foreign Powers whose interests involved the governance of Moslem populations, that is to say with Holland, France, Russia and Italy. He has also entered into treaty relations with Turkey and Persia. But still more significant from the point of view of the Arab national movement is the chain of pacts and treaties which now bind the Kingdom of Sa'udi Arabia[1] to its neighbours in the Yaman, Iraq and Egypt. Their conclusion did far more than put an end to contentions and strife: it opened up channels, which had hitherto been blocked, for cultural and economic interpenetration and for the freer play of the forces which are slowly shaping the Arab future.

8.

Not less striking than his successes in the field and in diplomacy was Ibn Sa'ud's achievement in the administration of his empire. In so vast an expanse of conquered territory, whose nomadic populations had for centuries defied the authority of all but their own chieftains and refused to be bound by any standards other than those of the tribal code, the task of establishing order and justice and the foundations of progress was difficult enough. It was made more difficult still by the lack of local resources for economic development and indeed for any but the barest needs of good government. But perhaps the worst difficulties that confronted Ibn Sa'ud at the start were those created by the zealotry of his own followers. Twenty years of intensive preaching had transformed the people of Najd into a nation of earnest fundamentalists who would brook no infringement of the sacred Law and no innovation on the practices of early Islam. They had been encouraged to regard the Hejaz as a sink of impiety and its conquest as a God-ordained mission of purification, and had come to fulfil that task with all the rigour of their literalist doctrine. Their fervour was of the uncompromising kind, that would stop at no obstacle

[1] As the former *Kingdom of the Hejaz and of Najd and its Dependencie*s is now officially styled.

or scruple, and it was all the more of an embarrassment to Ibn Sa'ud as it moved not only his forces to take the law into their own hands but also the theologians to condone and encourage the excesses of the troops.

In the belief that they were stamping out idolatry, the Wahhabi soldiery had visited the tombs and graveyard shrines of the Hejaz with wholesale destruction.[1] They tried also to demolish the dome of the Prophet's tomb. They took it upon themselves to browbeat the people of the Hejaz into conforming with their own ascetic way of life, down to giving up such amenities as tobacco and instrumental music. They embroiled Ibn Sa'ud in a dispute with the Egyptian Government over a question of not more than ceremonial significance at the very first pilgrimage held after the conquest of the Hejaz; and when the controversy was referred to the theologians of Najd, they gave a ruling which substantially endorsed the attitude of the troops and left Ibn Sa'ud with no alternative but to resign himself to a rupture with Egypt and bide his time. He was clear-sighted enough to see that, while contact with the world outside the Peninsula was bound to soften the rigour of his Wahhabi purists, it would be folly to force the pace, however pressed he might be to secure their acquiescence; and he chose to wait until, as they gained experience and their horizon expanded, he could bring them by degrees to mind the spirit as well as the letter of the sacred Law and to distinguish between real and apparent transgressions. The task was not easy, and, in the pursuit of it, he has had at one time or another to face charges of impiety and to deal with open sedition. Yet in the space of a few years the change that has already come about in the attitude of the Wahhabis as a whole has made it possible for Ibn Sa'ud, without permitting himself the slightest deviation from orthodoxy, to keep the peace between his own followers and other

---

[1] It is a tenet of the Wahhabi doctrine to condemn the erection of a shrine or monument of any kind on the site of a tomb, the argument being that the existence of such a monument encourages the practice of addressing prayers to the holy man whose burial place it adorns, instead of praying to God alone as the Qoran prescribes.

Moslems, to put an end to the clashes which disturbed the pilgrimage, to heal the breach with Egypt, and to enter into treaty relations with Persia and the Yaman, both of them Shi'i states – a feat which, a few years previously, the Wahhabi divines would have condemned as an impious act of truck with the heretic.

Other problems confronting Ibn Sa'ud in the internal administration of his empire were those affecting the welfare of the tribes. He had first to establish order and justice, more particularly among the tribes of the Hejaz some of whom were large and powerful and a law unto themselves. They regarded themselves as a caste apart, and had successfully resisted the imposition of conscription, taxation and other obligations borne by the settled population. In their own roaming area, they behaved as absolute masters, compelling caravans – not excepting official caravans travelling with military escorts – to pay tolls. Their code had few of the inhibitions of common or criminal law: it made no ethical distinction between cattle-breeding and cattle-lifting, and, being strict in matters of personal honour, it held blood-feuds in high esteem and, in some cases, made it an obligation of honour to kill. Certain tribes had fallen into the habit of transgressing the nomadic code and taken to all forms of pillage and rapine, plundering even those travellers and pilgrims to whom a safe-conduct had been granted on payment of the toll. These practices had gone on for centuries. All the attempts of the Turks at checking them had ended in failure.

The contrast between that state of affairs and present conditions appears at first sight incredible. Raids are now illegal and tolls are a thing of the past; a uniform system of taxation is in force; scales of fees regulate the transport of pilgrims; and the right to punish offenders is vested in the State. In every way, the tribes of the Hejaz and of the whole kingdom, although still enjoying their nomadic freedom, are subject to the law of the land, and the astounding thing is that they obey it. The practice of raiding has in fact practically ceased, the word for 'tolls' (*Khawa*) has dropped out of the tribal vocabulary, and taxes are collected without opposition. It is a rare occurrence nowadays for a traveller to be molested or for a pilgrim to be robbed or squeezed. Respect for the law is as general in the countryside and on the highways as it is in the towns, and it is no exaggeration to say that the standard of public security is higher in Sa'udi Arabia than perhaps in any country in the world, not excluding the most civilised.

The change was brought about by the sheer exercise of Ibn Sa'ud's authority backed by the force at his disposal. At first, the tribes had been recalcitrant and defiant in spite of his stern warnings. He had taken pains to secure a willing acquiescence, in patient parleys with the chieftains whom he hoped to convince by invoking the example of Najd and of the benefits which the establishment of a reign of order had secured for its tribes. When it became clear to him that his arguments were of no avail, he had issued warnings to all the chieftains and sent them away laden with presents to ponder his words in good feeling. But the meditation did not bear the desired fruit, for presently news came of a fierce attack followed by plunder on the part of the Bani Harb tribesmen. Thereupon Ibn Sa'ud assembled a mustering of his armed followers and ordered them out against the offenders with ruthless injunctions. The Wahhabi soldiery fell upon the Bani Harb encampment and an appalling carnage had ensued in which some two hundred tribesmen lost their lives. The news rang through the Hejaz and drove the chieftains to fresh meditation in which they pondered the swiftness of the punishment as well as its severity. The episode was followed by two acts of similar retribution, but on a much smaller scale. Then the tribes settled down sullenly but in earnest to an acceptance of the new order.

9.

The new order has proved all the more beneficial as it became the groundwork for Ibn Sa'ud's scheme of social and economic reform. The scheme was one which, in its essentials, had matured long before in his mind. Its central feature was the settlement of nomads on the soil. An area of land adjoining a well or some other source of water was assigned in freehold to a tribal group, to be their fixed and permanent home. Henceforth they were to live there as an agricultural and pastoral community. They were to be provided with housing, implements and guidance in the arts of systematic cultivation and cattle-breeding; and each of those new colonies was intended in course of time to become a village unit, more or less self-contained in its local administration and economy.

The scheme had been initiated in Najd in 1910 when the first colony was founded, and the process had gone on in such rapid strides that, by the time Ibn Sa'ud came to the Hejaz, there were already over seventy colonies (of a size ranging from 400 to 6,000 inhabitants) in various parts of Najd. It was an attempt to grapple with the scourge of Arabia – the eternal penury of life in the desert. As an experiment in social planning, it may lead to permanent results, for it carries moral as well as material objectives. Its immediate aim was to discourage the practice of raiding by providing the tribes with new and dependable means of subsistence and thus removing the main incentive to inter-tribal looting. Another motive, so far at any rate as the Hejaz was concerned, was to devise a new source of sustenance for those of the tribesmen who had hitherto found a livelihood in the pilgrim-transport trade and whose trade seemed to be threatened by the displacement of the camel by the motor-car. But Ibn Sa'ud, with his profound knowledge of the psychology of the Beduin, had also more distant objects in view: to transform the errant life of the nomads into one centred around a fixed abode, with all that that would mean of new interests, new responsibilities and new values. His insight had led him to see through the acquired core of a nomad's psychology into the deeper instincts of the human being, and so to the conclusion that, if a tribesman were to become a householder and take root in the soil, he would cast off the core formed by the centuries and obey the instincts of man to cherish a home of his own. In that sense, Ibn Sa'ud's scheme is an experiment in moral regeneration and takes its place among the imaginative feats of creative statesmanship. If it can be applied to the rest of the Peninsula as extensively as it has been in Najd and (on a smaller scale) in the Hejaz, it will profoundly modify the character and the habits of the nomadic population and change the face of Arabia.

The change will be all the more rapid as Arabia adopts modern forms of transport and communication, and develops hitherto unused resources. That process is already well under way. When Ibn Sa'ud came to the Hejaz, the camel was still the universal means of transport. Since then, the motor-car has penetrated almost everywhere in Sa'udi Arabia, and although its use is still far from general the possibilities it opens up are immense. The old caravan tracks are being made fit for motor traffic, and already the traveller can drive in comfort from the Red Sea to the Persian Gulf, and from Jedda to Madina and on to Baghdad. In barely ten years, the transport of pilgrims has become entirely mechanised, and the one hundred thousand or more who come to the Hejaz annually travel to Mecca and Madina on petrol. There are wireless stations in the principal towns and, as he motors across from one end of his empire to another, Ibn Sa'ud's portable transmitters and receivers keep him in constant touch with his officials all over his dominions. He has also embarked on a systematic search for underground water and caused a number of artesian wells to be sunk. Prospecting for minerals has yielded abundant sources of oil, some gold and various ore deposits. And while the oil and the metals may not mean more than an increase of income, the new resources of water and the adoption of fast means of locomotion will accelerate the two most momentous changes taking place in the Peninsula to-day: the settlement of tribes on the land and the growing intercourse between the several disjected members of the Arab family – in each of which lies some promise of a new stability in an Arabia revived.

CHAPTER XVI

IRAQ, SYRIA AND PALESTINE AFTER THE WAR

I.

IN the countries forming the Arab Rectangle to the north of the Peninsula, the years that followed the War were also years of turmoil and strife. But whereas in Arabia itself the underlying causes of conflict had been inherent in its own political instability and in the rivalries of its Rulers, in the territories placed under British or French mandate the conflict was provoked and made inevitable by the action of the European Powers and was the natural sequel of the San Remo decisions and of the steps which Great Britain and France took to carry out their self-appointed 'tasks' in Iraq, Syria and Palestine.

The mandates had been assigned, not by the League of Nations, but by a body – the Supreme Council – composed of the representatives of France, Great Britain and Italy, each of whom had designs of her own on the former possessions of the Ottoman Empire. With the United States out of the way and Woodrow Wilson's prickly objections no longer hampering them, the prime ministers of France and Great Britain found it possible at last to reach agreement about the division of the spoils and to entrust each other with mandates in the territories which were to form their respective shares. The Covenant of the League of Nations,[1] which was already in force, contained specific provisions to govern the assignment and the scope of mandates; and, in the particular case of the Arab countries, it stipulated ex-

---

[1] The references throughout this chapter are to Article XXII of the Covenant.

pressly that the wishes of the populations concerned were to be a principal consideration in the selection of the Mandatory. The San Remo Conference disregarded that provision, and its decisions were a violation of it. The wishes of the populations concerned were known to the Allied representatives, if only from the report of the King-Crane Commission and the resolutions of the Damascus Congress. But in assigning the mandates they were guided solely by their own ambitions, modified only in so far as was necessary to reconcile the conflicting designs of France and Great Britain. Each Power grabbed as much as the other would let her, and henceforth described the administration of her share of the spoils as a task imposed upon her by sacred international obligations.

The Covenant was also violated in regard to another of its provisions. In the section dealing with the former possessions of the Ottoman Empire, it was laid down that certain communities had reached a stage of development where their existence 'as independent nations' could be provisionally recognised subject to their receiving mandatory tutelage, in the way of administrative advice and assistance, until such time as they would be able to stand alone. This did not mean that the recognition of independence was to be withheld until the time would come for terminating the mandate, but just the reverse, namely, that those communities were already entitled to the status of independent nations and that the mandate was to be no more than a temporary restriction on the free enjoyment of the prerogatives of independence. So far as Iraq and Northern Syria were concerned, the decisions of the San Remo Conference formally respected that provision, and recognised those two territories as independent states in name though not in fact. But in the case of Palestine they violated it in name as well as in fact. They gave the mandate for it to Great Britain, on terms in which the recognition of the independence of that territory was purposely omitted. And the reason given for the omission was that it was rendered necessary by Great Britain's obligations under the Balfour Declaration.

The provisions made in the Covenant for placing certain populations under a foreign mandate were intended as an application of a new principle which the Allies had openly espoused in many war-time and post-War utterances. In the Covenant, it was defined as 'the principle that the well-being and development of such peoples form a sacred trust of civilisation and that securities for the performance of this trust should be embodied in this Covenant'. The first point that strikes the student perhaps is that, when the San Remo Conference assembled in April 1920, the Treaty of Versailles had already been ratified and had come into force on January 10, 1920; and that the Covenant, being part of the Treaty, was then a binding instrument on the Allies. The decisions of the San Remo Conference were taken at a time when the Covenant was the legal, and the only legal, instrument defining the principles on which a mandate might be assigned and held, and they are valid or invalid according as they conform to those principles or deviate from them. Both in the selection of the mandatory and in the differentiation made as between Palestine and the rest of the Arab territories, the San Remo Conference had transgressed the stipulations of the Covenant and come to decisions which violated not only the moral but also the legal obligations of the Allies.

In the case of Syria, they went further in their disregard of 'the well-being and development' of its people by deciding upon its dismemberment into three separate States. The country had a unity of its own in more ways than one. In spite of the great diversity of its physical features, it was geographically one and formed a self-contained unit enclosed by well-defined natural frontiers. In the economic field, it had developed its agricultural and commercial life on a foundation of natural resources, and the whole country was criss-crossed with a close network of inter-dependent lines of activity, linking region to region, the countryside to the cities and the coast to the interior. It had also cultural and historical traditions of unity: ever since the Arab conquest, except for the interlude of the Crusades, it had formed one political unit and kept the language and the customs which it had begun to acquire in the seventh century. On every essential count, it was clear that the well-being and the future development of the country were bound to be retarded if its unity were to be destroyed. Nor had indications been lacking to show the strength of feeling in the country itself on the subject of unity. But all those considerations were ignored; and the Supreme Allied Council, mindful only of the appetites of its members, found that the only way to satisfy Great Britain and France was to divide Syria between them. And the division was made on lines roughly corresponding to the partition envisaged in the Sykes-Picot Agreement with one important difference, that the Brown area reserved for international administration was now to be administered by Great Britain exclusively, which was what Mr. Lloyd George and some of his colleagues had had in view all the time while they professed humanitarian and altruistic sympathy with Zionist aims.

Iraq, on the other hand, was placed under a single mandate. The Sykes-Picot Agreement had, it is true, provided for its partition into French and British spheres. But by the time the San Remo Conference had assembled France was no longer a candidate. Although the negotiations begun in London in December 1918 (when Mr. Lloyd George had asked Clemenceau to agree to the inclusion of Northern Iraq as well as Palestine in the British sphere) had not led to a final settlement at the time, an agreement had been arrived at after Clemenceau's fall from power in January 1920; and, in return for a free hand in Syria and a substantial share of the Mosul oil, France had given up all territorial ambitions in Iraq. The Franco-British bargain was actually clinched at San Remo while the Conference was in session; and, as soon as the deal was concluded,[1] the Supreme Council formally assigned to Great Britain a mandate for the whole of Iraq.

[1] On the 24th of April, in a convention entitled *Memorandum of Agreement between M. Philippe Berthelot and Sir John Cadman*, Cmd. 675 (1920).

2.

Thus had come into being the three 'A' mandates which, between them, covered the whole of the Arab Rectangle. Iraq, consisting of the vilayets of Basra, Baghdad and Mosul, was constituted into a single state under British mandate. Syria was parcelled out into three new states coinciding almost exactly with the three units into which it had been divided after the Allied occupation: what had hitherto been *O.E.T.A.* (South) became the British-mandated territory of Palestine, while *O.E.T.A.* (East) and *O.E.T.A.* (West) became the State of Syria and the State of the Lebanon respectively, both of them subject to a French mandate but otherwise treated as two distinct political entities. In other words, what the San Remo decisions purported in effect to do was to improvise some semblance of international approval for the post-War division of the spoils, and to give the existing régimes, hitherto described as provisional military administrations in occupied enemy territory, an appearance of legality and a charter of permanence, to serve the ulterior motives which France and Great Britain had obviously had in mind when they set up those 'temporary' administrations.

The decisions of the San Remo Conference need to be studied in their moral as well as their political implications, for they were the starting point of a new chapter in the history of the Arab Movement – that of insurgence against the two Powers of the West. Politically, the decisions were unwise, in that they ran counter to the deepest wishes of the people concerned and to a tide of national consciousness which the War and the defeat of the Turks had swelled to a level from which there could be no receding; and their enforcement could only be achieved by the constant use of force and other means of repression. On the moral plane, they stand out as one of the more flagrant instances of international sharp practice, in which the breach of faith was all the more reprehensible as it was bound to provoke armed resistance and an unpredictable toll of human life and suffering.

Apologists of the San Remo Conference lay stress on the difficulties which Great Britain had to contend with in her relations with France, and represent its decisions as a compromise which, however imperfect, was the only means of averting a breach between the two Powers. There is also a tendency, even among historians of repute, to attribute those difficulties to French intransigence and, in the main, to France's insistence on the execution of the Sykes-Picot Agreement which Great Britain had offered to tear up. And the general inference is that, had France been well disposed instead of hostile to the Arab revival, had she taken a broad instead of the narrowest view of the possibility of Franco-Arab co-operation, and had she agreed to replace the Sykes-Picot Agreement by some workable arrangement to be devised by the two Powers in consultation with the Arabs, the worst features of the San Remo decisions would have been avoided.

On a close examination of the facts, that inference cannot be sustained, at any rate not in its entirety. The argument on which it rests overlooks Great Britain's share of the responsibility and the problem created solely by her desire, announced only after the Armistice, to add Mosul and Palestine to her share of the spoils. This claim entailed such a departure from the terms of the Sykes-Picot Agreement and such an accession of influence to Great Britain in the Arab countries that the French became profoundly apprehensive about their own position in the Near East and withheld their consent. The difference between the two Powers was not, as some would have it, the difference between a far-seeing and broad-minded Foreign Office magnanimously renouncing their rights in the discredited Agreement, and a bigoted, grasping Quai d'Orsay intent only upon their pound of flesh. In actual fact, it was Great Britain who, while her politicians proclaimed the invalidity of the Sykes-Picot Agreement, was claiming not only the whole of the region assigned to her in the Agreement, but Palestine and the Vilayet of Mosul into the bargain. The French were thus thrown on to the defensive; and their insistence on the execution of the Agreement, which certain historians regard as the crux of the Anglo-French difficulties, was essentially a tactical retort to the new British pretensions.

It is altogether true to say that the French Government as a whole were fundamentally hostile to the Arab revival and that their policy was inspired by a desire to arrest its development as a political force; just as it is true to say that the British were moved by genuine sympathy with Arab aspirations and even by a desire to see them partly fulfilled, subject, of course, to the concurrent fulfilment of British aspirations. But it is misleading to represent the San Remo decisions as the inevitable outcome of French intransigence. The worst features of those decisions were those that came into being as a direct result of Great Britain's demands for additional territory.

One of the most iniquitous of those decisions was that which placed Faisal's Administration in Damascus at the mercy of the French. Even on the narrowest interpretation of the McMahon pledges, it was universally admitted that an obligation lay on Great Britain to 'recognise and uphold' an Arab Government in the interior of Syria. The obligation was clear and unmistakable, and had been publicly recognised by the British Government, and never so eloquently as in Mr. Lloyd George's own utterances.[1] Yet he gave way at San Remo to the French demand for a mandate over the interior as well as the coastal regions of Syria. It was the price which France was asking in return for her consent to the inclusion of Mosul and Palestine in the British sphere. Mr. Lloyd George paid it at the expense of the debt which Great Britain had admitted she owed to the Arabs, and he consented to the assignment of the mandate to France without a corresponding guarantee that the independence of the Arab Government would be recognised and upheld by her. And when, two months later, the French marched into Damascus and expelled Faisal, the British Government were somewhat perturbed, but soon regained their composure and took refuge in the thought that they

[1] See Chapter XIV, Section 11, *supra*.

could not contemplate going to war with France over Syria, as indeed they could not.

In the eyes of the Arab leaders, the most mischievous feature of that cynical bargain was that it involved the partition of Syria and paved the way for its further dismemberment. For reasons noticed earlier in this chapter, the imposition of any barrier across the lines of social and economic traffic was bound anyhow to dislocate the economy of the country as a whole and retard its development. The frontier that was laid down in December 1920 as a natural corollary of the San Remo decisions did much more than that: it also created a new and formidable obstacle to the cultural and political aims of the Movement, and one that was more disastrous in its implications than any of the centralising measures of the Turkish régime. Subsequent events have shown that there was justification for those fears. After the French occupation of Damascus in July 1920, the British sphere was extended to include the region east of the Jordan, and the frontier provisionally laid down in December of that year was eventually prolonged to run all the way from the Mediterranean to the Syrian Desert and into Iraq (map facing p. 304). It started at an arbitrary point between Acre and Tyre, cut across the countryside in a roughly easterly direction and continued beyond the limits of sedentary habitation; and it is no exaggeration to say that, in following its destined course as the permanent dividing line between the French and British spheres, it violated almost every known law of physical and human demarcation. It has stood ever since as a crippling obstacle to trade and other forms of intercourse; as an artificial wall on either side of which each of the two Powers has established her own language and currency, and instituted altogether different systems of administration, of education and of economic regulation and planning.

The harm done by the partition will become clearer as this narrative proceeds. All that need be noticed now is that, when it was decided upon at San Remo in utter disregard of the wishes and the needs of the people concerned, it aroused greater resentment in the minds of the leaders than the mere assignment of the mandates. It was regarded – and rightly so – as a retrograde and wasteful measure which violated not only the promises made but also the principles of common decency in the treatment of weaker nations, that is to say, the very principles which the mandates were originally created to serve. In the eyes of thoughtful Arab leaders, and especially among those who had been the most ardent advocates of Anglo-Arab friendship, the ulterior motives of the two Powers stood revealed in all their sordid nakedness. The disillusion was complete, but alongside of it there were created a feeling of contempt for the Powers of the West and a wave of hot resentment which presently turned to despair and vented itself in the wild upheavals that followed. All kinds of erudite reasons may be dug up to account for this or that aspect of the upheavals. But they were essentially the product of outraged feelings and of the psychological revulsion provoked by the San Remo decisions. For eighteen months since the Armistice, the Arabs had waited in suspense and apprehension, dubious of the blandishments of the Allies but held in check by Faisal to await the final verdict of the Peace Conference. Now it had come, with what seemed to them a sentence of servitude imposed upon them not for any guilt but for the disparity between European might and their own weakness; and, in their despair, they rose to hit wildly at the superior forces of the Allied battalions; and the most serious rising had, as we have seen, broken out in Iraq within a few weeks of the announcement of the San Remo decisions.

3.

In so far as it was primarily an insurgence against the dictation of the Allied Powers, the Iraq rebellion may be held to have achieved its main objective at once. Twelve years were still to elapse before the mandate was abolished and the country's status as a sovereign independent state formally recognised at Geneva. But the seed was sown in 1920 when the British Government, in face of the appalling cost of the rebellion, decided upon a change of policy, or at any rate of tactics. As is customary when a great Power yields to the violence of a subject people, the new policy was given out as being merely a continuation of the old; and the fact was stressed that it had always been the British Government's intention to set up an Arab government in Iraq and regulate their relations with that government by means of a treaty of alliance. Outwardly, the change amounted to a change of method: the mandatory relation was to be preserved but was now to be regulated by treaty and not merely by an instrument fashioned at Great Britain's discretion. In effect, however, the change was fundamental in that it revived the discarded doctrine of 'the consent of the governed'. It implied that Iraq's consent would be a condition of any arrangement, and that Great Britain would in future have to attain her ends by negotiation instead of, as at San Remo, by dictation. The rebellion had shown that, beneath a surface of disunion and factiousness, Arab national consciousness was already a force, that a policy based on coercion was anyhow costly and might even prove futile, and that British interests could more profitably be furthered on a plane of agreement by mutual consent – a lesson which France has since shown signs of having learnt in Syria and which Great Britain has yet to learn in Palestine.

The new policy had been worked out in its broad lines at the Cairo Conference[1] in the spring of 1921, but an earlier manifestation of it had been the appointment of a provisional Arab Government in the preceding November, as an earnest of new intentions. In the following summer, Faisal proceeded to Iraq as a candidate for the throne. The ground had been prepared by his British friends and his numerous Arab partisans, and although there were many dissentient voices his candidature obtained an enormous majority of the

[1] See Chapter XIV, Section 13, *supra.*

suffrage. He was formally proclaimed King of Iraq on the 23rd of August, 1921.

Thus opened a reign which lasted twelve years until Faisal's death on the 8th of September, 1933, just long enough to see Iraq through all the stages of its constitutional formation and of its political emancipation. The debt which the country owes to its first king can scarcely be over-stated. His gifts and his experience fitted him to play a determining part in the handling of some of its most difficult problems, and it is the unanimous verdict of all those who are in a position to judge that his influence was the decisive factor in the creation of the modern state of Iraq. His role was not confined to inspiring and guiding the conduct of affairs: he played a leading part in the multifarious activities of statecraft whose pivot he was in virtue of his position. And yet, engrossed as he became in the country's immediate problems, he never lost sight of the broader aims of the Arab Movement and of the part which Iraq might play, as an example to the other Arab countries under mandate, and a pioneer in their march towards the common goal.

The emancipation of Iraq was accomplished in four stages, marked by the conclusion of four different treaties of alliance with Great Britain, namely, those of October 1922, January 1926, December 1927 and June 1930. This multiplicity was perhaps inevitable: it was the reflection of the gap between the British and Iraqi notions of what the treaty should aim at, and of the attempts made to bridge it. In the British mind, the treaty was to be a new robe for the mandate and would have to grant Great Britain a right of control in the affairs of the new state. In the minds of the Iraqi leaders, the claim to a right of control and indeed to a mandate of any kind was not one that they were prepared to admit, and in their understanding the treaty would have to be one of alliance between two independent partners entering freely into ties for the furtherance of their mutual interests. This conflict of aims was made more acute still by the psychological conflict between the British desire to play for safety and the impatience of Iraqi leaders, sharpened by their feelings of mistrust. Their former eagerness for British assistance in the building up of the new state had been damped by their experience of Colonel A. T. Wilson's omnipresent, omnivorous and omnipotent bureaucracy, and had given way to a belief that the word Mandate was only a new label for the old methods of colonial exploitation and that foreign assistance, as understood at San Remo, could only mean foreign domination. An influential group of leaders with a considerable following took the view that no treaty would be acceptable that did not recognise the complete and absolute independence of Iraq.

The gap was as wide on the psychological as on the political approach, and the only bridge across it proved to be King Faisal's personality. In conducting the negotiations for each of the four treaties in turn, he had to exert himself on a dual task: to persuade the British Government into a less stringent insistence on safeguards, and to plead with his own people for a broader view of their true interests and a more realistic conception of their own limitations in the field of self-government and of the value of Anglo-Arab co-operation.

The decisive treaty was that which was concluded at Baghdad on June 30, 1930, and ratified later in the year. It was concluded on the understanding that Great Britain would sponsor the admission of Iraq as a sovereign independent state to membership of the League of Nations in 1932, and that it would come into force as soon as Iraq had been admitted to the League. It provided for an alliance between Great Britain and Iraq for a period of twenty-five years, during which the two parties undertook to consult each other fully with a view to harmonising their common interests in matters of foreign policy. The defence of the new state and all other responsibilities hitherto assumed by Great Britain in virtue of her mandate were to devolve upon the King of Iraq. The two parties were to give each other certain facilities: to Great Britain, the use of specified stations for Air Force bases and of the existing means of communication; to Iraq, British assistance in the form of a military mission to advise on the building up of the national army. In the event of war, the two countries were to regard themselves as allies.

Outwardly, the treaty met with hostile criticism in both countries. In England, it was attacked mainly on the ground that it did not contain sufficient safeguards to ensure the security of imperial communications, and the attacks were led, as was to be expected, by statesmen who had held office in the days when the British Government's attitude was still inspired primarily by motives of strategic safety. In Iraq, the criticisms were to a large extent the captious manifestations of the old distrust. But in both countries the Government and the bulk of opinion supported the treaty. And when the Permanent Mandates Commission at Geneva expressed doubts as to the fitness of Iraq to shoulder all the responsibilities of independence, it was on Great Britain's assurances alone that the objections were dropped. The stand taken by the British Government did much towards creating a better feeling in Anglo-Arab relations. It provoked a wave of satisfaction and gratitude which swept over the remains of bitterness and rancour, and its effect on the Arab mind was not confined to Iraq.

On the 3rd of October, 1932, at a session of the Assembly in Geneva, Iraq was formally admitted to membership of the League, by the unanimous vote of the fifty-two nations present. The Anglo-Iraq Treaty of 1930 came automatically into force on that date and one of the three mandates assigned in the Arab countries by the San Remo Conference was thereby extinguished.

4.

By the time she was received into the League, Iraq was already exercising many of the prerogatives of self-government, including those of diplomatic representation abroad. The heavy hand laid on her by Great Britain after the War had, after Faisal's accession, gradually but rapidly relaxed its hold, concurrently with the establishment of constitutional government and the growth of a national army and civil service. Parliamentary institutions had come into being as far back as the end of 1924, with departments of state presided over by Iraqi ministers. The powers of the British High Commissioner which had formerly been supreme were gradually restricted, and the functions of the British officials in the public departments had, as time went on, been increasingly subjected to the authority of Iraqi ministers. The conduct of foreign relations was still in effect controlled by Great Britain, but the King of Iraq had his representatives in certain countries abroad and received foreign envoys accredited to his court; and his formal consent and that of his parliament were necessary to validate agreements concluded in his name. So far as the machinery of democratic government went, Iraq entered the League as a going concern; and the credit for that belongs in great measure to England.

The British contribution to the building up of Iraq is one of the most remarkable instances of post-War reconstruction. Just as hard things may legitimately be said of the British Government's piratical attempt to grab Iraq after the War, so it can without exaggeration be said that the modern state of Iraq owes its existence largely to the efforts and the devotion of its British officials. There were two reasons for this. One was that the British Government, as they discovered that the country was more of a hornet's nest than an imperial Garden of Eden, became increasingly anxious to ensure that the régime of Arab independence which had sooner or later to come should possess real stability. The other was that, by a lucky accident of circumstance, Iraq was fortunate in getting the services of an unusually capable and conscientious band of British officials. Those two factors in combination helped to set up the Arab Administration more rapidly and more securely on its feet. The achievement is all the more striking as Iraq, with its large tribal population, its sectarian divisions and the scarcity of its means of communication in proportion to its size, is a particularly difficult country to administer on the usual lines of bureaucratic routine.

The population numbers a little over three millions and is predominantly Moslem. The Christian minorities, made up of six distinct sects, amount to some 120,000 souls; and there is a Jewish community of approximately 80,000, mostly residing in Baghdad. But the line of sectarian demarcation runs also through the Moslem element dividing it almost equally into the two broad categories of Sunni and Shi'i adherents. Racially, the population is predominantly Arab, roughly in a ratio of three to one; of the remaining quarter the largest group is that of the Kurds, who number approximately 500,000 souls, entirely contained in the northern half of the Vilayet of Mosul, and belong to the Sunni Moslem faith. The Assyrians, of whom much has been heard in recent years, form another distinct non-Arab group and, like the Kurds, are concentrated in the Mosul region. They numbered about 35,000 and belong to the Nestorian Church. The existence of these and a few other minorities, and of a large tribal population, created problems of a political and administrative nature, which obstructed the task of reconstruction and even threatened to thwart it.

The tribes were perhaps the most serious difficulty. Tribes are always a problem in the establishment of orderly government, but in Iraq it was rendered more complex by a variety of local factors such as land, water and religion. Several tribal groups, more particularly in the Middle Euphrates, belonged to the Shi'i sect and acted in closer solidarity with the Shi'i divines in Najaf and Karbala than with the predominantly Sunni Government in Baghdad. Disputes over the ownership of land and water-rights were frequently arising between them and the officials of the central government; and the disputes, aggravated by intrigues on the part of politicians in Baghdad and by the dislike of the tribesmen for the bureaucracy and all that a bureaucracy stands for, did not take long to develop into a conflict followed by a resort to arms. Another source of disturbance sprang from the unsettled conditions on the south-west border and the interchange of predatory visits between the tribes of Iraq and those owning allegiance to Ibn Sa'ud.

The problem of the Kurds was also a difficult one. In numbers they amounted to one-sixth of the total population with whom they had scarcely anything in common save for the religious bond with the Sunni Moslems. Their deep attachment to their own language and customs made it more natural for them to look to reunion with their fellow-Kurds in Turkey and Persia than to a minority status in an Arab State. When Turkey finally agreed in 1926 to the incorporation of the Vilayet of Mosul in the state of Iraq, it fell to the Government in Baghdad to persuade the Kurds who had thereby become Iraqi subjects into a willing acquiescence in their new citizenship; and this it had to strive for at a time when symptoms of a budding national consciousness were appearing among the Kurds, and their characteristic aversion to any manner of subjection was more than ever in evidence.

The Assyrians were for the most part immigrants from South-Eastern Anatolia, who had fled from Turkish punishment during the War, sought refuge in Iraq and become the protégés of the British military command with whom large numbers of them had taken service. They had nothing whatever in common with the Arab (or, indeed, the non-Arab) inhabitants of Iraq; and the fact that from the earliest days, they had ostentatiously placed themselves on the side of the occupying Power had emphasised their aloofness. The problem afterwards created by their presence in Iraq was in many ways unique; but its main difficulty was caused not by their numbers or their poverty or their peculiar needs but rather by the psychological effect of their association with the mandatory Power which lasted throughout the period of mandatory control. It acted as yet another barrier between them and the people in whose midst they had taken refuge; and, as it increased their sense of detachment, it obscured their sense of proportion and led them into extravagant expectations and a dangerous reliance on their own warlike qualities.

In their efforts to solve all those problems the Arab Government were remarkably successful in certain directions but failed in others. Their worst failure was over the tribal problem. Recruited as they were mainly from the urban classes, both the politicians and the officials lacked the necessary knowledge of tribal life, understanding of its needs and interest in its welfare. The gulf between townsman and tribesman was still too wide, and no one other than King Faisal could have bridged it. But he achieved only partial success. Although he did a great deal towards reconciling the chieftains to the idea of co-operation with the Government, he allowed his feelings as son of the King of the Hejaz to impinge upon his duties as King of Iraq and used the tribes as a pawn in the conflict with Ibn Sa'ud. It was not until 1930, when he had made his peace with the latter, that he began to apply himself in earnest to the task of tribal pacification, and the success he achieved then was in the nature of a personal triumph. But he died in the midst of it and, after his death, trouble broke out again in the region of the Middle Euphrates. The Government of Iraq have succeeded in restoring the peace and have followed it up with measures which reveal greater attentiveness to, and perhaps more sympathy with, tribal needs and grievances. But it is scarcely possible to tell yet whether a lasting harmony has been attained.

King Faisal and his Government were more successful in their handling of the minorities. The problem was one with which Arab leaders were intimately conversant, since it involved the very issues which they had formerly debated with the Turks; and the policy they adopted rested on understanding and tolerance. They recognised, because they felt it so deeply, the importance of cultural values and of communal freedom, and the concessions they made were both generous and wise. The result was a series of special enactments and measures arrived at in agreement with the leaders of each minority, which have proved workable. The only exception was the Assyrian minority. In their treatment of that problem, the Government of Iraq had gone to even greater lengths in the way of concessions. But the extravagant claims put forward by the Assyrian Patriarch and a truculent group of chiefs made agreement impossible. Nothing can excuse the acts of savagery with which the Assyrians were visited after their armed insurgence in the summer of 1933, and the massacre which took place is a shameful blot on the pages of Arab history. This does not alter the fact that the Government of Iraq had previously done everything in their power to meet all the reasonable needs of the Assyrians, and that the offers which they had made were not only fair but generous. The failure to come to terms was due primarily to Assyrian intransigence and to the ill-advised attitude of certain Assyrian leaders. A share of the responsibility falls on British shoulders, too, partly because the open favouritism of the British military authorities in Iraq and of Anglican prelates in England was interpreted by those Assyrian leaders to mean a greater measure of support than was intended, and partly because the mandatory Power did not pay sufficient heed to the warnings of trouble which British officials in Iraq kept sending to the Colonial Office in the years preceding the outbreak.

It was fortunate for Iraq that, in many important respects, Great Britain's interests marched with her own, and that this community of interests embraced foreign as well as domestic questions. The British desire to control the sources of oil in the Vilayet of Mosul resulted not only in the incorporation, thanks entirely to British diplomacy, of that province into the Arab State, but also in effective Anglo-Iraqi co-operation towards the solution of the Kurdish problem. Similarly, Great Britain's interest in the preservation of peace on the Iraq border caused her to take the initiative in bringing about, first, a personal reconciliation between King Faisal and King 'Abdul-'Aziz Ibn Sa'ud and, later, the establishment of friendly relations between the Governments of Iraq and of Sa'udi Arabia. In almost every department of the public service, the Arab Government had the benefit of sympathetic British guidance; and the British officials, taking their cue from their own Government, gave invaluable help in the laying of good foundations. Their work in Iraq was in marked contrast with the vagaries of the French administration in Syria and the Lebanon, and with the sterility and the wastefulness of the British bureaucracy in Palestine. And the progress achieved in Iraq between 1921 and 1932, for all its imperfections, is a credit to both countries and an example of what Anglo-Arab co-operation can do when it rests on the right foundations.

5.

The French mandate in Syria and the Lebanon has no such achievement to its credit. Its record is largely one of wasteful conflict; and it is no exaggeration to say that, in the period from 1920 to 1936, that is to say in the years between San Remo and the conclusion of the Franco-Syrian Treaty, the harm done in the name of the mandate to French and Arab interests was far greater than its incidental benefits. The change of policy implied in the treaty of 1936 has altered the very basis of the Franco-Arab connexion and improved the outlook for the future. But the story of the mandate prior to that is for the most part the story of a tussle between French ambitions and Arab national aspirations, which lasted sixteen years to the serious detriment of both.

The main underlying cause was one of mutual distrust. Just as the colonial methods of the French had a bad name among Arab leaders, so was the Arab Movement, in the eyes of the French, a source of trouble and a menace. Both attitudes were inspired by suspicion and fear. The Arabs, drawing their own conclusions from hearsay reports (often garbled) of French rule in North Africa, were afraid that French intervention would mean anything but freedom and equality. Their experience of European political activity in Syria before the War had caused them to believe that France's support of the Catholic missions and her partisanship with the Maronites had an ulterior motive, and that, in any case, it had revived the flames of sectarian dissension

368

which both the Christian and the Moslem leaders in the Movement were genuinely bent on extinguishing. They also believed that France was fundamentally inimical to the Movement in the sense that she was opposed to the political emancipation of the Arabs, at any rate in the Mediterranean countries; and this belief had been strengthened by what they had seen of French efforts to keep the Revolt confined to the Peninsula and of the lengths to which Husain, Faisal and Lawrence had had to go to defeat those efforts. On their side, the French were moved by two main considerations. They knew that the establishment of an independent Arab Government in Damascus would have political repercussions and give an impetus to national consciousness in all the other Arab countries, and they feared the consequences in their North African empire. They also considered the Arab Movement a hindrance to their ambitions in Syria, partly on account of its gospel of unity and independence, and partly because of its ties with the British. They suspected British political officers stationed in Damascus of working secretly to undermine French influence, and they believed that Faisal had become the willing instrument and the Movement the unwary stalking-horse of a policy perfidiously designed to queer France's pitch in Syria.

It was in that frame of mind that the French Government, having obtained the mandate at San Remo, had decided to march into Damascus, expel Faisal and occupy the interior of the country. In that frame of mind, too, was a policy laid down for the administration of the mandated territory, which, as it revealed itself in actual measures and enactments, showed that the apprehensions of the Arabs were well grounded.

6.

At San Remo, the French Government had asked for and obtained the mandate 'for Syria and the Lebanon', thus endowing each of those territories with a separate identity. The reason was that they intended to pursue a different policy in each. The Lebanon was the stronghold of their influence in the Near East. Within the frontiers assigned to it in the *Règlement Organique* of 1861,[1] there lived a population, predominantly Christian, which included the Maronites – France's oldest friends – and those other sects, also in communion with Rome, who looked to France as their traditional protectress. Syria, on the other hand, was predominantly Moslem, and Damascus the stronghold of the Arab Movement. The policy adopted by the French aimed at strengthening the first and weakening the second, which they proceeded to do in a series of high-handed and shortsighted measures, and with a callous indifference to the human consequences of their acts.

The first of those measures was one to enlarge the Lebanon at the expense of Syria. On the 31st of August, 1920, a decree issued by Général Gouraud brought into being the 'State of the Greater Lebanon' with boundaries including, in addition to the former Sanjaq of the Lebanon (map facing p. 176), the territories immediately to the north, east and south of it, in such a way as to give the new state the coast-towns of Tripoli, Bairut, Sidon and Tyre, and the inland town of Baalbeck with the rich plain of the Biqa' into the bargain. The new state was roughly double the size of the former Sanjaq in area and in population. Its new boundaries gave it a considerable accretion of Moslem citizens, thus reducing the preponderance of its Christian element to a bare majority, and control of the ports of Tripoli and Bairut which between them served practically the whole of the sea-borne trade of Syria. •On both those grounds, the aggrandisement of the Lebanon was a shortsighted act: by depriving Syria of its normal outlets to the sea, it created a movement of irredentism which will have sooner or later to receive satisfaction; and by the annexation of regions inhabited mostly by Moslems, it exposed the Christian majority to the fate of becoming in course of time a minority in a state designed to ensure its predominance. But worse still, it introduced a new bone of conten-

[1] See Chapter III, Section 10, *supra.*

370

tion in a country already rich in motives of dissension; and if the measure is also to be judged in the light of its human consequences, of the passions it aroused, of the bitterness it engendered and of its effect in resuscitating sectarian hatred, then the French deserve condemnation for an act which is as remarkable for its mischievous disregard of moral values as for its inherent short-sightedness.

Having thus enlarged the citadel of their influence, the French proceeded to break up the unity which the rest of the country had enjoyed under Faisal's Arab Administration. They devised a scheme for its partition into a number of states. In its final form, the scheme led to the creation, out of a territory of little more than 2,000,000 inhabitants, of three separate states endowed with four distinct administrations, (map, p. 304), namely:

(1) The Government of Latakia, with its capital at Latakia, comprising the coastal region between the enlarged Lebanon and the Sanjaq of Alexandretta;

(2) The State of the Jabal al-Duruz, with its capital at Suwaida, comprising the mountainous region between Damascus and the Transjordan frontier;

(3) The State of Syria, with its capital at Damascus, comprising the remainder of the mandated area;

(4) The Sanjaq of Alexandretta which, although nominally included in the State of Syria, was endowed with a separate administration of its own.

The reasons which the French gave to justify this measure were that it had been taken in response to the wishes of the people immediately concerned, that is to say, of the Druzes, of the 'Alawis[1] and of the Turkish element in the Sanjaq of Alexandretta; that the existing diversity in points of religious allegiance, racial origin and political maturity made it inevitable; and that it was dictated by a clear-sighted and benevolent conception of the true interests of the

---

[1] One of the Shi'i sects of Islam, also known as Nusairis, whose numbers in Syria amount to approximately 150,000 souls concentrated in the northern coastal regions.

people of Syria. But the real reason was their hostility to the Arab Movement, and the real motive their desire to set up obstacles in its way. The measure had two main objectives: to foster the growth of separatist tendencies and to turn Arab Syria into an inland state. The chain formed by the Greater Lebanon, the Government of Latakia and the Sanjaq of Alexandretta, all three of which were to be administered by a French governor with absolute powers, was to act as a wall shutting off the State of Syria from the sea. The creation of regional governments functioning quite independently of each other as so many separate instruments of the French will was primarily a device for promoting disunity. It was designed to stimulate the growth of a regional as opposed to a national outlook and so to counteract the unifying efforts of the Movement.

In their administrative methods, the officials of the mandatory Power showed that they were inspired by the same motive. They subjected Arab nationalists to a system of police supervision combined with Martial Law jurisdiction which recalled, and in some ways outdid, the severity and the partiality of the Hamidian tyranny. They muzzled the nationalist Press, subsidised venal newspapers and tried to stifle all outward expression of Arab sentiment. They reserved appointments in the public departments and the local councils to those whom they tested and found subservient; and they used their administrative power to secure the return of their nominees in public elections. They played upon the fears of the Christian and other minorities in order to drive a wedge between them and the Moslem majority.

In the economic field, the policy of the mandatory Power was handicapped by the weakness of the franc in relation to the currency in force in the mandated territories. They created a new 'Syro-Lebanese' currency based on the franc, thereby inflicting upon those territories the contingent losses and depreciation of a weak and unstable monetary system. The measure aroused a general outcry in the Lebanon as well as in Syria, which was unfair to the French to the extent that it seemed to ignore their national monetary difficulties and the fact that it would have been scarcely possible for them to do otherwise than peg the new currency to their own. But where they laid themselves open to blame was over the management of the new currency, which they entrusted to a French bank on conditions which favoured its shareholders at the expense of Syrian and Lebanese fiscal autonomy. They showed the same kind of partiality in the grant of concessions and monopolies, and frequently made improper use of the administrative machine to further the interests of French companies and concession-holders. How much of the stagnation and other economic ills endured by the country under the mandate was directly attributable to the policy and how much to other causes over which the French had less control it is impossible to tell. But although some of the grievances were wrongly held against them, there was a good deal in their fiscal and economic methods to account for the discontent they caused.

Among the major causes of discontent was the threat to the supremacy of Arabic. One of the rewards of the Revolt had been the liquidation of the language dispute between Turks and Arabs. The cultural motive behind the Movement – probably the deepest impulse and certainly the most constructive force animating it – had asserted itself after the victory in the immediate enthronement of Arabic as the sole medium of the national life and in a wholesale transformation of the educational system; and nowhere had the change been more to the popular liking than in the schools and the law-courts. But the French mandate, with needs and a policy of its own in regard to language and education, had resuscitated the old dispute; and it was precisely the schools and the law-courts that became, as they had been in the days of Turkish rule, the main bones of contention.

France's interest in Syrian education, which went back to the days of the early missions, had become an instrument of policy long before the War. But this policy, of which the object was to spread French influence, was not specifically directed against Arab influence. It was naturally in conflict with the spirit of the Arab Movement, since its aim was to promote education in the French tongue and spirit; and it had led to the endowment of a considerable section of the Christian population, more particularly in the Lebanon, with a mental equipment which was more French than Arab. But there is no evidence that the policy was inspired then by a deliberate anti-Arab motive. After the War, however, when the Movement had become a political power and France had the upper hand in Syria, the policy became consciously anti-Arab; and the educational activities of the mandatory authorities, while promoting French cultural influence for its own sake, aimed also at undermining the props of the Arab cultural influence.

The most visible manifestations of that policy were the compulsory teaching of French in all State schools and its use in the courts of justice on a footing of equality with Arabic. In themselves, those measures were not indefensible. But they were carried to excess, with a singular disregard of their psychological effect and, still more, of the claims of education and justice; and, as the officials who applied them were quite often unable to understand or make themselves understood by the public, there were frequent and sometimes scandalous abuses. Serious denials or miscarriages of justice occurred merely because the French magistrate who tried the case knew no Arabic and had to rely on indifferent interpreters. In some districts, where the official in charge was more than usually zealous, school-children were taught to sing *la Marseillaise*, who were scarcely able to read their own mother tongue. In subtler ways, the expansion of Arabic culture was impeded by a studied neglect of Arabic-speaking schools and institutions, the failure to provide means for training the teachers they needed, and an ostentatious readiness to help French-speaking schools. Text-books were specially composed for History classes of all standards, in which the Arab achievement in Syria was watered down and the ties uniting her to the rest of the Arab world represented as fictitious.

The errors of French policy were made worse by the vagaries of the officials. In some glaring cases, the fault lay in the carelessness with which persons who afterwards revealed themselves as manifestly corrupt or incompetent were chosen to posts of executive power. But the fundamental cause was that the French service as a whole had had no previous experience of, and was psychologically unfit to deal with, many of the problems they were faced with. The great majority of them had received their training in North Africa and other French possessions of which the inhabitants were culturally and politically less advanced and more amenable to dictation than those of Syria; and they approached their tasks in the mandated territories with minds accustomed to the summary methods of French rule in the colonies. This applied equally to the civilians and to the numerous army officers who occupied posts in the administration. Even when the ability or the honesty of an official was not in question, his understanding was usually deficient and his manners often arrogant or boorish. A good deal of the resentment felt against the policy was directly caused by the tactlessness and lack of judgment displayed in its execution.

The result was that the undeniable benefits of French rule, both in the moral and the material fields, were eclipsed by its errors and excesses or neutralised by the handicaps under which it was exercised. Thus the impetus it gave to trade and industry was largely offset by the weakness and the instability of the franc. The development of the country's resources and of its means of communication would have stood a better chance of recognition had it not been for the undue protection given to French individuals and companies. The genuine efforts made by successive high commissioners to establish a sound system of administration were to a large extent stultified by the dearth of qualified officials, the frequent changes brought into the organisation of the territories under mandate, the wasteful duplication of services believed necessary for the maintenance of stricter French control, and the resulting extravagance and lack of proper checks on public expenditure. Even the magnificent educational achievement which forms an imperishable monument to the work of the French missions became associated – and not without reason – in the popular mind with the sundry other devices used to spread and strengthen French political influence.

7.

The history of the French mandate falls naturally into three parts. The first, from 1920 to 1926, seems like a dark age of blindness and folly and waste, in which the mandatory Power and her officials sowed the seeds of trouble and reaped its harvest in the rebellion with which the period closes. The second, from 1926 to 1936, was a period of negotiation in which France, chastened by the losses of the rebellion and the discredit it had brought upon her administration, tried but failed to come to an understanding with the nationalist leaders in Syria. The third, from 1936 to the present day, is the period in which substantial agreement was at last reached, a definite term set to the mandate, and a new era opened in Franco-Arab relations.

The first period was essentially a military dictatorship in which three generals of the French army – Gouraud, Weygand, Sarrail – held the office of high commissioner in succession and exercised their powers under martial law. In point of statesmanship, foresight, scruple and regard for the wishes of the people and their interests, it stands out as the most deficient of the three; and the policy and methods described above had freer play in it than in the periods that followed. Even when martial law was formally abolished early in 1925, the high commissioner remained vested with such drastic powers as to enable him, whenever he wished, to flout the fundamental principles of common law in his treatment of Arab nationalists. He had all the resources of a supreme autocrat: unfettered legislative and executive powers, influence over the judiciary, and a large army of which he was *ex officio* commander-in-chief; and he exercised his will as arbitrarily in the State of Syria with its puppet Arab administration as in the three States which were under undisguised French rule.

The rebellion began in July 1925, when Général Sarrail had been some eight months in office. It broke out in the Jabal al-Duruz, and its immediate causes were largely of his own making in the sense that it was his high-handed and offensive treatment of certain Druze leaders that ignited the flame. The deeper causes lay in the discontent engendered by French policy and methods, and in particular by the methods of the Governor of the Jabal al-Duruz who had allowed himself to be carried away by his zeal for efficiency into an outrageous tyranny over the inhabitants. It began as an explosion of violent indignation and developed into a national rising.

A full account of the Syrian rebellion has yet to be written, but the salient facts are known. The first punitive column sent out against the rebels suffered a serious reverse on the 21st of July, and its remnants only just managed to get back to Suwaida, where they remained besieged for over two months. Another and much larger force, over 3,000 strong, marched out on the 2nd of August and met with a similar disaster, losing about one-third of its strength and a quantity of guns and ammunition. The rebels then advanced on Damascus; and, although their first intrusion into its suburbs was repulsed with heavy losses, they remained masters of the countryside around it. Towards the end of September, the French succeeded in relieving Suwaida but were unable to hold it and withdrew the garrison. By that time, several nationalist leaders in Damascus and others living in exile abroad had joined the Druze forces, and the rebellion took on the character of a national insurgence. It never became general, but it spread to beyond Damascus into the regions of Homs, Hama and Tripoli, and there was one rebel incursion which at one time seriously threatened Bairut. But it was national in the sense that the leaders of the Movement had thrown in their lot with that of the Druze chieftains and, in unison with them, had proclaimed that the object of the revolt was henceforth to secure the country's independence and its unity.

In their efforts to suppress the rebellion, the French were guilty of some unpardonable acts of severity. They bombed villages without warning and they frequently let their troops loose on the villagers without restraint. They armed a large number of Armenians and Circassians and, for a time, allowed them to kill, loot and burn indiscriminately. On two separate occasions, when large groups of rebels had penetrated into the streets of Damascus, they bombarded the inhabited quarters from the air and from field guns mounted on the roof of the citadel, which is in the heart of the city. This act of savagery, first committed without warning in October, received strong official condemnation in France and was followed by the recall of Général Sarrail, who had ordered it. It was repeated in the following May by his successor, Sénateur de Jouvenel, after due warning this time but with a large toll of lives (running into four figures) and an appalling destruction of residential and commercial property. When the rebellion broke out, France was in the throes of 'Abdul-Karim's revolt in the Rif, and her resources were already severely taxed. But even when due allowance is made, nothing can excuse the acts of barbarism which were committed in Syria, with and without official cognisance, in France's name.

The rebellion remained active through the greater part of 1926. But as the French re-asserted their authority by the sheer weight of force, it took on the character of a desultory guerilla and finally died down in the spring of 1927. Its cost in human lives and material devastation cannot be ascertained exactly, but there is no doubt that it was even more disastrous, both for the country itself and for the mandatory Power, than the Iraq rebellion of 1920. And, as in the case of Iraq, it caused the Mandatory to announce a change of policy. During his term as high commissioner, which lasted only a few months, de Jouvenel proclaimed the Lebanon a republic and made it known that France's policy envisaged the conclusion of a Franco-Syrian treaty of alliance to replace the mandate, on the basis of the British precedent in Iraq ; and he tried to open negotiations to that end with the Arab nationalist leaders. But the negotiations led to an immediate deadlock, and it was left to his successor, an experienced civil servant, to try and build up a new edifice on the ruins of the first six years.

The second period of mandatory rule opened with M. Ponsot's appointment in August 1926. He was the first high commissioner with civilian administrative experience, and his tenure of office lasted seven years, that is to say longer than those of his four predecessors together. He made a sincere attempt to improve the methods of administration and to come to an understanding with the leaders in Syria. But he achieved only partial success. He did put a stop to some of the worst administrative abuses without, however, doing away with the essential tyranny of the bureaucracy or curbing its extravagance or insolence. He gained the confidence of the nationalists by his scrupulous neutrality in the first public elections he held, but failed to come to terms with them, or even narrow the differences, on the fundamental points at issue. The efforts of his immediate predecessor, who appears to have been equally sincere in his desire to arrive at an agreement, had led to a deadlock mainly on the issues of Syrian unity and of whether or not the frontiers of the enlarged Lebanon were to be regarded as permanent; and when Ponsot retired, after seven years of unhurried but painstaking negotiations, those two issues stood substantially where he had found them. He turned out to be an improvement on his predecessors in method and manners rather than in breadth of view. For, when it came to discussing an organic law for Syria and, later, the terms of the projected Franco-Syrian treaty, his views were found to be almost indistinguishable from those which had prevailed at the Quai d'Orsay from the earliest days of the mandate.

In his fourth year, M. Ponsot proclaimed a republic in Syria. He had failed to come to an agreement with the nationalists over certain provisions of the proposed organic law, and his way out of the deadlock was to promulgate the organic law exactly as they had drawn it up but with the addition of a new article suspending the operation of the six clauses which were in dispute. The overriding article, he explained, was only intended to tide over the period which would have to elapse before a treaty could be negotiated and concluded. He announced it as his intention to hold elections under the new constitution with the least possible delay so that he might open negotiations for a treaty with a properly constituted representative government, and he used his influence with two of the nationalist leaders to persuade them into co-operation. The elections were held, but not until eighteen months had elapsed. M. Ponsot was not only slow by temperament and a born Fabian: he was also manœuvring for position in the electoral battle, for he had succumbed to the temptation of using his power to influence the elections. At last in June 1932, a constitutional government came into office, with a puppet President of the Republic and a Chamber of Deputies which was only nominally representative of the electorate.

It was only during his last year in office that Ponsot presented the Syrian Government of the day with concrete proposals in the form of a draft treaty. He had previously announced it as being his intention to model the treaty on the Anglo-Iraqi Treaty of 1930; but his draft was found to fall far short of it. Several of its clauses had exact parallels in the Anglo-Iraqi Treaty, but there were important differences on points of principle affecting the sovereignty, the unity and even the internal autonomy of the proposed independent Arab State, which made it altogether unacceptable. The two nationalist leaders who had had the public spirit to join an unpopular Government on the strength of the High Commissioner's declared intentions resigned, and deadlock reigned again. And when M. Ponsot retired in the summer of that year, the problem of Syria was no nearer a solution than when he had first applied himself to it, except in so far as the passage of time and their longer experience of the French mandate had made the Arab nationalists more determined than ever to seek their political liberation.

By that time, more than six years had elapsed since the suppression of the Syrian rebellion; and the French Government, having regained their former confidence in their ability to hold the country by force, decided to send as successor to Ponsot a strong man of the type that stands no nonsense. Their choice fell upon one of their ablest diplomats, M. de, Martel, who was Ambassador in Tokyo at the time. The new High Commissioner lost no time. He had barely assumed office in October 1933 when he sent for the Syrian Prime Minister and demanded his immediate acceptance of the draft treaty. The Prime Minister, who was a nominee of the French and carried little weight in the country, complied; but when the treaty came up to the Chamber of Deputies for ratification a few days later, an overwhelming majority of the members declared themselves in favour of its rejection. M. de Martel's retort to this rebuff was fully in accordance with the spirit of his strong mission. He suspended the Chamber for an indefinite period, restricted the functions of the Government to those of a mere channel for the execution of his orders and enacted legislation to enable him to impose his will with an appearance of legality. He made it known that he intended henceforth to concentrate his efforts on furthering the economic interests of the country, and that, while he was so engaged, his wish was that political issues were to remain in abeyance. He was as good as his word, and from that moment he exhibited an active interest in various economic schemes and a studied indifference to the resentment caused by his high-handed attitude, until, two years later, a sudden explosion of feeling roused him from his complacency and showed him that, in imagining that passions could be suppressed by decree, he had been living in a fool's paradise of his own making.

The upheaval was brought about by yet another of M. de Martel's virile measures. In the first half of January

1936, meetings were being held in the principal towns of Syria to honour the memory of a revered nationalist leader; and, while a wave of emotion and political agitation was sweeping the country, police raids were suddenly carried out upon the offices of the nationalist party on the strength of some denunciation. No incriminating papers were found, but the offices were nevertheless closed by the authorities and several leaders were arrested and deported on various charges and, as had happened before under mandatory rule, without the waste of time that a trial would have entailed. The reaction this time was immediate. The shops in Damascus remained closed in protest, and this was followed by a general stoppage of business throughout Syria, accompanied with unrest and disturbances. The mandatory authorities retorted with a series of further arrests and other punitive measures which only hardened the popular will; and there ensued a movement of passive resistance of a kind hitherto unknown in the annals of Syria or of any other Arab country, which was as remarkable for its universality as for its discipline and perseverance – both of them unfamiliar traits in the Arab character. The general strike paralysed the life of the country and had lasted six weeks with scarcely a symptom of flagging when there was a sudden change of tactics on the part of the French. On the 25th of February, the High Commissioner made an announcement which opened out a prospect of immediate negotiations for a treaty. He also made it known that he was prepared at once to decree a general amnesty and the release of political internees, and that he was inviting the heads of the nationalist party to confer with him. The announcement came as a surprise and was universally welcomed. A conference took place at which M. de Martel's assurances as to the basis and the scope of the projected negotiations satisfied the nationalist leaders, and they gladly accepted his proposal that a Syrian delegation on which they were to be in a majority should go to Paris at once to enter into direct negotiations with the Quai d'Orsay. As soon as this arrangement was made, that is to say on the 1st of March, the general strike was called off, and the third phase in the history of the French mandate began.

The change in the French attitude was unexpected and took the country by surprise. It turned out to be a change in tactics rather than a change of heart, but it was destined to lead by an accident of electoral fortune to a fundamental revision of the mandatory policy. The credit for the Franco-Syrian reconciliation seems to belong mainly to M. de Martel who, once he had convinced himself of the futility of his policy of repression, had the sagacity and the courage to declare himself in favour of its reversal. He seems to have seen the light all of a sudden and by some occult process, and his conversion was not less striking than that of Saul of Tarsus who, like himself, had been fond of breathing out threatenings and slaughter against the people of Damascus. The fact that barely two weeks earlier he had somewhat foolishly insulted the nationalist leaders in one of his official *communiqués* did not deter him, when he had seen his mistake, from making due amends; and to that treatment the President of the nationalist party responded with all the innate courtesy of an Arab gentleman. An era of understanding and co-operation was thus opened, which has lasted to the present day, and the marked improvement in Franco-Arab relations which began then was largely the outcome of M. de Martel's initiative and of the feelings of respect it inspired among his erstwhile victims.

The Syrian Delegation arrived in Paris and began negotiations before the end of March. They discovered at once that there was still a wide gap between the French conception of a treaty and their own; and when they received what purported to be the final proposals of the Quai d'Orsay they found them unacceptable. What they asked for was a treaty modelled on the Anglo-Iraqi Treaty of 1930 in all its essential provisions and based on the recognition of the unity of Syria. But the French Government, while admitting the justice of the claim, were not prepared to grant it yet. Then it was that the timely accident occurred in the form of an electoral victory for M. Blum and his party. With him in office in place of M. Sarraut, negotiations were resumed on a broader basis and resulted in the conclusion, on the 9th of September, of a Franco-Syrian treaty of alliance. A few weeks later, negotiations were opened in Bairut between M. de Martel and a delegation representing the Lebanon, which resulted in the conclusion, on the 13th of November, of a parallel Franco-Lebanese treaty.

The treaties were both modelled on the Anglo-Iraqi precedent and were practically indentical with it and with each other. They were both intended to come into force within three years and automatically replace the mandate as soon as Syria and the Lebanon would be admitted to membership of the League of Nations as sovereign independent states, and to remain in force for a period of twenty-five years renewable by consent. The unity of Syria was recognised. The obligations implied in the alliance were the same as in the Anglo-Iraqi Treaty. The most significant difference between the two new treaties was in the provisions relating to military occupation: in Syria, the French were to retain a garrison in the Jabal al-Duruz and another in the Latakia region for five years from the coming into force of the treaty, and were to be allowed the use of two air-bases at specified points in Syrian territory for the whole of its duration; in the Lebanon, they were to retain the right, throughout the period of the treaty, of stationing military forces of all arms, without restriction as to the locality or the number of the garrisons. France undertook to sponsor and secure the admission of both states to membership of the League within three years of the ratification of the treaties.

Nothing was said in the Franco-Syrian Treaty about the frontiers of the enlarged Lebanon. The feeling among a large and powerful section of the Lebanese population was against a modification of the 1920 boundaries, and the French Government who look to the Lebanon as the bulwark of their power in the eastern Mediterranean were not prepared to disregard the feeling. In abstaining from making an issue of the question, the Syrian Delegation showed wisdom as well as practical sense. They stuck to their contention that the enlargement of the Lebanon was unfair to Syria and harmful to the Lebanon as well. But they took the view that, if their contention were sound, the play of natural forces was bound in time to vindicate it by exposing the artificiality of the present frontiers; and that the day would come when the Lebanese themselves would seek a modification, if not the total abolition, of the barriers. This expectation may, or may not, be realised; but in staking the future upon it the Syrians showed statesmanship and proved that their long-suffering advocacy of the doctrine of consent had been no mere weapon of political agitation but that they practised what they preached.

The treaties were ratified by the respective Chambers before the end of the year. In the Lebanon, trouble broke out because the Government in power tried to stifle the voices of those who wanted to press for an immediate settlement of the question of the frontiers on the basis of a return to the pre-1920 boundaries. The trouble led to serious disturbances in Bairut and Tripoli: but, with the help of French troops, order was restored and the Government carried the treaty through without opposition in the Chamber and in spite of the opposition outside it. In Syria, a general election was held in November which resulted in a sweeping victory for the nationalist party, and the Chamber thus returned ratified the treaty unanimously. But although two years have elapsed since their conclusion, both treaties are still awaiting French ratification.

The conclusion of the Franco-Syrian Treaty was greeted with genuine satisfaction not only in Syria but in the other Arab countries as well. In retrospect, even in the short perspective of two years, it stands out as an unmistakable turning-point in the century-old history of France's relations with the Arab world; and the goodwill and desire for co-operation which are now in evidence in the counsels of the Arab Movement may prove a factor of incalculable importance, not only in Syria itself but in North Africa as well.

It is too early to tell whether the change of policy represents a change of vision on the part of the French or merely a tactical move in the grand manner. But if it does mean that they have at last realised the futility of the policy of coercion and that they intend henceforth to secure their interests on a basis of friendly co-operation, there is no reason why Franco-Arab friendship should not rapidly develop into a constructive force. The Syrian adventure has already cost France several thousand French lives and some 14 milliard francs of expenditure from the French Treasury alone on the military services of the mandate;[1] and their decision to terminate it will not only put an end to that insane wastage but also give Franco-Arab friendship its first trial.

8.

Lastly comes Palestine – the most notorious and least successful of all the mandatory ventures.

For the historian, the study of the Palestine problem is beset with peculiar difficulties. In the first place, the material is enormous and widely scattered. In the second place, it is to an unusual degree conflicting and inconsistent. Thirdly, a large proportion of it which on inspection appears relevant and promising turns out, when sifted, to rest upon false assumptions or questionable data. Lastly, the passions aroused by Palestine have done so much to obscure the truth that the facts have become enveloped in a mist of sentiment, legend and propaganda, which acts as a smoke-screen of almost impenetrable density.

I do not claim that the present study has necessarily mastered all those difficulties. But I have been made acutely aware of their existence by my research, and they have led me to the conclusion that the most formidable obstacle to an understanding, and therefore to a solution, of the Palestine problem lies not so much in its inherent complexity as in the solid jungle of legend and propaganda

[1] The equivalent, on a rough computation of the average value of the franc, of some £120,000,000

which has grown up around it. To the ordinary tasks of a student dealing with the facts is thus added an obligation to deal with the pseudo-facts and dethrone them from their illegitimate eminence. It is as much his duty to expose the fallacies as to assert the truth, and the duty is all the more imperative as he is dealing with a tragedy in enactment, in which innocent lives are being sacrificed every day and human beings kept in anguish and suffering.

9.

There is in existence already a considerable body of literature in English and other European languages on the history of the British mandate in Palestine. But it has to be used with care, partly because of the high percentage of open or veiled propaganda, and partly because the remoteness of the indispensable Arabic sources has militated against real fairness, even in the works of neutral and fair-minded historians. A similar inequality vitiates the stream of day-to-day information. Zionist propaganda is active, highly organised and widespread; the world Press, at any rate in the democracies of the West, is largely amenable to it; it commands many of the available channels for the dissemination of news, and more particularly those of the English-speaking world. Arab propaganda is, in comparison, primitive and infinitely less successful: the Arabs have little of the skill, polyglottic ubiquity or financial resources which make Jewish propaganda so effective. The result is, that for a score of years or so, the world has been looking at Palestine mainly through Zionist spectacles and has unconsciously acquired the habit of reasoning on Zionist premises.

Another vast body of information comes from official British sources; but here, too, the requirements of true impartiality are not met. Nor can they be, so long as the British Government continue to withhold some of the basic documents from publication. The effect of their reticence is that their reports and statements and interpretations of policy, far from clarifying the issues and contributing to the enlightenment of public opinion, present the problem in an unreal light and a false perspective. The harm done by that concealment is particularly apparent in parliamentary debates. Down to a few years ago, members of the House of Lords and of the House of Commons were wont from time to time to appeal to the Government to make the facts fully known by publishing the documents relating to the war-time undertakings. But the request was consistently rejected, until the members wearied of repeating it and the debates went on, year after year, in the twilight of half-truth and with the issues still further obscured by the propaganda and the efforts of Zionist sympathisers to impress their point of view on the minds of the members. The fact that a number of members of both Houses are Jews is in itself a guarantee that the Zionist case does never go by default; and as no such representation is open to the Arab side, the one-sidedness of the debates is further accentuated. A striking example is provided by the debate in the Commons on March 24, 1936, which stands out in the pages of the official report as a remarkable exhibition of Zionist influence in Parliament, in which a measure which the Government proposed towards meeting one of the Arab grievances and which the Zionist Organisation had rejected was overwhelmingly defeated.

Another mine of one-sided information is provided by the Minutes of Proceedings of the Permanent Mandates Commission. In them, the student will find a full and admirably clear summary of the discussions at which the annual reports of the mandatory Power are reviewed at Geneva. He will also find a startling inequality in the knowledge and interest revealed in regard to the Zionist as compared with the Arab case. The members of the Commission enjoy the benefits of a well-equipped Zionist office in Geneva, which supplies them all the year round with information in a form and a language suited to their comprehension. There is no similar channel on the Arab side. Even such sources as the Arabic Press of Palestine, which provide a valuable body of comment on the operation of the mandate as it affects the Arab population, are not used. Petitions and memoranda drawn up in Arabic have to be submitted at Geneva in translation. It requires more than mere transposition to turn good Arabic into readable English or French, and the Arabs of Palestine are so notoriously unskilled in the art of presenting their case in a foreign language that the rendering is usually a travesty. The result is that the knowledge possessed by the members of the Commission is visibly one-sided and their examination of the working of the mandate reads as though it were conducted for the most part by advocates of the Zionist case.

The cumulative effect of all that inequality tends to hinder the efforts made to arrive at an equitable decision. It endows the legends and half-truths spread by the propaganda with an appearance of truth, and lends substance to the misconceptions which prevail almost everywhere in the countries of the West, and not least in England itself. The valuable corrective which public opinion might provide as a check on policy is not forthcoming. Too great stress cannot be laid on the importance of removing those misconceptions: they are playing a mischievous part in obscuring the fundamentals of the problem, in the minds not only of the general public but also of writers, politicians and officials many of whom reveal, in the very discharge of their professional duties concerning Palestine, an abysmal ignorance of the background and of the real issues. Space does not permit of the copious quotations that might be made from ministerial speeches and official reports and White Papers, in which a startling ignorance is revealed of the real nature and extent of Great Britain's commitments and of the less obvious facts of the situation in Palestine. Until the fullest light is thrown on it and the significant facts are brought into their true perspective, it is idle to hope for a return to sanity.

10.

Perhaps the best approach to the problem is to begin with

a review of the rights, claims and motives of each of the three parties concerned, as they stood at the end of the War.

The rights of the Arabs are derived from actual and long-standing possession, and rest upon the strongest human foundation. Their connexion with Palestine goes back uninterruptedly to the earliest historic times, for the term 'Arab' denotes nowadays not merely the incomers from the Arabian Peninsula who occupied the country in the seventh century, but also the older populations who intermarried with their conquerors, acquired their speech, customs and ways of thought and became permanently arabised. The traditions of the present inhabitants are as deeply rooted in their geographical surroundings as in their adoptive culture, and it is a fallacy to imagine that they could be induced to transplant themselves, even to other Arab surroundings, any more than the farmers of Kent or York-shire could be induced to go and settle in Ireland. It may seem superfluous to point this out, but the fallacy is one on which the Palestine Royal Commission have raised a new edifice of false hopes; and the fact needs stressing, therefore, that any solution based on the forcible expulsion of the peasantry from the countryside in which they have their homesteads and their trees, their shrines and graveyards, and all the memories and affections that go with life on the soil, is bound to be forcibly resisted.

In addition to those natural rights, the Arabs had acquired specific political rights derived from the Sharif Husain's compact with Great Britain and the help they gave her, in Palestine amongst other theatres. The thesis that Palestine west of the Jordan was excluded from the British pledges can no longer be maintained. The texts now available show that the Sharif Husain was given a general promise relating to its independence in the McMahon Correspondence and a specific promise securing the political and economic freedom of its Arab population in the message conveyed to him by the late Commander Hogarth. There is also the pledge contained in the Declaration to the Seven. Taken together, these undertakings amount to a binding recognition of Arab political rights; but, here again, the real position has become obscured by a mass of contentious literature and utterances, abetted by official concealment. In spite of its circulation in the Arab countries, the McMahon Correspondence has remained hidden from public knowledge in England and in the Western world at large. As for Hogarth's message and the Declaration to the Seven, they lie buried in Whitehall in a sea of oblivion. The Report of the Royal Commission does not mention either; and it is obvious that important decisions of the British Government have been taken in the last eighteen years without reference to their contents. The point needs stressing not only because of its historical interest but for its practical bearing on the solution of the Palestine problem. It would be vain to seek a solution that does not take into account the significance of those undertakings and the importance which is attached to them in the Arab world as evidence of the validity of Arab political rights.

In other words, the Arab claims rest on two distinct foundations: the natural right of a settled population, in great majority agricultural, to remain in possession of the land of its birthright; and the acquired political rights which followed from the disappearance of Turkish sovereignty and from the Arab share in its overthrow, and which Great Britain is under a contractual obligation to recognise and uphold.

Thus in their opposition to the British mandate, the Arabs are animated by the motive of self-preservation as well as that of self-determination. Their attitude is not dictated by any hostility to the Jewish race. Both in the Middle Ages and in modern times, and thanks mainly to the civilising influence of Islam, Arab history remained remarkably free from instances of deliberate persecution and shows that some of the greatest achievements of the Jewish race were accomplished in the days of Arab power, under the aegis of Arab rulers, and with the help of their enlightened patronage. Even to-day, in spite of the animosity aroused by the conflict in Palestine, the treatment of Jewish minorities settled in the surrounding Arab countries continues to be not less friendly and humane than in England or the United States, and is in some ways a good deal more tolerant. Nor is the Arab attitude hostile to Great Britain, but just the reverse. The expression *anti-British* is so freely bandied about in reference to the Arab insurgence that it has given rise to the legend that the Arabs are fundamentally hostile to everything English. In actual fact, they are 'anti-British' only in the political connotation of that overworked epithet, in the sense that they are determined to resist the present policy in Palestine by every means in their power.

The rights of the Jews are of a different order. In the minds of many people in the West, and more particularly in the Protestant countries, Zionism appears as a new embodiment of the old Jewish yearning for the Holy Land, and one that is destined to bring about the fulfilment of the Biblical prophecies. That is only one more of the prevalent misconceptions. There does exist a school of 'spiritual' Zionists, sponsored by some of the most eminent names in Jewry, whose aims are primarily cultural and whose mainsprings are to be found in the idealistic and religious sentiments which had hitherto inspired Judaism in its affection for Palestine.[1] But their influence in international politics has become relatively insignificant. The real power is wielded by the exponents of 'political' Zionism which is not a religious but a nationalist movement aiming at the establishment of a Jewish state in Palestine on a basis of temporal power backed by the usual attributes of possession and sovereignty. It is against that school of Zionism that the Arab resistance in Palestine is directed.

The motives animating Zionism[2] sprang from a humane concern over the precarious position of the Jews in certain countries in Europe. It had come into being as a reaction against anti-Semitism, in the last quarter of the nineteenth century,

---

[1] See Chapter XIII, Section 8, *supra*.
[2] Unless otherwise stated, the terms *Zionism* and *Zionist* are to be read as referring to 'political' Zionism.

with the specific object of providing a remedy through the creation of a national state to which Jews might migrate and in which they could live in peace, freedom and the dignity of self-government. The motive was altogether humanitarian and generous, but whether the remedy proposed was a wise one is open to question. It rested on the theory that the Jews of the world formed one race and so could become one nation; and, in the eyes of many thoughtful Jews, it carried, in addition to the defects inherent in all racial nationalisms, the drawback that it implied a challenge to the position and the citizenship acquired by Jews in the countries of their adoption. But the crucial point in the Zionist programme is that it looks to Palestine as the only acceptable home of the proposed Jewish state. Such had not been the original intention of Theodor Herzl, the founder of Zionism; but when, in 1903, the British Government offered to make Uganda available for Jewish colonisation, a majority of Zionist pioneers overruled Herzl, rejected the offer and carried the vote in favour of a Palestinian state.

The Zionists base their claims on the historic connexion of Jewry with Palestine, which they represent as entitling the Jews to return to their ancient homeland. The connexion is too well-known to need recapitulation; but what does need stressing, in view of the widespread misconceptions that prevail, is that an historic connexion is not necessarily synonymous with a title to possession, more particularly when it relates to an inhabited country whose population claims, in addition to an ancient historic connexion of their own, the natural rights inherent in actual possession. Ever since the Dispersion, the Jews have been a minority – and most of the time a very small minority – in Palestine, living mainly in the cities sacred to Judaism and enjoying no distinctive rights other than those enjoyed from time to time by the other minorities. At the end of the War, they numbered barely 55,000 souls, that is to say less than 8% of the total population of which the Arabs formed over 90%. In the intervening eighteen centuries, the Jews of the

Diaspora had maintained a distant but living connexion with the Holy Land, which stands out as an impressive and moving example of faith and devotion. It was a tie of the spirit, strengthened by the messianic hope and altogether unconcerned with political aspirations. It was similar in kind to the bond uniting the Moslems or the Catholics of the world to Mecca and Madina or the Vatican City, and just as undesirous of sovereignty, titles to possession or economic preference and of the other 'rights' which the Zionists were the first to claim in its name.

The Zionist claim is based not solely on that ancient connexion but also on the assistance the Jews gave the Allied cause in the War and the promises made to them in return. Some of the reports that have been current about specific Jewish help are now known to be unfounded. Others turn out on examination to refer to services rendered by Jews as citizens to the countries of their adoption. Nevertheless, it is manifest that the Allies did get the benefit of important Jewish services which, but for the Balfour Declaration, would probably not have been forthcoming; and that the contention of the Zionists that they had a claim on the gratitude of the Allies is justified. As for the promises, they are contained in the Balfour Declaration which, it must be remembered, had before its issue received the approval of the President of the United States and was subsequently endorsed by the principal Allied Powers.[1] It has therefore the additional sanction of a wide international recognition. It does not fulfil the Zionist aspiration to a Jewish *national state* but it pledges England's goodwill and assistance towards the establishment of a Jewish *national home* in Palestine. And it curtails Zionist prospects still further by stipulating that the establishment of a

---

[1] Italy's endorsement calls for special notice on account of the substitution of the words 'juridical and political rights' for 'civil and religious rights' in that part of the Balfour Declaration which purports to safeguard the rights of the non-Jewish communities in Palestine. It seems as though the Italian Government had known or guessed that the Arabs would never surrender their political rights, and the emendation is all the more significant as it was made on the instructions of a Jewish statesman – Baron Sonnino, who was Italian Foreign Minister at the time (May 1918).

national home for Jews must be conditioned by two obligations: to safeguard the civil and religious rights of the non-Jewish population of Palestine, and to safeguard the rights and political status enjoyed by Jews in other countries.

In so far, then, as it is based upon the historical connexion of the Jews with the Holy Land, the Zionist claim to political rights and economic preference in Palestine rests on no substantial foundation. But in so far as it rests upon the Balfour Declaration, it is justified to the extent allowed by the two reservations. The unfortunate thing for Zionism – and herein lies the tragedy of the Palestine problem – is that Great Britain's promise lacks real validity, partly because she had previously committed herself to recognising Arab independence in Palestine and partly because the promise involves an obligation which she cannot fulfil without Arab consent.

The consent of the Arabs seemed assured after Commander Hogarth's visit to King Husain in January 1918. But when they realised that the safeguards conveyed by Hogarth were not being observed, that the immigration of Jews into Palestine was not merely a humanitarian enterprise, and that, judging from Zionist declarations and activities, one of the purposes of that immigration was to establish a Jewish majority and thereby, by a vote of the majority, a Jewish state in Palestine, all prospect of securing their consent disappeared. Nor are their apprehensions groundless. For it must be remembered that, although appearing to content themselves with the *national home* envisaged in the Balfour Declaration, the Zionists had by no means given up their ideal of the *national state*, but had accepted the Declaration *faute de mieux* and in the hope that, by steady effort and pressure, they could swell the national home to the dimensions and the power required for its translation into a national state. Of that, they made no secret. On more than one occasion after the issue of the Balfour Declaration, Dr. Weizmann frankly stated in public that Zionism aimed at making Palestine 'just as Jewish as America is American and England is English'.

The motives which impelled the British Government to issue the Balfour Declaration have already been summarily analysed.[1] The determining motive was the desire to occupy Palestine for strategic reasons; and, in obedience to it, they made promises to the Zionists which, had they realised the true position, they would probably have hesitated to make. Ignorance is not seldom a factor in international muddles, and sometimes their source. The Arab charge that there was throughout a conscious fraud perpetrated by an omniscient and deliberate British Government cannot be sustained: it does not take into account the element of ill-informed and haphazard decision which creeps into the shaping of policy, especially in war time and in regard to matters which, to the prime minister of a great Power occupied in defending her very existence, would have seemed of secondary importance. This cannot exonerate Mr. Lloyd George's Government from blame, for nothing can excuse – or, for sheer duplicity, surpass – the message sent through Commander Hogarth to King Husain in January 1918 about the safeguards of the Balfour Declaration, or that other message which was sent to him a month later over the Foreign Secretary's signature to bamboozle him into believing that the Sykes-Picot Agreement was a figment of Turco-Bolshevist imagination. But when a great country with well-established traditions of fair dealing and political sagacity appears to stoop to the level of Hamidian trickery, it behoves the Arabs to remember that war and rectitude are not natural companions, and to try to understand and not only condemn what appears to them to be a deliberate deception. There is little doubt that, while the Balfour Declaration was under consideration, the British Government – or at any rate, several members of the Cabinet – did not realise the strength of the Arab claim to Palestine or the extent to which the available land in it was necessary to the existence and the natural expansion of its rural population; and that, to their harassed minds in the third and most critical year of the War, such questions must have

[1] See Chapter XIII, Section 7, *supra*.

appeared, if not unimportant, at any rate shelvable. Others, not aware of the nature of the forces behind the Sharif Husain's leadership, made light of his pretensions and felt confident that it would not be difficult, when the time came, to silence the funny old man in Mecca – 'that old marmoset', as Sir Mark Sykes would say – with a few courteous but strong phrases, and a sackful or two of gold into the bargain. What with that and with the confusion caused by the multiplicity of departments (Foreign Office, India Office, War Office, Admiralty, Arab Bureau in Cairo, Foreign Department in Delhi) dealing directly with the shaping of Arab policy, it is scarcely surprising that the British right hand was sometimes completely ignorant of what the left hand had done or was about to do, and that serious mistakes were made.

But where Great Britain's policy appears altogether indefensible is in the period after the War when the incompatibility of her promises to the Arabs and to the Jews had become manifest; when it became clear that the Zionists were out for a Jewish majority and were using the Balfour Declaration as a means and the label of National Home as a screen to establish the Jewish state, and that the Arabs were determined upon defending their own existence as a majority for the sake of their existence on the land; when there was no doubt left that the problem was fundamentally one in which an aspirant nation from abroad aimed at ousting from its secular holding the nation in possession at home. History shows that a conflict of that kind, if allowed to develop, can only be resolved in blood. Even on the assumption that the British Government had chosen, from some motive or other, to turn a blind eye to the teachings of history, there were enough indications in the earliest years of the mandate in Palestine to show them what to expect. Not only in such warnings as they had had from the penetrating report of the King-Crane Commission and from other, often British, sources; but also in the opening acts of the tragedy itself. They saw that Zionist colonisation involved the actual wiping out of villages and the eviction of their peasantry; that the money which the Zionists brought and the resulting prosperity – if real prosperity there were – did not make up in Arab eyes for the loss of all that a peasant holds dear and sacred in his village surroundings; that the peasants were defenceless against the process of dispossession and the legalised but relentless pressure that went with it; that the sense of helplessness against the inexorable advance of Zionist colonisation had led to obviously unpremeditated outbreaks on the part of a population who are by nature peaceful and hospitable to strangers, and was bound, if allowed to continue, to cause unpredictable losses in lives and property. They learnt from actual experience that the policy they were carrying through by sheer force was, for all the optimism in ministerial speeches and official reports, a policy which was in effect laying in stores of dynamite.

Yet, seeing that, the British Government remained to all outward appearances unmoved. It is not easy to arrive at the underlying motive of their attitude: whether it is that they are more deeply committed to the Zionists than they allow to appear, and more amenable to their pressure; or that they believe that a Jewish state would be a stronger and more dependable ally of Great Britain's than an Arab state in that important corner of the world; or that they are above all concerned with retaining for as long as they can their absolute strategic and economic hold on Palestine. The available evidence does not throw enough light on the deeper motives of their attitude. Nor can it be explained rationally, or even psychologically: only historically, by analogy with Ireland where the same obstinate persistence in an unwanted policy and the same blindness to the writing on the wall were shown and continued to be shown until Ireland was lost. Even now when, by steps which it did not take a prophet to foretell, their policy has turned Palestine into a shambles, they show no indication of a return to sanity, that is to say to the principles of ordinary common sense and justice which are held in such high honour in England.

II.

The appointment of a Royal Commission of inquiry in the summer of 1936 gave rise to the hope that a thorough investigation would take place and bring the facts to light. But that expectation has been disappointed. The Report which appeared in July 1937 is in many ways a masterly exposition; but it is also an incomplete survey, and its value as an authoritative summing-up is somewhat impaired by the failure of the Commissioners to maintain an even level of thoroughness in their investigation of the origins of the problem.

The Report has certain outstanding merits. It contains valuable information which had not appeared in any official publication before. It performs a signal service to the truth by exposing some of the fallacies on which successive British Governments had based their acts and pronouncements since the inception of the mandate; and, although its authors take every precaution against ruffling the waters of official complacency, their strictures amount to a serious and well-deserved indictment. Its analysis of the policy hitherto pursued in execution of the mandate is carried far enough to reveal that the one was by definition unworkable and the other on results a failure – two undeniable facts which, although known to every independent observer in Palestine, had lain hidden from the outside world behind the smoke-screen of legend and propaganda. To that extent, the Report marks an important step forward towards the rehabilitation of the truth. It exposes the invalidity of those numerous declarations in which, on frequent occasions between 1918 and 1937, Prime Ministers and Secretaries of State would assert that the policy of a national home for Jews in Palestine was not incompatible with the obligations undertaken towards the Arabs.

In other ways, however, the Commissioners missed their unique opportunity. Like the members of the Permanent Mandates Commission, they appear to have allowed their judgment to be influenced by the skill and the completeness with which the Zionist case is always presented, and to have unconsciously overlooked that, since the Arabs were not so well equipped with the resources of presentation, a duty lay on the inquirers to examine their claims with still greater thoroughness. The Report shows that, in actual fact, the Commissioners did the very reverse, in their examination both of the political and economic grievances of the Arabs and of the historical background in which those grievances are rooted.

To a certain extent, the fault for that is attributable to the Arab boycott, which was called off only a few days before the Royal Commission's departure from Palestine. Until then, the Commissioners had devoted some seven or eight weeks to the hearing of British and Jewish evidence. When the boycott was called off, they did not find it possible to allocate more than five days to the hearing of Arab evidence. For that, the Arabs have only themselves to thank. But the fact remains that the Commissioners heard only a fraction of the argument which might have been tendered on the Arab side. The number of Arab witnesses who appeared before them was approximately 12 as against a total of nearly 100 British and Jewish witnesses. An important part of the Arab evidence reached them through the medium of translation, and somewhat faulty translation at that. The fact that the Commissioners did not find it possible to extend their stay in Palestine meant that they were deprived of the time required for probing the Arab evidence with the patience and thoroughness which they had devoted to the British and the Jewish evidence.

With regard to the historical background, the insufficiency of the Commissioners' inquiry is inexplicable. They go fully into the question of the obligations implied in the Balfour Declaration but leave their investigation of the obligations contracted towards the Arabs deliberately incomplete. They quote and analyse some of (though by no means all) the relevant portions of the McMahon Correspondence, and yet make no mention of the pledge given to King Husain in January 1918 about the scope of the Balfour Declaration. Nor do they make any reference to the Declaration to the Seven of June 1918. They give prominence to the Faisal-Weizmann Agreement, but do not mention the safeguards of Arab political and economic freedom on which Faisal had relied. The reason they give for not going more fully into the historical background is as follows:

> 'We have not considered that our terms of reference required us to undertake the detailed and lengthy research among the documents of twenty years ago which would be needed for a full re-examination of this issue. We think it sufficient for the purposes of the Report to state that the British Government have never accepted the Arab case.'

The explanation is a puzzling one: on the one hand, it was precisely the fact that the British Government had never accepted the Arab case that was the underlying cause of the disturbances which the Royal Commission had been appointed to investigate; on the other, there is an unexplained inconsistency between the readiness of the Commissioners to probe some of the documents of twenty years ago and their deliberate neglect of the remaining and not less relevant documents. For, lower down in their Report, they state that:

> 'We must now consider what the Balfour Declaration meant. We have been permitted to examine the records which bear upon the question. . . .'

It is not clear why the Commissioners, while making a point of examining the records relating to the Balfour Declaration, felt that an examination of the records relating to the promises made to the Arabs would have fallen outside their terms of reference.

This inequality is of more than academic interest, for it not only impairs the value of the Commission's survey but also vitiates their fundamental conclusions. By not carrying their inquiry to its proper limits, the Commissioners found themselves defenceless against the argument that Zionist and Arab rights in Palestine stood on an equal footing, and were persuaded into adopting it, thus giving the weight of their endorsement to a claim which is historically invalid and, so far as natural rights go, fictitious. And, having adopted the claim as valid, they based their proposals for a solution upon it.

The solution proposed by the Royal Commission rests on the argument that, since Arabs and Jews have equal rights to the possession of Palestine, the country should be divided between them. The form which the division should take is outlined in the Partition scheme with which the Report concludes. The Commissioners recommended that a portion of Palestine west of the Jordan, far larger than the area of present Jewish settlement, be detached from the rest to form a Jewish state; that zones of permanent British mandate be created around the cities of Jerusalem, Bethlehem and Nazareth, ostensibly to guard the Holy Places contained in them; and that the rest be merged with Transjordan to form an Arab state. The Arab State and the Jewish State are to be recognised as sovereign independent national entities, eligible for membership of the League of Nations and tied to Great Britain by treaties of alliance in place of the existing mandate. A new mandate would be devised for the British zone.

The outstanding feature of the Partition scheme is that it complicates the problem which it purports to solve. The scheme envisages the conversion of the proposed Jewish national home into a Jewish state, and the extension of the present area of Zionist colonisation to an area several times its size, which includes a settled Arab population of some 300,000 souls, and in which Jewish authority would be supreme. In other words, it meets the Arab objections to the Balfour Declaration by recommending that the Zionists be given far more than was actually promised them on the broadest possible interpretation of the Declaration; and it faces the difficulties arising out of the displacement of the Arab population by recommending displacement on a much vaster scale.

In support of their scheme, the Commissioners adduce eloquent arguments which reflect greater credit upon their humane concern for a solution than upon their insight or practical sense. They claim for it that it was devised to meet three essential requirements. 'It must be practicable. It must conform to our obligations. It must do justice to the Arabs and the Jews.' Yet it is demonstrable that the scheme does not fulfil any of those three conditions. It is not practicable. It does not conform to Great Britain's obligations. It does not do equal justice to the Jews and to the Arabs. There is reason to believe that the Commissioners may have drawn up their scheme somewhat hurriedly, for the section on Partition has an air of hasty improvisation which is in striking contrast with the thoughtful tenor of the rest of the Report; and the impression it gives of insufficient preparation is strengthened by the errors and inconsistencies it contains. The probability is that the Commissioners did not make up their minds finally on the subject of Partition until a late stage in the preparation of the Report, and that they did so only when fresh testimony had led them to believe that some such scheme as they decided to put forward would find favour with certain Arab and Zionist leaders and stand a chance of being generally accepted. If that inference is correct, it would explain what seems otherwise incomprehensible, namely, the Commissioners' belief that Partition offered a prospect of peace in Palestine.

The weakness of the Royal Commission's scheme seems attributable in the main to a confusion between what is desirable and what is fair and practicable. In face of the abominable persecution to which Jews in Central Europe are nowadays subjected, it is not only desirable but also urgent that room be found for the relief of the greatest possible number. A duty lay on the Commissioners, as it does on every human being, to do their utmost for suffering Jewry; and the Report shows, to its eternal credit, that its authors were acutely conscious of that duty. But they did a disservice to it in formulating a scheme which is neither fair nor workable.

The scheme is based on the expectation that the Arabs would, or could be made to, renounce their natural and political rights in any part of Palestine; that frontiers may be laid down in defiance of physical features and of ingrained habits of human intercourse; that trade and good government can thrive in a small country not larger than Wales, after its dissection into some half-dozen entities made up of separate states, enclaves and corridors; and that a population of 300,000 settled people, deeply attached to their homes and their culture, would submit to either of the alternatives proposed for them by the Royal Commission: forcible eviction or subjection to a Jewish state to be established over their heads. It runs counter to the lessons of history, the requirements of geography, the natural play of economic forces, and the ordinary laws of human behaviour. It reproduces some of the most discredited and dangerous features of the Treaty of Versailles. It pays scant regard to the doctrine of consent. In drawing it up, the Commissioners appear to have overlooked that it is no more feasible to drive a peasantry from its soil than to impose an alien government upon an unwilling population, except by constant resort to force; and that the use of superior force to hold down a nationally-conscious people, while it may for a time achieve its immediate purpose, is bound sooner or later to defeat its own ends.

The moral and political objections to the scheme may be judged in the light of the preceding chapters of this narrative. By no stretch of the word can it be said to conform to the obligations incurred by Great Britain, if the obligations are examined as a whole, with due regard to all the relevant records, and not selectively in the manner of the Royal Commission. Nor is there any justification for the claim that it does justice to both the Arabs and the Jews. The claim is set forth in the concluding pages of the Report with a wealth of argument and an eloquent appeal to the spirit of compromise; but it turns out on examination to rest rather on verbal niceties than on a basis of substance. In substance, the scheme offers the Jews a good deal more and the Arabs a good deal less than they possess or was promised to them; and the appeal for compromise is in effect an appeal to the Arabs to get out and make room for a Jewish state. The Commissioners would have stood on firmer ground had they put forward a scheme based on real compromise, that is to say on equivalent sacrifices on the part of all the three parties concerned. But what the Partition scheme does is to require different things of each: of the Arabs, the real and substantial sacrifice of something they own and want to keep; of the Zionists, the nominal sacrifice of something they do not own but want to have; and of the mandatory Power no sacrifice whatever. For the scheme has been so devised as to allow Great Britain to retain her strategic and economic position, enable the Zionists to become absolute masters of western and northern Palestine, and achieve those two aims at Arab expense.

The array of moral, political and practical obstacles in the way of the scheme is formidable and renders it manifestly inapplicable. There is no need to analyse it in greater detail: it can never be carried into execution. The labours of the Technical Commission appointed in the spring of 1938 to study the ways and means of its application are not yet completed. They have spent three months in Palestine, at a time when the revolt against Partition was in full swing; and, although they were precluded by the boycott from hearing Arab evidence, the probability is that they will have seen for themselves that the unwillingness of the Arab peasantry to be dislodged from their soil is genuine and deep-seated.

12.

One of the most prevalent misconceptions is that the trouble in Palestine is the result of an engineered agitation. It is variously attributed to the intrigues of the *efendi* class, to the political ambitions of the Grand Mufti, to the agents and the subsidies of Italy and Germany, to Communist machinations; and the opinion is commonly expressed – and sometimes quite genuinely – that, had the Arab masses been left unmisguided to reap the full harvest of benefits brought to them by the mandate, there would have been no trouble. The blindness of that view is clear to-day. Former outbreaks had similarly been explained; but, after inquiry by one or other of the commissions appointed by the mandatory Power, the underlying causes had always been found to have lain in the profound attachment of the Arabs to their soil and their culture. The rebellion to-day is, to a greater extent than ever before, a revolt of villagers, and its immediate cause is the proposed scheme of Partition and, more particularly, that aspect of it which envisages the eventual displacement of a large Arab peasantry to make room for the immigrant citizens of the proposed Jewish state. The moving spirits in the revolt are not the nationalist leaders, most of whom are now in exile, but men of the working and agricultural classes who are risking their lives in what they believe to be the only way left to them of saving their homes and their villages. It is a delusion to regard it as the work of agitators, Arab or foreign. Political incitement can do much to fan the flames of discontent, but it cannot keep a revolt active, month after month, in conditions of such violence and hardship.

Far from its being engineered by the leaders, the revolt is in a very marked way a challenge to their authority and an indictment of their methods. The rebel chiefs lay the blame for the present plight of the peasantry on those Arab landowners who have sold their land, and they accuse the leaders of culpable neglect for failing to prevent the sales. The peasants have had no say in the great majority of the land transactions which have led to their eviction. The landowner who has the legal title disposes of the land at his discretion, and one of the provisions of the deed of sale is that the land is to be surrendered to the purchaser free from all occupants or rights of tenancy. The revolt is largely manned by the peasantry, that is to say by the people whose life and livelihood are on the soil but who have had no say whatever in its disposal; and their anger and violence are as much directed against the Arab landowners and brokers who have facilitated the sales as against the policy of the mandatory Power under whose aegis the transactions have taken place. The fact that some of those landowners have served on national Arab bodies makes them only more odious to the insurgent peasantry and has rendered it less amenable to the influence of the political leaders as a whole.

Another serious misconception relates to the economic results of Zionist enterprise. The belief is widespread that the Arab population has greatly benefited by it, and many thoughtful people are genuinely bewildered by what appears to be ingratitude on the part of the Arabs and a perverse inability to recognise the value of the further benefits that would be conferred upon them by a continuation of it. This appears all the more puzzling as the establishment of a British administration has resulted in a visible improvement in the government of the country and in the material lot of the Arab population.

The explanation is twofold. In the first place, while it is true that Jewish capital and initiative have greatly contributed to the economic development of the country, to the enrichment of a number of Arab landowners and to a rise in the wages of Arab labour, it is also true that they have created new needs and new burdens. The public services called into being by the policy of the mandate – special measures of public security, duplication rendered necessary by the imposition of Hebrew as an official language, swelling of the wages bill in public contracts solely in order to give employment to Jewish labour – have necessitated the setting up of an abnormally large and costly bureaucracy for such a small country, and the ear-marking of a considerable portion of the budget to unproductive expenditure. The establishment of Jewish industries, especially those which were artificial in the sense that they depended on raw materials imported from outside, led to the imposition of protective tariffs and a consequent rise in the price of commodities. The rapid influx of population resulted in an abnormal rise in the cost of living everywhere, in the villages as well as in the towns. In the absence of full statistical data, it is impossible to tell to what extent the economic benefits have been offset by the corresponding burdens; but it is an undeniable fact, and one that is generally overlooked, that, save for the enrichment of a number of landowners and middlemen, the economic position of the Arab population as a whole, and more particularly that of the villages, is scarcely better or worse than it has been for generations.

In the second place, the economic aspect is overshadowed by the moral and political issues. To the Arabs the problem is now essentially one of self-preservation. This had not always been so. In the early years of the mandate, the main source of Arab discontent was the denial of independence. Fears for the future were already in evidence and had indeed been among the underlying causes of the earlier outbreaks. But Zionist settlement had not yet made great strides, and Arab apprehensions were more concerned with its ultimate aims than with its tangible results. A profound change has come about since, due to the unprecedented flood of Jewish immigration and settlement which began in 1932 and caused, as well as an appearance of general prosperity in the country, a sharp rise in Arab apprehensions. The fears of the Arabs had now a more tangible basis. At the rate at which immigrants had come in during 1935, the Jews who had formed 8% of the total population in 1918 might acquire a majority in another ten years. Even if Jewish capital and initiative had been bringing undiluted material benefits, those fears would still have been the paramount factor in the Arab attitude and would have led inevitably to some such outbreak as occurred in 1936. But the final hardening of the Arab attitude took place in 1937 when it became known that the Royal Commission had recommended Partition and that the British Government had adopted the recommendation in substance. The Royal Commission's scheme, proposing as it did the subjection or displacement from their homes and villages of a large Arab population in the area proposed for a Jewish state, translated Arab fears of eventual dispossession into a certainty.

The problem became, in Arab eyes, a problem of self-preservation. In face of such issues, economic considerations are naturally lost sight of. The acts of violence which broke out after the appearance of the Royal Commission's Report are causing as much ravage to the Arab countryside as to that part of it which has passed into Jewish hands. The disturbances have since assumed the character of a rebellion in which the leading part is played by peasants and labourers who, in despair, have resorted to violence as the only means left to them of resisting Partition.

13.

No lasting solution of the Palestine problem is to be hoped for until the injustice is removed. Violence, whether physical or moral, cannot provide a solution. It is not only reprehensible in itself: it also renders an understanding between Arabs, British and Jews increasingly difficult of attainment. By resorting to it, the Arabs have certainly attracted an earnest attention to their grievances, which all their peaceful representations in Jerusalem, in London and in Geneva had for twenty years failed to do. But violence defeats its own ends; and such immediate gains as it may score are invariably discounted by the harm which is inseparable from it. Nothing but harm can come of the terror raging in Palestine; but the wise way to put an end to it is to remove the causes which have brought it about. The fact must be faced that the violence of the Arabs is the inevitable corollary of the moral violence done to them, and that it is not likely to cease, whatever the brutality of the repression, unless the moral violence itself were to cease.

To those who look ahead, beyond the smoke-screen of legend and propaganda, the way to a solution is clear: it lies along the path of ordinary common sense and justice. There is no room for a second nation in a country which is already inhabited, and inhabited by a people whose national consciousness is fully awakened and whose affection for their homes and countryside is obviously unconquerable. The lesson to be drawn form the efforts hitherto made to lay the foundations of a Jewish state in Palestine is that they have turned the country into a shambles – not because of any inherent Arab hatred of Jews or lack of feeling for their plight, but because it is not possible to establish a Jewish state in Palestine without the forcible dislodgement of a peasantry who seem readier to face death than give up their land. On that ground alone, and without taking the political issues into account, the attempt to carry the Zionist dream into execution is doomed to failure; and the first step along the road to a solution is to face that fact objectively and realise its implications.

Once the fact is faced that the establishment of a Jewish state in Palestine, or of a national home based on territorial sovereignty, cannot be accomplished without forcibly displacing the Arabs, the way to a solution becomes clearer. It is not beyond the capacity of British, Jewish and Arab statesmanship to devise one. There seems to be no valid reason why Palestine should not be constituted into an independent Arab state in which as many Jews as the country can hold without prejudice to its political and economic freedom would live in peace, security and dignity, and enjoy full rights of citizenship. Such an Arab state would naturally be tied to Great Britain by a freely-negotiated treaty which should contain provisions for the safeguarding of British strategic and economic interests, for ensuring the safety and the inviolability of the Holy Places of all faiths, for the protection of all minorities and minority rights, and for affording the Jewish community the widest freedom in the pursuit of their spiritual and cultural ideals.

A solution on those lines would be both fair and practicable. It would protect the natural rights of the Arabs in Palestine and satisfy their legitimate national aspirations. It would enable the Jews to have a national home in the spiritual and cultural sense, in which Jewish values could flourish and the Jewish genius have the freest play to seek inspiration in the land of its ancient connexion. It would secure Great Britain's interests on a firm basis of consent.

And it would restore Palestine to its proper place, as a symbol of peace in the hearts of Judaism, Christianity and Islam.

No other solution seems practicable, except possibly at the cost of an unpredictable holocaust of Arab, Jewish and British lives. The relief of Jewish distress caused by European persecution must be sought elsewhere than in Palestine, for the country is too small to hold a larger increase of population, and it has already borne more than its fair share. It is for Great Britain who has taken the lead in this work of charity at Arab expense to turn to the vast resources of her empire and to practise there some of the charity she has been preaching. It is also for the other countries that pride themselves on being civilised and humane to revise the niggardly decisions of the Evian Conference and consent to some of the sacrifices which Arab Palestine has been bullied into making on a scale that has taxed her capacity.

The treatment meted out to Jews in Germany and other European countries is a disgrace to its authors and to modern civilisation; but posterity will not exonerate any country that fails to bear its proper share of the sacrifices needed to alleviate Jewish suffering and distress. To place the brunt of the burden upon Arab Palestine is a miserable evasion of the duty that lies upon the whole of the civilised world. It is also morally outrageous. No code of morals can justify the persecution of one people in an attempt to relieve the persecution of another. The cure for the eviction of Jews from Germany is not to be sought in the eviction of the Arabs from their homeland; and the relief of Jewish distress may not be accomplished at the cost of inflicting a corresponding distress upon an innocent and peaceful population.

The renunciation will not be easy. Jewish hopes have been raised to such a pitch that the non-fulfilment of the Zionist dream of a Jewish state in Palestine will cause intense disillusionment and bitterness. The manifold proofs of public spirit and of capacity to endure hardships and face danger in the building up of the national home are there to testify to the devotion with which a large section of the

Jewish people cherish the Zionist ideal.   And it would be an act of further cruelty to the Jews to disappoint those hopes if there existed some way of satisfying them, that did not involve cruelty to another people.   But the logic of facts is inexorable.   It shows that no room can be made in Palestine for a second nation except by dislodging or exterminating the nation in possession.

APPENDIX A

THE McMAHON CORRESPONDENCE

(COVERING LETTER TO NO. 1)

The Amir 'Abdullah to Mr. Ronald Storrs

Mecca, Ramadan 2, 1333.
[*July* 14, 1915.]

Complimentary titles.

I send my affectionate regard and respects to your esteemed self, and trust that you will ensure, as you know how to, the acceptance of the enclosed note which contains our proposals and conditions.

In this connexion, I wish to give you and your Government my assurance that you need have no anxiety about the intentions of our people, for they realise how closely their interests are bound to those of your Government. Do not trouble to send aeroplanes or warships to distribute news and reports as in the past: our minds are now made up.

What we would request is that you should make it possible for the Egyptian Government to resume the consignment of the bounty of grain for the poor of Mecca and Madina, which was stopped last year. The arrival of this year's grain, together with last year's, would be valuable here for the promotion of our mutual interests. To a person of your quick understanding, this hint will suffice.

I beg of you not to send us any communications until you hear that our plans have matured, except for the reply to this letter and its enclosure, which should only be sent through the bearer. Perhaps you will think fit to give him a written warrant to enable him to pass through to you whenever we think it necessary to send him. He is dependable.

Compliments.

No. 1

The Sharif Husain's First Note to Sir Henry McMahon

Mecca, Ramadan 2, 1333.
[*July* 14, 1915.]

Complimentary titles.

Whereas the entire Arab nation without exception is determined to assert its right to live, gain its freedom and administer its own affairs in name and in fact;

And whereas the Arabs believe it to be in Great Britain's interest to lend them assistance and support in the fulfilment of their steadfast and legitimate aims to the exclusion of all other aims;

And whereas it is similarly to the advantage of the Arabs, in view of their geographical position and their economic interests, and in view of the well-known attitude of the Government of Great Britain,[1] to prefer British assistance to any other;

For these reasons, the Arab nation has decided to approach the Government of Great Britain with a request for the approval, through one of their representatives if they think fit, of the following basic provisions which, as time presses, have not been made to include matters of relatively smaller importance, since such matters can wait until the time comes for their consideration: –

1. Great Britain recognises the independence of the Arab countries which are bounded: on the north, by the line Mersin-Adana to parallel 37° N. and thence along the line Birejik-Urfa-Mardin-Midiat-Jazirat (ibn 'Umar) – Amadia to the Persian frontier; on the east, by the Persian frontier down to the Persian Gulf; on the south, by the Indian Ocean (with the exclusion of Aden whose status will remain as at present); on the west, by the Red Sea and the Mediterranean Sea back to Mersin.

2. Great Britain will agree to the proclamation of an Arab Caliphate for Islam.

3. The Sharifian Arab Government undertakes, other things being equal, to grant Great Britain preference in all economic enterprises in the Arab countries.

4. With a view to ensuring the stability of Arab independence and the efficacy of the promised preference in economic enterprises, the two contracting parties undertake, in the event of any foreign state attacking either of them, to come to each other's

[1] i.e., in view of the overtures made to the Arabs by Lord Kitchener in 1914, as related in Chapter VII.

assistance with all the resources of their military and naval forces; it being understood that peace will be concluded only when both parties concur.

In the event of one of the two parties embarking upon a war of offence, the other party will adopt an attitude of neutrality, but, if invited to join, will agree to confer with the other party as to the conditions of joint action.

5. Great Britain agrees to the abolition of Capitulations[1] in the Arab countries, and undertakes to assist the Sharifian Government in summoning an international congress to decree their abolition.

6. Clauses 3 and 4 of the present Agreement are to remain in force for a period of fifteen years. Should either party desire an extension, due notice of one year before the expiry of that period will have to be given.

Therefore, since the entire Arab nation is (God be praised!) united in its resolve to pursue its noble aim to the end, at whatever cost, it requests the Government of Great Britain to return an answer, whether negatively or in the affirmative, within thirty days of the receipt of this message, in default of which it reserves its right to complete freedom of action, just as we will consider ourselves absolved from the letter and the spirit of the declaration which we made earlier through 'Ali Efendi.[2]

Compliments.

No. 2

Sir Henry McMahon's First Note to the Sharif Husain

Cairo, August 30, 1915.

Complimentary titles.

We have the honour to tender the gratitude due to you for the sentiments of sincere friendship for England which you display, and it pleases us, moreover, to learn that Your Lordship and your people are at one in believing that Arab interests are in harmony with British interests, and vice-versa.

In earnest of this, we hereby confirm to you the declaration of Lord Kitchener as communicated to you through 'Ali Efendi, in which was manifested our desire for the independence of the Arab

---

[1] i.e., the long-established Conventions by which foreigners in the Ottoman Empire enjoyed financial and juridical privileges.
[2] The messenger who had carried the secret communications between the British Agency in Cairo and the Amir 'Abdullah in Mecca. See Chapter VII, Section 3, *supra*.

countries and their inhabitants, and our readiness to approve an Arab caliphate upon its proclamation.

We now declare once more that the Government of Great Britain would welcome the reversion of the caliphate to a true Arab born of the blessed stock of the Prophet.

As for the question of frontiers and boundaries, negotiations would appear to be premature and a waste of time on details at this stage, with the War in progress and the Turks in effective occupation of the greater part of those regions. All the more so as a party of Arabs inhabiting those very regions have, to our amazement and sorrow, overlooked and neglected this valuable and incomparable opportunity; and, instead of coming to our aid, have lent their assistance to the Germans and the Turks; to that new despoiler, the German, and to that tyrannical oppressor, the Turk.

Nevertheless, we are fully prepared to despatch to Your Lordship whatever quantities of grain and other charitable gifts may be owed by Egypt to the Holy Land of Arabia and the noble Arabs. These will be forwarded, on a sign from Your Lordship, to whatever locality you may indicate.

We have made the necessary arrangements for facilitating the journeys of your messenger to us.

Compliments.

No. 3

The Sharif Husain's Second Note to Sir Henry McMahon

Mecca, Shawwal 29, 1333.
[September 9, 1915.]

Complimentary titles.

We received your note of the 19th Shawwal, [August 30,] with gratification, and have given it the fullest consideration, notwithstanding the obscurity and the signs of lukewarmth and hesitancy we descried in it in regard to our essential clause. We find it necessary to affirm to Your Excellency our sentiments of amity with Great Britain and our readiness to ensure her a favoured place in all circumstances and in every manner, for in that way can the true interests of our co-religionists best be served.

Your Excellency will suffer me to say, in explanation of what I mean by lukewarmth and hesitancy, that your statements in regard to the question of frontiers and boundaries – namely that to discuss them at this stage were unprofitable and could only result in a waste of time since those regions are still occupied by their sovereign government, and so forth – reflect what I might almost describe as reluctance or something akin to reluctance, on your part.

The fact is that the proposed frontiers and boundaries represent not the suggestions of one individual whose claim might well await the conclusion of the War, but the demands of our people who believe that those frontiers form the minimum necessary to the establishment of the new order for which they are striving. This they are determined to obtain; and they have decided to discuss the matter, in the first resort, with that Power in whom they place their greatest confidence and reliance, and whom they regard as the pivot of justice, namely Great Britain.

In this, they are moved by considerations of the reciprocity of interests, the requirements of territorial organisation, and the wishes of the populations concerned; and also by their desire to see the foundations of their future life settled beforehand, so as to avoid finding themselves, when their new life is being established and organised, in opposition to or conflict with Great Britain or one of her allies – which God forbid! It should be noted that, in drawing up their proposed delimitation, they have not outstepped the bounds of the regions inhabited by their race.

For our aim, O respected Minister, is to ensure that the conditions which are essential to our future shall be secured on a foundation of reality, and not on highly-decorated phrases and titles. As for the caliphate, God have mercy on its soul and comfort the Moslems for their loss!

I am confident that Your Excellency will realise beyond all doubt that I have had nothing to do with the proposing of those boundaries, which include only populations of our race, and that they were proposed by our people who regard them as being, to put it briefly, vitally and economically essential – as indeed they are.

In conclusion, we believe in all sincerity that your loyalty will prevail, whether you are satisfied with us or displeased; and that you will not wish to seize upon the fact that some of our people are still with the utmost zeal furthering Ottoman designs, as stated in your letter under reference, as an excuse for treating our aspirations with such lukewarmth and hesitancy. I think Your Excellency is above denying that our demands are fundamental, nay, that they are the very substance and essence of our existence, be it from the material, the spiritual or the moral point of view. Up to this very moment, I have been endeavouring, in person and with all my powers, to enforce the prescriptions of our Sacred

Law in my country and in all that concerns me in relation to the rest of the empire, until God issue His decree.

For these reasons, and the better to set your mind at ease, I may state that the people of all those countries, including those of whom you say that they are zealously furthering German and Ottoman designs, are awaiting the result of the present negotiations, which depend solely upon whether you reject or admit the proposed frontiers, and upon whether or not you will help us to secure their spiritual and other rights against evil and danger. Please communicate to us the decision of the British Government on this point, for our guidance as to what suits their policy, and as to what steps it behoves us to take. For the rest, it is God Who decrees the past and the future, He ordains all things, exalted be His Name!

With regard to our request for the despatch of the people's bounty, with the customary purses from the Ministry of Auqaf and all that it is usual to send with the Pilgrimage convoy, I had in view that their despatch would be a means of substantiating the terms of your proclamations to the world, and more particularly the Moslem world, in which you stated that your hostility was solely directed against the usurpers of the caliphate and, hence, of the rights of all Moslems. To say nothing of the fact that the said bounty comes from specific endowments which have nothing to do with politics. If you decide to send them, let the bounty due on account of the past two years be consigned in a special steamer to Jedda as usual in the name of the people, and let the skipper or the special officer who is usually charged year by year with the duty of delivery communicate with the authorities at Jedda on arrival at the port, and ask for the competent official who is to take delivery of the grain against the proper receipt to be signed by the receiving officer. It should be noted that only the signature of that officer may be accepted, and the skipper or special officer should be instructed that if any obstruction is attempted, he should threaten to return with his cargo to the port of departure. The consignment is to be formally received by the committee known as the 'Committee for dealing with the People's Bounty'.

If you should wish to reply to this note, let the reply be sent by the bearer.

Compliments.

No. 4

Sir Henry McMahon's Second Note to the Sharif Husain

Cairo, October 24, 1915.

Complimentary titles.

I have, with gratification and pleasure, received your note of the 29th Shawwal, 1333, and its tokens of sincere friendship have filled me with satisfaction and contentment.

I regret to find that you inferred from my last note that my attitude towards the question of frontiers and boundaries was one of hesitancy and lukewarmth. Such was in no wise the intention of my note. All I meant was that I considered that the time had not yet come in which that question could be discussed in a conclusive manner.

But, having realised from your last note that you considered the question important, vital and urgent, I hastened to communicate to the Government of Great Britain the purport of your note. It gives me the greatest pleasure to convey to you, on their behalf, the following declarations which, I have no doubt, you will receive with satisfaction and acceptance.

The districts of Mersin and Alexandretta,[1] and portions of Syria lying to the west of the districts of Damascus, Homs, Hama and Aleppo[2], cannot be said to be purely Arab, and must on that account be excepted from the proposed delimitation.

Subject to that modification, and without prejudice to the treaties concluded between us and certain Arab Chiefs, we accept that delimitation.

As for the regions lying within the proposed frontiers, in which Great Britain is free to act without detriment to the interests of her ally France, I am authorised to give you the following pledges on behalf of the Government of Great Britain, and to reply as follows to your note:

(1) That, subject to the modifications stated above, Great Britain is prepared to recognise and uphold the independence of the Arabs in all the regions lying within the frontiers proposed by the Sharif of Mecca;

(2) That Great Britain will guarantee the Holy Places against all external aggression, and will recognise the obligation of preserving them from aggression;

[1] The port of Mersin lay in the Vilayet of Adana, and the port of Alexandretta in the Vilayet of Aleppo.

[2] The cities of Damascus, Homs and Hama lay in the Vilayet of Syria, of which Damascus was the capital. Aleppo was the capital of the vilayet of that name.

(3) That, when circumstances permit, Great Britain will help the Arabs with her advice and assist them in the establishment of governments to suit those diverse regions;

(4) That it is understood that the Arabs have already decided to seek the counsels and advice of Great Britain exclusively; and that such European advisers and officials as may be needed to establish a sound system of administration shall be British;

(5) That, as regards the two vilayets of Baghdad and of Basra, the Arabs recognise that the fact of Great Britain's established position and interests there will call for the setting up of special administrative arrangements[1] to protect those regions from foreign aggression, to promote the welfare of their inhabitants, and to safeguard our mutual economic interests.

I am confident that this declaration will convince you, beyond all doubt, of Great Britain's sympathy with the aspirations of her friends the Arabs; and that it will result in a lasting and solid alliance with them, of which one of the immediate consequences will be the expulsion of the Turks from the Arab countries and the liberation of the Arab peoples from the Turkish yoke which has weighed on them all these long years.

I have confined myself in this note to vital questions of primary importance. If there are any other matters in your notes, which have been overlooked, we can revert to them at some suitable time in the future.

I have heard with great satisfaction and pleasure that the Sacred Kiswa[2] and the charitable gifts which had gone with it, had arrived safely and that, thanks to your wise directions and arrangements, they were landed without trouble or damage in spite of the risks and difficulties created by the present deplorable war. We pray Almighty God that He may bring a lasting peace and freedom to mankind.

I am sending this note with your faithful messenger, Shaikh Muhammad ibn 'Aref ibn 'Uraifan, who will lay before you certain interesting matters which, as they are of secondary importance, I have abstained from mentioning in this note.

Compliments.

[1] And not 'special measures of administrative control', as in the version printed in the Report of the Palestine Royal Commission, Cmd. 5479, 1937, p. 19. The Arabic text is: *tadābir idariya khāssa*.
[2] The embroidered pall which is annually sent to Mecca from Egypt to be used as a covering for the Ka'ba.

420

No. 5

The Sharif Husain's Third Note to Sir Henry McMahon

Mecca, Zul-Hejja 27, 1333.
[November 5, 1915.]

Complimentary titles.

With great gratification have we received your note of the 15th
Zul-Hejja [October 24] to which we would reply as follows.

First, in order to facilitate agreement and serve the cause of
Islam by the removal of possible sources of hardship and tribula-
tion, and in earnest of the particular esteem in which we hold
Great Britain, we no longer insist on the inclusion of the districts[1]
of Mersin and Adana in the Arab Kingdom. As for the vilayets of
Aleppo and Bairut and their western maritime coasts, these are
purely Arab provinces in which the Moslem is indistinguishable
from the Christian, for they are both the descendants of one fore-
father. And we Moslems intend, in those provinces, to follow
the precepts laid down by the Commander of the Faithful, 'Umar
ibn al-Khattab (God have mercy upon him!), and the caliphs
who came after him, when he enjoined upon the Moslems to treat
the Christians on a footing with themselves, saying: they are to
enjoy the same rights and bear the same obligations as ourselves.
They will have, moreover, their denominational privileges, as far
as the public interest allows.

Secondly, since the provinces of Iraq were part of the former
Arab Empire, and indeed were the seat of government in the days
of the Caliph 'Ali ibn Abu-Taleb (God's favour be upon him!) and
of all the caliphs after him; and since it was in those very provinces
(and more particularly in Basra which was the first centre of Arab
culture) that the civilisation of the Arabs and the expansion of
their power flourished – a fact that gives them in the eyes of all
Arabs, both far and near, the precious significance of an unforgettable heritage; for these reasons, we should find it impossible to
persuade or compel the Arab nation to renounce that honourable
association. On the other hand, since the safeguards referred to
in your clause 5 concerning Great Britain's interests are naturally
secured – for the safeguarding of British interests with which are
bound up our own is one of our main concerns – we should be
willing, in our desire to facilitate agreement, to allow those parts

---

[1] The word used by the Sharif is *wilayat*, and he is obviously using it in
the general sense of 'district' since there was no Vilayet of Mersin but a
Vilayet of Adana in which were contained the port and district of Mersin.

which are now occupied by British troops[1] to remain so occupied for a period to be determined by negotiation, without prejudice to the rights of either party or injury to the natural wealth and resources of those parts. It being provided that, during the period of the occupation, the Arab Kingdom shall receive suitable pecuniary assistance towards the burden of expenditure which a nascent kingdom inevitably has to bear; and that the agreements in force with certain Chiefs in those parts will be respected.

Thirdly, your advocacy of speedy action seems to us to entail risks as well as advantages. In the first place, premature action might give rise among those Moslems who do not as yet appreciate the realities of the situation, to the criticism that, by proclaiming a revolt, we are seeking the disruption of Islam. In the second place, we have to consider what our position would be against Turkey who is aided by all the might of Germany, in the event of one of the Entente Powers weakening to the extent of being compelled to make peace with the Central Powers: what attitude would Great Britain and her remaining allies adopt to preclude the possibility of the Arab nation being left alone to face Turkey and her allies? We would have had no anxiety had the conflict lain between us and the Turks alone. These aspects of the question have to be considered, especially as, if we were to enter the War in an informal way, it might be contended by some of the belligerents that they have a right, in concluding the peace, to interfere in our affairs.

Fourthly, the Arabs firmly believe that, after the War, the German-ridden Turks will try to give them constant provocation, in religious as well as temporal matters, and to wreak the utmost vengeance upon them. On their side, the Arabs have resolved and vowed to fight the Turks and continue fighting them until not one of them (save for women and children) remains in any of the Arab countries. Our present deliberation is on account of the considerations stated above.

Fifthly, the moment the Arabs feel confident that, when the time comes for the conclusion of peace in Europe, Great Britain and her allies will not leave them in the lurch face to face with Turkey and Germany, but that they intend to help them and advocate their case effectively in the peace negotiations, from that moment will Arab participation in the War undoubtedly serve the general Arab interest.

Sixthly, our previous communication dated the 29th Shawwal, 1333, makes it superfluous for us to reply to clauses 3 and 4 of your

[1] At that time, British troops were in occupation of the town and province of Basra, and were advancing on Ctesiphon. This was a few weeks before General Townshend's retreat to Kut.

letter, relating to forms of administration, advisers and officials, especially as it is clear from Your Excellency's declarations that there will be no interference in our internal affairs.

Seventhly, we request a clear and final reply, in the shortest possible time, to the questions and problems set forth above, so that the necessary action may be taken with the least possible delay. In our desire to secure agreement which should be satisfactory to both sides, we have gone to the furthest lengths of concession. For we know that the outcome of this war for us can only be either to achieve victory, which will secure to the Arabs a life worthy of their ancient glory, or to find destruction in the attempt. Were it not for the determination shown by the Arabs to realise their aspirations, I would have elected to retire to some mountain-top. But they pressed me to lead the movement to its goal.

Compliments.

No. 6

Sir Henry McMahon's Third Note to the Sharif Husain

Cairo, December 13, 1915.

Complimentary titles.

Your note of the 27th Zul-Hejja, 1333, has reached me, and I was glad to find that you consent to the exclusion of the vilayets[1] of Mersin and Adana from the boundaries of the Arab countries.

I have also received with the utmost pleasure and satisfaction your assurances that the Arabs are resolved on following the precepts of the Caliph 'Umar ibn al-Khattab (the blessing of God be upon him!) and of the other early caliphs, which guarantee equal rights and privileges to all creeds alike.

Your statement that the Arabs are prepared to recognise and respect all our treaties with other Arab Chiefs is of course taken to apply to all territories to be included within the frontiers of the Arab Kingdom, for Great Britain cannot repudiate agreements already concluded between her and those Chiefs.

As for the two vilayets of Aleppo and Bairut, the Government of Great Britain have fully understood your statement in that respect and noted it with the greatest care. But as the interests of their ally France are involved in those two provinces, the question calls for careful consideration. We shall communicate again with you on this subject, at the appropriate time.

---

[1] The word used in the Arabic text is *wilayat*, which shows that Sir Henry McMahon, like the Sharif, was using it in its general connotation of 'district'. See footnote p. 421.

The Government of Great Britain, as I have previously informed you, are prepared to give all the guarantees and assistance in their power to the Arab Kingdom. But their interests in the Vilayet of Baghdad necessitate a friendly and stable administration, such as you have outlined. The proper safeguarding of those interests calls for fuller and more detailed consideration than the present situation and the speed with which these negotiations are being conducted permit.

We fully approve your desire to proceed warily, and do not wish to impel you to hasty action which might obstruct the success of your objectives. But, at the same time, we deem it imperative that you should turn your endeavours to uniting the Arab peoples to our joint cause and to urging them to abstain from aiding our enemies in any manner whatsoever. On the success of your endeavours, and on the efficacy of the measures which, when the time comes, the Arabs will find it possible to take in aid of our cause, will the strength and permanence of our agreement depend.

In these circumstances, the Government of Great Britain have authorised me to declare to your Lordship that you may rest confident that Great Britain does not intend to conclude any peace whatsoever, of which the freedom of the Arab peoples and their liberation from German and Turkish domination do not form an essential condition.

In token of our good faith, and as a contribution to your endeavours in our joint cause, I am sending the sum of £20,000 with your trusted messenger.

Compliments.

No. 7

The Sharif Husain's Fourth Note to Sir Henry McMahon

Mecca, Safar 25, 1334.
[January 1, 1916.]

Complimentary titles.

I have received your note of the 9th Safar, 1334 [December 13, 1915], with the bearer of this, and noted its contents which have filled me with the utmost satisfaction and gratification, inasmuch as they set my mind at rest over one point, namely the arrival of Muhammad Sharif al-Faruqi and his interview with you.[1] You

---

[1] Sir Henry McMahon's note made no mention of Faruqi. But the Sharif had heard from him direct, and had also had an oral message from McMahon concerning him, with the emissary who carried the notes between Mecca and Cairo.

will now have satisfied yourself that our attitude was not prompted by personal desires, which would have been foolish, but was the result of the decisions taken and the desires expressed by our people; and that our role in the matter was confined to conveying and putting into effect those desires and decisions, thus merely discharging a duty with which our people had invested us. It is, in my view, most important that Your Excellency should realise that.

As for your statements concerning Iraq and the compensation to be paid during the period of occupation, I would illustrate the friendly sentiments animating us towards Great Britain and the confidence we repose in her, both in word and in deed, in the spirit as well as the letter, by leaving the assessment of the compensation to her wisdom and sense of fair play.

With regard to the northern parts and their coastal regions, we have already stated, in our previous note, the utmost that it was possible for us to modify. We made those modifications solely in order to achieve the ends which, Almighty God willing, we desire to attain. In that same spirit, we have felt bound to steer clear of that which might have impaired the alliance between Great Britain and France and their concord during the calamities of the present war. On the other hand – and this Your Excellency must clearly understand – we shall deem it our duty, at the earliest opportunity after the conclusion of the War, to claim from you Bairut and its coastal regions which we will overlook for the moment on account of France.

I find it superfluous to point out that this arrangement also serves Great Britain's interests best; that it safeguards them as fully – if not more – as it secures our rights; and that no other arrangement is possible by which it could fall to Great Britain to achieve the aim, which she has at heart, of seeing her friends in contentment and happiness. All the more so as the proximity of the French to us would be a source of difficulties and disputes such as would render the establishment of peaceful conditions impossible. To say nothing of the fact that the people of Bairut are resolutely opposed to such a dismemberment, and would drive us to take a stand which might cause concern and trouble to Great Britain on a scale not far short of her present preoccupations, owing to what we firmly believe to be the community, and indeed the identity, of your interests and our own, and to be the only explanation of our unwillingness to deal with anyone else but Great Britain in these negotiations.

Thus any concession designed to give France or any other Power possession of a single square foot of territory in those parts is quite out of the question. In proclaiming this, I place all my reliance on the declarations which concluded your note, and this reliance is such that, at our death, it shall be inherited by those who live after us.

Your Excellency may rest assured, and Great Britain may rest assured, that we shall adhere to our resolve to which reference has already been made, and which was made known to Storrs – that able and accomplished man – two years ago. We are only waiting for an opportunity in consonance with our situation. It appears to be drawing nearer, and the hand of destiny seems to be driving it towards us in timely and unmistakable fashion, as though to provide us and those who think like us with weapons for meeting the criticism and facing the responsibilities in store.

Your statement that you do not wish to impel us to hasty action which might obstruct the success of your objectives renders further explanation superfluous, except that we shall have to let you know in due course our requirements in the way of arms, ammunition and so forth.

Compliments.

No. 8

Sir Henry McMahon's Fourth Note to the Sharif Husain

Cairo, January 30, 1916.

Complimentary titles.

With great pleasure and satisfaction have we received your note of the 25th Safar, 1334, from the hand of your faithful messenger who never fails to give us your oral messages as well. We fully realise and appreciate the motives which animate you in the momentous issue with which we are concerned, and we do not question the fact that you are working for the good of the Arab nation without any ulterior motive whatsoever.

We have noted what you say with regard to the Vilayet of Baghdad, and we shall examine the matter with the utmost care after the defeat of the enemy, when the time comes for the conclusion of peace.

As for the northern regions, we note with great satisfaction your desire to avoid anything that might impair the alliance between Great Britain and France. It has not escaped you that it is our firm determination not to allow anything, however small, to stand in the way of our ending this war in complete victory. Moreover, when victory is attained, the friendship between Great Britain and France will be stronger and closer than ever, cemented as it will have been by the shedding of British and French blood – the blood of those who have fallen fighting side by side in the cause of right and freedom.

The Arab countries are now associated in that noble aim which can be attained by uniting our forces and acting in unison. We pray God that success may bind us to each other in a lasting friendship which shall bring profit and contentment to us all.

We are very glad to hear that you are endeavouring to gain all the Arab tribes over to our joint cause, and to prevent them from giving any assistance to our enemies. We leave it to your discretion to choose the most suitable opportunity for the initiation of more decisive measures.

You will doubtless inform us, through the bearer of this note, of the ways in which we can help you. You may rest assured that all your requests will always be carefully considered and most expeditiously dealt with.

You will surely have heard that Sayyed Ahmad al-Sharif, the Sanusi, has lent an ear to the intrigues of our enemies and started hostilities against us, and you will doubtless be sorry to hear that he has so far lost sight of Arab interests that he has thrown in his lot with our enemies.[1] He has now fallen a victim to his own misguided ways, and met with adversity at every turn. This may yet convince him of his error and lead him back into the path of reason and of peace, out of pity for his poor followers whom he is guiding to destruction.

Your faithful messenger who carries this note to you will give you all our news.

Compliments.

---

[1] In November 1915, as a result of Turkish incitement and active help, the Sanusi Chief invaded Egypt and began hostilities which lasted until the following March when he was finally driven out of Egyptian territory. For a brief summary of the Sanusi campaign see Chapter XI, Section 2.

APPENDIX B

THE ANGLO-FRANCO-RUSSIAN AGREEMENT
(April–May 1916)

GENERALLY KNOWN AS

THE SYKES-PICOT AGREEMENT

[The Sykes-Picot Agreement was concluded in the form of diplomatic notes exchanged between the Governments of the three Powers, in which the claims of each Power to portions of the Ottoman Empire after its dismemberment were recognised by the other two. Notes defining the Russian share were exchanged in Petrograd on April 26, 1916, between the Minister of Foreign Affairs (M. Sazonoff) and the French Ambassador (M. Paléologue), and in London a few weeks later between the Secretary of State for Foreign Affairs (Sir Edward Grey) and the Russian Ambassador (Count Benckendorff). Notes defining the British and French shares were exchanged in London on May 9 and May 16, between Sir Edward Grey and the French Ambassador (M. Paul Cambon).

The text reproduced below is only that of the Anglo-French section of the Agreement, since that section alone dealt with the future of Arab territories. It is my own translation of the French version published in A. Giannini, *Documenti per la Storia della Pace orientale*, Rome, 1933.]

TEXT OF THE AGREEMENT

CONCLUDED IN LONDON ON MAY 16, 1916

1. France and Great Britain are prepared to recognise and uphold an independent Arab State or a Confederation of Arab States in the areas shown as (A) and (B) on the annexed map,

under the suzerainty of an Arab Chief. France in area (A) and Great Britain in area (B) shall have a right of priority in enterprises and local loans. France in area (A) and Great Britain in area (B) shall alone supply foreign advisers or officials on the request of the Arab State or the Confederation of Arab States.

2. France in the Blue area and Great Britain in the Red area shall be at liberty to establish such direct or indirect administration or control as they may desire or as they may deem fit to establish after agreement with the Arab State or Confederation of Arab States.

3. In the Brown area there shall be established an international administration of which the form will be decided upon after consultation with Russia, and after subsequent agreement with the other Allies and the representatives of the Sharif of Mecca.

4. There shall be accorded to Great Britain

(a) The ports of Haifa and Acre;
(b) Guarantee of a specific supply of water from the Tigris and the Euphrates in area (A) for area (B).

His Majesty's Government, on their part, undertake that they will at no time initiate negotiations for the concession of Cyprus to any third Power without the previous consent of the French Government.

5. Alexandretta shall be a free port as regards the trade of the British Empire and there shall be no differentiation in treatment with regard to port dues or the extension of special privileges affecting British shipping and commerce; there shall be freedom of transit for British goods through Alexandretta and over railways through the Blue area, whether such goods are going to or coming from the Red area, area (A) or area (B); and there shall be no differentiation in treatment, direct or indirect, at the expense of British goods on any railway or of British goods and shipping in any port serving the areas in question.

Haifa shall be a free port as regards the trade of France, her colonies and protectorates, and there shall be no differentiation in treatment or privilege with regard to port dues against French shipping and commerce. There shall be freedom of transit through Haifa and over British railways through the Brown area, whether such goods are coming from or going to the Blue area, area (A) or area (B), and there shall be no differentiation in treatment, direct or indirect, at the expense of French goods on any railway or of French goods and shipping in any port serving the areas in question.

6. In area (A), the Baghdad Railway shall not be extended southwards beyond Mosul, and in area (B), it shall not be extended northwards beyond Samarra, until a railway connecting

429

Baghdad with Aleppo along the basin of the Euphrates will have been completed, and then only with the concurrence of the two Governments.

7. Great Britain shall have the right to build, administer and be the sole owner of the railway connecting Haifa with area (B). She shall have, in addition, the right in perpetuity and at all times of carrying troops on that line. It is understood by both Governments that this railway is intended to facilitate communication between Baghdad and Haifa, and it is further understood that, in the event of technical difficulties and expenditure incurred in the maintenance of this line in the Brown area rendering the execution of the project impracticable, the French Government will be prepared to consider plans for enabling the line in question to traverse the polygon formed by Banias-Umm Qais-Salkhad-Tall 'Osda-Mismieh before reaching area (B).

8. For a period of twenty years, the Turkish customs tariff shall remain in force throughout the Blue and Red areas as well as in areas (A) and (B), and no increase in the rates of duties and no alteration of *ad valorem* duties into specific duties shall be made without the consent of the two Powers.

There shall be no internal customs barriers between any of the areas mentioned above. The customs duties to be levied on goods destined for the interior shall be collected at the ports of entry and remitted to the Administration of the area of destination.

9. It is understood that the French Government will at no time initiate any negotiations for the cession of their rights and will not cede their prospective rights in the Blue area to any third Power other than the Arab State or Confederation of Arab States, without the previous consent of His Majesty's Government who, on their part, give the French Government a similar undertaking in respect of the Red area.

10. The British and French Governments shall agree to abstain from acquiring and to withhold their consent to a third Power acquiring territorial possessions in the Arabian Peninsula; nor shall they consent to the construction by a third Power of a naval base in the islands on the eastern seaboard of the Red Sea. This, however, will not prevent such rectification of the Aden boundary as might be found necessary in view of the recent Turkish attack.

11. The negotiations with the Arabs concerning the frontiers of the Arab State or Confederation of Arab States shall be pursued through the same channel as heretofore in the name of the two Powers.

12. It is understood, moreover, that measures for controlling the importation of arms into the Arab territory will be considered by the two Governments.

APPENDIX C

(February 8, 1918)

[The text of the original communication has often appeared in the Arabic Press in facsimile reproduction from a photostat copy supplied by the late King Husain.

The original communication was in Arabic. The version given here is my own rendering from the Arabic text.]

[*Translation*]

The Acting British Agent, Jedda to King Husain

Jedda, February 8, 1918.

Complimentary titles.

I am directed by His Britannic Majesty's High Commissioner[1] to forward to Your Majesty the text of a telegraphic message which His Excellency has had from the Foreign Office in London for transmission as a communication from His Britannic Majesty's Government to Your Majesty. The text is *verbatim* as follows:

Begins. The loyal motives which have prompted Your Majesty to forward to the High Commissioner the letters addressed by the Turkish commander-in-chief in Syria to His Highness the Amir Faisal and to Ja'far Pasha have caused His Majesty's Government the liveliest satisfaction. The steps taken by Your Majesty in this connexion are only a token of the friendship and mutual sincerity which have always inspired the relations between the Government of the Hejaz and His Majesty's Government. It would be superfluous to point out that the object aimed at by Turkey is to sow doubt and suspicion between the Allied Powers and those Arabs who, under Your Majesty's leadership and guidance, are striving

---

[1] i.e., Sir Reginald Wingate, High Commissioner for Egypt.

431

nobly to recover their ancient freedom. The Turkish policy is to create dissension by luring the Arabs into believing that the Allied Powers have designs on the Arab countries, and by representing to the Allies that the Arabs might be made to renounce their aspirations. But such intrigues cannot succeed in sowing dissension among those whose minds are directed by a common purpose to a common end.

His Majesty's Government and their allies stand steadfastly by every cause aiming at the liberation of the oppressed nations, and they are determined to stand by the Arab peoples in their struggle for the establishment of an Arab world in which law shall replace Ottoman injustice, and in which unity shall prevail over the rivalries artificially provoked by the policy of Turkish officials. His Majesty's Government re-affirm their former pledge in regard to the liberation of the Arab peoples. His Majesty's Government have hitherto made it their policy to ensure that liberation, and it remains the policy they are determined unflinchingly to pursue by protecting such Arabs as are already liberated from all dangers and perils, and by assisting those who are still under the yoke of the tyrants to obtain their freedom. Ends.

Compliments.

J. R. BASSETT,
Lt.-Col.
Acting British Agent,
Jedda.

APPENDIX D

(June 16, 1918)

[This Declaration was made in reply to a memorial submitted to the Foreign Office, through the Arab Bureau in Cairo, by seven Arab leaders domiciled in Egypt.

The Declaration was read out by an officer of the Arab Bureau at a meeting of the seven Arab leaders, which had been specially convened for the purpose on June 16, 1918, in Cairo.

The text reproduced here is my own rendering of the Arabic text which is in the possession of one of the seven memorialists.

In Arab circles this Declaration is usually known as the Declaration to the Seven.]

[*Translation*]

DECLARATION TO THE SEVEN

His Majesty's Government have considered the memorial of the Seven with great care.   They fully appreciate the reasons for the desire of its authors to retain their anonymity,[1] but the fact that the memorial is anonymous has in no way detracted from the value which His Majesty's Government assign to that document.

The territories mentioned in the memorial fall into four categories:—

    (i) Territories which were free and independent before the outbreak of the War;

    (ii) Territories liberated from Turkish rule by the action of the Arabs themselves;

---

[1] The memorialists were Rafiq al-'Azm; Shaikh Kamel al-Qassab; Mukhtar al-Sulh; 'Abdul-Rahman Shahbandar; Khaled al-Hakim; Fauzi al-Bakri; Hasan Himadeh.

    (iii) Territories liberated from Turkish rule by the action of
          the Allied armies;

    (iv) Territories still under Turkish rule.

With regard to the first two categories,[1] His Majesty's Government recognise the complete and sovereign independence of the Arabs inhabiting those territories, and support them in their struggle for freedom.

With regard to the territories occupied by the Allied armies,[2] His Majesty's Government invite the attention of the memorialists to the proclamations issued by the commander-in-chief on the occasions of the capture of Baghdad (March 19, 1917) and of the capture of Jerusalem (December 9, 1917). These proclamations define the policy of His Majesty's Government towards the inhabitants of those regions, which is that the future government of those territories should be based upon the principle of the consent of the governed. This policy will always be that of His Majesty's Government.

With regard to the territories in the fourth category,[3] it is the desire of His Majesty's Government that the oppressed peoples in those territories should obtain their freedom and independence. His Majesty's Government will continue to work for the achievement of that object. They are fully aware of the difficulties and perils which threaten those who are striving for the [liberation?][4] of the inhabitants of those territories.

In spite of those obstacles, however, His Majesty's Government believe that the difficulties can be overcome, and they are prepared to give every support to those who are striving to overcome them. They are ready to consider any scheme of co-operation which does not conflict with the military operations in hand or with the political principles proclaimed by His Majesty's Government and their allies.

[1] i.e., the independent states of the Arabian Peninsula, and the Hejaz as far north as 'Aqaba.
[2] In June 1918, when this statement was issued, those territories comprised the greater part of Iraq (inclusive of Basra and Baghdad) and the southern half of Palestine (inclusive of Jerusalem and Jaffa).
[3] i.e., the hitherto unliberated portions of Iraq and Syria.
[4] This word is obscure in the Arabic source.

APPENDIX E

ANGLO-FRENCH DECLARATION

(November 7, 1918)

[This Declaration was issued in Palestine, Syria and Iraq, in the form of an official *communiqué* emanating from General Headquarters, Egyptian Expeditionary Force, dated November 7, 1918.

The text was given out to the Press, on the authority of the military censorship department, with instructions that it be given special prominence. Copies of it were posted on the public notice-boards in all towns and a great many villages in the Arab territories then occupied by the Allied forces, that is to say throughout the length and breadth of Palestine, Syria and Iraq.

The Declaration appears to have been originally drawn up in French. Official versions that have appeared in English are obvious translations, not excluding that which was circulated in answer to a question in the House of Commons on the 25th July 1921.

The version here given is my own rendering of the authoritative French text as printed in one of the leaflets officially distributed at the time.]

[Translation]

ANGLO-FRENCH DECLARATION

November 7, 1918.

The goal envisaged by France and Great Britain in prosecuting in the East the War set in train by German ambition is the complete and final liberation of the peoples who have for so long been oppressed by the Turks, and the setting up of national governments and administrations that shall derive their authority from the free exercise of the initiative and choice of the indigenous populations.

In pursuit of those intentions, France and Great Britain agree to further and assist in the setting up of indigenous governments and administrations in Syria[1] and Mesopotamia[2] which have already been liberated by the Allies, as well as in those territories which they are endeavouring to liberate, and to recognise them as soon as they are actually set up.

Far from wishing to impose this or that system upon the populations of those regions, their [i.e., France's and Great Britain's] only concern is to offer such support and efficacious help as will ensure the smooth working of the governments and administrations which those populations will have elected of their own free will to have; to secure impartial and equal justice for all; to facilitate the economic development of the country by promoting and encouraging local initiative; to foster the spread of education; and to put an end to the dissensions which Turkish policy has for so long exploited. Such is the task which the two Allied Powers wish to undertake in the liberated territories.

---

[1] In official parlance, this name was still used to denote the whole of geographical Syria, from the Taurus range to the Egyptian frontier.

[2] The term is used here to denote the region made up of the former Ottoman Vilayets of Basra, Baghdad and Mosul, which has throughout this book been referred to (and is now universally known) as Iraq.

APPENDIX F

THE FAISAL-WEIZMANN AGREEMENT

(dated January 3 (?), 1919)

[The source I have used is a photostat reproduction of the original document.

Versions of the Agreement have appeared in the Press, but none that I have seen may be described as being both exact and complete. The version given in D. H. Miller's collection of texts[1] is in every respect identical with the original except that it omits the stipulation inscribed by Faisal on the Agreement itself.

The Agreement was in English; Faisal's stipulation was in Arabic, and was inscribed in the space immediately following the last Article. A rough summary in English of Faisal's stipulation, made by T. E. Lawrence at the time, has gained currency – notably in *The Times* of June 10, 1936, and in the Report of the Palestine Royal Commission – as being a reliable rendering of the original. In actual fact, Lawrence's 'translation' is a loose and somewhat misleading paraphrase.

The Agreement is dated January 3, 1919, but I have queried the date. From the internal evidence in the text of Faisal's stipulation, it seems probable that it was signed at a later date, and in any case not earlier than January 4.]

TEXT OF THE
FAISAL-WEIZMANN AGREEMENT

His Royal Highness the Amir FAISAL, representing and acting on behalf of the Arab Kingdom of HEJAZ, and Dr. CHAIM WEIZMANN, representing and acting on behalf of the Zionist Organisation, mindful of the racial kinship and ancient bonds existing between the Arabs and the Jewish people, and realising

[1] David Hunter Miller, *My Diary at the Conference of Paris*, Vol. III.

that the surest means of working out the consummation of their national aspirations, is through the closest possible collaboration in the development of the Arab State and Palestine, and being desirous further of confirming the good understanding which exists between them, have agreed upon the following Articles:

ARTICLE I

The Arab State and Palestine in all their relations and undertakings shall be controlled by the most cordial goodwill and understanding and to this end Arab and Jewish duly accredited agents shall be established and maintained in their respective territories.

ARTICLE II

Immediately following the completion of the deliberations of the Peace Conference, the definite boundaries between the Arab State and Palestine shall be determined by a Commission to be agreed upon by the parties hereto.

ARTICLE III

In the establishment of the Constitution and Administration of Palestine all such measures shall be adopted as will afford the fullest guarantees for carrying into effect the British Government's Declaration of the 2nd of November, 1917.

ARTICLE IV

All necessary measures shall be taken to encourage and stimulate immigration of Jews into Palestine on a large scale, and as quickly as possible to settle Jewish immigrants upon the land through closer settlement and intensive cultivation of the soil. In taking such measures the Arab peasant and tenant farmers shall be protected in their rights, and shall be assisted in forwarding their economic development.

ARTICLE V

No regulation nor law shall be made prohibiting or interfering in any way with the free exercise of religion; and further the free exercise and enjoyment of religious profession and worship without discrimination or preference shall for ever be allowed. No religious test shall ever be required for the exercise of civil or political rights.

Article VI

The Mohammedan Holy Places shall be under Mohammedan control.

Article VII

The Zionist Organisation proposes to send to Palestine a Commission of experts to make a survey of the economic possibilities of the country, and to report upon the best means for its development. The Zionist Organisation will place the aforementioned Commission at the disposal of the Arab State for the purpose of a survey of the economic possibilities of the Arab State and to report upon the best means for its development. The Zionist Organisation will use its best efforts to assist the Arab State in providing the means for developing the natural resources and economic possibilities thereof.

Article VIII

The parties hereto agree to act in complete accord and harmony in all matters embraced herein before the Peace Congress.

Article IX

Any matters of dispute which may arise between the contracting parties shall be referred to the British Government for arbitration.

Given under our hand at LONDON, ENGLAND, the THIRD day of JANUARY, ONE THOUSAND NINE HUNDRED AND NINETEEN.

[*Translation*]

Provided the Arabs obtain their independence as demanded in my Memorandum dated the 4th of January, 1919, to the Foreign Office of the Government of Great Britain, I shall concur in the above articles. But if the slightest modification or departure were to be made [*sc.* in relation to the demands in the Memorandum] I shall not then be bound by a single word of the present Agreement which shall be deemed void and of no account or validity, and I shall not be answerable in any way whatsoever.

FAISAL IBN HUSAIN (*in Arabic*)
CHAIM WEIZMANN

APPENDIX G

RESOLUTIONS OF THE
GENERAL SYRIAN CONGRESS[1]

(Damascus, July 2, 1919)

We, the undersigned, members of the General Syrian Congress assembled in Damascus on the 2nd of July 1919 and composed of delegates from the three zones, namely the southern, eastern and western,[2] and furnished with credentials duly authorising us to represent the Moslem, Christian and Jewish inhabitants of our respective districts, have resolved to submit the following as defining the aspirations of the people who have chosen us to place them before the American Section of the Inter-Allied Commission. With the exception of the fifth clause, which was passed by a large majority, the Resolutions which follow were all adopted unanimously:—

1. We desire full and absolute political independence for Syria within the following boundaries: on the north, the Taurus Range; on the south, a line running from Rafah to al-Jauf and following the Syria-Hejaz border below 'Aqaba; on the east, the boundary formed by the Euphrates and Khabur rivers and a line stretching from some distance east of Abu-Kamal to some distance east of al-Jauf; on the west, the Mediterranean Sea.

2. We desire the Government of Syria to be a constitutional monarchy based on principles of democratic and broadly decentralised rule which shall safeguard the rights of minorities, and we wish that the Amir Faisal who has striven so nobly for our liberation and enjoys our full confidence and trust be our King.

3. In view of the fact that the Arab inhabitants of Syria are not less fitted or gifted than were certain other nations (such as the Bulgarians, Serbs, Greeks and Rumanians) when granted inde-

---

[1] The text given here is my own rendering of the text published at the time in the Arabic Press.

[2] i.e., the three O.E.T.A.s.

pendence, we protest against Article XXII of the Covenant of the League of Nations which relegates us to the standing of insufficiently developed races requiring the tutelage of a mandatory power.

4. If, for whatever reason that might remain undisclosed to us, the Peace Conference were to ignore this legitimate protest, we shall regard the mandate mentioned in the Covenant of the League of Nations as implying no more than the rendering of assistance in the technical and economic fields without impairment of our absolute independence. We rely on President Wilson's declarations that his object in entering the War was to put an end to acquisitive designs for imperialistic purposes. In our desire that our country should not be made a field for colonisation, and in the belief that the American nation is devoid of colonial ambitions and has no political designs on our country, we resolve to seek assistance in the technical and economic fields from the United States of America on the understanding that the duration of such assistance shall not exceed twenty years.

5. In the event of the United States finding herself unable to accede to our request for assistance, we would seek it from Great Britain, provided always that it will not be allowed to impair the unity and absolute independence of our country and that its duration shall not exceed the period mentioned in the preceding clause.

6. We do not recognise to the French Government any right to any part of Syria, and we reject all proposals that France should give us assistance or exercise authority in any portion of the country.

7. We reject the claims of the Zionists for the establishment of a Jewish commonwealth in that part of southern Syria which is known as Palestine, and we are opposed to Jewish immigration into any part of the country. We do not acknowledge that they have a title, and we regard their claims as a grave menace to our national, political and economic life. Our Jewish fellow-citizens shall continue to enjoy the rights and to bear the responsibilities which are ours in common.

8. We desire that there should be no dismemberment of Syria, and no separation of Palestine or the coastal regions in the west or the Lebanon from the mother country; and we ask that the unity of the country be maintained under any circumstances.

9. We desire that Iraq should enjoy complete independence, and that no economic barriers be placed between the two countries.

10. The basic principles proclaimed by President Wilson in condemnation of secret treaties cause us to enter an emphatic protest against any agreement providing for the dismemberment

of Syria[1] and against any undertaking envisaging the recognition of Zionism[2] in southern Syria; and we ask for the explicit annulment of all such agreements and undertakings.

The lofty principles proclaimed by President Wilson encourage us to believe that the determining consideration in the settlement of our own future will be the real desires of our people; and that we may look to President Wilson and the liberal American nation, who are known for their sincere and generous sympathy with the aspirations of weak nations, for help in the fulfilment of our hopes.

We also fully believe that the Peace Conference will recognise that we would not have risen against Turkish rule under which we enjoyed civic and political privileges, as well as rights of representation, had it not been that the Turks denied us our right to a national existence. We believe that the Peace Conference will meet our desires in full, if only to ensure that our political privileges may not be less, after the sacrifices of life which we have made in the cause of our freedom, than they were before the War.

We desire to be allowed to send a delegation to represent us at the Peace Conference, advocate our claims and secure the fulfilment of our aspirations.

[1] *sc.* the Sykes-Picot Agreement.
[2] *sc.* the Balfour Declaration.

APPENDIX H

RECOMMENDATIONS OF THE KING-CRANE COMMISSION WITH REGARD TO SYRIA-PALESTINE AND IRAQ[1]

(August 28, 1919)

---

1. *Syria-Palestine*

A. We recommend, as most important of all, and in strict harmony with our Instructions, that whatever foreign administration (whether of one or more Powers) is brought into Syria, should come in, not at all as a colonising Power in the old sense of that term, but as a Mandatory under the League of Nations with the clear consciousness that 'the well-being and development', of the Syrian people form for it a 'sacred trust'.

(1) To this end the Mandate should have a limited term, the time of expiration to be determined by the League of Nations, in the light of all the facts as brought out from year to year, in the annual reports of the Mandatory to the League or in other ways.

(2) The mandatory Administration should have, however, a period and power sufficient to ensure the success of the new state; and especially to make possible carrying through important educational and economic undertakings, essential to secure founding of the State.

(3) The mandatory Administration should be characterised from the beginning by a strong and vital educational emphasis in clear recognition of the imperative necessity of education for the citizens of a democratic state, and for the development of a sound national spirit. This systematic cultivation of national

---

[1] Text copied from *Editor and Publisher* (New York), issue dated December 2, 1922.

spirit is particularly required in a country like Syria, which has only recently come to self-consciousness.

(4) The Mandatory should definitely seek, from the beginning of its trusteeship, to train the Syrian people to independent self-government as rapidly as conditions allow, by setting up all the institutions of a democratic state, and by sharing with them increasingly the work of administration, and so forming gradually an intelligent citizenship, interested unselfishly in the progress of the country, and forming at the same time a large group of disciplined civil servants.

(5) The period of 'tutelage' should not be unduly prolonged, but independent self-government should be granted as soon as it can safely be done; remembering that the primary business of governments is not the accomplishment of certain things, but the development of citizens.

(6) It is peculiarly the duty of the Mandatory in a country like Syria, and in this modern age, to see that complete religious liberty is ensured, both in the constitution and in the practice of the state, and that a jealous care is exercised for the rights of all minorities. Nothing is more vital than this for the enduring success of the new Arab State.

(7) In the economic development of Syria, a dangerous amount of indebtedness on the part of the new state should be avoided, as well as any entanglements financially with the affairs of the mandatory Power. On the other hand, the legitimate established privileges of foreigners, such as rights to maintain schools, commercial concessions, etc., should be preserved, but subject to review and modification under the authority of the League of Nations in the interest of Syria. The mandatory Power should not take advantage of its position to force a monopolistic control at any point to the detriment either of Syria or of other nations; but it should seek to bring the new State as rapidly as possible to economic independence as well as to political independence.

Whatever is done concerning the further recommendations of the Commission, the fulfilment of at least the conditions now named should be assured, if the Peace Conference and the League of Nations are true to the policy of mandatories already embodied in the Covenant of the League of Nations. This should effectively guard the most essential interests of Syria, however the machinery of administration is finally organised. The Damascus Congress betrayed in many ways their intense fear that their country would become, though under some other name, simply a colonial possession of some other Power. That fear must be completely allayed.

B. We recommend, in the second place, that the unity of Syria be preserved, in accordance with the earnest petition of the great majority of the people of Syria.

(1) The territory concerned is too limited, the population too small, and the economic, geographic, racial and language unity too manifest, to make the setting up of independent States within its boundaries desirable, if such division can possibly be avoided. The country is very largely Arab in language, culture, traditions, and customs.

(2) This recommendation is in line with important 'general considerations' already urged, and with the principles of the League of Nations, as well as in answer to the desires of the majority of the population concerned.

(3) The precise boundaries of Syria should be determined by a special commission on boundaries, after the Syrian territory has been in general allotted. The Commissioners believe, however, that the claim of the Damascus Conference to include Cilicia in Syria is not justified, either historically or by commercial or language relations. The line between the Arabic-speaking and the Turkish-speaking populations would quite certainly class Cilicia with Asia Minor, rather than with Syria. Syria, too, has no such need of further seacoast as the large interior sections of Asia Minor.

(4) In standing thus for the recognition of the unity of Syria, the natural desires of regions like the Lebanon, which have already had a measure of independence, should not be forgotten. It will make for real unity, undoubtedly, to give a large measure of local autonomy, and especially in the case of strongly unified groups. Even the 'Damascus Programme' which presses so earnestly the unity of Syria, itself urges a government 'on broad decentralisation principles'.

Lebanon has achieved a considerable degree of prosperity and autonomy within the Turkish Empire. She certainly should not find her legitimate aspirations less possible within a Syrian national State. On the contrary, it may be confidently expected that both her economic and political relations with the rest of Syria would be better if she were a constituent member of the State rather than entirely independent of it.

As a predominantly Christian country, too, Lebanon naturally fears Moslem domination in a unified Syria. But against such domination she would have a four-fold safeguard: her own large autonomy; the presence of a strong mandatory for the considerable period in which the constitution and practice of the new State would be forming; the oversight of the League of Nations, with its insistence upon religious liberty and the rights of minorities; and the certainty that the Arab Government would feel the necessity of such a State, if it were to commend itself to the League of Nations. Moreover, there would be less danger of a reactionary Moslem attitude, if Christians were present in the State in considerable numbers, rather than largely segregated outside the State, as experience of the relations of different religious faiths in India suggests.

As a predominantly Christian country, it is also to be noted that Lebanon would be in a position to exert a stronger and more helpful influence if she were within the Syrian State, feeling its problems and needs, and sharing all its life, instead of outside it, absorbed simply in her own narrow concerns. For the sake of the larger interests, both of Lebanon and of Syria, then, the unity of Syria is to be urged. It is certain that many of the more thoughtful Lebanese themselves hold this view. A similar statement might be made for Palestine; though, as the Holy Land for Jews and Christians and Moslems alike, its situation is unique, and might more readily justify unique treatment, if such treatment were justified anywhere. This will be discussed more particularly in connexion with the recommendation concerning Zionism.

C. We recommend, in the third place, that Syria be placed under one mandatory Power, as the natural way to secure real and efficient unity.

(1) To divide the administration of the provinces of Syria among several mandatories, even if existing national unity were recognised; or to attempt a joint mandatory of the whole on the commission plan: – neither of these courses would be naturally suggested as the best way to secure and promote the unity of the new State, or even the general unity of the whole people. It is conceivable that circumstances might drive the Peace Conference to some such form of divided Mandate; but it is not a solution to be voluntarily chosen, from the point of view of the larger interests of the people, as considerations already urged indicate.

(2) It is not to be forgotten, either, that, however they are handled politically, the people of Syria are there, forced to get on together in some fashion. They are obliged to live with one another – the Arabs of the East and the people of the coast, the Moslems and the Christians. Will they be helped or hindered, in establishing tolerable and finally cordial relations, by a single mandatory? No doubt the quick mechanical solution of the problem of difficult relations is to split the people up into little independent fragments. And sometimes, undoubtedly, as in the case of the Turks and Armenians, the relations are so intolerable as to make some division imperative and inevitable. But in general, to attempt complete separation only accentuates the differences and increases the antagonism. The whole lesson of the modern social consciousness points to the necessity of under-

standing 'the other half', as it can be understood only by close and living relations. Granting reasonable local autonomy to reduce friction among groups, a single mandatory ought to form a constant and increasingly effective help to unity of feeling throughout the State, and ought to steadily improve group relations.

The people of Syria, in our hearings, have themselves often insisted that, so far as unpleasant relations have hitherto prevailed among various groups, it has been very largely due to the direct instigation of the Turkish Government. When justice is done impartially to all; when it becomes plain that the aim of the common government is the service of all classes alike, not their exploitation, then can decent human relations be secured – a foundation which could not be obtained by dividing men off from one another in antagonistic groups.

The Commissioners urge, therefore, for the largest future good of all groups and regions alike, the placing of the whole of Syria under a single Mandate.

D. We recommend, in the fourth place, that Amir Faisal be made head of the new united Syrian State.

(1) This is expressly and unanimously asked for by the representative Damascus Congress in the name of the Syrian people, and there seems to be no reason to doubt that the great majority of the population of Syria sincerely desire to have Amir Faisal as ruler.

(2) A constitutional monarchy along democratic lines, seems naturally adapted to the Arabs, with their long training under tribal conditions, and with their traditional respect for their Chiefs. They seem to need, more than most people, a king as the personal symbol of the power of the State.

(3) Amir Faisal has come, too, naturally into his present place of power, and there is no one else who could well replace him. He has the great advantage of being the son of the Sharif of Mecca, and as such honoured throughout the Moslem world. He was one of the prominent Arab leaders who assumed responsibility for the Arab uprising against the Turks, and so shared in the complete deliverance of the Arabic-speaking portions of the Turkish Empire. He was consequently hailed by the Damascus Congress as having merited their full confidence and entire reliance. He was taken up and supported by the British as the most promising candidate for the headship of the new Arab State – an Arab of the Arabs, but with a position of wide appeal through his Sharifian connection, and through his broad sympathies with the best in the Occident. His relations with the Arabs to the east of Syria are friendly, and his kingdom would not be threatened from that side. He undoubtedly does not make so strong an appeal to the

447

Christians of the West Coast, as to the Arabs of the East; but no man can be named who would have a stronger general appeal. He is tolerant and wise, skilful in dealing with men, winning in manner, a man of sincerity, insight and power. Whether he has the full strength needed for his difficult task it is too early to say; but certainly no other Arab leader combines so many elements of power as he, and he will have invaluable help throughout the mandatory period.

The Peace Conference may take genuine satisfaction in the fact that an Arab of such qualities is available for the headship of this new state in the Near East.

E. We recommend, in the fifth place, serious modification of the extreme Zionist programme for Palestine of unlimited immigration of Jews, looking finally to making Palestine distinctly a Jewish State.

(1) The Commissioners began their study of Zionism with minds predisposed in its favour, but the actual facts in Palestine, coupled with the force of the general principles proclaimed by the Allies and accepted by the Syrians have driven them to the recommendation here made.

(2) The Commission was abundantly supplied with literature on the Zionist programme by the Zionist Commission to Palestine; heard in conferences much concerning the Zionist colonies and their claims; and personally saw something of what had been accomplished. They found much to approve in the aspirations and plans of the Zionists, and had warm appreciation for the devotion of many of the colonists, and for their success, by modern methods, in overcoming great natural obstacles.

(3) The Commission recognised also that definite encouragement had been given to the Zionists by the Allies in Mr. Balfour's often-quoted statement, in its approval by other representatives of the Allies. If, however, the strict terms of the Balfour Statement are adhered to – favouring 'the establishment in Palestine of a national home for the Jewish people', 'it being clearly understood that nothing shall be done which may prejudice the civil and religious rights of existing non-Jewish communities in Palestine' – it can hardly be doubted that the extreme Zionist programme must be greatly modified.

For a national home for the Jewish people is not equivalent to making Palestine into a Jewish State; nor can the erection of such a Jewish State be accomplished without the gravest trespass upon the civil and religious rights of existing non-Jewish communities in Palestine. The fact came out repeatedly in the Commission's conferences with Jewish representatives, that the Zionists looked forward to a practically complete dispossession of the present non-Jewish inhabitants of Palestine, by various forms of purchase.

In his address of July 4, 1918, President Wilson laid down the following principle as one of the four great 'ends for which the associated peoples of the world were fighting': 'The settlement of every question, whether of territory, of sovereignty, of economic arrangement, or of political relationship upon the basis of the free acceptance of that settlement by the people immediately concerned, and not upon the basis of the material interest or advantage of any other nation or people which may desire a different settlement for the sake of its own exterior influence or mastery.' If that principle is to rule, and so the wishes of Palestine's population are to be decisive as to what is to be done with Palestine, then it is to be remembered that the non-Jewish population of Palestine – nearly nine-tenths of the whole – are emphatically against the entire Zionist programme. The tables show that there was no one thing upon which the population of Palestine were more agreed than upon this. To subject a people so minded to unlimited Jewish immigration, and to steady financial and social pressure to surrender the land, would be a gross violation of the principle just quoted, and of the people's rights, though it kept within the forms of law.

It is to be noted also that the feeling against the Zionist programme is not confined to Palestine, but shared very generally by the people throughout Syria, as our conferences clearly showed. More than seventy-two per cent – 1,350 in all – of all the petitions in the whole of Syria were directed against the Zionist programme. Only two requests – those for a united Syria and for independence – had a larger support. This general feeling was duly voiced by the General Syrian Congress in the seventh, eighth and tenth resolutions of the statement.

The Peace Conference should not shut its eyes to the fact that the anti-Zionist feeling in Palestine and Syria is intense and not lightly to be flouted. No British officer, consulted by the Commissioners, believed that the Zionist programme could be carried out except by force of arms. The officers generally thought that a force of not less than 50,000 soldiers would be required even to initiate the programme. That of itself is evidence of a strong sense of the injustice of the Zionist programme, on the part of the non-Jewish populations of Palestine and Syria. Decisions requiring armies to carry out are sometimes necessary, but they are surely not gratuitously to be taken in the interests of serious injustice. For the initial claim, often submitted by Zionist representatives, that they have a 'right' to Palestine, based on an occupation of 2,000 years ago, can hardly be seriously considered.

449

There is a further consideration that cannot justly be ignored, if the world is to look forward to Palestine becoming a definitely Jewish State, however gradually that may take place. That consideration grows out of the fact that Palestine is the Holy Land for Jews, Christians, and Moslems alike. Millions of Christians and Moslems all over the world are quite as much concerned as the Jews with conditions in Palestine, especially with those conditions which touch upon religious feeling and rights. The relations in these matters in Palestine are most delicate and difficult. With the best possible intentions, it may be doubted whether the Jews could possibly seem to either Christians or Moslems proper guardians of the holy places, or custodians of the Holy Land as a whole.

The reason is this: The places which are most sacred to Christians – those having to do with Jesus – and which are also sacred to Moslems, are not only not sacred to Jews, but abhorrent to them. It is simply impossible, under those circumstances, for Moslems and Christians to feel satisfied to have these places in Jewish hands, or under the custody of Jews. There are still other places about which Moslems must have the same feeling. In fact, from this point of view, the Moslems, just because the sacred places of all three religions are sacred to them, have made very naturally much more satisfactory custodians of the holy places than the Jews could be. It must be believed that the precise meaning in this respect of the complete Jewish occupation of Palestine has not been fully sensed by those who urge the extreme Zionist programme. For it would intensify, with a certainty like fate, the anti-Jewish feeling both in Palestine and in all other portions of the world which look to Palestine as the Holy Land.

In view of all these considerations, and with a deep sense of sympathy for the Jewish cause, the Commissioners feel bound to recommend that only a greatly reduced Zionist programme be attempted by the Peace Conference, and even that, only very gradually initiated. This would have to mean that Jewish immigration should be definitely limited, and that the project for making Palestine distinctly a Jewish commonwealth should be given up.

There would then be no reason why Palestine could not be included in a united Syrian State, just as other portions of the country, the holy places being cared for by an international and inter-religious commission, somewhat as at present, under the oversight and approval of the Mandatory and of the League of Nations. The Jews, of course, would have representation upon this commission.

The recommendations now made lead naturally to the necessity of recommending what power shall undertake the single Mandate for all Syria.

(1) The considerations already dealt with suggest the qualifications ideally to be desired in the mandatory Power: First of all, it should be freely desired by the people. It should be willing to enter heartily into the spirit of the mandatory system, and its possible gift to the world, and so be willing to withdraw after a reasonable period, and not seek selfishly to exploit the country. It should have a passion for democracy, for the education of the common people and for the development of the national spirit. It needs unlimited sympathy and patience in what is practically certain to be a rather thankless task; for no Power can go in honestly to face actual conditions (like land-ownership, for example) and seek to correct these conditions, without making many enemies. It should have experience in dealing with less developed peoples, and abundant resources in men and money.

(2) Probably no Power combines all these qualifications, certainly not in equal degree. But there is hardly one of these qualifications that has not been more or less definitely indicated in our conference with the Syrian people and they certainly suggest a new stage in the development of the self-sacrificing spirit in the relations of peoples to one another. The Power that undertakes the single Mandate for all Syria, in the spirit of these qualifications, will have the possibility of greatly serving not only Syria but the world, and of exalting at the same time its own national life. For it would be working in direct line with the high aims of the Allies in the War, and give proof that those high aims had not been abandoned. And that would mean very much just now, in enabling the nations to keep their faith in one another and in their own highest ideals.

(3) The Resolutions of the Peace Conference of January 30, 1919, quoted in our instructions, expressly state for regions to be 'completely severed from the Turkish Empire', that 'the wishes of these communities must be a principal consideration in the selection of the mandatory Power'. Our survey left no room for doubt of the choice of the majority of the Syrian people. Although it was not known whether America would take a Mandate at all; and although the Commission could not only give no assurances upon that point, but had rather to discourage expectation; nevertheless, upon the face of the returns, America was the first choice of 1,152 of the petitions presented – more than sixty per cent – while no other Power had as much as fifteen per cent for first choice.

And the conferences showed that the people knew the grounds

upon which they registered their choice for America. They declared that their choice was due to knowledge of America's record; the unselfish aims with which she had come into the War; the faith in her felt by multitudes of Syrians who had been in America; the spirit revealed in American educational institutions in Syria, especially the College[1] in Bairut, with its well-known and constant encouragement of Syrian national sentiment; their belief that America had no territorial or colonial ambitions, and would willingly withdraw when the Syrian State was well established as her treatment both of Cuba and the Philippines seemed to them to illustrate; her genuinely democratic spirit; and her ample resources.

From the point of view of the desires of the 'people concerned', the Mandate should clearly go to America.

(4) From the point of view of qualifications, too, already stated as needed in the Mandatory for Syria, America, as first choice of the people, probably need not fear careful testing, point by point, by the standard involved in our discussion of qualifications; though she has much less experience in such work than Great Britain, and is likely to show less patience; and though her definite connexions with Syria have been less numerous and close than those of France. She would have at least the great qualification of fervent belief in the new mandatory system of the League of Nations, as indicating the proper relations which a strong nation should take toward a weaker one. And, though she would undertake the Mandate with reluctance, she could probably be brought to see how logically the taking of such responsibility follows from the purposes with which she entered the War, and from her advocacy of the League of Nations.

(5) There is the further consideration that America could probably come into the Syrian situation, in the beginning at least, with less friction than any other Power. The great majority of Syrian people, as has been seen, favour her coming, rather than that of any other Power. Both the British and the French would find it easier to yield their respective claims to America than to each other. She would have no rival imperial interests to press. She would have abundant resources for the development of the sound prosperity of Syria; and this would inevitably benefit in a secondary way the nations which have had closest connexion with Syria, and so help to keep relations among the Allies cordial. No other Power probably would be more welcome as a neighbour to the British with their large interests in Egypt, Arabia and Iraq; or to the Arabs and Syrians in these regions; or to the French with

---

[1] The Syrian Protestant College founded in 1866, see Chapter III, Section 4, *supra*.

their long-established and many-sided interests in Bairut and the Lebanon.

(6) The objections to recommending at once a single American Mandate for all Syria are: First of all, that it is not certain that the American people would be willing to take the Mandate; that it is not certain that the British or French would be willing to withdraw, and would cordially welcome America's coming, a situation which might prove steadily harassing to an American administration; that the vague but large encouragement given to the Zionist aims might prove particularly embarrassing to America, on account of her large influential Jewish population; and that, if America were to take any mandate at all, and were to take but one mandate, it is probable that an Asia Minor Mandate would be more natural and important. For there is a task there of such peculiar and world-wide significance as to appeal to the best in America, and demand the utmost from her, and as certainly to justify her in breaking with her established policy concerning mixing in the affairs of the eastern hemisphere. The Commissioners believe, moreover, that no other Power could come into Asia Minor, with hands so free to give impartial justice to all the peoples concerned.

To these objections, as a whole, it is to be said that they are all of such a kind that they may resolve themselves; and that they only form the sort of obstacles that must be expected in so large and significant an undertaking. In any case they do not relieve the Commissioners from the duty of recommending the course which, in their honest judgment, is the best course, and the one for which the whole situation calls.

The Commissioners, therefore, recommend, as involved in the logic of the facts, that the United States of America be asked to undertake the single Mandate for all Syria.

If for any reason the mandate for Syria is not given to America, then the Commissioners recommend, in harmony with the express request of the majority of the Syrian people, that the mandate be given to Great Britain. The tables show that there were 1,073 petitions in all Syria for Great Britain as mandatory, if America did not take the Mandate. This is very greatly in excess of any similar expression for the French.

On the contrary – for whatever reason – more than sixty per cent of all the petitions presented to the Commission directly and strongly protested against any French mandate. Without going into discussion of the reasons for this situation, the Commissioners are reluctantly compelled to believe that this situation itself makes it impossible to recommend a single French Mandate for all Syria.

The feeling of the Arabs of the East is particularly strong against the French. And there is grave reason to believe that the attempt to enforce a French Mandate would precipitate war between the Arabs and the French, and force upon Great Britain a dangerous alternative. The Commissioners may perhaps be allowed to say that this conclusion is contrary to their own earlier hope, that – because of France's long and intimate relations with Syria, because of her unprecedented sacrifices in the War, and because the British Empire seemed certain to receive far greater accessions of territory from the War – it might seem possible to recommend that France be given the entire Mandate for Syria. But the longer the Commission remained in Syria, the more clear it became that that course could not be taken.

The Commissioners recommend, therefore, if America cannot take the mandate for all Syria, that it be given to Great Britain; because of the choice of the people concerned; because she is already on the ground and with much of the necessary work in hand; because of her trained administrators; because of her long and generally successful experience in dealing with less developed peoples; and because she has so many of the qualifications needed in a mandatory Power, as we have already considered them.

We should hardly be doing justice, however, to our sense of responsibility to the Syrian people, if we did not frankly add some at least of the reasons and misgivings, variously expressed and implied in our conferences, which led to the preference for an American Mandate over a British Mandate. The people repeatedly showed honest fear that in British hands the mandatory power would become simply a colonising power of the old kind; that Great Britain would find it difficult to give up the colonial theory, especially in case of a people thought inferior; that she would favour a civil service and pension budget too expensive for a poor people; that the interests of Syria would be subordinated to the supposed needs of the Empire; that there would be, after all, too much exploitation of the country for Britain's benefit; that she would never be ready to withdraw and give the country real independence; that she did not really believe in universal education, and would not provide adequately for it; and that she already had more territory in her possession – in spite of her fine colonial record – than was good either for herself or for the world.

These misgivings of the Syrian people unquestionably largely explain their demand for 'absolute independence', for a period of 'assistance' of only twenty years, their protest against Article XXII of the Covenant of the League of Nations, etc. They all mean that whatever Power the Peace Conference shall send into

Syria, should go in as a true mandatory under the League of Nations, and for a limited term. Anything else would be a betrayal of the Syrian people.

It needs to be emphasised, too, that under a true mandatory for Syria, all the legitimate interests of all the nations in Syria would be safeguarded. In particular, there is no reason why any tie that France has had with Syria in the past should be severed or even weakened under the control of another mandatory Power, or in an independent Syria.

There remains only to be added that, if France feels so intensely concerning her present claims in Syria as to threaten all cordial relations among the Allies, it is, of course, possible to give her a Mandate over the Lebanon (not enlarged) separated from the rest of Syria, as is desired by considerable groups in that region. For reasons already given, the Commissioners cannot recommend this course, but it is a possible arrangement.

II. Iraq[1]

In view of the Resolutions, passed by the Peace Conference on January 30, 1919, and of the Anglo-French Declaration of November 7, 1918 – on the eve of the Armistice – both of which documents class Syria and Iraq together to be treated in the same way, and make to them the same promises and assurances, the Commissioners recommend that the Peace Conference adopt for Iraq a policy in general parallel to that recommended for Syria, in order that the Anglo-French Declaration may not become another 'scrap of paper'.

1. We accordingly recommend, as most important of all, and in strict harmony with our instructions, that whatever foreign administration is brought into Iraq, should come into Iraq not at all as a colonising power in the old sense of that term, but as a mandatory under the League of Nations, with clear consciousness that the 'well-being and development' of the people form for it a sacred trust. To this end the Mandate should have a limited term, the time of expiration to be determined by the League of Nations, in the light of all the facts as brought out from year to year, whether in the annual reports of the mandatory to the League or in other ways.

The entire text of the first recommendation for Syria, with its subordinate recommendations, applies point by point to Iraq as truly as to Syria.

[1] For the sake of uniformity I have replaced 'Mesopotamia' by 'Iraq' throughout, and made certain orthographical changes in proper names.

If the Peace Conference, the League of Nations, and the appointed mandatory Power loyally carry out the policy of mandatories embodied in the Covenant of the League of Nations, the most essential interests of Iraq would be fully safeguarded – but only so.

2. We recommend, in the second place, that the unity of Iraq be preserved: the precise boundaries to be determined by a special commission on boundaries, after the Mandate has been assigned. It should probably include at least the Vilayets of Basra, Baghdad, and Mosul. And the Southern Kurds and Assyrians might well be linked up with Iraq. The wisdom of a united country needs no argument in the case of Iraq.

3. We recommend, in the third place, that Iraq be placed under one mandatory Power, as the natural way to secure real and efficient unity. The economic, political, social and educational development of the people all call for such a unified mandate. Only waste, confusion, friction, and injury to the people's interests could come from attempting a division and 'spheres of influence' on the part of several nations. But this implies that the mandatory Power shall not itself be an exploiting Power, but shall sacredly guard the people's rights.

4. Since it is plainly desirable that there be general harmony in the political and economic institutions and arrangements of Iraq and Syria; and since the people themselves should have chief voice in determining the form of government under which they shall live, we recommend that the Government of Iraq, in harmony with the apparent desires of its people, be a Constitutional Monarchy, such as is proposed for Syria; and that the people of Iraq be given opportunity to indicate their choice of a Monarch, the choice to be reviewed and confirmed by the League of Nations. It may be fairly assumed that the 1,278 petitions from Syrians for the independence of Iraq – 68.5 per cent of the total number received – reflect the feeling in Iraq itself; and such contact as we have been able to secure with Iraqis confirms the assumption, and leads to the belief that the programme, presented at Aleppo by representative Iraqis, headed by Ja'far Pasha, Military Governor of the Aleppo District, and practically parallel to the Damascus Programme, would be generally supported by the Iraqi people. Whether this support extends to each item in the programme alike, and so to the naming of a king from the sons of the King of the Hejaz, we have not sufficient data to determine, and so have recommended that a plebiscite be taken upon that point; although there is British evidence that many Iraqis have expressed themselves in favour of one of the sons of the King of the Hejaz as Amir.

5. The Iraqi Programme expresses its choice of America as mandatory, and with no second choice. Undoubtedly there has been a good deal of feeling in Iraq against Great Britain, and the petitions specifically charge the British authorities in Iraq with considerable interference with freedom of opinion, of expression, and of travel – much of which might be justified in time of military occupation. But feeling so stirred might naturally breed unwillingness to express desire for Great Britain as mandatory.

On the other hand, the material in the pamphlet called 'Copies and Translations of Declarations and other Documents relating to Self-Determination in Iraq' was called out by an attempt on the part of the British Government in Iraq to secure the opinions of leading men of all groups concerning 'self-determination'. This material, just because reported directly to British officials, is doubtless somewhat more favourable to the British than it would otherwise be; but it gives unquestionably good evidence of much opinion likely to choose a British Mandate. And after all, the range of choice of a mandatory, of sufficient power and experience and of essential justice, is decidedly limited, and it is by no means improbable that if the Iraqis were confronted by a refusal of America to take a Mandate for Iraq, they would make Great Britain at least second choice, as the majority of the Syrians did. There is supplementary evidence also upon this point.

Now it seems so unlikely that America could or would take a Mandate for Iraq, in addition to the possible consideration of Syria and Asia Minor, that the Commissioners recommend that the Peace Conference assign the Mandate for Iraq to Great Britain: because of the general reasons already given for recommending her as mandatory in Syria, if America does not go in there; because she is probably best of all fitted for the particular task involved, in view of her long relations with the Arabs; in recognition of the sacrifices made by her in delivering Iraq from the Turks, though with no acknowledgment of right of conquest, as her own statements expressly disclaim; because of the special interests she naturally has in Iraq on account of its nearness to India and its close connexions with Arabia; and because of work already done in the territory.

These reasons make it probable that the largest interests of the people of Iraq as a whole will be best served by a British Mandate, in spite of the fact that from the point of view of world-interests, in the prevention of jealousy, suspicion, and fear of domination by a single Power, it were better for both Britain and the world that no further territory anywhere be added to the British Empire. A British Mandate, however, will have the decided advantage of tending to promote economic and educational unity throughout

457

Iraq and Syria, whether Syria be under Great Britain or America, and so will reflect more fully than ever before the close relations, in language, customs, and trade between these parts of the former Turkish Empire.

In a country so rich as Iraq in agricultural possibilities, in oil, and in other resources, with the best intentions, there will inevitably be danger of exploitation and monopolistic control by the mandatory Power, through making British interests supreme, and especially through large Indian immigration. This danger will need increasingly and most honestly to be guarded against. The Iraqis feel very strongly the menace particularly of Indian immigration, even though that immigration should be confined to Moslems. They dread the admixture of another people of entirely different race and customs, as threatening their Arabic civilisation.

Respectfully submitted,

HENRY C. KING,
CHARLES R. CRANE.

INDEX

INDEX

461

INDEX

462